IRON WAR

IRON
WAR

DAVE SCOTT, MARK ALLEN
& THE GREATEST RACE EVER RUN

MATT FITZGERALD

BOULDER, COLORADO

3002 Sterling Circle, Suite 100
Boulder, Colorado 80301-2338 USA
(303) 440-0601 · Fax (303) 444-6788 · E-mail velopress@competitorgroup.com

Distributed in the United States and Canada by Ingram Publisher Services

Library of Congress Cataloging-in-Publication Data
Fitzgerald, Matt.
Iron war: Dave Scott, Mark Allen & the greatest race ever run / Matt Fitzgerald
with Bob Babbitt.—1st ed.
    p.   cm.
ISBN 978-1-934030-77-6 (alk. paper)
1. Ironman triathlons. 2. Scott, Dave. 3. Allen, Mark, 1958- I. Babbitt, Bob. II. Title.
GV1060.73.F575   2011
796.42'57—dc23
2011027408

This paper meets the requirements of ANSI/NISO
Z39.48-1992 (Permanence of Paper).

Cover design by theBookDesigners
Interior design by Katie Jennings
Interior illustrations by Charlie Layton

Text set in Eidetic Neo and Eidetic Modern

For information on purchasing VeloPress books, please call (800) 811-4210 ext. 2138
or visit www.velopress.com.

11   12   13   /   10   9   8   7   6   5   4   3   2

IN MILITARY AFFAIRS THE STRENGTH OF AN ARMY is the product of its mass and some unknown x. . . . That unknown quantity is the spirit of the army, that is to say, the greater or lesser readiness to fight and face danger felt by all the men composing an army, quite independently of whether they are, or are not, fighting under the command of a genius, in two- or three-line formation, with cudgels or with rifles that repeat thirty times a minute. Men who want to fight will always put themselves in the most advantageous conditions for fighting.

— LEO TOLSTOY, *WAR AND PEACE*

CONTENTS

CHAPTER 1

THE MOMENT

A hero is no braver than an ordinary man,
but he is brave five minutes longer.

— RALPH WALDO EMERSON

T wo men run shoulder to shoulder down the middle of the Queen Kaahumanu Highway on Hawaii's Big Island, pressing southward toward
the coastal town of Kailua-Kona. The road they travel cuts a narrow
artery through a vast black lava field that supports no life save for a few
scattered tufts of hardy fountain grass. Hazy clouds above trap muggy hot-
ness below like the lid of a steaming kettle. A slick coat of rank sweat—a
microcosm of the smothering atmosphere—bastes the skin of the hard-
breathing runners, sealing in the heat churned out by the fiery furnaces
of their muscles.

Both men are tall and lean, with the characteristic legs of elite triathletes—lither than those of cyclists, more muscular than those of runners—extending sinuously beneath skimpy 1980s running shorts. Each
man hides a thousand-yard stare behind sport sunglasses, but their slack
cheeks betray a deathly weariness.

They are not alone. A caravan of mopeds, bicycles, cars, Jeeps, and
trucks has formed behind the athletes, the spectators aboard these con-
veyances having been drawn into the convoy by the spreading news of the
spectacle they now behold. A few of the motorized vehicles and most of
the bikes should not be where they are, as the highway is closed to normal

transit, but the race marshals have lost control and no longer care. Caught up in the same hypnosis as everyone else, they simply follow and watch.

It is a strange apparition, this silent caravan, a sort of motley roving amphitheater, made stranger still by its silence. Those watching dare not speak a word for fear of breaking the spell in which all are complicit. Aside from the occasional shout of encouragement from a volunteer at a roadside drink station, the only sound to be heard is the rhythmic huffing of the athletes' exhalations and the soft slapping of their feet against the pavement.

"Right on!" screams one young man as the runners approach the drink station he's staffing. *"Right! On!"* he repeats, cheering not for one runner or the other but for the performance itself, losing his mind in excitement as he witnesses the consummation of every fan's notion of the best thing that could possibly be happening in this, the most anticipated showdown in the history of triathlon—the sport's two towering heroes running each other into the ground, obliterating records and annihilating all other competitors, *eight hours* into a duel in which they have never been more than a few feet apart.

The man on the right, dressed in green, black, and white Brooks apparel, is Dave Scott, six-time winner of this race, the Ironman World Championship. The runner in yellow, black, and white Nike apparel is Mark Allen, six-time loser of Ironman, winner of everything else.

They continue. Each man runs not as fast as he can but as fast as the *other* can, having already swum 2.4 miles, bicycled 112 miles, and run 24 miles, with the balance of a marathon left to run, all in tar-melting heat. That is why the pair remains as if tethered wrist to wrist after racing nearly a full-day shift, well ahead of 1,284 of the best triathletes in the world. Each is trying with all his might to break the body, mind, or spirit of the other, but although all of these elements in both have been stretched to the breaking point, none has yet broken.

Within their minds a pitched battle is being waged between unimaginable suffering and an equally intense desire to resist that suffering and win. The pain in their thighs, especially, is so severe that in any other context they would find it impossible to walk a single step. Yet each continues to run sub-six-minute miles because each still believes the pain is worth the hope of winning.

An expectant crowd waits at the finish line in downtown Kailua-Kona. All they know of the great struggle taking place on the Queen K Highway is what little information the race announcer provides in sporadic updates based on garbled two-way radio reports from the field. Yet these crumbs are more than enough to captivate them.

While the multitude waits, the competitor who is currently in twenty-seventh place in the race encounters Dave Scott and Mark Allen and their silent caravan head-on (it's an out-and-back course) and stops cold to watch them. He has devoted months of hard training to preparing for this day. For several seconds he claps and shouts like any other spectator, momentarily indifferent to his own performance.

A photographer leaps off the back of his chauffeured motorcycle and attempts to capture close-up images of the combatants while sprinting alongside them. Immediately he recognizes his mistake. Although young and fit himself, he quits in exhaustion after fifty yards. Before leaping back on his motorcycle, he watches the runners speed away down the road, the camera slung from his neck briefly forgotten.

Seated on the trunk of a convertible some fifty feet behind Dave and Mark, his shoes resting on the back seat, is Bob Babbitt, the 38-year-old publisher of San Diego–based *Competitor* magazine. His face is frozen in a faint grin. He believes he is watching the greatest race ever run. The cover line for the next issue of his publication has already come to him: *Iron War.*

IRONMAN IN 1989 means more to the young sport of triathlon than any other major championship means to any other sport. It is virtually the sport itself—the only race that really matters. Fans and sponsors don't care how many other triathlons you win if you don't win Ironman. That's why short-course specialist Mike Pigg, feared in two-hour races, is competing in this race even though it's way too long for him. It's why Scott Molina, winner of numerous events in cooler places, kept doing Ironman, despite being no good in the heat, until he cherry-picked a victory last year, taking advantage of Dave's absence and Mark's bad luck. Hell, even duathlon star Kenny Souza, dominant in run-bike-run events, feels compelled to try, and he can't really swim.

Mark Allen is virtually unbeatable in other triathlons and has amassed nine wins in nine races this year ahead of Hawaii, two of those wins over Dave Scott. But those victories count for little in his reckoning.

"When you come to Ironman, you have to put everything you've done before it in the garbage can," Mark told *ABC Sports* before the 1987 Ironman. "It all means zero."

It is this race Mark wants, and he is snakebit here. Dave and the island have his number.

Dave Scott dominates Ironman as few athletes have ever dominated a major championship in any sport. Before today he has raced it seven times, won it six times, and finished second once. And then there's *how* he wins—crushingly, wielding a force field of invincibility like a weapon. At the start of the marathon leg of the 1983 Ironman, trailing Scott Tinley by twenty seconds, Dave looked into an ABC television camera trained on him and snarled, "I'm going to *bury* this guy," then promptly fulfilled the promise.

They call him the Man.

Mark Allen is his only equal, almost untouchable in triathlons held everyplace except Hawaii. His nickname is Grip. As in "death grip."

Seldom do the two greatest champions of a generation in sport, each with a career prime that will ultimately span more than a decade, achieve their finest moments on the very same day, but Dave Scott and Mark Allen appear to be doing just that. On this day, they are not merely the best in the sport; they are literally the best by miles. Here in the final stretch of the marathon leg of the race, Dave and Mark are *three miles* ahead of their nearest challenger. With every stride they are redefining the possible, on pace to run a sub-2:40 marathon in almost 90-degree heat following a four-and-a-half-hour cycling time trial and a fifty-minute all-out swim effort in open water—a feat that nobody would previously have believed to fall within the scope of human potential.

Earlier in the year, in anticipation of this collision, Bob Babbitt set out to fan the hype by creating a cover for his publication that depicted the two men standing back to back, fisted arms crossed against their chests, in the style of a classic boxing poster.

"Sure, I'll do it—if Dave comes here," said Mark, who was training in Boulder, Colorado, when Bob called.

"Yeah, I'll do it—if Mark comes here," countered Dave, born and raised and still living in Davis, California.

In the end a photographer traveled to both places to shoot each man with the same backdrop behind him, then spliced the two halves together. The rivals appeared to be as close as they are now. The cover line read, "SHOWDOWN ON THE KONA COAST."

It's not that Dave and Mark really hate each other. They just can't like each other. Only one race matters, and only one man can win it. They're like two ravenous tigers fighting over a kill. Dave was an Ironman legend before Mark even owned a bike. But the younger man was quickly dubbed his elder's heir apparent. Dave resented it, and Mark knew it.

"It was like coming home after a hard day at work and expecting the family to cater to him," Mark wrote of Dave in his 1988 book, *The Total Triathlete*. "When he got home, when he arrived in Hawaii, someone else was in his house getting all his attention. And that someone else was me."

Dave has beaten Mark five times in this event, but the overall rivalry is hardly lopsided. Mark defeats Dave routinely in most other triathlons. Each loss here deepens Mark's desire to turn the tables, and both men know—or at least one fears and the other has faith—that Mark is capable. Twice he has finished second to Dave, and twice he has amassed huge leads over his rival before falling apart. There is broad agreement that Dave keeps beating Mark in Hawaii not because Dave is simply better but because Dave has mastered the race and Mark has not.

"It's not so much Dave Scott has defeated me, or Scott Tinley, or whoever's come in ahead of me," Mark said dismissively in an interview for ABC television before the race they are now near completing. "It's always been the course—the elements, the wind, the heat, the humidity, and the distance under that sun for eight and a half hours."

In support of Mark's point, when Dave pulled out of the '88 Ironman two days before the race with an injury, Mark became the prohibitive favorite. But he suffered two flat tires on the bike and finished fifth. It seemed as if Fate was not content for Mark to become the Ironman champion except by beating his nemesis. If ever.

A year later Dave is healthy, and Mark's rotten luck appears to be behind him. Both men have transformed the agony of their disappointments at the '88 race into hunger for redemption. Both performed at the highest level of their careers in their summer buildup to this race. Mark went undefeated. Dave set an Ironman world record of 8:01:32 in Japan. Theirs were the only names mentioned in the obsessive "Who do you like this year?" conversations that ritually devour all other topics during race week in Kailua-Kona. Last year's winner, Scott Molina, has not returned to defend his crown, writing himself off as a one-time opportunist. Two-time winner Tinley, it is agreed, has been surpassed. Sure enough, with two miles left in the race, Dave and Mark are three miles ahead, inches apart.

The conflict between the two men goes deeper than mere professional self-interest. Under the surface of their Ironman battles is a clash of opposing ways of being. Mark is what some might call a New Age spiritual type. He meditates and favors alternative medicine. He trains smart and isn't afraid to take a day off when his body needs it. Dave's a good old-fashioned jock of the no-pain-no-gain school. He believes you win by outworking your competition in training and outsuffering it in races. Meditation? No, thanks.

Like many great athletes, Dave competes best when he competes angry. He feels that being pals with any of his rivals would weaken him as a competitor, so, in stark contrast to his peers, he trains utterly alone in his out-of-the-way hometown, the chief virtue of whose isolated desert environment, in his mind, is that it is not a place that is attractive to anyone else in the sport. It is Dave against the world, and he likes it that way.

Meanwhile, Mark trains with Tinley, Molina, Pigg, Souza—everyone, it seems, in triathlon's hypersocial birthplace and epicenter: sunny, beachy San Diego.

Generally mild-tempered, Dave goes to great lengths to gather so-called bulletin-board material—insults, perceived slights, and signs of disrespect—to feed the anger that he depends on to race as hard as he does. In 1987 Kellogg created a breakfast cereal called Pro-Grain. Mark Allen's face appeared on one version of the box along with the tagline "Ironman Food."

"What a joke," Dave scoffed at the time. "Mark has never won Ironman. And that cereal's not even good for you!"

Proving his point at Ironman that year, Dave again chased down Mark on the run, erasing a four-minute deficit and blowing by him to win by eleven minutes. Mark spent the night in a hospital.

As in any great sports rivalry, enmity is mixed with intimacy. In training, Dave and Mark think about each other like targets. Their blood warms whenever their paths cross off the racecourse, as they did at a press conference just two days ago, where they never greeted one another, never even made eye contact, despite being seated in adjacent chairs. As they run together now, each senses clearly how the other feels—whether he is strong or weak in any moment.

Who is ultimately stronger? The answer is undetermined. Dave does not know, nor does Mark, nor do the spectators who trail them in a reverent hush. One of these two men must soon break the other—in body, mind, or spirit. Who will it be? Not necessarily the faster man. The battle being waged now is about will as much as skill. Already both men have pushed deeper than ever before into the inferno of suffering that stands between every racer and his final performance limit. The winner of this fight is likely to be the man who dares to push deepest. Eight hours of racing are culminating in a game of chicken.

Endurance racing is steeped in the art of pacing. Each man has to hold back *something*. But how little does he gamble holding back? As they blaze southward toward the finish line in Kailua-Kona, Dave Scott and Mark Allen are risking everything, running in a shared state of unmasked desperation, to win—or not lose—*right now*.

It is one minute before three o'clock on the afternoon of October 14, 1989, and something is about to happen.

CHAPTER 2

A DROP
TOO MUCH

Nature sends no creature, no man into the world
without adding a small excess of his proper quality.

— RALPH WALDO EMERSON

D ave Scott was 13 years old in the fall of 1967 and in seventh grade
at Davis Junior High School in Davis, California. On weekday morn-
ings Dave could be seen waiting for the school bus outside his family's home. But he did not board the bus when it came. Instead, as the big
yellow coach rumbled by, he took off after it on his three-speed bike.

Five times a week young Dave Scott raced his own bus to school.

Davis was a small town then, agricultural and spread out. Fields of
onions and groves of almond trees and not much else bordered the flat,
straight country roads leading from the Scott residence, a comfortable
five-bedroom house situated at the edge of El Macero Country Club on the
outskirts of town, to the centrally located junior high building, some five
and a half miles away. There was seldom much traffic on those roads, and
at seven fifteen in the morning almost none. Just a boy on his bike and a
Blue Bird Type C running neck and neck. The kids on the starboard side
of the bus watched in detached amusement as their schoolmate pedaled
madly alongside their thrumming vessel. The bus would pull ahead between stops; Dave would leapfrog it as the driver paused to take on additional pupils.

The first time Dave raced the bus to school, the bus won, but narrowly enough that the defeat left him keenly motivated to give it another try. The next day he lost again, but his margin of defeat was even smaller. On his third try the seventh grader triumphed. By then Dave was hooked on the strenuous morning ritual, and he continued to race the bus daily, even through the worst of Davis's winter weather, with frost on the ground and blinding fog in the air.

Exactly one traffic light stood between home and school. Some days it was green when the bus reached it, other days red. If the driver was caught by that light, Dave knew he had him. But it felt like cheating. He wanted the bus to flow through so he could beat it fair and square.

YOUNG DAVE SCOTT could not remember a time when he did not feel the constant pressure of a tremendous energy threatening to split his body wide open. His only release was to engage in as much physical exertion as he could squeeze into a day, every day. He did not learn such drive or absorb it from his environment. He was born with it.

Dave's childhood was about as normal as an American childhood could be. Davis, where he was born and raised, was a wholesome, middle-class university town located thirteen miles west of Sacramento—a sort of upscale Levittown of the West, with broad, tree-lined streets; comfortable, unostentatious houses; and pridefully manicured lawns. The Scott home had been custom-built for the family of five but was typical in every detail—a two-story, flat-fronted colonial whose interior resembled the set of *Ozzie and Harriet*.

Dave grew up with an older sister, Patti, and a younger sister, Jane. His parents were Verne and Dorothy. A Michigan native, Dot had a generally easygoing disposition, but the full-time homemaker's devotion and loyalty to her husband and children became fierce when necessary. She kept meticulous scrapbooks that documented the noteworthy doings of each of her three equally beloved offspring, including everything from school play programs to clippings from local newspapers that listed the results of their sports competitions. While Dot was not an athlete herself, Dave may have inherited his endurance through her, as her brother, Jim Forshee, was among the best masters runners in the United States. Verne, like most fathers on Elmwood Drive, taught at the university. Neighbors knew Verne as a "Steady Eddy" type: hardworking and competent yet completely unassuming. A big values guy, Verne saddled his children with household chores to teach discipline and the value of a dollar (their allowances were tied to performance of those chores). He played practical jokes on the Walker family across the street and practiced a teasing sense of humor on everyone he liked. He rode a three-speed bike to work in the morning. That, and a little tennis and a little golf, constituted his exercise.

Verne came to know his son's appetite for physical exertion long before Dave began to race the bus to school. The Scott family Sunday service was at a church where Verne was an elder. Dave was miserable there, stuffed inside a wool suit and crammed into the middle of a pew, surrounded by old ladies wearing too much perfume. On one particularly hot summer Sunday, Dave decided he could stand it no longer. During a break in the service he scrambled from the pew, found his father, and tugged on his sleeve.

"Dad, do you mind if I go home?" he asked.

If Verne's instinct was to deny his young son's unwelcome request, that instinct was countered by the innocent unhappiness on Dave's face.

"Sure," Verne said gently. "Go on home."

No key was needed. The Scott home, like every house in Davis, stood unlocked when empty. Dave ran out of the church and had freed himself from his suit jacket before he reached the sidewalk. He took off toward home, a mile and a half away, at a full sprint. Three-quarters of a mile later he was still sprinting. He felt wonderful, utterly impervious to fatigue. Dave was hit by a powerful sense of rightness. His body and spirit fitted this challenge, this thumbing of his nose in the face of exhaustion, like a key in the lock it was made for.

Evidence of Dave's bone-deep will to endure first emerged in the pool. In 1960 a youth swim club called the Davis Aquadarts was formed. A year later Patti, Dave, and Jane joined. (The Scott family tended to do most things together.) Despite developing an ugly, thrashing freestyle stroke that no amount of coaching could break him of, Dave excelled in the pool, becoming one of the strongest swimmers his age not by virtue of superior talent but by outworking everyone else in practice and refusing to lose in competition—and every lap was competition. Verne, a man proud of his own professional work ethic, at first was pleased to see such willingness to suffer in his young son. But Verne soon recognized that Dave's drive far exceeded anything his father or anyone else could give him by example.

Unlike the other kids on the team, Dave cut no corners in workouts, always doing everything Coach Jerry Hinsdale asked and often more. His work ethic took him only so far, though. At age 12 Dave swam thirteen races at the California State Fair Swim Meet. He was beaten in all but one of them by a hotshot from the Midwest with a naturally beautiful swim stroke and the memorable name of Murphy Reinschreiber. Indeed, Dave never forgot him. Sixteen years later Dave found Murphy at a triathlon, approached him, and jabbed a finger into his chest.

"I remember you," he said. "You beat me in twelve out of thirteen races at the California State Fair Swim Meet in 1966. I'm here for payback!"

No youth sport is more demanding than swimming, which gives most kids all the activity they need. Not Dave Scott. Nowadays children with such energy are often called hyperactive, but in the 1960s Dave was able to avoid being labeled anything other than normal by grabbing for every sport within reach. From swimming Dave branched out to baseball and excelled with ball and glove, becoming a Little League all-star. He dabbled in tennis and golf as well and showed an aptitude for both, getting his golf handicap down to 11 by age 13. In junior high he took up basketball. When he reached high school Dave tried out for the football team and became a starter at tight end and flanker back. When Davis High School created a water polo team Dave signed up and became the school's first All-American in any sport.

Although Dave excelled in every sport, he was not the best in any. He tried harder than anyone to be the best, but it seemed there was always a Murphy Reinschreiber standing in his way—some born talent who made it look easy. Dave's lowest moment as a young athlete occurred on the basketball court during his sophomore year of high school. At the beginning of the season Dave's unmatched work ethic earned him a spot as a starting guard on the junior varsity team. But as the team's losses piled up Coach Dennis Pytel became increasingly disenchanted with Dave's graceless style of play and progressively more enamored of the lazier but more naturally coordinated kids on the bench. Coach Pytel demoted Dave from starter to second string to bench warmer over the course of the season. Eventually Dave found himself on the court only in garbage minutes at the very end of games. This struck Dave as the height of injustice. And he wasn't going to take it lying down.

In the last game of the season Coach Pytel summoned Dave with fifty-nine seconds left on the clock.

"Scotty, you're in," he said.

Dave hated being called "Scotty."

I'll not going **in**," Dave said

And he didn't. Why play a game in which his hard work counted for so little? The hardest worker should always win. It was only fair. Maybe, Dave thought, he just needed to work even harder. So he did.

As a football player Dave lifted weights, which introduced him to the concept of conditioning. Until then he had only practiced for and competed in sports. But general conditioning for sports was something else—something more he could do. So, while his teammates lifted weights only when required, Dave lifted year-round, which entailed some very late trips to the gym after all the practicing and competing were done.

Verne and Dot had an eleven-meter lap pool installed in their backyard so Dave would never be unable to swim when he needed to, whether before dawn or after dark. Members of the Walker family across the street often heard him splashing around very late at night, after the practicing and the competing in other sports, and the weight lifting, were done. If there was ever a spare moment between practices for his various sports and his extra conditioning workouts, Dave filled it by bouncing a basketball off the wall of the school gymnasium. Passing students would observe the statuesque youth going about what looked like some form of punishment with an incongruous enjoyment—hammering the inflated sphere against painted cinder blocks at a rate of two rebounds per second with impressive force and tirelessness and no regard for how conspicuous his behavior might appear to someone watching him. It was as though the young man *feared* stillness, like the sharks that stop breathing if they stop gliding forward.

In fact, Dave *was* one of those sharks, in a sense. At about the same time that he started racing the bus to school, Dave began to notice that on the very rare occasions when he missed a few days of activity for some reason—illness, family travel—he felt miserable. One day might be okay. But after two days he was edgy, and three days would send him right over the edge. Normally outgoing and positive, Dave would turn antisocial and irritable. His entire personality would change. Dave just wasn't Dave without the freedom to move.

In his early adolescence Dave began to foster a vision of perfection. Having discovered that a little exercise was good and more was better, Dave decided that he wanted to work toward becoming as fit as he could possibly be, if not the fittest man alive, if not the fittest mammal that had ever walked the earth. When he was younger, Dave had spent untold hours poring over the *Guinness Book of World Records*, reading and rereading each annual edition until it fell apart in his hands. He was fascinated by bests and superlatives and dreamed of earning his own page in a future edition of his favorite book through some feat of inexhaustibility. His vision of ultimate fitness filled Dave with excitement but also caused him to continually judge his current self unfavorably against his ideal. He developed a gently self-mocking sense of humor; like most self-deprecatory jokesters, Dave genuinely believed and privately fretted over everything he said. ("My swim stroke is horrendous," he half-joked to one writer.)

Dave was maturing into a magnificent human specimen: tall, tan, blond, and lean. Girls loved his eyes—not so much the eyes themselves as the hypnotically droopy lids and the femininely long lashes. But Dave was also becoming increasingly self-conscious about his appearance. Even at 5 or 6 percent body fat, he occasionally felt too flabby to be seen shirtless. Perhaps his only real flaw was a thin upper lip, inherited from Verne. As soon as he was able, Dave covered up the problem with a mustache that would become his trademark.

"My biggest motivator is to live up to my own standards," Dave told one of his earliest interviewers. "I create the fear that lives within me."

ON A WITHERINGLY HOT afternoon in September 1978, Linda Buchanan sat in her dorm room at UC-Davis doing homework. The room lacked air conditioning, so she had flung open a window for ventilation. Suddenly her attention was drawn away from her book by the sound of heavy breathing coming from the college green outside. She peered through the window frame and saw a shirtless, golden-skinned man running by in the blazing heat, wheezing with effort.

That's pretty crazy, she thought.

A few days later the scenario was repeated. It became a regular happening, and before long Linda found herself looking forward to seeing the suffering Adonis. Most of the UC-Davis students who did not know Dave Scott personally knew of him through similar encounters. He was that guy who never stopped moving.

As the son of a UC-Davis professor, Dave had been destined from birth to matriculate there. He became a physical education major, which would not have been Verne's first choice for his only son, but Dave couldn't have cared less; he loved the subject. Moreover, it was easy—no drain on the energy resources he needed for sports. Dave told his friends he never studied. Instead, he said, he placed his books under his pillow and slept on them, absorbing their contents through a form of osmosis.

The march toward physical perfection continued through college. Dave was named captain of the water polo team. Almost having no choice, the coach (the same Jerry Hinsdale who had coached Dave as a youth swimmer) placed him in charge of the team's conditioning program. Dave led his teammates on slogs through the 100-degree heat of Davis summers—runs that he would have done with or without them. The team practiced twice a day for a total of five hours during the preseason in August. After the last session of the afternoon, when his teammates went off to eat and pass out, Dave hustled over to Hickey Gym to pump iron in the tiny, airless, wood-paneled weight room.

"Come lift with me," Dave told the team's star goalie, Craig Wilson, after one long day of practice. "It's fun."

"You're completely psycho," Craig replied, backing away.

When he started at UC-Davis, Dave knew zero about nutrition. As a phys ed student, he began to learn the science of healthy eating, and he had an epiphany. Here was a whole new way to improve his body and its capacity. Dave had been raised on an All-American diet of roast beef and buttered potatoes for dinner and ice cream for dessert. He now learned all about the negative effects of such fattening staples. (He might not have done all of his assigned reading, but he did pay attention in class.) Then he considered how these consequences were surely compounded in his body by the incredible quantities in which he consumed food.

For Dave Scott was, on top of everything else, the hungriest man in the world. He had to be to support his extreme level of activity. A typical lunch in his freshman year of college consisted of thirteen grilled-cheese sandwiches. He once ate eight and a half pounds of ice cream in one sitting. But his greatest gustatory feat occurred on Thanksgiving 1973. The Scott home was always bustling with extended family, friends, and other guests, and in the hospitable spirit of his clan Dave brought along a few teammates to grub on Dot's home cooking. After eating a heaping plate of turkey and fixings, Dave said, "I think I'll have seconds. Anyone else?"

He gave his friends a challenging look. Dave could turn anything into a competition. They took seconds also.

Minutes later, having cleaned his plate again, Dave threw the same challenging look and announced, "Thirds, anyone?"

His friends were silent. One mumbled something about room for dessert. Dave took thirds. And fourths. And fifths. And sixths. *And sevenths!*

Upon swallowing his last bite, Dave immediately crumpled to the floor and slept under the dining room table for two hours.

More than half of the foods Dave gorged on that day would be self-proscribed at the following year's Thanksgiving dinner. At age 20 Dave transformed his diet. He made a long list of bad foods, which included red meat and all confections, and eliminated them from his meals and snacks. That was fine. But because the healthy foods that remained in his diet were less calorically dense than those he had purged, Dave had to increase the volume of his intake even further. A typical breakfast (as reported in *Sports Illustrated*) became six oranges; six apples; five rice-cake-and-banana sandwiches; ten ounces of cottage cheese (which Dave rinsed in a strainer to reduce its fat content); and a homemade puree of almond butter, onions, garlic, garbanzo beans, and lemon juice on rice cakes and wheat crackers.

"That's what I was up against," Mark Allen is fond of saying in public-speaking engagements. "If I was ever going to win Ironman, I had to beat a man who rinsed his cottage cheese."

UPON GRADUATING from college Dave started an adult swim club—Davis Aquatic Masters—with his sister Patti and his dad, Verne, who by then had taken up swimming as a way of bonding with his offspring. Verne handled administrative duties while Dave and Patti coached. Jane would eventually take her sister's place after Patti enrolled in nursing school and Jane graduated from UC–Santa Barbara. As a sports team captain Dave had discovered a passion for coaching that rivaled his love of training and competition, and he threw himself into the vocation with perfectionist zeal. He coached four workouts a day, five days a week, prowling the pool deck like a lion tamer while his swimmers swam and pushing each of them toward his or her own perfection with a good-humored refusal to accept excuses of any kind.

"Gee, I feel kind of flat today, Dave."

That's too bad. Next set starts in five seconds.

"Kid's sick. Up all night."

Four. Three.

"Just got back from a business trip."

Two, One,

Dave drew commitment from his swimmers by proving his own commitment to them. He not only knew all of his athletes by name but also remembered everyone's splits and routinely stunned and flattered swimmers by singling them out for individual instruction and correction that revealed a total knowledge of the person as a swimmer, whether a recent dog paddler or a national champion. Membership in the group grew from five to more than four hundred in a few years, and it became the largest masters swim club per capita in the country. Dozens of local residents became swimmers during Dave's tenure as coach of the Davis Aquatic Masters just to experience Dave.

Fifty five hours of coaching per week did not leave a lot of waking hours for his own training, but Dave managed. Davis residents often saw him jogging through town after eleven o'clock at night, and he took advantage of the privilege of possessing a key to Emerson pool to swim while others slept.

Although Dave was no longer on a team after college, he had an aspiration. Having been named an NCAA All-American in water polo in his last two seasons at UC-Davis, he set a goal to earn a spot on the national team and to compete in the Olympics. He scored a rare opportunity to train with the national team in Berkeley, California, but did not make the final cut. Dave had already hit the ceiling in swimming, where he never qualified for an NCAA championship, so he took it hard.

A second blow came later when Craig Wilson, his former team's star goalie, was chosen for the national squad. Craig did not work as hard as Dave, but he was more talented. Dave had always held fast to the belief that his hard work could trump another's talent. This belief was, in fact, his most treasured article of faith—practically his entire life's philosophy. Dave knew he was not the world's most talented athlete, but he clung tightly to the conviction that he could be the best anyway by being the man who never quit. His Olympic near miss rattled that conviction.

It did not, however, destroy the conviction. One way or another, Dave was going to persuade the cosmos to recognize and reward his work ethic. And so, when his dreams of ultimate success in the pool died, the broader dream stayed alive. Dave dropped water polo and explored different ways to challenge his body. He tried open-water swims. Then he learned about a brand-new sport that seemed worth a spin.

DAVE'S MAIDEN TRIATHLON was, by decree of fate, one of the world's earliest multisport races. The inaugural Turkey Triathlon was held in November 1976 in San Francisco and was organized by the local Dolphin Swim Club and South End Running Club. It was Patti, then in nursing school, who heard about it first and who invited her brother to join her. Dave not only leaped at the challenge but also recruited Verne and a few of his masters swimmers to make the seventy-mile journey with him.

The race consisted of a 9-mile bike ride along the city's tourist-packed, potholed embarcadero, followed by a hilly 4-mile run over Fort Mason to the San Francisco Yacht Club and back and ending with a 600-meter swim in the icy waters of San Francisco Bay. The race director was a crusty retired marine lieutenant colonel named Buck Swannack. His pre-race instructions struck Verne as little more than an excuse to say the word "survival" a couple of dozen times. There was no mention of course monitors or paramedics or directional signs or water stops.

"You're just going to *do it!*" Buck barked.

Nursing a sore knee, Dave planned to complete the ride and stay on his bike to keep his sister company through the run, after which he would ditch the bike and swim with her. That was the plan. But when the race started and the stud athletes (or the "peacocks," as Dave called them) shot ahead of them, instinct took over, and he dropped his sister to chase after the leaders. Whereas the peacocks who had come to race had their running shoes waiting for them in a makeshift transition area on a patch of grass at Rincon Park, Dave had to dump his bike there, run through a nearby parking lot to his car, pull his keys from their hiding spot under the bumper, and grab the "oil-changing, river-rafting, lawn-mowing" tennis shoes he had stashed inside the vehicle. Despite the detour, Dave passed every peacock but one, finishing the race thirty seconds from victory and claiming the coveted second-place prize of a frozen turkey.

Patti knew her brother well enough to be neither surprised nor upset by the competitive fever that had taken hold of him.

"I wanted to see what I could do," he told her.

"I know, Dave," she said.

Patti understood that these words meant something different on her brother's lips than they would on anyone else's, because he said them often. Coming from Dave they expressed nothing less than a soul-seizing desire to discover the ultimate limits of his physical and mental endurance and were based on his understanding that the way to fulfill this destiny was to try harder than anyone else did, or could, and to always try harder than he himself ever had. They codified the highest standard in a certain field of endeavor, a standard that very few athletes could dare to embrace. A hero's credo.

Dave's search for the right fit for his unique blend of athletic aptitudes and proclivities continued. There must be some sort of competition out there whose winner was the last man standing—not the fastest or the most coordinated or the most talented in any particular way but the man who tried hardest and never quit.

In September 1978 Dave flew to the island of Oahu to compete in the Waikiki Roughwater Swim, a major open-water race. The challenges that made open-water swimming different from pool swimming—surf, currents, brine, contact with other bodies—made the race a good fit for Dave, for whom the more grueling a challenge, the better. He did well, finishing ninth overall and second in his age group.

Still, though. Ninth. Second. That was not greatness. Dave needed something more grueling still.

At a meeting before the race Dave had been approached by a lanky, middle-aged navy commander named John Collins, who handed him a flyer promoting an event scheduled to take place the following January.

"It's called Iron Man," he said. "You do the same swim you're doing tomorrow, then you ride a bike 112 miles and run a marathon. We did the first one earlier this year—twelve of us. I think you'd be a good candidate."

Dave had finally discovered the particular athletic calling he'd been looking for his whole life. But he didn't know it yet. He was more than a little intrigued by the challenge and flattered by John's suggestion that he would fare well, but the event was too small. Twelve people? Come on. Dave craved glory on a big stage. And so, upon returning to Davis, he crumpled the flyer and threw it away.

The following spring Dave visited his sister Patti and her husband, Rick Baier, in Los Angeles. On a previous trip there Dave had met and befriended Rick's friend Mike Norton, a radiology intern at UCLA and a runner. Dave and Mike ran together whenever Dave came down from Davis, and they did so again on this fateful visit.

While they ran Mike told Dave about a lengthy feature article on the second Iron Man, which had also drawn only twelve participants, recently published in *Sports Illustrated.* When they got back to Mike's place he showed it to Dave.

"You should do the next one," he said, agreeing with John Collins's assessment that Dave was a good candidate for the three-sport, all-day endurance test.

Dave read the article with undisguised interest and some dismay. *Sports Illustrated.* If he had only accepted John Collins's invitation, he could have been reading about himself right now!

"Look at the times," Mike urged. "It took the winner more than eleven hours to finish the damn thing. You could beat that. You could win it!"

Dave needed no more convincing. A new vision took shape in his mind. Suddenly this Iron Man thing was a big deal. And it truly seemed custom-made for the unique athlete he was. When he left Los Angeles Dave was buzzing with the feeling that the pathway to his destiny had at last opened up before him.

When he got home Dave called his folks. Dot answered.

"Mom, I have a plan," Dave said. "And it starts now."

DAVE BEGAN TO TRAIN. He dropped $900 on a Raleigh Professional racing bike and rode it all over Yolo County, through blazing summer heat and valley winds. He ratcheted up his running and signed up for September's Sacramento Marathon, figuring the marathon leg of Iron Man should not be his first 26.2-miler. Knowing no better, Dave blitzed the race in 2:45, finishing twenty-third in a field of 1,850 runners, most of whom were far more experienced than he was.

One day in the middle of all this Dave's friend John Reganold bumped into Dave's girlfriend Sasha and asked about his training.

"Do you think he can do it?" John asked.

"Oh, yes," she said. "He already has."

"What do you mean, he already has?"

"He already did those distances. In a workout."

She was only exaggerating slightly. As a sort of dress rehearsal for Iron Man, Dave had risen very early on a Saturday morning and swum 5,000 yards at Emerson Pool, then linked up with a bunch of local cyclists who happened to have a 103-mile bike tour planned for that day—but Dave had not toured, he had *raced*, dusting everyone.

When he finished the ride Dave was met, by prearrangement, by Sasha, Jane, and Dot, whom he had instructed to bring drinks and snacks that he would use to refuel his muscles before he set out on the twenty-one-mile run that would complete the workout. They screwed up his order, bringing oranges when he'd asked for bananas. Dave threw a fit.

Dave harangued his volunteer support crew without pause as he drank and ate and made ready to run. Future viewers of his Ironman performances on ABC television would become familiar with, even charmed by, Angry Dave, but in this surprise debut, Dave's small audience was not amused. Dot, with a mother's tolerance and long-suffering, was probably more hurt than upset. Sasha, whose bond with Dave was not so deep, would not be his girlfriend much longer. And Jane, if she was like most sisters, would have been half annoyed, half amused by Dave's antics. Perhaps she would even have bitten her lip to suppress a laugh as Dave struggled to squeeze his feet, swollen from five hours of pedaling, into his running shoes.

Sasha went home, abandoning the plan to supply her boyfriend with additional drinks throughout his run. When Dave reached the next designated refueling stop eight miles down the road and found nobody there, he became even angrier. Within a few more miles he was so dehydrated that he no longer had the energy to be angry. Sixteen miles into the run, Dave saw—in double vision—the family sedan approaching. Dot had decided her boy had been punished enough and had come to his rescue with water. Dave thanked his mother by yelling at her some more.

He could apologize later. This new rage gave him energy, and he needed all the energy he could get.

The water blessed Dave with a strong second wind. As he floated blissfully through the last mile, he passed a group of friends standing together on the curb of a downtown Davis street. Unable to contain himself, Dave spontaneously shouted out a short description of the "workout" he had just done. All of them burst out laughing—not at what he had just done but at the childlike euphoria with which he shared it.

After completing his 127-mile Iron Man dress rehearsal, Dave reviewed it and concluded that, aside from the dehydration episode, it had been easy. It had been, in fact, the most fun he'd ever had. He then analyzed his times, extrapolated, and estimated that he could complete Iron Man in less than ten hours—or more than seventy-five minutes faster than anyone had done it yet.

Dave arrived in Oahu—accompanied by his ever-supportive parents and his best friend, Pat Feeney—brimming with confidence but outwardly humble, secretly intending to *race* an event that everyone else viewed as a test of survival. His goal was not merely to win but to blow people's minds.

Dave was not the only hotshot who had been lured to the third Iron Man by the second's publicity. More than 100 men and a few women had filled out the one-page registration form and paid the $5 entry fee, including some ringers. Future mountain bike world champion Ned Overend had come with his roommate Bob Babbitt. Future Boston Marathon race director Dave McGillivray's name was on the start list. He had recently run across the United States. Olympic cyclist John Howard had also made the trip and was considered the favorite to win. Dave was not intimidated.

Shortly after arriving on the island Dave learned that ABC had dispatched a television crew to film the race for *Wide World of Sports*—a Sunday-afternoon show that everyone watched in those days of thirteen channels. That buzzing feeling of stepping toward a long-awaited destiny returned.

Better still, someone tipped ABC's Jim Lampley that Dave was an athlete to watch, and so, as the sun peeked over the watery horizon off Ala Moana Beach on race morning, Jim hauled Dave in front of a camera and jabbed a microphone in his face.

"Dave, what athletic background do you bring to this event?" Jim asked.

"Uh, limited," Dave lied, chuckling. "I had a swimming background. I swam in college, and I've done quite a few rough-water swims over the last four or five years. My running background? I've only run one marathon. I've been running for about two years. Cycling? It's an unknown."

"Do you think the fact that you've only run one marathon is a big disadvantage here?"

"No," Dave said. "I usually train pretty hard year-round, so I think I can hang on with everyone at the end. I think I can pound it out, so to say, with anyone at the end."

Forget about athletic backgrounds, Jim. Forget about swimming, cycling, and running experience. My edge is mental. I can pound it out with anyone at the end. Nobody *can outlast me!*

The Dave Scott who introduced himself to the world in this manner was the Dave Scott the world would always know. In almost every interview after the first he mixed self-mockery and sandbagging with cocksure, often antagonistic, bravado. His answers always delivered a version of the same basic message.

I'm really not at my best right now, Jim, but I'll probably destroy all the clowns in this race anyway.

The 1980 Ironman was over as soon as it started. Dave had a four-minute lead when he waded out of the placid waters of Ala Moana Basin, where the swim had been moved, over Dave's protests, when a gale producing twelve-foot waves had come along and made the original Waikiki Beach swim course too dangerous to use. (This did not stop Dave from practicing there at the height of the storm on the day before the race, along with a friend who wound up having to be rescued by Coast Guard helicopter.) He ran straight across the beach and into the women's changing room. No matter. The first of the three women in the race would not need that space for another thirty minutes. Dave exchanged his swim brief for a pair of wool cycling shorts, a white cotton muscle shirt, and long tube socks, as if deliberately aiming to make ABC's footage of the race look vintage within just a year or two.

Dave threw a leg over his bike. Pat Feeney, who would serve as Dave's Ironman factotum throughout his career, then set about duct-taping Dave's right shoe to the right pedal. This was a trick they had picked up from the recently released film *Breaking Away*. Taping the feet to the pedals—a technique that would be made obsolete by the advent of clip-in shoes and pedals five years later—was purported to provide the advantage of better pedaling efficiency. It came with the obvious disadvantage of causing the rider to fall over if he stopped. Before the race Dave had thought he could live with this disadvantage, but in confronting the reality of the risk, he changed his mind.

"Let's just do the one foot," Dave said.

Pat shrugged. A physicist, he was tempted to point out that if Dave wasn't going to ride with both feet taped, he might as well ride with neither foot taped, but he held his tongue.

Dave rode off, one foot duct-taped to a pedal, with almost violent intensity, as though he had been given bad information about the distance of the race. He was expecting this John Howard guy to blow by him any minute. Little did Dave know he would be twenty miles down the road by the time John finally left the water, having no hope of catching the man with a limited athletic background—although he certainly tried, blazing through the 112-mile bike course in four hours, twenty-eight minutes, a time that few professional triathletes could match today despite the benefit of such innovations as clip-in pedals, aerobars, and carbon-fiber frames.

The day turned muggy, but Dave embraced the wet heat as a relief from the cold and rain of the Davis winter in which he had completed his training. His body seemed to come alive in the humidity, which had the opposite effect on almost everyone else. Dave liked anything that made a race harder, believing that every enhancement of the basic challenge increased his mental advantage over other competitors. The elements were just one more factor that made Iron Man seem like a thing he had been allowed to design himself, to ensure his own dominance.

There were no road closures, course markers, aid stations, or support staff. Dave had a single police motorcycle as an escort, and his parents followed him in a rented woodie wagon with a spare bike on top and food and drinks in the backseat. He ran red lights and stop signs and had a few close encounters with cross-traffic that had the right of way.

Two hours into the ride, Dave's taped left foot was killing him. Pat had wrapped it too tightly, cutting off circulation. Dave realized they probably should have practiced the technique before the race. He also decided he probably shouldn't adopt any more racing techniques from movies.

By the time Pat Feeney freed Dave's throbbing foot from the right pedal, Dave held a twenty-five-minute lead on John Howard. He had not seen a single competitor since the race had started six hours earlier. In the changing room (men's this time) he exchanged his cycling clothes, such as they were, for a skimpy pair of running shorts, no shirt. A race official then directed him to a scale, where he had to pass a weigh-in before being allowed to finish the race. Too much weight loss meant too much dehydration.

"Wow, you've only lost one pound!" the woman said.

In all the excitement she somehow failed to notice the liter bottle of water, full and weighing two pounds, that Dave held, having just received it from a fast-thinking Pat Feeney.

Dave started running, and again his pace seemed to betray a dangerous ignorance of how far he had to go, not to mention obliviousness to how far he had already come. But Dave was feeling totally at home as an athlete for the first time in his life. He had vowed to transform Iron Man from a test of survival into a race, and he was doing it. Every previous Iron Man finisher had walked significant stretches of the marathon and done little more than shuffle during the running parts. Dave clicked off steady sub-eight-minute miles and did not walk a single step except when he stopped to relieve himself in some bushes.

The finish line of the 1980 Iron Man was an almost invisible piece of string held up by race director Valerie Silk and a volunteer on a quiet street in Kapiolani Park. Expecting a little more fanfare, Dave fittingly ran right through it, stopping only when Valerie shouted after him, "You're done. You won."

A LEGEND WAS BORN. Dave's time of 9:24:33 bettered the existing course record by an hour and fifty-one minutes. Runner-up Chuck Neumann, who passed John Howard during the marathon, did not finish for another hour, by which time Dave had dressed; stretched; eaten massively; talked over the whole experience with Verne, Dot, and Pat; and done interviews.

"Are you going to retire?" asked Carol Hogan, a reporter for the *Honolulu Advertiser*.

Carol knew Dave from his past visits to Hawaii for open-water swims. She had a bit of a crush on him and had lost her reason in the excitement of the moment. Dave had just turned 26.

"Retire?" Dave said. "I'm just getting started!"

Word of Dave's stunning achievement spread rapidly through the burgeoning endurance subculture in California and beyond, and ABC's airing of its Iron Man coverage made him an instant idol to thousands more. Somewhere in all of this, he acquired a nickname. First it was "the Iron Man." Then just "the Man."

Dave had hoped that winning Iron Man would open a door, and it did. Aspiring triathletes found his address and phone number and contacted him seeking advice and training plans. Born teacher that he was, and a willing responder to the flattery of being approached as an authority, Dave doled out his expertise freely at first. Then he started charging: $150 to $275 per one-year plan. He went into business under the name Dave Scott Triathlon Training and soon expanded from coaching into daylong clinics. Verne, always watchful for ways to share in his children's passions, organized a triathlon in Davis.

Sponsors came calling. Nike, Anheuser-Busch, Peak Performance vitamins, and helmet maker Bell exchanged cash for the rights to Dave's name and image.

In the summer of 1980 Dave found himself sitting in the family room of his parents' home, talking with Verne and Dot about what a whirlwind the past few months had been and where it all might lead.

"You know, you don't have to do that crazy race again," said Verne, who may have still had a vestige of hope that he could steer his son toward a more intellectual profession than ultraendurance racing.

"Well, I'm going to," Dave said.

The Man was nothing if not his own man.

In due time Verne would come to appreciate the full measure of what his son had found in Ironman. Not in triathlon generally but in that specific event, with its crazy distances, its extreme conditions, its mystique.

"There's no other race that draws out my physical talents as this one does," Dave told ABC before his 1989 showdown with Mark Allen.

Dave was not the fastest guy over short distances, but he seemed able to sustain his maximum speed almost indefinitely. Heat did not slow him down, as it was supposed to. And most importantly, at the end Dave could, as he said, "pound it out with anyone"—because his greatest athletic ability was his *inability* to quit.

Beyond matching up ideally with Dave's talents, Ironman also made his thirty-hours-a-week workout habit something other than freakishly pointless. Suddenly it was perfectly rational. Ironman actually rewarded working harder than anyone else alive. That was precisely how you won it. And Dave set about working harder than he ever had before as he prepared to defend his Ironman title.

TRIATHLON TRAINING METHODS had not been normalized when Dave won his first Ironman, and even to the extent that the sport's earliest pioneers had figured out what seemed to work, Dave did not care to follow anyone else's lead. So when he began training to defend his title, he simply continued the experiment he had started the previous summer. He discovered that about 30,000 yards of swimming, 400 miles of cycling, and 70 miles of running per week, plus four hard weight lifting sessions, were his limit. If he pushed any further, he broke down.

Dave did most of his training alone. Each workout was a private game, like his old seventh grade game of racing the bus to school. Games provided the telos that enabled Dave to pursue his mission of "seeing what he could do." To continually redefine his physical limits Dave could not just jump into the pool or hop onto his bike or lace up his running shoes and try hard. He needed a concrete challenge, a clear representation of his present limit, to go after. There had to be some way he could *win* every single swim, ride, and run he did. This approach was woven into the fabric of his nature.

There wasn't much variety in these games. Any other athlete, no matter how driven, would have found Dave's training routine dizzyingly monotonous. There weren't all that many places to ride and run in Davis anyway, but Dave waved off whatever diversity there was in favor of covering the same routes over and over again, day after day, month after month, and ultimately year after year. By October 1989, when his climactic Ironman duel with Mark Allen occurred, Dave had ridden his favorite among a handful of cycling routes, an out-and-back on Highway 31 to the hills east of Davis, some 3,000 times.

Millions of laps in the pool in his formative years had left Dave with no need for variety or scenic distractions in workouts. Endless repetition in training allowed him to monitor progress easily and precisely. All Dave wanted from his bike rides and runs were the same things the pool gave him: the structure and measurability required to play the simple game of improving his times.

Dave memorized the distance of every ride, and key segments of every ride, and memorized his best time for every ride and key segment so he could chase these standards repeatedly in his pursuit of perfection. His favorite game was time trialing the last twelve-and-a-half-mile segment of the ride that took him to Lake Berryessa and back. If asked today what his best time for that stretch of road was, he would gladly supply the number without a moment's hesitation: 26:50.

On those rare occasions when he rode or ran with another person (and then only one, typically), the partner became the focus of the game. Among the few athletes Dave permitted to join him on rides with any regularity was Mike Norton, who really had no business training with Dave because he was nowhere near the same level as an athlete. But that disparity was not a problem that the right game couldn't solve. During a long out-and-back ride, for example, Dave might propose, after making some silent calculations, that Mike turn around at the next crossroads, and then he would continue for another three miles before reversing his own direction and trying to catch Mike before he got home.

Although Mike Norton allowed Dave to dictate the games they played in their occasional shared workouts, most other athletes, and especially Dave's fellow elite athletes, resisted such unilateral control, so Dave avoided them—which was as easy as staying put in Davis, where there were no other pros.

He did entertain the occasional visit from an elite racer living within driving distance of Davis. Mike Pigg, who hailed from Arcata, among the redwoods of Humboldt County, visited twice.

Pigg had been taking classes at a community college and working part time as a mechanic's assistant for a trucking company when he saw Dave Scott win Ironman on *Wide World of Sports* and was inspired to give triathlon a try. He was still fairly new to the sport and as much Dave's fan as his peer when he convinced Dave to let him come to Davis for a week of training. Dave was surprised by Pigg's appetite, which rivaled his own. Before their first ride together Pigg poured three kinds of cereal into a mixing bowl and emptied it in minutes.

Pigg was no less Dave's match on the bike. On their longest ride together Dave found himself hanging on to Pigg's back wheel by a thread, concentrating so completely on survival that he missed a turn. By the time he discovered his mistake they were far from home and badly in need of energy. They stopped at a convenience store, where Pigg inhaled a box of Ding Dongs and a bottle of chocolate milk and Dave devoured a loaf of bread. The last leg of their 130-mile expedition was completed in the dark.

Pigg left after four days. Both men were exhausted. Dave simply couldn't figure out how to train with Pigg without racing him. Although the two men remained friends and mutual admirers, years would pass before Pigg returned to Davis.

WHILE TRAINING for the 1981 Ironman Dave developed a pain in his knee while running. His response was to continue running every day. The pain worsened. Dave kept running. Soon he couldn't run at all, or even walk without pain. Now Dave was forced to rest. He took a few days off, but the pain persisted. His mood turned dark, as it always did when he was deprived of physical exertion. But this time his disappointment turned to apathy. He stopped caring—or seemed to. Dave's knee healed eventually, but he did not resume training. Instead he sat all day in a beanbag chair inside his apartment. He binged on foods he normally avoided. Within a month he had gained fifteen pounds.

Dave's girlfriend, who shared his apartment, became concerned. Although she had first known Dave only as a shirtless, golden-skinned man running past her dorm window, Linda Buchanan, then a member of the UC-Davis swim team, had joined Dave's swim club after her graduation and had soon become his sweetheart, roommate, and a top triathlete herself. From her own experience as an athlete she understood the frustration of setbacks in training, but the meltdown she was witnessing in Dave was something else entirely. She tried to cheer him up at first, but he didn't want that, so she let him be and simply rode out the storm beside him, trusting that whatever demon had a hold on him would let go eventually. Only after the 1981 Ironman took place without Dave did the storm clouds disperse.

Months later Dave was hit with another injury, and again he plunged into the slough of despond. Linda rode out this second dark period as gamely as she had the first, but after a third episode she dumped the most eligible bachelor in Davis and moved to San Diego. It wasn't that she was fed up with Dave's unpredictability. In fact, Linda had no idea why she had left Dave and could not articulate a clear reason when he beseeched her for an explanation. Years would pass before Linda would figure out that dashing, exciting, kind, charismatic Dave Scott did not satisfy her because what she really needed was the love of a beautiful, exciting, kind, charismatic woman.

Dave went into a tailspin. Prone to terrible insomnia during periods of stress, he slept poorly. Although uninjured, he stopped training. He returned to the beanbag chair and went back to bingeing. His friends did what little they could to get him going again, but in vain. Dave did manage to make a trip to Bass Lake, California, to compete in a triathlon he was obligated to race for his sponsors, but he would have been better off staying home. He finished twenty-seventh, getting his ass handed to him by second-rate pros and amateurs who would forever after be able to say, "I beat Dave Scott."

It was that humiliation and the mockery inspired by his bad showing—which, of course, reached his ears eventually—that finally jolted Dave out of his funk and got him back on track. Like other perfectionists, Dave never tired of criticizing himself, but he was acutely sensitive to criticism from others—which is to say he fed off it.

On the rebound from Linda Buchanan, Dave plucked another comely young swimmer from the pool, his future wife, Anna Pettis. One day they happened to find themselves in neighboring lanes of the Davis Civic Center pool. By coincidence, they also completed their separate workouts at the same time and left the building together. They stepped outside into a downpour. Dave, who'd had his eye on Anna for a while, offered her a ride home. She was a bundle of nerves the whole way, because Dave was a local hero, larger than life, and because he was 29 and she was 21, and because Dave was flirting with her and Anna thought he was still seeing Linda. When they reached her building, Dave asked her out. Afraid to say no, she said yes, only later finding out that Dave was, in fact, single.

No sooner had Anna fallen for Dave's looks, charm, and celebrity than Dave hit another bump in the road, and she encountered his vulnerable side. She tried everything under the sun, from encouragement to guilt trips, to coax him out the door during these low moments. When the most obvious measures failed, she got creative. She bought a bike and rode it with him but gave that up after crashing and breaking a collarbone. When creative measures failed, she tried the absurd. More than once Anna offered to drive her car ahead of Dave, blaring motivational music while he rode his bike. But for all her efforts, she never found any solution that really worked.

The trigger for one of these downswings could be anything from stress in a relationship to an injury to simple burnout from his frenzied training highs. It was hard to predict, but Anna did her best. She developed antennae with exquisite sensitivity to early warning signs of coming trouble. But even when she foresaw rough patches on Dave's road, she could not steer him around them. Dave had to go through them on his own, and Anna took comfort in knowing that he always came out the other side eventually.

Anna could no more explain Dave's struggle than cure it. Perhaps, she speculated, his energy and will were just too strong for his body, like an engine too powerful for its supporting chassis. His drive to see what he could do seemed to guzzle all his resources and then demand more, leaving him defenseless on many fronts. Dave was like a human dragster, precariously combining extreme power and structural lightness for maximum speed, hence as likely to explode as to go really fast when the lights turned green.

Dave's perfectionism was also mixed up in his pattern of ups and downs. The kinds of small setbacks and interruptions to his training that other people would roll right over drove him around the bend. He was like a straight-A student who, when he gets a B+ on a quiz, says, "To hell with it!" and drops out of school.

Naturally, as a perfectionist, Dave likely hated himself for going off the rails. So he punished himself by going even farther off the rails.

During one dark period Dave told Scott Molina that he had just eaten eleven PowerBars in a sitting instead of working out.

"What are you doing?" Molina told him. "You're punishing yourself—for what? You're just making yourself more miserable!"

Although Dave was able to hide most of his weakest moments from Scott Molina and his other competitors by holing up in Davis, he never hid his personal struggles from the public. On the contrary, he seemed compelled to expose his vulnerabilities openly in the media. He told a *Sports Illustrated* writer about "personal troubles" that had laid him low lately. He seemingly mistook a CBS cameraman for a therapist during the bike leg of the 1983 Kauai Loves You Triathlon, confessing his lovelorn, lonely state to America. Later the same year he told an ABC reporter, "There are periods when I like to sit in my beanbag chair and let the days go by." And in his 1986 book, *Dave Scott's Triathlon Training*, Dave admitted to having "battled emotional problems."

Despite all of this, Dave's image as "an unshakable monolith and a single-minded endurance maniac" (as one journalist described him) persisted. How? Because of Ironman. After the setbacks that followed his game-changing Ironman victory in 1980, Dave somehow always—almost always—managed to pull himself together for the only race that really mattered. His awe-inspiring October triumphs would obliterate all memory of his twenty-seventh place finishes at short triathlons in June.

Ironman would become the balance point of Dave's dynamic equilibrium. Year after year he would go as far off the rails as he could possibly go without flushing any chance of winning Ironman; then he would pull himself together to salvage his claim to the title that had become his identity. He was like a procrastinating genius who doesn't read a book all semester and then crams like mad in the last week before exams, rallying at just the point where he must rely on the full scope of his genius to pass every test.

Dave typically wallowed until he was written off—until he was able to grab on to some sign of dismissal that enraged him, putting him in that happy place of fury, discovered during his 127-mile Ironman rehearsal, where he was able to work harder and suffer more than any other athlete could. When he arrived on the starting line in Kona, it did not matter how badly Dave had embarrassed himself at races earlier in the season or what sorts of rumors about his mental state had circulated—everyone else was scared shitless of him because they remembered what he had done to them the previous year after similar embarrassments and rumors.

He didn't always inspire such fear, though. Dave's jaw-dropping one-hour victory in the 1980 Ironman gave him a lot of slack to waste afterward, but his legend would not have survived if he had not eventually followed up with further feats of fortitude—and he wasted every inch of that slack. After getting injured and going off the rails in the summer of 1980, Dave did not start the 1981 Ironman, which John Howard won. The next summer the same pattern was repeated. This time Dave got back on track in time to cram for the 1982 Ironman but not in time to attain peak fitness. The new golden boy of triathlon, Scott Tinley, passed Dave early in the run and relegated the Man to second place, breaking his course record in the process.

Ironman was then moved from February to October. Dave prepared for the October 1982 Ironman as just one of five one-time winners of the race. He was in danger of becoming a historical footnote. Dave felt a consuming need to win again. His usual competitive anger was intensified by a terrible fear of irrelevance as he drove his body through the heat and wind of another Davis summer toward vengeance in his third Ironman—which just happened to be Mark Allen's first.

CHAPTER 3

GET A GRIP

Courage is the fear of being thought a coward.

— HORACE SMITH

Mark Allen was born in a shack in Glendale, California. The shack stood in the backyard of a house whose owner rented it to Mark's struggling parents. Mark's father, Ken Allen, whose friends called him by his unusual middle name, Space, would later become an ob-gyn, but in January 1958 he was still a poorly paid medical lab technician who lacked any special skills that might have helped him bring his first child safely into the world. Nevertheless, baby Mark arrived healthy. Exceptionally healthy.

Three years after Mark's arrival a second son, David, was born to Space and his wife, Sharon, also at home. A few months later they took the infant to the hospital, worried about David's development. The doctor ran some tests. He returned to the room where they waited wearing an expression that stopped their breath.

"I'm afraid I have some bad news, Mr. and Mrs. Allen," he said.

David had Down syndrome. Some cases are more severe than others, and David's was very severe. Space and Sharon cared for him at home until he was 10 years old, by which time they had a third son, Gary. Then they made the heartbreaking decision to place David in an institution, where he has remained ever since.

Isolated from his first brother by misfortune and from his second by a significant age gap, Mark grew up as an only child in all but name. This circumstance may have strengthened a deeply self-reliant nature that Mark evinced early and seemed to have inherited from Space. Father and son alike kept their own counsel.

When Mark was still a preschooler, Space enrolled at St. Louis University School of Medicine, and the family moved to the Midwest. For the next year they lived in poverty in a low-income housing project near campus. Crime was rampant in their midtown neighborhood. Mark could see a small playground below from his bedroom window, but he was afraid to use it. When Sharon shopped for groceries she would honk the car's horn outside their building until Space came down to help her carry the bags up to the flat. The stench of urine never left the elevator. The walls were so thin that at night Mark could hear the screams and weeping of a woman being beaten by her husband in a neighboring apartment.

FIVE-YEAR-OLD MARK ALLEN felt no safer inside the slum tenement building his family inhabited in St. Louis than he did outside it. The source of his fear was his father. Mark would later use the words "rough" and "abusive" to describe Space's treatment of him. Besides administering frequent "negative reinforcement," as the adult Mark Allen would delicately characterize his paternal handling, Space endlessly criticized his eldest son's imperfections. He did not erupt in fits of temper. On the contrary, he was icy and distant, paying Mark little attention except to pass judgment and to express his disappointment in no uncertain terms.

Mark long repressed his memories of the worst that happened to him during these years. The details would remain lost deep inside him for almost a quarter century. But the effect that Space's tough parenting had on his eldest son was profound. Mark internalized the judgments that his father passed on him. The self-trusting part of Mark knew he was a good kid: smart, friendly, funny, and blessed with many talents. But he struggled to fully believe in his own worth, to love himself as he deserved. There was an emptiness inside him of which he was constantly, dully aware.

To cope with this emotional undernourishment, Mark developed a strong desire for outside validation. Like many sons of fathers who withhold their blessings, he had an unquenchable thirst to distinguish himself. By the time he started school most of his greater efforts were motivated by hopes of proving his worth—to his father, to himself, and to the world. Yet nothing he did ever seemed enough.

"All along I felt I was hopelessly lost in a sea of the ordinary," Mark once explained. "I always wanted to do something that would stand out, something others would look at and say, 'That's incredible.'"

MARK STARTED FIRST GRADE two weeks late. His family had just moved from St. Louis to Sacramento. Space had earned his medical degree and scored an internship at a hospital just down the road from the University of California-Davis, where Dave Scott's father, Verne, was on the civil engineering faculty. Mark's classmates did not know what to make of him. He spoke sparingly and expressed little emotion. But he was not quiet in the empty way of some kids. Mark's silence was intense. His piercing, green-eyed stare suggested that a lot was going on behind it. He seemed to exist halfway in the reality occupied by his fellow students and halfway in some other reality, visible to himself alone.

Kids who are hard to peg attract nicknames, and Mark would have many. His first nickname at school was "the Kid," an appellation that referred both to his scrawny body and to his inscrutability. Later he would become "Twanger" (a bastardization of "Twain," as in Mark Twain, whose unruly curls of chestnut hair Mark Allen shared) and later still "the Enigma" and "Zen Master," monikers recognizing the unique spiritual presence that Mark's older peers came to see in his semiabsence from the here and now.

Mark's new first grade classmates had been learning to read since day one of the school year. Mark did not even know the alphabet. But he knew that Space expected him to be the best student in his class, so he studied the reader he had been issued with all the focus and willpower a 6-year-old boy could muster. Before long he had surpassed everyone to become the strongest reader in the entire first grade. He tasted a delicious triumph, a feeling of satisfaction so bracing he never forgot it.

The next year the Allen family moved 100 miles southwest to Palo Alto, where Space started a residency at Stanford University. That summer the Olympics took place in Mexico City. Mark was captivated by the swimming events and the medal-winning exploits of Mark Spitz, Don Schollander, and other American heroes. By then Mark probably knew the story of his father's swimming experience. Growing up on a farm in upstate New York during the Great Depression, Space had never learned how to stay afloat in water. After graduating from high school he enlisted in the navy to avoid being drafted into the army and possibly sent to the front line of the Korean War. But in order to join the sailors' ranks, he first had to pass a test that consisted of swimming from the edge of a pool to the middle and back. Space survived the test, but barely.

Eighteen years later Space still feared the water. This fear did not trickle down to his first child, as parental fears often do. If anything, Space's phobia probably made the pool even more intriguing to Mark. But it did give him a late start. At age 10 Mark could manage no more than an exhausting dog paddle. Observers would have assumed, based on his skill and his size, that he was about half his actual age.

Sharon often took Mark to a local public outdoor pool to play in the water. Mark's favorite part of the swimming-pool experience was the diving board, which stood at the deep end. There was a rule that you had to be able to swim twenty-five yards without stopping before you were allowed into that part of the pool. This distance represented the outer limit of Mark's swimming range. Enforcing the rule was a matter of lifeguard discretion. One day Mark was dog-paddling across the pool toward the diving board when a lifeguard called out to him, "Hey, kid! Can you swim twenty-five yards?"

Nothing made Mark more determined to do something than being told he could not do it. A mere suggestion of inability, like this lifeguard's skeptical question, was often enough to set him to the task. *I'll show him I can swim*, Mark thought. *I'll show everyone!*

Mark passed the test, but barely. A short time later he spotted an advertisement for youth swim club tryouts in the *Palo Alto Times.* He begged his parents to take him. Within a year of his first lesson Mark had become an exceptional competitive swimmer. His meteoric progress in the pool filled him with a delicious triumph. That was reward enough, but an even greater and unexpected reward was the pride that Space, who had never before shown any pride in his son, took in Mark's accomplishments in the water. The more Mark won, the more supportive of his swimming—and of his general being, it seemed—his father became. Mark drank up the approval thirstily.

One day, when Mark was 12 years old, Space swung by the hospital to see some patients and brought Mark with him. They first stopped by the nurses' station, where Space introduced Mark to an attractive woman in her mid-20s.

"Mark, meet Nurse Carole," Space said. "Everyone calls her Toot." Addressing the woman, he continued, "Mark's my oldest. He's going to be an Olympic swimmer."

Mark blushed and rolled his eyes, pretending without success to hate the overblown praise. Toot rolled her eyes with him as though to say, "He lays it on thick, doesn't he?" Mark did not know that his father had fallen in love with the pretty nurse. Toot also did not know some things.

Space's pride in Mark's swimming did not last long beyond this introduction to his future stepmother. It became apparent that Mark, though gifted, would never in fact become an Olympic swimmer. Mark had fallen victim to a version of the Peter Principle, rising to the level where he was no longer the best. The ride was over. Almost as suddenly and unexpectedly as Space had gotten behind Mark's exploits in the pool, he turned away. He stopped coming to races. He stopped listening, even *pretending* to listen, when Mark tried to talk about his swimming. Almost completely incapable of expressing deep feelings openly or airing grievances directly with another person—especially his father—Mark found himself powerless to alleviate the bereavement Space's indifference caused in him. He had come to rely on the approval that winning earned him, and the loss of that approval tormented him.

Around the time Space stopped paying attention to his eldest son, Mark hit another wall as a swimmer. He became a classic athletic head case. A choker. If someone got even a half-stroke lead on him, his race was done. Without fail, if the guy next to him seemed bigger, stronger, or more focused, Mark choked. There was a fear lurking inside him that became paralyzing, utterly self-sabotaging, under the right stimulation.

Mark heard a voice in his head at the most critical moments of the race. The same confidence-crushing script played over and over: *I can't do it! This guy's too strong! I'm going to lose again!* Despite his talent, his love of swimming, his willingness to work hard, and a burning desire to win, Mark carried a deep sense of self-doubt into his racing that made him weak in the moments when he most needed to be strong. Any endurance athlete can fall prey to a voice of negativity and self-pity in crisis moments, but in Mark that mutinous inner voice had a special personal significance. It *hated* him.

Life improved for Mark after Space divorced Sharon, married Toot, and moved with his new wife to Elko, Nevada. Mark was required to visit his dad occasionally and dreaded each trip. His best friend, Eric Bunje, always noticed that Mark seemed out of sorts for a few days after returning to Palo Alto. But when Eric invited his friend to talk about it, a wall went up. Otherwise, with Space out of the way, Mark began to feel truly free for the first time in his life.

On weekends he and Eric planned long bike rides. Mark on his ten-speed Gitane, Eric on his Schwinn, both in street clothes, they pedaled from Mark's home on High Street to an A&W restaurant and split a gallon of root beer, or rode to Foothills Park and ate submarine sandwiches, or dragged themselves over the coastal mountains to San Gregorio State Beach—a seventy-mile round-trip.

Mark remained dedicated to his swimming, but he needed more success, more recognition, than he was finding in the pool, so he decided to test the waters of another sport. One day the coach of the Palo Alto High School cross-country team was approached by a scrawny kid with a piercing, green-eyed stare and hair like Mark Twain's who asked if he could race. Not join the team or train with the runners—he couldn't do that because swim practice conflicted with cross-country practice. Just do the races. Mark's self-doubt got the best of him during his first race, when he faked a stomachache and dropped out. But he redeemed himself at his next opportunity and soon became one of the team's top runners—logging just a few runs per week on his own.

Mark's explorations at this time were not limited to the physical but included the spiritual. If he seemed to others to exist partly in another reality, it was because he did, showing a strong spiritual sensibility when he was still quite young. One of Mark's childhood friends observed an early sign of this sensibility in the strong pull that nature exerted on him; before Mark had even reached his teens he demonstrated an adult appreciation for the beauty of a fiery sunset or the grace of a gliding hawk. Later Mark developed a curiosity about religions and spiritual traditions. The same childhood friend noticed that when Mark visited the homes of religious friends, he asked lots of questions. He felt pulled toward sages, prophets, and wise men depicted in movies, figures like Chief Sitting Bull. Space's father no doubt intrigued Mark. An osteopath, he had been more or less adopted into a Native American tribe in New Mexico and had learned the tribal language, spiritual ways, and other customs.

After her divorce Sharon chose spiritual exploration as her primary means of self-reinvention. Through her Mark was exposed to Zen Buddhism and transcendental meditation. On his own he discovered the works of Carlos Castaneda, an anthropologist and best-selling author who narrated psychedelic stories of a youthful shamanistic apprenticeship in Mexico. Mark had been forced to attend Sunday school briefly when he was younger and had chafed against it. Christianity was too rule-bound and institutionalized for his taste. He much preferred the primitiveness of the shamanism Castaneda described, the ubiquity of nature in its lore and rituals, and the immediacy of the supernatural. Too bad such practices existed only in Mexico and other faraway places.

Mark hungered for a spiritual path he could really latch on to. He judged each one he sampled by feel. He knew the right path would feel right when he found it. It would lead him into deep connectedness with all things and would fill the emptiness that troubled his soul, that became a confidence-crushing inner voice of doubt in competition, and that motivated all of his searches in life. But nothing seemed a perfect match. So he kept searching.

Midway through his senior year of high school Mark left home, with Sharon's hands-off support, to participate in tryouts for a lifeguarding job in San Diego. He qualified and returned to Southern California immediately after his high school graduation to laze away his days on the beach for $6 an hour until it was time to begin his studies at UC–San Diego in the fall. He lived in a low-rent apartment in the town of Oceanside with Gary Hardin, a fellow lifeguard and a former swimming teammate in Palo Alto. The days passed in a haze of mellow pleasure.

Mark had recently learned to surf. His first ride was an awakening. He was instantly hooked and quickly bought a board. Surfing brought Mark a joy he had never experienced in any other hobby—not playing baseball, not taking kung fu lessons, not riding a unicycle, not even swimming. Surfing had the element of exertion that Mark liked in swimming, but it was also thrilling, a pure adrenaline rush. And there was something wonderful about the idea of taking a free ride on water instead of struggling through it—something magical, mystical, about partnering with nature to create these little performances of ephemeral beauty.

For Mark, the pleasure of surfing was completely intrinsic to the activity, whereas the satisfaction of swimming was largely contingent on winning. Only winning really satisfied Mark in the pool because that was the point, especially for those who were attracted to the sport as a means to be extraordinary. Winning swim races momentarily answered in the affirmative the silent question that followed him everywhere: *Do I have something to offer in this world?* On his surfboard Mark was filled, also briefly, tantalizingly, with a very different feeling: peace. It did not answer the question that dogged him. It made him forget it.

Mark spent as much time as he could riding waves throughout the summer. Years later an interviewer would ask him what he thought he might have been if he had not become a triathlete. A surf bum, he said, only half joking.

MARK QUIT SWIMMING after his first year at UCSD. The coach was terrible and the athletics department unsupportive, asking him to pay his own way to the national championships, for which he qualified despite training only a few days a week. Enough of chlorine. Mark would rather surf, where he couldn't lose. But his decision was short-lived. The athletic department hired an infectiously enthusiastic young coach, Bill Morgan, who had himself just graduated from UCSD. Bill befriended Mark and persuaded him to get back into the pool. It wasn't a hard sale. Swimming was still Mark's best escape from the sea of the ordinary.

Mark wound up using all four years of his college eligibility, and achieved some of his finest successes as a swimmer, qualifying for the championships of the NAIA in ten events. But he would have done more, perhaps even won a few of those championship events, if his shaky confidence had not bedeviled him still. In race after race Mark started strong and finished poorly. His talent and fitness would carry him to the decisive last lap, and then that voice of doubt and fear would enter his head, and he would fall apart.

I can't do it! This guy's too strong! I'm going to lose again!

Mark's most spectacular collapse occurred during his senior year in a 200-yard individual medley, a grueling event that comprises a 50-yard butterfly leg, a 50-yard backstroke leg (Mark's specialty), a 50-yard breaststroke leg, and finally a 50-yard freestyle leg. He started incredibly well, reaching the 150-yard mark in 1:27, on pace for a nation-leading time of 1:56. But what should have been his fastest leg, the closing 50 freestyle, was his slowest—a pathetic thirty-two-second slog, putting him at the wall in 1:59. Still a great time, but not what might have been.

Bill Morgan nearly had to help Mark climb out of the pool, so weakened was he from his implosion.

"What happened?" Bill asked.

Mark threw up his arms in speechless frustration.

MARK GREETED HIS GRADUATION from college with both relief and dread. On the one hand, he felt relieved to be freed from the grind of taking classes that were not always his own first choices (he had majored in biology at his father's quiet insistence) and the "black-line fever" of swimming endless laps in the pool. He looked forward to having more time to surf and hang out with friends, enjoying the beach-centered, cannabis-scented San Diego lifestyle. On the other hand, the pressure to follow his dad's plan for his life intensified. Space wanted his eldest son to become a doctor too, even though it seemed to Mark that he did not really like being a doctor himself.

Every few weeks Space phoned Mark to have the same conversation.

"Have you decided what you're going to do with your life?" he would ask.

"No, Dad. Not yet."

In his first summer out of college Mark reluctantly struck a compromise. He worked full time as a lifeguard and took surfing trips to Mexico and Hawaii. But he also studied for the Medical College Admission Test. Mark dragged himself to the university library several times a week to listen to study tapes. Again and again he would snap out of daydreams and realize he hadn't absorbed a single word in minutes. *Why am I doing this?* he asked himself.

Blessed—or, in this case, cursed—with a steel-trap mind, Mark aced the test despite his halfhearted preparation. Only then, when the two conflicting plans for his life (or rather his father's plan and his own unscripted preference) formed a crossroads, did Mark discover that he just couldn't do it—could not bear to give himself over to four years of medical school, several more years of internship and residency, and after that a career that he knew he would loathe as much as his dad hated his own career in medicine.

Mark braced himself and broke the news in the next monthly phone call from his sire. He still did not know what he was going to do with his life, besides maybe lifeguarding for another year or so. He only knew he was not going to be a doctor.

IN 1981 IT WAS next to impossible for a former college swimmer to work as a lifeguard in Southern California without getting involved in lifeguard competitions, which combine open-water swimming and barefoot beach running. In trying his hand at these races, Mark rediscovered his talent for running and excelled in the few low-key competitions he participated in, earning a new nickname along the way: Animallen. Mark had the ideal crossbred body for these hybrid races. A late growth spurt had brought him to a swimmer's height of six feet, but he was built like a greyhound, with long tubes of springy muscle stretched across bird bones. His rib cage was massive, housing huge lungs that served him well on land and in the water. Mark had run a sub-five-minute mile in tennis shoes after swim practice one day in college when a teammate who said he couldn't run challenged him to a race.

Some of the other participants in these lifeguard competitions also dabbled in the fledgling sport of triathlon. Among them was Mark's friend Reed Gregerson, who informed him one day that he had signed up for the fifth Ironman triathlon in Hawaii, which Mark had heard about but had never given much thought to before.

The race took place on February 6, 1982. Reed acquitted himself well, finishing fifth. Two weeks later, on Sunday, February 21, taped coverage of the race was broadcast on ABC's *Wide World of Sports*. San Diego's own Scott Tinley had won, and there were viewing parties all over the county. Mark and his live-in girlfriend, Bernice "Bunny" Stein, hosted one at their apartment in Del Mar. Mark did not know Tinley but was keen to catch a glimpse or two of Reed.

Those ninety minutes of television changed Mark's life.

Reed got little love from ABC's cameras, but another familiar face did: Reed's on-and-off girlfriend Julie Moss, a cute 23-year-old college student with ginger-colored hair from nearby Carlsbad, whom Reed had met in lifeguarding school. Julie had signed up for Ironman not because she had any personal interest in the ordeal but because she hoped that training with Reed might extend their relationship. He dumped her before the race, but she followed through with her Ironman commitment in the hope that she could win him back with a show of grit.

The plan worked—and then some. Julie made her television debut when she passed the women's race leader, Pat Hines, eight miles into the marathon. Julie built up a big lead over the next ten miles, but with eight miles remaining in the race, she began to weaken. At first her decline wasn't so bad. She merely had to interrupt her running with walking breaks. But the downward slide continued and indeed went further than imaginable. As day gave way to dusk and dusk to night, Julie's race also descended into darkness. Her stride became a shuffle, her shuffle a spastic, two-legged limp. The freckled waif, her small head lost underneath a baby-blue baseball cap, looked like a half-starved prisoner of war being prodded with a bayonet to walk barefoot over broken glass as she made the turn onto Ali'i Drive, the homestretch, still leading but losing ground quickly to another 23-year-old college student, Kathleen McCartney. A scant quarter mile from the finish line, Julie suddenly collapsed in a heap, falling like a condemned building imploding into its own foundation. She dropped in the way that already-unconscious people do—a way that betokens no quick rise. Yet within two minutes Julie was back on her feet. After peeling her body off the pavement, she steadied herself briefly with the fingers of both hands on the road, doubled over, before pulling herself upright. The television camera held a rear angle on Julie as she paused in that bottom-up position, presenting an excellent view of a murky stain on the seat of her light-blue running shorts and dark, semisolid matter dribbling down her inner thighs.

Mark watched transfixed as Julie continued to wobble toward the finish line. Incredibly, she seemed to regain mastery of her limbs as she went, first swinging her upper appendages in an almost jaunty straight-armed fashion and then breaking into a herky-jerky quasi run. She survived to within about 100 yards of the finish line before dropping to the asphalt again. Two male race volunteers detached themselves from the spellbound and appalled crowd that tightly surrounded her by this time and helped lift her to her feet. At first it appeared clear that she would fall the moment they let go of her arms, which were held outspread from her body. But seconds later she pulled free from her concerned rescuers, waving them away like a dangerously plastered sorority girl refusing an escort home.

Julie had stumblingly halved the distance to the finish line when she made the mistake of trying to run again and instantly planted her face on the street. As volunteers struggled to restore her to a standing posture a second time, Kathleen McCartney slipped by, unnoticed in the darkness and crowdedness and confusion, to win the race. Julie now crawled toward the finish line. The six-deep crowd of spectators, many in tears, who lined the barricades on either side of her applauded, less with sympathy than with awestruck respect, as Julie inched through the last bit of her personal Via Dolorosa and collapsed one last time, right on top of the finish line.

Mark's own cheeks were wet with tears when he stood up to turn off the television. He could not imagine ever subjecting himself to such a pointlessly extreme torment. Yet he could not stop thinking about the race, and about Julie Moss especially. The courage Julie had shown in finishing Ironman was the very quality Mark had lacked as an athlete ever since his father had turned away. Seeing such courage in girl-next-door Julie Moss made Mark believe he could find it in himself and made him want it more than ever. Over the ensuing days, Mark came to recognize that overcoming the choker within him was his greatest present need in life. And the way to do it had already been revealed to him.

Two weeks after he saw Julie Moss crawl across the finish line in soiled shorts, Mark decided he would do the next Ironman. It was only seven months away, because the race organizers had elected to move the event from February to October so participants could train for it in the summer instead of having to prepare over the fall and winter months.

When Mark got his next monthly call from his dad, Space asked what he'd been up to and Mark gushed about this cool race he had seen on television, where you had to swim 2.4 miles in the ocean, then ride 112 miles, then run a marathon—and it was in Hawaii, where it was really hot and windy. Mark's dad showed little interest in the contest.

"And my friend Reed did it, and he said it was the hardest thing he'd ever done," Mark added.

Silence.

"And they're doing it again in October."

Silence.

"And I just signed up for it."

More silence. Then, "So, have you decided what you're going to do for a living?"

Mark was undaunted by his father's indifference. He knew what he needed. Mark emptied his small savings and bought a used racing bike, certain he would never regret the risk he was taking. Indeed, the thrill of the risk itself was worth the risk.

In April, three weeks into his training, Mark rose early on a Saturday morning and drove his old Volkswagen Squareback to the inaugural La Jolla Half Marathon. But he did not compete. Mark was not quite ready to run that far. Instead he watched some friends run. While he was there he bumped into Julie Moss for the first time since she'd returned from Ironman as a sudden folk hero. To Mark she seemed nine feet tall.

"I saw you on TV," he told her. "You were amazing."

"Well, I don't know about amazing," Julie said, blushing. "I crawled. I lost. But thanks!"

"No, really," Mark insisted. "It inspired me."

Julie studied his face and saw the truth of his words.

"Anyway, if anybody should be doing triathlons, it's you," she said. "You'd kick ass. It's not that different from a lifeguard competition."

"As a matter of fact, I'm going to," Mark said. "I'm doing the next Ironman in October."

"Are you serious? That's awesome! You'll probably win it." Julie paused. "Don't tell Reed I said that!"

Julie had just passed the California lifeguard certification test. A couple of weeks later she started her job training. On her first morning her new supervisor pulled up in a bright yellow lifeguard Jeep. It was Mark Allen.

Reed also worked as a lifeguard. Three peas in a pod. Reed and Julie both planned to return to Ironman in October, so the couple formed a little training clique with Mark, swimming together at every opportunity, running on the beach, and going for long bike rides on days off. Reed found it harder and harder to keep up with Mark on those rides, while Julie quickly learned not to even try. She had said he would kick ass; he started with hers.

WHILE MARK WAS TRAINING for the October 1982 Ironman, a bored young Sacramento lawyer named Jim Curl and an executive from Speedo swimwear, Carl Thomas, were working together to develop a national series of triathlons of a shorter and more welcoming format than the famous Ironman. The inaugural event of the United States Triathlon Series (USTS), which would be the world's premier triathlon race series for the next decade, took place at Torrey Pines State Beach in Del Mar, just north of San Diego, on June 12. Mark was among more than 600 athletes who gathered at the race site just after dawn on that Saturday morning. Most of them, like Mark, were first-timers.

A tremendous "I was there when" excitement charged the atmosphere. There was a shared, unspoken awareness that USTS San Diego would be remembered as a milestone in the young sport's development, a quantum leap toward mainstream legitimacy. The event wore the trappings of a bona fide, professionally organized sporting event, including police support and sponsor signage—simple things that had been missing from the rinky-dink triathlons that had taken place here and there over the previous few years. Participants racked their bikes in long, mass bike racks, a new innovation that spared racers from having to return to their cars to execute transitions. A $2,000 prize purse was on the line. No doubt about it: This was the big time.

A celebrity element contributed to the excitement. All of the sport's few emerging stars were there. As Mark milled about in the parking lot where the transition area had been set up, nervously wondering what the heck he should be doing, he saw Dave Scott, whom he recognized from the Ironman broadcast he'd watched four months earlier. Mark also spotted the man who had beaten Dave in that race, local boy Scott Tinley. Striking and charismatic, Tinley always burned the candle at three ends, partying as hard as he trained and working the business side of sport as aggressively as he partied. Tinley would soon parlay his rising popularity into his own signature line of performance apparel and a back-page column in *Triathlete* magazine, which would be founded a few months later. Present as well was Scott Molina, who had cannonballed 600 miles from northern California in a VW Squareback just like the one Mark drove. Known as a blue-collar triathlete, Molina had been born and raised in the industrial San Francisco exurb of Pittsburg, one of seven children. He'd skipped college and had become a husband and father before his twenty-third birthday. When he raced his first triathlon he was living in a trailer and working as a clerk in a liquor store and as a short-order cook at the local K-Mart.

The morning was cool and cloudy, typical of San Diego in June. As the competitors crowded against the water's edge, which served as a start line, scores of spectators watched from the beach and from a concrete terrace behind them. A horn blasted, and all 600-plus racers dived into the surf together for a chilly 2-kilometer swim. Mark happily discovered that he was a stronger swimmer than all but a handful of his competitors, nestled comfortably into the lead pack, and left the water on the heels of none other than Dave Scott.

On the bike, Dave, wearing a collared shirt, dropped Mark like it was child's play, and another strong cyclist also got away from him. But he held off everyone else and completed the 35-kilometer bike leg in third place. Mark lost valuable time when, rookie that he was, he racked his bike at the wrong transition spot and struggled to put on a woman's running shoes before realizing his mistake and locating his own Nikes. A spirited crowd of onlookers thronging around the bike racks sent Mark onto the run course feeling like a superstar. He quickly passed the guy who had passed him on the bike and moved into second place, four minutes behind Dave. Then he heard footsteps.

Mark swiveled his head and saw a pack of three runners quickly reeling him in: Tinley, Molina, and a dark-haired stranger wearing bib number 6. The trio soon caught Mark and moved in front of him. As Tinley slid past him, he turned to Mark and spoke.

"Who are you?" he said somewhat irritably.

"My name is Mark Allen," Mark struggled to say between breaths.

"Oh, I heard about you," Tinley said, seemingly relieved that it was not a completely unknown party who was challenging him. "Someone told me to watch out for you."

These words filled Mark with as much pleasure as any words that had ever been spoken to him.

Spirits buoyed, Mark tried to hang on to the others, but they were running too damn fast. If he didn't let them go, he wouldn't finish. It was that simple. Mark fell back into his own rhythm as the others drifted ahead of him.

When Mark was half a mile from the turnaround point on the 15-kilometer out-and-back run course, Dave Scott came chugging by in the opposite direction like a gas-powered machine, radiating strength and confidence. Then came Scott Tinley and Scott Molina together, without the third guy. Mark was within sight of the turnaround when he encountered the dark-haired fellow wearing bib number 6. He had clearly slowed down and was obviously hurting. Minutes after making the turn, Mark caught him, but the moment he did, the other surged. He was not going to go down without a fight.

Number 6 was Dale Basescu, a former standout college swimmer also competing in his first triathlon. Dale was exactly the kind of guy who had always intimidated the hell out of Mark in the pool. He had an actor's good looks and a chiseled body. He gave off the same aura of confidence Mark had just seen on Dave Scott, and, like Dave, he was as tough as an alligator.

Dale's countermove shook Mark like a bully's two-handed shove to the chest. His spirit nosedived as he considered the pain he would have to embrace to match the stranger's increased tempo. That old tape loop began to play in his head.

I'm no match for this guy. Look at him. He'll never crack. Fifth place is good enough. Hell, it's my first triathlon! Why suffer any more than I am already if I'm going to lose anyway?

But Mark did not quit this time. Instead of shamefully caving in to the voice of doubt and negativity as he'd always done in the past, instead of allowing those tired old self-sabotaging refrains to talk him into submitting to yet another alpha male, Mark fought back. That voice had always hated him. Now Mark hated it right back. He silenced the mutinous mouth inside him.

No! To hell with that. Not this time. I don't care. I'll die trying.

Mark lifted his chin, pressed his hips forward, and began beating the ground with his feet. He clawed his way back onto Dale's shoulder. Over the next four miles, the pair fought an escalating battle of speed and will. Certain that he could make Mark crack—for he had enforced his will on the likes of Mark Allen many times before—Dale turned up the pace another notch. Mark threw it right back at him, plunging into an abyss of pain unlike any he had felt before. Dale could hear him wheezing and knew the tall, lanky stranger had pinned the needle. Mark's audible struggle for breath suggested an imminent collapse, but he confounded his foe's expectations and held on. Mark had a murderous chokehold on his choker self, and no amount of suffering would make him release it. He ran utterly mindlessly, giving himself over entirely to the effort to prevail, and when Dale accelerated yet again, when everything Mark had wasn't enough, he found a way to run harder still.

Out of the corner of his eye Dale now noticed something disturbing about Mark's face. It was an asymmetrical rictus grin, an unconscious and locked gaping of the right side of his mouth. The crooked grimace lent a borderline crazed appearance to Mark's visage and caused Dale to fear that the young man he was battling was somehow impervious to pain, or perhaps even enjoying his own suffering. It rattled him.

The race's homestretch was a short but tough hill leading back into Torrcy Pines State Beach. Dale and Mark were still side by side when they hit the base of the hill, but Mark suddenly unleashed a savage kick. Dale prided himself on his ability to dig deeper and hurt more than other athletes. In a battle of wills, he almost always triumphed. But Mark exerted a kind of mental dominance Dale had rarely seen, and it crushed him. Mark had done to Dale what others had been doing to Mark his whole life. Suddenly, in this new sport, he was as strong as he had been weak as a swimmer. Preyed upon in sports for fourteen years until then, he was now the predator.

But how? And why? One reason was physical. Mark had a body born for triathlon; he was that rare good swimmer who also turned out to be a great cyclist and a phenomenal runner. Ability is always the substrate of confidence. A second reason was mental. The competitor in Mark had finally had enough time and distance to process the damage he had endured and transform a source of quaking weakness into a fuel for ruthless strength, becoming like a bone that is more unbreakable for having healed from a past break. Body and mind together had found their niche.

A need to prove his value as a human being still powered Mark's racing. Inner doubts continued to plague him. Success was still the only proof of self-worth he recognized. But he had the coward inside him against the ropes.

After crossing the finish line behind Mark, Dale approached him and shook his hand. Mark was still hyperventilating, but he was ecstatic in spite of his exhaustion. Having congratulated Mark, Dale walked away in search of friends and told them about his race.

"I think I just got beat by the guy who's going to be the greatest triathlete ever," he said.

MARK AND DALE struck up a friendship after their duel. They didn't train much together, but they sometimes hooked up for a bite to eat. Dale had no clue how adrift Mark had been before the moment of their meeting, but he could plainly see how excited he was about triathlon. He seemed reborn, almost manic in his blind optimism for a wide-open future, like an infatuated new lover or a freshly baptized believer.

"I really found what I'm supposed to be doing," Mark told Dale more than once, over tacos. "It's the right thing for me. I know it."

Mark told his dad the same thing in their next call. He shared the results of that talk with Dale during another cheap Mexican dinner. More than a few young men and women were having similar conversations with their parents at that time, and Mark's had gone no better than most.

"Are you saying this is what you're supposed to be doing as a *job?*" Space had asked, incredulous.

"Well, yeah, maybe."

"But you haven't *done* anything. You haven't won *anything*."

"No, but I've been right up there with the big dogs. Dad . . ."

Silence.

IN 1982 SAN DIEGO was the center of the triathlon universe. Most of the top talents who weren't there already when the triathlon bug bit them moved to "America's Finest City" sooner or later. Nearly every bright light in the young sport's constellation of stars, with the notable exception of Dave Scott, called San Diego home. As a fanatical young triathlete with tremendous promise, Mark was quickly drawn into the orbit of San Diego's elite endurance set. He soon found himself sharing lanes with Scott Tinley, Julie Moss, and other big names at the UCSD pool and trading pulls with them on weekly group rides along the Pacific Coast Highway.

One morning Mark rode through Otay Lakes, an area of suffocating inland heat and relentlessly rolling hills south of San Diego, with Scott Tinley and Murphy Reinschreiber, the very guy who had beaten Dave Scott in twelve out of thirteen races at the 1966 California State Fair Swim Meet. Mark dropped his partners repeatedly throughout the long ride. About three hours into the ordeal, Tinley noticed something about Mark's hands.

The standard hand position on a high-performance road bike is at the outer sides of the top portion of the handlebar, right next to the brake levers. Cyclists typically drop their hands into the bullhorns, or the lower section, when they wish to become aerodynamic and ride fast on flat or downhill terrain. They move their hands close to the center of the handlebar when climbing, to attain a more upright position. Tinley noticed that whenever Mark moved his grip from the standard position to either the bullhorns or the climbing position, he and Murphy began to suffer. The next time Mark moved his grip, Tinley drew Murphy's attention to it.

"See that?" he said. "It's the grip of death."

When Tinley next rode with Mark, he did not call him "Mark." He called him "Grip." The nickname quickly spread; eventually its literal source was forgotten, and it came to be understood as a reference to the mental death grip Mark put on other athletes through his newfound capacity to outsuffer all comers.

On another ride, after his grip-of-death reputation had been cemented, Mark was joined by Paul Huddle, then a newcomer to the San Diego scene who had not yet experienced the death grip. He didn't have to wait long. Mark effortlessly dropped Paul on the way out from their starting point and collected him again on the way back. Paul was once more hanging on to Mark's back wheel for dear life when he heard Mark's rear tire spring a leak. Paul eased up, expecting Mark to stop to fix it, only to watch him disappear ahead. Five miles up the road Paul caught Mark, who had at last stopped to change his tube. He had ridden five miles on a deflating rear tire before he noticed it. On subsequent rides Paul made a game of seeing what else Mark wouldn't notice, which turned out to be anything short of being hit by a truck, so singularly internal was his focus when pedaling hard.

Mark and Paul became close friends and seasonal housemates in a house they rented with a couple of others every summer in Boulder, Colorado. One morning they were eating cereal together at the breakfast table when Paul realized that Mark was staring at him. Mark did this often, and it unnerved Paul. The most unsettling thing about Mark's wordless watching was the Mona Lisa smile that accompanied it, an almost perfect facsimile of the world's most enigmatic smile: faint and frozen, simultaneously demanding and defying interpretation. Suddenly Paul couldn't take it anymore.

"What?" Paul shouted.

Mark flinched, seeming to return from somewhere far away.

"What?" Mark quietly echoed.

"What the hell are you staring at?"

"Nothing."

Paul realized that Grip was not, in fact, trying to read the secrets of his soul. Mark's mind was far away; Paul might as well have not been in the room.

The more time Mark's housemates spent with him, the more mysterious he became in some ways. Living with Mark exposed them to his spiritual practices, of whose existence they saw no hint in the workout experiences they shared with him. Mark kept crystals in his bedroom, which he used to heal himself by placing them on his body at chakra points and which the clownish young duathlete Kenny Souza, who also shared the house in Boulder, liked to rearrange when Mark wasn't looking. Mark also practiced self-hypnosis, and he habitually regaled his roommates with descriptions and interpretations of his frequently fantastical dreams. One day Mark excitedly told Kenny that he had fallen asleep wishing he could make time stand still and then dreamed of a square waterfall floating in a void. He explained that it was not water falling but time, and the pink mist rising from the bottom of the water-fall represented eternity in suspension.

Mark read a great deal of spiritual literature. His roommates became accustomed to seeing all kinds of spiritual reading material left around the house. For a while Mark's personal bible was a book titled *Constructive Living* by David K. Reynolds, which presented a self-help philosophy based on the tenets of accepting the reality of everything you feel and unswervingly doing what you need to do in life. There was a spirit of self-reliance in Reynolds's philosophy that validated Mark's natural outlook.

"Feeling pressured by others, by time, by circumstances is just another feeling," goes a typical Reynolds teaching. "The feeling causes you trouble when you believe you must respond to it or fight it or remove it. Just feel the pressure and continue doing what you need to do."

One night Mark dreamed that he was surfing at Torrey Pines State Beach, the site of his first triathlon. He kept trying to paddle through the whitewater to reach the break but was repeatedly waylaid by other surfers who were struggling and needed his help. Mark got so caught up in helping others that he never did reach the break. When he woke up Mark decided the dream was telling him he was giving too much energy to his training buddies, and he needed to pull back from them for a time and focus on himself.

Losing energy to others was a constant concern for Mark, one that caused him generally to keep a certain distance from his friends. Most of the other guys trained together daily, but Mark ran and rode alone at least a few times every week. It was a matter of rational self-interest. Mark saw plainly what everyone else seemed to miss—that it was impossible for a bunch of world-class endurance athletes with healthy egos to train together without being sucked into a back-and-forth game of mileage one-upmanship that flung one athlete after another into the abyss of overtraining fatigue. Mark had been quick to realize that his body could not handle the volume his peers shouldered, so he stayed away from their most epic group rides and runs and attempted to compensate for doing less by doing it faster, developing a reputation for the brutal intensity of his regimen that the media celebrated.

Among those who read about Mark's high-intensity training approach with dubious interest was Phil Maffetone, a New York–based chiropractor and endurance sports coach who had recently developed a training philosophy, based on the use of heart rate monitors, that was well summarized in the slogan "Go slow to get faster." Phil cold-called Mark and volunteered his opinion that Mark was training too intensely. Phil advised Mark to get a heart rate monitor and to avoid letting his heart rate creep above 155 beats per minute while riding his bike and running, except during the thick of the racing season, and then only a few times a week.

Dave Scott probably would have told Phil to get lost. Mark found Phil's system appealing, mainly because Mark's current "go hard or go home" approach, although effective, left him constantly nursing minor injuries. He tried the method and discovered that he had to reduce his cycling speed and running pace to a grandmotherly crawl to keep his heart rate below the prescribed threshold. Phil told him to stick with it and explained that in doing so he would teach his muscles to function more and more efficiently, enabling him to ride and run faster and faster at that threshold intensity. Mark stuck with the program and discovered that it worked.

After buying into the Maffetone Method, as it became known, Mark began to moderate his efforts even in many of the workouts he did with friends, who quickly learned to exploit Mark's restraint for their own self-preservation. Ray Browning, another top racer of the day, figured out that when two or more athletes wearing heart rate monitors rode close together the monitor with the freshest batteries would overwhelm the signal of any other devices in its vicinity and display its wearer's heart rate on those other devices. Ray had just installed fresh batteries in his monitor before starting one long ride in the hills east of San Diego with Mark and a few others. As they climbed an especially tough hill, Ray began to struggle, and his heart rate spiked to 178 beats per minute. Meanwhile, Grip was cruising along comfortably at his limit of 155. Ray pulled his bike close to Mark's, and suddenly the reading on Grip's device jumped to 178. Alarmed, Mark slowed down dramatically until the reading dropped back to 155, and Ray survived to the top, snickering at his cleverness.

Mark not only allowed himself easy days in training; he gave himself a whole season of rest each year, quitting his training cold turkey after his last race of the season, usually Ironman, and waiting until New Year's Day to resume. For six weeks he would not swim a single lap or run a single step, and his bike gathered dust in his garage. Instead he surfed and indulged in other interests. When ABC's coverage of Mark's first Ironman was broadcast, Mark missed it because he was attending a meditation retreat. This habit of letting his fitness fields lie fallow and getting away from sport in the winter was an early indication that, as much as Mark needed it, triathlon did not give him everything he needed.

MARK TOOK THIRD PLACE in his second triathlon, USTS Los Angeles, and won his third, the Horny Toad Triathlon, in San Diego, defeating Scott Tinley and Scott Molina and picking up $1,000, or as much money as he made in a month of lifeguarding. The funds were badly needed. Mark was practically living on ramen noodles in those days. When he told his father about the prize haul, Mark noticed a change in Space's tone. Suddenly he wasn't so skeptical.

A photograph of Mark taken during the Horny Toad Triathlon appeared on the cover of the September 1982 issue of *San Diego Running News*. When it was published Mark stopped by a running-shoe store to grab a few copies. He found the publication stacked near the checkout counter and began to browse through a copy, lingering in the hope that the pretty girl behind the cash register would recognize him. She did not. Mark knew his disappointment was juvenile, but he couldn't help himself. He'd always wanted to do something that truly impressed people, and as a 24-year-old man he valued the fair sex's attention more than anyone else's.

A few weeks later Mark flew to Hawaii for Ironman. Unable to afford a hotel room, he slept on a pullout couch in the apartment that Reed Gregerson and Julie Moss had rented in Kailua-Kona while they slept together in the bedroom. Mark was still dating Bunny Stein, who had just started medical school in Texas. But would anyone have blamed Mark if, as he lay on that pullout couch waiting for sleep to overtake him, he imagined being in his friend's place—in the arms of the woman who had inspired his rebirth?

Ironman did not go well. Mark failed to finish. Nor did he finish his next race, the Malibu Triathlon, in which he developed hypothermia. Officials pulled Mark from the race when he came out of the ocean with blue skin and started shouting, "Where are the bikes?" as he stood right in front of them. Nevertheless, Mark had shown enough promise to receive an invitation to join the J. David professional triathlon team after that race. The offer came through another of Mark's lifeguarding buddies, George Hoover, whose mother, Nancy Hoover, was the romantic partner and a business partner of Jerry David Dominelli, head of the La Jolla-based J. David brokerage firm. Judging by his lifestyle, Jerry had more money than God, and Nancy used much of their wealth philanthropically. When her son got into triathlon, he and his sporting friends became one of her pet charities. Mark immediately quit his lifeguarding job and joined his new teammates on a flight to Nice, France, where a new event calling itself the World Triathlon Championship was to be held. Upon arriving, they checked into one of the finest hotels in the city.

Mark could not sleep the night before the race. He had never been to Europe. He was about to make his debut as a professional athlete. His mind and heart raced as he lay in bed. At one o'clock in the morning, giving up on sleep, Mark laced up his running shoes, left the hotel, and went for an easy run along the Promenade des Anglais. Pacing beside the water under the soft light of elegant streetlamps, he savored the fresh night air. A deep satisfaction washed over him. Its origin eluded him for a moment, but he soon traced it: He was going to win. Not just that—he was going to be a winner. He stood on the verge of escaping the sea of the ordinary once and for all.

It's all in front of me, he thought.

Hours later, 24-year-old Mark Allen won the World Triathlon Championship.

GEORGE HOOVER lived with his mother, who lived with Jerry Dominelli in a sprawling estate valued at $2.2 million in Rancho Santa Fe, one of the most exclusive zip codes in America. After Nice in 1982 George invited Mark to occupy one of the mansion's many spare bedrooms, and he did. Although Mark was not hung up on material things, his splendorous new lodgings surely enhanced the excitement of his new beginning—and Mark's exclusive new address could not have failed to impress his dad, which was worth something in itself.

One day, several months later, George Hoover returned to the boys' wing of the Dominelli estate looking distressed. He had just seen his mother.

"Bad news, Grip," he said.

Mark had felt it coming. Something had been not quite right from the beginning. The money had been almost too easy, coming with too few strings attached.

George informed Mark that Jerry Dominelli had just fled the country, and that J David was bankrupt. The operation had not actually invested any money but instead had shifted it from the base to the peak of a pyramid of suckers and exploiters—a Ponzi scheme. George was deeply distressed. He felt responsible for having ruined the careers of several of his closest friends.

In fact, the only athlete whose career was ruined by the fiasco was George. He never quite recovered from the blow of his mother's downfall and imprisonment and quit the sport three years after the scandal broke, at age 25. For Mark, the worst of it was perhaps having to endure an I-told-you-so monologue regarding the viability of triathlon as a career in his next monthly call with his dad. But Space had precious little time to gloat before Nike, exhibiting once again its uncanny ability to identify the single best athlete to sponsor in a given sport before anyone else did, swooshed in to grab Mark ahead of the 1984 racing season, making him the highest-paid triathlete in the world—fifty grand a year plus bonuses.

Among the next-best-compensated triathletes was Julie Moss, who had optioned the story of her Ironman crawl for a TV movie and been sponsored by Speedo, Yoplait, and Specialized bikes, and whom Mark continued to see often at races. She broke up with Reed Gregerson one last time and started dating Dale Basescu. Mark got engaged to Bunny Stein. Then Dale broke up with Julie. Mark broke up with Bunny.

Dale received a call from Mark shortly after these latest decouplings. Mark asked if Dale cared to join him for an easy run the following morning. They agreed to meet at Dale's place. From the moment Mark arrived, Dale could tell Mark wanted to talk about something. Not until they were midway through the run did he come out with it.

"So you and Julie split up, right?" Mark said.

"Yeah, we're not together anymore," Dale said.

"Do you mind if I ask her out?"

Dale laughed in appreciation of Mark's old-world propriety.

"Of course not," he said. "Go for it!"

Mark did not go for it right away. Handsome yet reticent, Mark was more often the pursued than the pursuer with women. In the end he and Julie met in the middle. Mark next bumped into Julie at a triathlon in New York City. After the race she mentioned to Mark, feigning offhandedness, that she had neglected to reserve a hotel room before making the trip east. Mark, playing along, invited her to stay in his room.

She did not sleep on the pullout couch. They became a couple. Mark now had the love of the woman who had inspired his rebirth. He had become a winner and muzzled the inner voice that called him a loser. He had a job that entailed playing outdoors all day in the most beautiful city in America and traveling around the world to show off his talents on destination beaches. He had a six-figure income, including prize winnings. And he'd even won back his father's support. There were moments when Mark Allen was able to convince himself that he had everything he would ever need.

CHAPTER 4

PAIN COMMUNITY

You desire to know the art of living, my friend?
It is contained in one phrase: Make use of suffering.

— HENRI-FRÉDÉRIC AMIEL

It is one minute before three o'clock on the afternoon of October 14, 1989, and Dave Scott and Mark Allen are running beyond known human limitations on the Kona Coast of Hawaii. Meanwhile, Mike Atkinson is caught up in an adolescent's Saturday rituals in Waterloo, Ontario, Canada—playing video games, hanging out at the mall with friends—unaware that the thirteenth Ironman World Championship is taking place. If he did know, he wouldn't care. He has never heard of Dave Scott and Mark Allen.

Nevertheless, Mike will one day be among the persons best able to explain how—or at least why—Dave and Mark are able to achieve what they are now achieving in the greatest race ever run. As a prominent sociologist of sport and the world's foremost triathlon ethnographer, Mike will define triathlon as a kind of "pain community." This concept will be used to reveal that Dave Scott and Mark Allen are exploding the limits of human endurance together on the Queen K Highway at this moment because they have cultivated an inexhaustible appetite for a certain kind of suffering, which, thanks to a perfect storm of circumstances, is being stoked to a never-before-seen degree of intensity.

MICHAEL ATKINSON was born in the charming southern Ontario city of Kingston and raised mostly in the town of Bedford, near Halifax. His was a typical middle-class Canadian family of the 1970s and '80s. Mike's father, Tony, taught at the local university. Mike and his brother, Spartacus, played the usual sports, mainly hockey, until they were weeded out by the sudden elevation of competitiveness that occurs at the start of high school. Over the next decade, as he completed high school and discovered a love for sociology at the University of Waterloo, pursued a master's degree in that subject at McMaster University, and earned a doctoral degree at the University of Calgary, Mike got little exercise beyond the occasional set of bench presses or recreational game of ice hockey. Lack of exertion wrought predictable effects on his physique.

One evening in 1999 Mike, then a PhD candidate at Calgary, played a pickup game of hockey with several of his undergraduate students. Not ten minutes after the first face-off, Mike was spent. Lungs heaving, he coasted with his hands on his knees as the other players, only slightly younger, whizzed around him. For the first time in his life he felt old.

A week later Mike began training for a marathon. His stated goals were to lose weight and to feel healthier. He achieved these goals well before he ran the marathon. But when he crossed the finish line Mike felt such unexpected euphoria that he immediately decided to run a second marathon—only faster. Staying lean and fit were now side benefits. The new main objective was to grab another dose of that incredible finish-line feeling. And then another. After three years mere marathons were no longer enough. Guessing that an even greater challenge would yield an even better finish-line feeling, Mike moved on to multisport racing, completing seventeen duathlons and seven triathlons between 2005 and 2007.

"Triathlon is like heroin in a lot of ways," Mike says. "Once you get hooked on it, it's like 'Wow, I don't care what anyone says, I'm staying on this stuff.'"

As junkies find other junkies, Mike traded his old bookish friends for a whole new set of athlete friends. He married a triathlete, joined running and triathlon clubs, and trained regularly in groups. A sociologist cannot operate in any particular social environment, no matter how far removed from his work, without studying and analyzing it, much as an artist cannot contemplate a landscape without applying a creative eye. And so, almost despite himself, as Mike trained and socialized with his athlete compadres he also surreptitiously studied and analyzed them, trying to figure out whnt made them tick. Epiphany came one day when Mike went for a five-hour bike ride with his friend John.

It was one of those wet, windy, miserable days when the elements seem to have been conjured by a malicious supernatural intelligence bent on making a single target, or two, feel wretched. Mike just didn't have it that day. He faltered with many miles left to go.

"I don't think I can make it," he told John.

"Yes, you can," John said. "You've got more than enough to do this. Keep pushing."

"I don't know," Mike lamented.

"Listen," John said, "you wouldn't be here right now if you didn't want to be, so just stop thinking yourself out of it. We'll take it stroke by stroke. Just stay with me and you'll make it."

He was right—Mike made it home. And as he relished a hot shower and basked in the pride of having toughed it out, he thought, *You know, I never would have finished that ride if John hadn't been there to talk me through it.* Mike was reminded of how he saw this phenomenon play out day after day in group training sessions. People pushed their physical boundaries together as they never would individually. With a flash of in-spiration, Mike rediscovered triathlon as a sort of intentional community centered on suffering. He recognized suddenly that the pain that everyone acknowledges as a big part of the triathlon experience was in fact *the very essence* of the sport and that it served distinctly social purposes, helping men and women satisfy needs not met in their everyday lives.

Mike spent the next four years interviewing triathletes and develop-ing his idea. He heard the same things over and over. Either Mike was right or everyone he talked to was in on a vast conspiracy to make him believe he was. All of the triathletes he questioned acknowledged that the sport hurt intensely, yet they described the pain as rewarding and as a major factor in their continued involvement in the sport.

One interviewee, a 36-year-old triathlete named Ashley, told him, "I trained for nearly a year before I entered a race, but all of that training, all of the adjustment to becoming more athletic didn't prepare me for how much it hurts. I never spent a minute of my life gasping for air with mus-cles in my body cramping like that." She added, "It's terrifying when you start, but after a year or so in the sport the pain of the race becomes like a drug. You become addicted to the adrenaline surge you feel when you are hurting and the release you go through when it's over."

Among the questions Mike was most keen to answer was why that finish line feels so damn good. His interviews led him to the conclusion that crossing a triathlon finish line satisfies a pair of specific needs that people experience with particular urgency today. One is the need to challenge the body and mind in ways that everyday life no longer does. In his best-known paper, "Triathlon, Suffering, and Exciting Significance," Mike notes that numerous sociologists have observed how the ever-increasing comfortableness of the modern lifestyle has bled everyday life of "exciting significance" and how sports have increasingly stepped into the gap to give people a way to live adventurously, even a little dangerously, in an otherwise too-easy world.

"People are really tired of living a sort of dull, boring, and sedentary lifestyle," Mike says. "Most triathletes have white-collar desk jobs. They don't use their bodies. They use their minds or their voices all day, and they really like the physical aspect of doing something grueling like triathlon."

Mike offers Oliver as a typical case. Oliver told Mike that, before he discovered triathlon, each day brought the same, safe, unexciting routine. He woke in his soft bed, enjoyed a hot shower, and ate an instant breakfast. He spent an hour in the car on autopilot and then nine dreary hours sitting at a desk, earning his ample biweekly paycheck without taxing himself on any level. Upon returning to his empty house Oliver mechanically switched on the television, nodded off, then woke up the next day and did it all again. He explained to Mike, "I had money; I had stability; but I had nothing to make me feel alive, to make my body and mind work in different ways."

Triathlon changed all that and brought Oliver back to real living.

"I think that's the essence of being human, to feel alive, to move beyond the comforts of familiarity," Oliver said. "It's about saying to yourself that you don't want to feel dead on earth."

Despite all the evidence to the contrary, pleasure is not the magnetic north of all human behavior. People are more complex than that. As Oliver realized, it can be better to feel anything—even pain—than to feel nothing. Sometimes pleasure and pain are derived from the same source. There is no pleasure in doing a triathlon, but it metes out a kind of suffering that is satisfying in the context of our soporific modern existence with its all infernal conveniences. Driving your muscles, heart, and lungs against the gravitational press of extreme fatigue does indeed make you feel as alive— as fully present in reality—as any experience life has to offer. It's an acquired taste but, once acquired, addictive.

In the hardest moments of a long race, the athlete's entire conscious experience of reality boils down to a desire to continue pitted against a desire to quit. Nothing else remains. The athlete is no longer a student or a teacher or a salesman. He is no longer a son or a father or a husband. He has no social roles or human connections whatsoever. He is utterly alone. He no longer has any possessions. There is no yesterday and no tomorrow, only now. The agony of extreme endurance fatigue crowds out every thought and feeling except one: the goal of reaching the finish line. The sensations within the body—burning lungs, screaming muscles, whole-body enervation—exist only as the substance of the desire to quit. What little of the external environment the athlete is aware of—the road ahead, the competitor behind, the urgings of onlookers—exists only as the substance of the desire to continue. The desire to continue versus the desire to quit—the athlete is this and this alone until he chooses one or the other. And when the choice is made he briefly becomes either persevering or quitting until, after he has stopped at the finish line or, God forbid, short of it, the stripped-away layers are piled back on and he becomes his old self again. Only not quite. He is changed, for better or worse.

Many sports provide forms of exciting significance without subjecting participants to the kind of suffering triathlon does. Yet triathlon and other endurance sports have gained popularity over the past few decades at a far greater rate than playful pastimes such as tennis and pickup basketball. Mike Atkinson believes that triathlon is more attractive than less painful alternatives precisely because of the suffering element. Although many sociologists before Mike observed that sports in general have moved in to provide the exciting significance that is lacking in everyday life, no one before him identified suffering specifically as a source of exciting significance. His colleagues always treated suffering—which has a small place in most sports—as a negative that athletes had to put up with to gain the real rewards.

In triathlon, however, the suffering is so central and the other rewards so peripheral that *one could only do it for the suffering*. And since triathlon has gained popularity faster than more pleasant sports, Mike reasoned, it must be because people feel a specific need to suffer, not just a need for any old kind of exciting significance. Why?

Mike's ethnographic work in the triathlon community has led him to the conclusion that the need to suffer stems from an underlying need to feel special, distinct from, and above one's neighbors in meaningful ways.

People today don't just want to escape their boring lives, Mike argues—they want to take pride in being among the minority that does. Human beings are competitive. We constantly compare ourselves against our neighbors, and we are happier when we compare favorably, less happy when we compare unfavorably. Driving a better car than one's neighbor is satisfying. But proving oneself tougher than one's sedentary neighbor by completing a triathlon is more satisfying because it says more than the car does about *who one is*, especially in an environment where most people, like the poet T. S. Eliot's character J. Alfred Prufrock, vaguely despise themselves for having allowed the modern world to make them so soft.

Simply put, crossing the finish line feels good in large measure because it makes people feel good about themselves in comparison to others. One of Mike's more hard-core interview subjects, a moderately experienced 29-year-old triathlete named Chris, told him, "Most of my friends take the weekend to lounge around the house or relax on the couch. I couldn't think of a stupider way to spend life." Although most triathletes do not bask as consciously in a sense of superiority as Chris does, even the most outwardly humble enjoy the thrill of proving themselves tougher than average. If they didn't, if it was all about the private, personal challenge, then people would not gather in the pain communities of triathlons at all. They would cover great distances in the water and on bikes and in running shoes all alone, and no one else would know.

Some of the best feelings in life are experienced in moments of overcoming immense challenges to claim meaningful rewards—moments of discovering what one is made of. A person needs to be tough to survive in this world. It is a great comfort to the soul to know that one is tougher, more courageous, more capable of enduring suffering than the next person. And the only way to know this is to prove one's capability in a socially recognized way. Robinson Crusoe would have gained little satisfaction from completing a triathlon alone on his remote island because he had no neighbors to be tougher than, no fellow pain community members to make the finish line meaningful, its crossing excitingly significant.

But in today's real world, triathlon is one of the best ways to demonstrate toughness and courage, and the finish-line feeling is one of the best feelings imaginable. There is nothing like it. It is a deep, warming satisfaction—an embracing, healthful pride—a moment of well-earned self-love. People weep at triathlon finish lines. Strong grown men who shed tears nowhere else do so openly at triathlon finish lines. People lift their arms and faces to the sky and shout at the top of their lungs. Some speak in tongues. At triathlon finish lines people allow themselves to do things they never do in the rest of their lives because they feel something they never feel in the rest of their lives. Something that not only rewards all the suffering but makes all the suffering rewarding.

THE TENS OF THOUSANDS of triathletes who have discovered the finish-line feeling in recent years owe a debt of gratitude to the men and women who first rebelled against this soul-killingly cosseted modern life to create the sport of triathlon in the mid-1970s.

It all started in San Diego, where a vital community of over-the-top exercise fanatics had recently coalesced. Most of the community's members were lifelong athletes, former hyperactive kids of the kind who stared longingly out the window during class and threw tantrums when Mom called them home at dusk. For reasons few of them fully understood, at least not in Mike Atkinson's terms, these exercise fanatics felt dissatisfied with the usual challenges of open-water swim races, century bike rides, and marathons. They craved new challenges.

The archetype of these fanatics was Tom Warren, who owned a thriving beachside bar called Tug's Tavern. A former competitive swimmer, Tom could no longer be classified as any particular kind of athlete by the time he had reached his late thirties, which coincided with this moment of special ferment. He swam, he biked, he ran, and he lifted weights—pretty much all day long. He competed in just about every local race of any kind, including hybrid swim-bike events that he organized under his own bar's sponsorship and usually won. But Tom's local reputation was built mainly on the zany feats of endurance that he performed spontaneously apart from organized events. In 1974 he pedaled a $75 beach cruiser home to San Diego from a vacation in Canada, wearing surf shorts and a dress shirt to prevent sunburn. He told people it was to save the cost of airfare, but that wasn't the real reason. Another time he jumped off a cruise ship that was preparing to dock at a Caribbean port and swam a half mile to shore. He told people it was to save time, but that wasn't the truth. On another occasion a friend saw Tom running along the boardwalk late at night. The friend asked why, and Tom explained that he'd been at home looking at his training log, had realized he'd miscalculated his running mileage for the week, and had decided to correct the error by running the extra miles instead of changing the number in his log. And that *was* the real reason.

It wasn't so much boredom with everyday life or J. Alfred Prufrock-style self-disgust that impelled Tom Warren and his fellow fanatics to pursue greater endurance challenges at this time. After all, they had been spared the worst of such modern afflictions by having been swimmers, cyclists, or runners since childhood. Instead, what drove them toward new athletic horizons was the sudden influx of new participants into *their* sports—an unwanted incursion of recent couch potatoes who had become unbearably bored with their own everyday lives and disgusted by their own softness.

A sea change was occurring in American society. The pampering of modern life had crossed a threshold beyond which the average person simply could not tolerate it any longer—something had to be done.

"At the same time," Mike Atkinson says, "there was already alarm over the growing obesity crisis. People were being pushed to get outdoors and become active."

Kenneth Cooper's 1968 book *Aerobics*, followed by Frank Shorter's gold medal in the 1972 Olympics, had kicked off the so-called running boom. Suddenly everybody was running marathons. Just as suddenly the exercise fanatics who had been running marathons all along didn't feel so special.

Human beings are competitive. The members of San Diego's community of exercise fanatics depended on challenging themselves more than the average person to enjoy feeling tougher, more driven, and more disciplined than the average person. So if the average person was now running marathons, Tom Warren and his buddies had to do more.

The first triathlon took place on the afternoon of September 25, 1974, on San Diego's Fiesta Island, a small lump of dirt peeking through the sparkling waters of Mission Bay and connected to the mainland by a 100-yard man-made isthmus. Tiny as it is, the island is a popular training spot for local runners and cyclists because of the flat, lightly trafficked road circumnavigating its perimeter. Hosted by the San Diego Track Club, this first triathlon comprised a bike leg of two laps around the island, followed by multiple short swims and runs. On that day forty-six aerobic thrill seekers went where no human had gone before. All of them agreed that, whatever it was they had done, it was an exercise worth repeating.

Among the athlete-adventurers participating in the second Mission Bay Triathlon, held in May 1975, was a 38-year-old navy lieutenant named John Collins, who three years later would organize the first Iron Man. The early Mission Bay Triathlons were filled with military men, who dominated the ranks (so to speak) of the sport's pioneering generation. Mike Atkinson would say that's no accident because the U.S. armed forces, like all military organizations, necessarily promote an ethos that glorifies suffering. No community values the willingness and capacity to endure combined physical and mental stress more highly than a volunteer army, and therefore no community is more attractive to young people who have learned to value suffering elsewhere. The military is the ultimate pain community. Back then military training and conditioning were the best available way to satisfy the needs of young men who loved to play outdoors, sweat, compete, strengthen their bodies, and test their endurance limits. Triathlon was, in a sense, a product of the efforts of some of these men to create an even better way to meet those needs.

In 1976 John Collins was promoted to commander and transferred from Coronado Island, off the San Diego coast, to Oahu, where he found and immersed himself in a community of athlete-adventurers much like the one he had just left behind. There was something in the air, for sure. All across the island navy men and others were avidly filling their free time with ass-kicking exercise, as past generations never had. Barriers were falling. Marathoners ran farther; swimmers rode bikes.

Yet something was still missing as late as 1977, after the first several triathlons had been contested. The preservation of the finish-line feeling—the special high chased by these endurance pioneers—required a new dimension of extremism. The first swim-bike-run races were a step in the right direction, but they literally didn't go far enough. In a word, the Mission Bay Triathlons were just too damn short.

It was John Collins who provided the missing element, spontaneously, offhandedly, utterly without expectations, at an awards ceremony following a relay running event in which teams had circled the entire perimeter of Oahu. Some beer had been consumed, and, right on schedule, the old argument about who were the tougher athletes—runners or swimmers—broke out. The runners naturally took the side of runners, and the few swimmers present defended their breed. John, who liked to ride a bike, submitted that cyclists deserved consideration also. The debate eventually evolved into a brainstorming session for ways to prove which type of athlete was truly the toughest. John suggested that a race combining Oahu's 2.4-mile Waikiki Roughwater Swim, 112-mile Round the Island Bike Race, and Honolulu Marathon should do the trick.

"Whoever won that ought to be called Iron Man," he said.

Iron Man. Interesting choice. Not a name to describe the most gifted or fittest athlete but a title befitting the toughest competitor. He who can bear the most pain. The best sufferer. Everyone who took part in that beer-enlivened dispute shared the same understanding of the matter's essence. All had passed through a generational looking glass into a world where suffering had become the main thing in the sports they loved. So together they blindly fumbled their way into creating a race that, unlike any other, would test the capacity to suffer, and fitness, and talent—in that specific order.

Many a big idea conceived over beers is never carried to full term. Nine times in ten these great notions seem less great or more daunting in the light of solitary sobriety than they did through the lens of inebriate groupthink. Ironman nearly met this fate. But one of John's old navy buddies, Dan Hendrickson, a fellow endurance frontiersman who had already enjoyed many a past adventure with John—often in company with the two men's wives, who were both badass athletes themselves—kept pestering Collins to follow through. So he did. The race was announced at the annual Waikiki Swim Club Banquet in October 1977. The first Iron Man Triathlon would take place on February 18, 1978, four months after the banquet. Plenty of time to train for a novel three-sport, 140.6-mile survival test. Fifteen men signed up.

Twelve started. The race was about as casual as two kids racing each other to the next mailbox. No roads were closed. The distances were approximately measured. Two men, both minimally employed fitness junkies, separated themselves from the rest to engage in an epic war of attrition in an undiscovered realm of competitive muscle-powered travel. John Dunbar, a 24-year-old taxi driver, traded the lead with Gordon Haller, a navy guy, throughout the day. They fought harder than seemed sane with so little at stake. Gordon finally broke John halfway through the marathon and won in eleven hours, forty-six minutes, fifty-eight seconds. John was seen running into parked cars and heard deliriously accusing his support crew of poisoning him as he reeled toward the finish line to claim his second-place prize of—nothing.

Gordon was not exactly awed by his feat. On days off from his job as a communications specialist he routinely ran 20 miles, cycled 100 miles, and swam 1.5 miles between sunup and sundown.

Despite its laughably humble trappings, Iron Man seemed a thing of destiny to the adventurous few who experienced it. Strange and small as it was, the race radiated that magical energy that marks a true happening.

The first Iron Man participants and witnesses knew deep in their bones, despite surface reasons to believe otherwise, that they were at the beginning of something special and lasting.

When the force of destiny is behind such a happening, strange coincidences help it grow. *Sports Illustrated* is not a magazine that regularly publishes lengthy features about two-year-old sporting events involving twelve participants, but it published a sprawling feature about the second Iron Man, which took place in February 1979.

SI writer Barry McDermott just happened to be in Hawaii covering a golf tournament that wrapped up a few days before the race and sort of stumbled upon it. He couldn't believe his ears when his editor requested 4,000 words on the competition. Barry selected the obvious theme for his account—perhaps the only theme he could have chosen. By way of describing the twelve racers he met on Oahu, he wrote, "They all shared a common reason for being there, a very compelling reason (some call it a curse): an addiction to inordinate amounts of exercise." The race itself he described as "a legal way to prove their toughness." Precisely.

None of the protagonists in Barry's story, which is to say none of the race's top competitors, was a world-class athlete in any of the three disciplines. The most talented cyclists, swimmers, and runners had other places to be: in the Tour de France, in the pool at the U.S. Olympic Training Center, on the start line of the Boston Marathon. What was exceptional about returning champion Gordon Haller, revenge-seeking John Dunbar, and first-timer Tom Warren (who had prepared for Oahu's sultriness by riding a stationary bike in a sauna) was not their talent but their tremendous appetite for training and their insatiable lust to challenge the outer limits of human endurance and tolerance for pain.

To come away with a fabulous story Barry McDermott needed to do little else than stick a tape recorder in front of these three eccentrics. Among the best lines he captured was one spoken by Tom Warren, which beautifully encapsulates the spirit that animated the first triathlons.

"I'm only in mediocre shape right now," said the man who worked out three times a day year-round. "But sometimes it's better that way."

A pool swimmer or track runner would have never said such a thing. If he had, he would have been branded a heretic. For the conventional endurance athlete, the race was all about performance—get as fit as you can to go as fast as you can. But for Tom Warren and his fellow iron men, who sought to separate themselves from the ranks of conventional endurance athletes so recently swelled by erstwhile couch potatoes, it was now all about suffering. The point of racing Iron Man was to attain a new height of toughness. Whatever added to the suffering the racers endured between the start and finish lines was good, even if the thing that did so was inadequate physical preparedness. Sure, a little extra fitness might have enabled Tom to complete Iron Man faster than eleven hours, fifteen minutes, and fifty-six seconds, and win by a wider margin than forty-eight minutes, but it would also have attenuated the suffering. And where was the satisfaction in that?

Barry's piece greatly excited the public imagination, *SI* having accurately read the American zeitgeist in devoting ten full pages to the Iron Man spectacle. The following year the ABC television network sent a camera crew to Oahu to cover the third Ironman (no longer Iron Man), Dave Scott's first, for *Wide World of Sports.* John Collins's brainchild, and the sport of triathlon, had passed a tipping point.

And then it passed another tipping point. Julie Moss's crawl in the February 1982 Ironman changed everything. Hers were the hands and knees that launched a thousand new triathletes. If the first two Ironman television specials created a healthy stream of interest in triathlon participation generally, and in Ironman participation specifically, the horrifyingly uplifting image of Julie willing her completely destroyed body through the final yards of the fifth Ironman opened the floodgates. Hundreds upon hundreds among the millions who watched Julie totter like a giraffe on ice and collapse onto the street in a seemingly lifeless heap, only to raise herself by some impossible means and stagger some more, leaped up from their recliners (at the same time as Mark Allen) and shouted, "Wow! I want to do that!"

Julie's crawl, her shocking display of voluntary suffering, was the image that caused the popularity of Ironman and triathlon to explode. A graph of triathlon's historical growth curve would show a dramatic upturn beginning precisely at the date of the television broadcast that got Julie an invitation from David Letterman (which she turned down because she feared he'd make fun of her). The lesson could not be clearer: This new sport and its grandest event appealed to a widespread and intense desire to *suffer.* Yes, people wanted to play in the water and on bikes. Yes, they wanted to have beautiful bodies like those of the triathletes on their television screens. Yes, they wanted to get back outdoors. But what they *really* wanted was to hurt like hell in pursuit of an outlandish goal.

JULIE'S CRAWL brought so many people to Ironman that Ironman soon could take no more. In 1983 race owner Valerie Silk established a qualifying system for Ironman entry. Each year since then, getting to Ironman has become more difficult as the number of qualifying events around the world and the number of athletes competing for a fixed number of Ironman slots have increased. This raising of the bar has been all to the good, because when the recent couch potatoes began racing Ironman, the original iron men no longer felt so special. To regain their distinction once again, they either had to do something even crazier or find a way to achieve distinction within the sport of triathlon in the form it took. Fortunately, those who followed that first wave have been able to do the latter.

"Ironman used to be a small group of dedicated people who were looked at as crazy," Mike Atkinson says. "But it grew, and every group, once it gets big enough, starts to define standards. You have to have some way of creating status hierarchies within groups—to measure who you are by comparison to other people. So now, if you want to be considered a serious triathlete, you've got to do Hawaii at some point."

Today there are double, triple, and even deca-Ironman races, but they haven't really caught on, and they probably never will because even those endurance fanatics who are most addicted to the pursuit of the ultimate finish-line feeling are able to pursue it without end at the original Ironman distance. Because the distance hasn't changed. Ironman remains long enough to test the capacity to suffer, and fitness, and talent—in that specific order. The ever-rising level of competition at Ironman gives even the most committed seekers (or abject addicts) all they need to continue their quest to suffer more than they ever have before.

The effect of competition on the human capacity to endure has been measured, and it is large. A seminal 1968 study at UC-Berkeley found that young men lasted 20 percent longer in a stationary bike ride to exhaustion when each subject was matched against a peer of roughly equal fitness than when the test was tackled alone.

This effect is not equal in all situations, however. The more important a test of endurance is perceived to be, the stronger the competition effect becomes. Thus, athletes are generally more motivated and more willing to suffer in major championship races such as Ironman than in smaller events. Likewise, because winning is the formal objective, athletes fortunate enough to have a legitimate chance of winning such races are generally readier to sacrifice and suffer than less gifted athletes. And because the particular composition of an important race can make it even more important, the best athletes are likely to reach farthest beyond existing limits when they must defeat their most accomplished and renowned rivals to claim victory—and they may reach higher still when they face their archnemesis on his best day.

The magnitude of the satisfaction that a triathlete experiences upon crossing a finish line is directly proportional to the amount of suffering he has overcome to get there. This reward knows no ability. Even the slowest of the slow can push themselves beyond existing limits and finish with tremendous satisfaction. But winning often demands and inspires the greatest suffering and thus confers the greatest sense of pride. Often, because of the nature of competition, it is precisely he who has the most guts who is the fastest and experiences the most intense fulfillment at the finish line.

Theoretically, then, the most deeply satisfying experience a triathlete could have in the sport (and among the best in life) would occur at the finish line of a race in which he has overcome as much suffering as he could possibly ever endure, and knows it.

THIS IS THE POSSIBILITY that stands before Dave Scott and Mark Allen as they match strides along the center of the Queen K Highway. Together they constitute an ephemeral and ultraexclusive pain community within a pain community. Not one element of their circumstances could be altered to make the moment more "excitingly significant" to either—to make either man more willing to embrace the pain he is now bearing and however much additional pain lies between where he is and the end.

The winner of this race will take home $20,000; the runner-up $12,000. It's not about the money. A much greater reward motivates Dave Scott and Mark Allen to bear the extraordinary suffering they now bear: the reward of suffering itself; maybe the greatest finish-line feeling anyone has ever felt.

Dave's closest pursuers in the 1980 Ironman were his parents, Verne and Dot.

LEFT: "I keep the intensity high," said Dave, shown here in 1984, of his training.

BELOW: Mark crushed the competition at the 1984 Las Vegas Triathlon.

Mark found himself in the rarefied company of Scott Molina, Dale Basescu, and Scott Tinley in his first triathlon, USTS San Diego in 1982. Dave won the race; Mark finished fourth.

ABOVE: Weight management was never Mark's problem, as he showed during this break in a 1982 swim workout.

LEFT: Tom Warren, winner of Iron Man in 1979, apotheosized the new generation of endurance seekers.

ABOVE: Mark posed with fellow elites Sylvaine Puntous, Scott Tinley, Julie Moss, Kurt Madden, Patricia Puntous, Ardis Bow, and Scott Molina in 1984.

LEFT: Dave, shown in 1984, was ahead of his time in his commitment to weight lifting.

ABOVE: Mark, Scott Tinley, and Dave put their feet up together after a USTS race in 1985.

LEFT: Scott Molina liked to run . . . and drink beer.

RIGHT: Scott Tinley looked ready to win before the 1985 Ironman, which Dave and Mark boycotted.

BELOW LEFT: Mark claimed his first win at San Diego's Horny Toad Triathlon on August 8, 1982.

BELOW RIGHT: Dave posed for the cover of *Triathlon* after winning his fourth Ironman in 1984.

Before Mark owned a bike, and before Scott Tinley knew who Mark was, they competed against each other in a run–bike–run race hosted by Tom Warren and Tug's Tavern in 1981.

CHAPTER 5

YOU AGAIN

It is an unhappy lot which finds no enemies.

— PLUBIUS CYRUS

In September 1976 Dave Scott, then 22 years old, flew to Oahu to compete in the Waikiki Roughwater Swim. So charmed was Dave by the island that he immediately decided to return the following year, maybe every year. Hawaii's kiln-like heat, choppy waters, and defiant topography brought out the best in an athlete designed for extreme environmental challenges. Not much of a tourist, Dave judged the places he visited by how much he enjoyed working out in them, exercise being the only recreation he had time for or interest in. Consequently, Dave did little sightseeing in Hawaii. He did not visit any volcanoes or take home any lava rocks as souvenirs.

Ten months later Mark Allen, then 19 years old, vacationed in Hawaii with his father and stepmother, one of Toot and Space's friends, and Mark's current girlfriend during the summer break after his first year of college. In the middle of their week on the Big Island, the group drove a rental car to the top of the volcano Mauna Kea and got out to admire the view from 13,796 feet.

Mauna Kea is dormant. It last erupted forty-six centuries before Mark's party peered into its quiescent crater. In traditional Hawaiian mythology all volcanic activity is the handiwork of the goddess Pele. Jealous in nature, Madam Pele cooks up eruptions to communicate rage and to punish. More than a few ancient stories begin with slights against Pele and end with burning lava shooting into the sky. It is from Pele, in fact, that we get our expression "Don't blow your stack." In times past native Hawaiians soothed Pele's temper by hiking to the rims of volcanoes to make offerings to the deity (and some still do, though less avidly).

Pele is best known outside Hawaii today for her curse. The curse of Pele sounds ancient but is actually of recent origin. It would have to be, because the curse is directed against people who remove lava rocks from the island, and Hawaiian tourism dates back only as far as airplane travel. Urban legend holds that the curse was invented by a fed-up park ranger who sought to discourage lava pilfering, which is in fact a violation of federal law if not a crime against a sovereign divinity, punishable by hard luck and misfortune.

Some people believe in the curse. Others don't. The people who believe in it most fervently are those who number themselves among the curse's victims—those who have taken lava home from Hawaii and have subsequently suffered health problems, accidents, financial calamities, and the like. Each year the Thomas A. Jagger Museum at Volcanoes National Park, site of Pele's "home" volcano, Kilauea, receives dozens of packages containing returned lava, letters of apology, and often propitiatory bottles of gin from contrite objects of Pele's vengeance.

The gin goes back to the late nineteenth century, when George Lycurgus, a Greek hotelier who operated an inn at the edge of Kilauea, got into the habit of entertaining tourists by performing sham prayers and tossing empty gin bottles (whose contents he had himself consumed) into the crater as gifts to Pele. A more traditional choice would have been ohelo berries.

As Mark Allen and his traveling companions wandered along Mauna Kea's crater rim, an extraordinary piece of lava, shaped like a wave and sparkling with little golden flecks, caught the attention of Mark and his stepmother simultaneously. They both reached for it, but Toot grabbed it first.

"It's mine!" she teased. "You can have it after I kick the bucket."

They poked around a little while longer and then returned to the car, only to discover that they had locked themselves out. Toot knew about the curse of Pele, but as a self-described "good little Catholic girl," she dismissed the curse as a toothless Hawaiian myth. It never crossed her mind that this little nuisance might be a kind of warning from the island goddess. So instead of putting the lava back where she had found it, Toot fetched a wire toilet-paper holder out of a nearby public bathroom and used it to jimmy the lock.

Frequent visitors to Hawaii, which Space had first seen as a navy man in 1950, Toot and her husband kept a Hawaiian-themed room in their home in Elko, Nevada, and Toot found a nice place to display her stolen gem there. A few years later the couple moved to Guam. They packed up most of their possessions, including that gorgeous bit of lava, and put them in storage.

Toot suffered no special misfortune during this time. Perhaps Madam Pele chose to hold out for later opportunities for vengeance, if not against Toot directly then against someone close to her, on her home turf.

OCTOBER 1982

Mark Allen returned to Hawaii in October 1982 to compete in his first Ironman. Grip was not the only newbie who had been lured to Kona by the Julie Moss effect. The previous Ironman had drawn 580 athletes. The first "postcrawl" Ironman eight months later brought in 850. And there were other changes. Race director Valerie Silk, who had taken over management of Ironman from John Collins in 1980, had signed Bud Light to a title sponsorship deal. The race entry fee was bumped up to $85. Valerie and her growing staff invested much of the additional funds in upgraded infrastructure, enhanced pre-race and post-race events, and greater governmental support. Scores of overseas athletes participated. All in all, the event had a very different feel from past Ironmans—grander scale, better organization, and slicker packaging.

Mark was intimidated—not so much by the general hoopla as by the island. It was not his ideal place to exercise. He felt assaulted by Kona's kiln-like heat, its choppy waters, and its defiant topography while training in the days before the race. Mark liked the island as a visitor, appreciating its beauty and especially its history and culture, but it seemed as if the island somehow did not like him as an athlete.

The most active worry in Mark's mind, however, on the long night before the race was the prospect of being pressed together with more than 800 other bodies in Kailua Bay as part of a floating mass of humanity that would suddenly become a seaward-drifting riot at seven o'clock on race morning. Mark's stomach turned somersaults when he imagined himself moshing against that many thrashing bodies in open water. Contact-averse, he had little enjoyed the mass swim starts he had experienced in his first few triathlons, and this one promised to be much bigger, faster, and more violent. Mark hatched a plan to spare himself the worst of the kicking and clawing by exploiting his swimming experience and sprinting hard from the start to get ahead of the masses.

That tactic worked well—perhaps *too* well, it seemed initially. When the cannon fired Mark put his head down and swam as hard as he could. After a minute or so he lifted his eyes to sight on the orange guide buoys ahead. He saw only one other swimmer, directly in front of him. At first he feared he had swum off course, but the other swimmer seemed to know where he was going, so Mark put his head back down and followed him all the way to the turnaround buoy at 1.2 miles and then back toward shore. Still not seeing the bright swim caps and wheeling arms, hearing the splashing, or feeling the presence of a single other athlete, Mark wondered if he and this man he was blindly following had been left far behind by the lead pack. But when he climbed out of the water on the other's heels, a race official pointed at him and shouted, "Two!"

That meant he was in second place, virtually tied for the race lead. Exhilaration filled the young first-timer, who just a few months earlier had felt he was letting his life drift away but who now seemed to encounter fresh evidence daily that he had discovered a thing he had been born to do. Forgetting himself, Mark placed a hand on the leader's shoulder and used it to slingshot himself ahead on the ramp that led to the transition area so he could see whose wake he'd ridden with such unexpected success. It was Dave Scott. Neither Dave nor Mark could have known that the competitive dynamic just established, of Mark shadowing Dave during the Ironman swim, would persist for years to come. Nor would it be the last time the pair made physical contact during Ironman.

While Mark paused to rinse the brine off his body under a makeshift shower, Dave went straight to the changing room. Rolling out of transition a minute ahead of Mark, Dave hit the early miles hard, tearing along the Queen Kaahumanu Highway through the sprawling black lava fields of the Kona coast in an effort to make his youthful challenger believe that pursuit was futile. After pedaling alone for ninety minutes, Dave assumed he'd succeeded in that effort. But at thirty-eight miles Mark pulled alongside him, looking as though he'd just woken from a refreshing nap. This was the moment when Dave Scott and Mark Allen met.

"Hi, Dave; I'm Mark Allen," Mark said.

"Yeah, I know who you are," said Dave, who not only knew who Mark was but had already dismissed the newcomer as too scrawny to constitute a legitimate threat at Ironman.

Mark's excitement made him garrulous, and he pressed the conversation.

"Hey, after we finish biking, do you want to go for a run?" he joked.

"Yeah, sure," Dave said without mirth. He then shifted into a higher gear and pulled away from the annoying gadfly.

Ironman's bike course was a simple out-and-back that hugged the coast between Kailua-Kona and the small village of Hawi (pronounced hah-VEE), some fifty miles away. Mark stayed within range of Dave all the way to the turnaround. Hawi was the worst possible place for a racer's bicycle to break down. At that point you were as far as you could get from where you needed to end up. Naturally, it was there that Madam Pele first struck Mark Allen—if you believe in such things. Mark attempted a gear change and felt something give, then heard the clatter of metal against asphalt. His machine was now stuck in its highest gear. He stopped to examine the drivetrain and found that the rear derailleur had spontaneously disintegrated—a one-in-a-million race-ender.

Mark hitched a ride back to town with a local in a pickup truck. He arrived just in time to watch Dave Scott become the first two-time Ironman champion. Although disappointed not to have finished, Mark left the island in good spirits.

I was right there with the best guy in the world, he thought. *Who knows? If everything goes right, maybe I can win this race someday.*

1983

When Mark returned to Kona the following October, he did so with a different identity. The talented but untested newcomer had been transformed into an established professional racer with two victories at the Nice Triathlon (a.k.a. the World Triathlon Championship), a generous contract with Team J. David, and a central place in San Diego's elite triathlete clique.

Mark met with no uncanny disaster during the 1983 Ironman. Instead, the race was spoiled for him before it even started by something that had happened in another race, weeks earlier. At Nice Mark utterly destroyed the 75-mile bike leg and started the run with a ten-minute lead on

Dave Scott. But he began to pay for his aggression halfway through the 20-mile run. Dehydrated and hypoglycemic, he became light-headed, then dizzy. His eyes lost the ability to focus, seeing only a soup of colors, light, and shadows. He was out on his feet—a punch-drunk fighter helpless before the final blow. That blow seemed to come when, with three miles to go, Mark tilted his head back to take a swig of water from a bottle and lost his equilibrium, pivoting backward to the ground like an axed oak. He dragged himself to his feet and steadied his body briefly with his fingertips on the road, exactly as Julie Moss had done in the February 1982 Ironman. Despite his addled state, Mark was conscious of the visual echo. *I look like Julie Moss*, he thought with a crazy sense of inflated significance. Somehow Mark righted himself fully and resumed running, only to stagger straight into a parking meter. Spectators' cheers turned to gasps of horror as the race leader loped close enough to permit a clear look into his vacant, unseeing eyes. Some were so moved by Mark's shocking perseverance that they started to run with him, urging him to keep moving as Dave Scott stalked closer and closer from behind. By the time Mark reached the finish line, a crowd of hundreds surrounded him, pleading for him.

It was a pyrrhic victory. In winning the race, Mark had lost his mojo. He arrived in Kona with no conscious memory of his purgatory on the French Riviera, but his body seemed to remember, as he raced uncharacteristically gun-shy, losing a minute to Dave in the swim, another three minutes on the bike, and eleven for good measure on the run.

It was not Mark but his J. David teammate Scott Tinley who nearly took down the Man that day, as he had done once before. Dave had arrived in Kona less fit than in previous years, his training having been curtailed by the dark period that followed his breakup with Linda Buchanan. But he believed he could will his way to a third Ironman title nevertheless.

"A lot of things had worn me down that year, but that race meant a lot to me," Dave said afterward. "I wanted to salvage the year for myself."

Dave, as always, led the race out of the water. Tinley, a weak swimmer, came out of the bay seven minutes behind Dave but laid down a heroic effort on the bike and caught up five miles before the bike-run transition. Tinley sportingly handed a water bottle to Dave as he passed but then negated any goodwill he'd earned by pedaling ahead and standing out of the saddle to piss on the fly, wetting Dave with the hot, rank spray.

The bike course ended at the Kona Surf Hotel on the far end of coastal Ali'i Drive, seven miles south of the start line at Kailua Pier. Tinley charged out of the hotel's vast parking lot to start the marathon twenty seconds in front of Dave. An ABC camera followed Dave out of the transition area and onto the run course in pursuit of the only man to have beaten him in Hawaii. As always, Dave treated the camera's presence like a confessional.

"I feel terrible," Dave volunteered. For a moment it seemed as if that was all he had to say. Then he spoke again: "But I'm going to *bury* this guy."

Half a mile up the road, Dave was back in the lead. His advantage ballooned to five minutes over the next fifteen miles. Tinley conceded defeat in his thoughts and began to focus on staying ahead of Mark Allen. But Dave had dug deep enough in his effort to "bury" his would-be usurper to expose the shallowness of his fitness, and suddenly he was in trouble.

"At about sixteen miles I was seeing dancing buffalo on the side of the road," he said later.

His lead shrank. Dave's buddy Pat Feeney, whose job was to give Dave split times and gap information throughout the race, grimly reported the dire numbers in the waning miles and worsened their deflating effect on his disintegrating friend by coloring the data with commentary.

"You've only got 2:20 on Tinley!" Pat shouted to Dave at the twenty-one-mile point. "He looks *great!*"

Gee, thanks, Dave thought.

Behind him Tinley had been getting similar information from his wife, Virginia. Between six and sixteen miles, it was all bad. Eventually the demoralized chaser snapped at her, "Why don't you just go away?" She complied. When he learned later from other spectators that Dave was struggling, Tinley went after him with everything he had. Preferring to die by his own hand, if at all, Dave ran himself into a new dimension of pain over the last two miles and crossed the finish line thirty-three seconds ahead of Tinley, blind with exhaustion, vowing never to participate in this stupid race again.

Fifteen long minutes passed before Mark Allen came down Ali'i Drive. On the one hand, he felt good about finishing third in the biggest triathlon in the world in just his second year in the sport. On the other hand, he knew he'd missed an opportunity to beat the best when he was not at his best.

1984

Dave's vow to retire from Ironman did not last. Another summer of bad racing and shadowy days in the beanbag chair provoked him to return to Kona and once more exorcise his mounting frustrations in the lava fields. Mark, meanwhile, enjoyed a terrific season and came to the island not merely believing but knowing he could win. Triathlon's fans and media largely agreed. Dave was down; Mark was rising. This was Grip's year.

Dave heard these prognostications and absorbed them with dark relish. He was like a loner with a triple black belt having sand kicked in his face by a lifeguard who is showing off for the popular crowd and has no idea. The first punch couldn't come soon enough.

On race morning Mark showed signs of cracking under the weight of expectation that had been placed on him—and that he had placed on himself. In the predawn darkness, Dave seemed loose and confident as he went about his last-minute preparations. Forty minutes before the cannon fired he was seen standing in line at a portable toilet, casually discussing how ready he felt with adoring age-group competitors. Mark, by contrast, seemed tense, shrinking into himself. There was a subtle deference in the way he sidled up to Dave at the start line.

When the cannon sounded Mark, per routine, slipped into Dave's wake, where he stayed for the next fifty minutes and change. In the transition area Dave was forced to stand around and wait while frantic volunteers tried to find the three-time champion's misplaced bag of cycling clothes. Dave remained remarkably calm through the crisis. Mark did not. Seizing the opportunity, he launched himself into the bike ride, hoping to shake the Man much earlier than he'd anticipated when mentally rehearsing the race under self-hypnosis, as he was wont to do. It appeared a crafty, opportunistic move, but Dave showed little concern as he rolled off the pier in pursuit.

Mark took the lead from former Olympic swimmer Djan Madruga at twenty-three miles. Shortly thereafter a car pulled alongside him. Inside were Mark's current fiancée, Bunny Stein, and his future fiancée, Julie Moss. (Things were getting complicated.)

"You've got a huge lead!" Bunny shouted through the wind.

"How much?" Mark demanded, disappointing his betrothed by failing to respond with the ebullience she'd expected.

Nearly three minutes, he was told. He picked up his pace. *Let's finish this now*, he thought.

By the halfway point in Hawi, Mark's advantage had grown to eight minutes. Nevertheless, he wore a grim expression as he made the turn, whereas Dave managed a smile for the spectators gathered there.

With thirty miles left in the bike leg, a press car pulled up next to Dave. Inside were Dave's friend Liz Barrett and a few other partisan journalists wearing forlorn expressions.

"Don't give up on me yet!" Dave shouted. "I haven't even put on my running shoes!"

When Mark arrived at the Kona Surf Hotel and hopped off his bike, he learned that he had an insurmountable lead of nearly twelve minutes. He removed his cycling togs and suited up in a red-white-and-blue running outfit with the letters "USA" stenciled on the shirtfront, an odd choice in a race where athletes did not officially represent their nations and where almost all of the top male contenders were Americans. At last Mark not only relaxed but openly celebrated. He knew there was no way Dave could catch him now. He could cruise the marathon at 90 percent and still win comfortably. Intoxicated by the certainty of his victory, Mark traded high fives with spectators as he ran down Ali'i Drive toward town. He was so happy that he didn't even notice it was 98 degrees and he was becoming severely dehydrated.

Mark was all smiles as he passed the Hot Corner, a rollicking spectator zone featuring music and a live announcer at the corner of Ali'i Drive and Hualalai Road. After blazing through Kailua Village, he made a right turn onto Palani Road and began to climb Pay-'n'-Save Hill (as it was known, owing to the presence of a certain supermarket on its north side) toward the Queen K Highway, where he would turn left and enter the desolate, scorching lava fields. At the base of the hill Mark felt fantastic. At the top of the hill, not even half a mile later, he was out of gas. His pupils shrank to pinhole size; his terrified eyes seemed to see Dave in the distance behind him, closing in.

Back at the Kona Surf, Dave looked anything but defeated. He blazed into the bike-run transition barking threats and commands at the race volunteers. The time for smiling had passed.

"Don't knock me off my bike!" he roared.

The volunteers, none of whom was positioned to knock him off his bike, scattered like zoogoers fleeing an escaped tiger.

"Where's my bag? Where's my bag?" Dave yelled as he yanked off his cycling shorts, mooning a TV camera behind him.

A surviving volunteer handed Dave his transition bag with a flinch, as though handing a morsel between cage bars. Dave dressed in such furious haste that he pulled his singlet on backward. He sprinted under the marathon "START" banner with his eyes far down the road, behaving very much like a person who believed he had a chance.

At the base of Pay-'n'-Save Hill, with twenty miles yet to run, Dave had already swallowed four minutes of Mark's advantage. Mark should have known that the only way to build a twelve-minute lead on a fit Dave Scott in the bike leg of Ironman was to ride too hard to survive the marathon. Letting fear get the best of him, he had written a check on the bike that he could not cash on the run.

Presently Dave learned that Mark was walking. He licked his chops. Mark looked like a drunk driver failing a roadside sobriety test when Dave glided past him at twelve miles, his lips briefly forming a faint, pitiless smile as he took the lead.

You again.

Sometime after Dave had vanished into the horizon, having replaced the old game of catching Mark with a new game of trying to better his course record and left his rival to fester in the searing heat, Mark became aware that a moped bearing a race medical volunteer had pulled abreast of him. Mark intensified his concentration on the movement of his limbs, trying to appear sober—or sane—or whatever.

"Are you okay?" the medic asked.

"I'm fine," Mark hissed, keeping his eyes on the ground in front of him, having learned the hard way that putting them anywhere else threatened his equilibrium.

"I'm just going to ask you a few questions," said the medic.

"Knock yourself out," Mark answered testily.

"What's your name?" the medic began.

"Mark Allen!" Mark barked. *Good grief*, he thought. This was humiliating enough as it was.

"What day is it?"

Mark briefly considered making a smart retort but decided that answering the question straight would rid him of the nuisance quicker. Of course it was Sunday. Wait, no, it was Saturday. Or was it? Mark realized with a burst of mortification that he had no clue. Meanwhile, the second hand was ticking.

"I'm fine. Leave me alone," Mark said at last.

Several cups of Gatorade and water put a little life back into Grip's legs, and he resumed running—not all the way to the finish line but enough to get him there in fifth place, forty-one minutes behind Dave. Bunny Stein met her wobbly fiancé in the finish area and dragged him away from the throng and back onto the relatively isolated pier, where his day had started with such promise. Together they stared silently into the water.

"Are you sure this race is good for you?" Mark's mother, Sharon, asked him later.

1985

Mark did not come back to Hawaii in 1985. But then, neither did Dave Scott, nor defending women's champion Sylviane Puntous, nor most of the other big stars. The pros banded together and boycotted the event for failing to offer prize money, vowing never to return if Valerie Silk did not share the loot Ironman took from *ABC Sports*, Bud Light, and other sponsors with the men and women who made the race good television and attractive to corporate backers. Meanwhile, the organizers of the Nice Triathlon, Ironman's main competitor for status among triathlons, saw an opportunity and moved their 1985 race date closer to Ironman's, making it almost impossible for any pro to compete in both—and they increased their prize purse to $75,000.

All of the sport's biggest stars flocked to the French Riviera for the race that still billed itself as the World Triathlon Championship. Mark Allen won for the fourth time. Dave Scott dropped out with a flat tire. The following weekend Dave was married to Anna Pettis. The weekend after that, in Kona, Dave, working as a TV commentator for ABC, watched Scott Tinley—the lone notable boycott-buster—win Ironman and break Dave's course record. It was hard to watch. Dave needed this race. It was *his* race—his only race.

1986

Loath to see a French event usurp Ironman as the world's preeminent triathlon, La Jolla real estate developer Steve Drogan donated $100,000 of his own money to fund a prize purse for the 1986 race. Dave decided to skip Nice and reclaim his race. Mark chose *his* race, Nice, and won yet again, easily.

"It feels good to win this one five times before Dave could win Ironman five times," Mark told reporters with a forced laugh at the finish line.

He wasn't fooling anyone. Dave could live with Mark's having Nice. But Mark, in his heart, wanted very much to take Dave's race from him. Grip later confessed his dissatisfaction.

"For some reason I didn't feel as fulfilled as I thought I would," he said. "I didn't feel I had stretched my capabilities to push beyond what I already knew I could do. I only had to put out maybe an 80 to 85 percent effort to do it, and there's a huge difference between going 85 percent and putting out 100 percent."

Mark had discovered what all great athletes discover sooner or later: Winning easily gives little satisfaction. Much more satisfying is a hard-fought victory—or loss—that stretches you beyond preexisting limits. When Mark got started in triathlon, every win felt good because he was not accustomed to winning at such a level, and because winning brought him the attention and respect—especially from his father—that he had always craved. But winning had become old hat. Mark had now won twenty-two races. He had not yet, however, become all he believed he could be.

After Nice Mark flew to Hawaii to represent sponsors at Ironman and to watch the race. Just watch. But Kona cast its spell on him. He had to admit, there was no race like it. Ironman was the first; the hardest; and, with prize money available and all of the top racers back, the most competitive. Nice could never match it. Ironman was also Dave Scott's race, and Dave Scott had become, along with the race he virtually personified, the embodiment of the challenge Mark now recognized as his next great goal in life. To discover his ultimate powers, Mark had to beat Dave Scott at Ironman.

Three days before the race Mark formally entered the pro men's field. Dave couldn't have been happier. He was motivated enough already to beat the scab and cherry picker Scott Tinley (as Dave then chose to think of a person whom he otherwise liked and respected). But Dave had heard about Mark's empty gloating after Nice, and he welcomed the opportunity to make him pay for his loose lips.

Mark again followed Dave like a duckling from the start line to the swim exit. He continued to shadow Dave through 105 miles of the bike leg, ahead of the rest of the field, until Mark stopped pedaling briefly to pee from the saddle. Dave chose the moment to surge ahead, and he was able to start the marathon with a one-minute lead. He had never raced so angry. His fanged expression startled spectators who watched him charge up the hill leading out of the Kona Surf Hotel parking lot. Some stepped back reflexively from the curb as though fearing they might be bitten.

Now came Dave's turn to piss. He stopped at the side of the road and whipped out his junk. The camera-bearing motorcycle traveling with him stopped too.

"Turn off the camera!" Dave shouted.

He resumed running. But his fury was not spent.

"I want a split, and I want it *now!*" Dave shouted at a race marshal on a scooter also riding alongside him.

That year, for the first time, Ironman had assigned spotters to provide time gaps to professional racers. But it was easier to tell the man in second place how far behind the leader he was than to tell the leader how much time he had on the man in second place. Receiving no immediate answer from the marshal, Dave became angrier still.

"Where's Allen?" he barked.

Okay, now it was out: That was what he really wanted to know. Smiling malevolently, the marshal gestured backward with a thumb. Dave swiveled his head. There was Mark, about sixty yards behind him.

You again.

That was it. Almost visibly steaming, Dave took off like a shot. His lead grew to 100 yards, then 200, then a quarter mile. He requested no more time gaps. He knew he didn't need them.

Dave crossed the finish line at 8:28:37, demolishing by twenty-two minutes the course record Tinley had set the previous year and having run a 2:49 marathon in 100-degree heat. Mark finished eight minutes back, telling himself that the fatigue in his legs from having won Nice two weeks earlier was worth at least that much time. If he had started the race fresh, he would have won for sure.

Dave's most attentive listener among the hundreds who heard his victory speech at the following night's awards banquet at the Kona Surf was Mark Allen. The now two-time runner-up sat far forward in his seat, feverish with envy. What Dave had on that stage seemed worth ten times more than everything Mark had achieved in his career to that point. He felt like a starving man watching the thief of his eggs eat an omelet. Perhaps Mark even began to sense that this clawing need inside him wasn't about sport at all.

1987

A massive wave of expectation carried Mark through the next year. The Kellogg company came calling and signed Grip to a deal that made him a pitchman for its new Pro-Grain breakfast cereal (which was its failed, sugary Star Wars C3PO's cereal in a different box), promoting it as "Ironman food." No matter that Mark had never won Ironman (although he had won *an* Ironman—in Japan the previous year). He would take care of that come October—a six-figure bonus from Kellogg said he would. Weeks before the race Kellogg purchased the back cover of the January 1988 issue of *Triathlete* for a Mark Allen/Pro-Grain Ironman victory advertisement. It was as good as done.

Around the same time Mark signed a book deal with a similar understanding. He and collaborator Bob Babbitt would pen the first chunk of the largely biographical manuscript before Ironman and would write the last part, which would describe his hard-earned first Ironman victory, immediately after he won the 1987 race. It hardly needed to be said that another failure would severely compromise this plan. Mark knew he would not fail.

Grip planned his entire season around Hawaii for the first time in his career. He skipped Nice, the lucrative race he had owned even more thoroughly than Dave had owned Ironman. He trained harder than ever, completing more than 15,000 miles of combined swimming, cycling, and running, or the equivalent of more than 100 Ironman races, between the time he started his buildup in January and his departure for Kona in early October.

Mark's confidence of winning Ironman was supported in no small measure by Dave Scott's announcement after the 1986 Ironman that he would skip the race in 1987. The star-crossed rivals did square off at other races, however, including the Bermuda International Triathlon in August, which Mark won and from which Dave, along with half of the men's pro field, was disqualified for drafting on the bike. After the race a fuming Dave Scott announced that he would defend his Ironman title after all.

"I want to race Mark at his best," he said flatly.

The news shook Mark, who came face to face with Dave, just hours after the announcement had been made, in the lobby of the hotel where both were staying. They had no choice but to speak, and there was only one thing to talk about.

"I hear you're doing Ironman," Mark said, his voice so tight it almost cracked.

"Yeah, I'm going back," Dave said good-humoredly, enjoying Mark's discomfiture.

As they parted Mark cursed himself under his breath. *I gave him my power!* he lamented. *Why did I let him have my power? I've got to get it back!*

Mark's arrival in Kailua two months later was treated like a crown prince's attendance at his father's deathbed. The whole hype-filled week before the race had the feel of a coronation. Mark was in the spotlight, and Dave had been pushed to the wings. The heir apparent was far more visible in Kona than in past years, and more celebrated. He did some promotional work for Kellogg on the island, signed scores of specially made posters at the race expo, and was seen breakfasting with Julie Moss at the Aloha Café and lunching with her at Amy's Café the day before the race.

The tension between Dave and Mark was palpable. They had been able to engage in brief but comfortable small talk together in Kona the previous October. Mark's low-key approach to that year's race had made a semblance of friendship possible. That possibility had ended.

At a meeting for professional racers held two days before the race, Dave sat on a chair facing a rotating cast of race officials, who reviewed the race rules and answered questions. Mark sat on the floor facing Dave, staring at him, daring Dave to look his way. He did not. Mark quietly gloated, feeling he'd reclaimed the power he'd given to Dave in Bermuda. That feeling did not last long.

Toward the end of the meeting Dave spoke up, voicing a concern about getting accurate time-gap information during the marathon.

"When I'm out there in first place on the run," he began. Then he caught his "slip" and corrected it before continuing, "Or whoever . . ."

A few days before the race Dave and Mark sat down separately for interviews for ABC's television coverage of the event.

"If there's one thing you can count on in this race," Mark said, "it's that Dave Scott is not going to die. Which means, as someone who's going to compete against him, I know that I have to go a little faster, push a little harder, and that when it gets tough for me I'm going to go beyond that, one or two or three or ten steps, until hopefully I get to the point where the guy's behind me."

Mark spoke these words in reasonable and earnest tones, but the nuances of his body language—his unblinking eyes and mumbling lips—seemed vaguely grasping, uncentered, as though he knew he was forcing something he shouldn't.

By contrast, Dave's mouth formed an insolent smile and his eyes twinkled as he told the camera, "Mark's had a great year. But I think he would throw away all those victories from January to October if he could just win Ironman. And I think he feels that pressure."

Mark had not actually raced in January, February, or March. Dave was pressing buttons, aware that Mark was listening live to his interview in the shadows of the Kona Surf Hotel meeting room that was being used as a television studio as Mark awaited his turn before the camera.

Having learned the hard way that dropping Dave on the bike was not the way to beat him, Mark planned to restrain himself through the cycling portion of the contest and then choose his moment to strike on the run. He did just that.

Once more Mark shadowed Dave through the swim. But this time Mark followed so closely that he repeatedly slapped Dave's feet with his hands. Midway through the swim Dave flipped over and swam a few backstrokes while glaring at Mark, or trying to, through his goggles. Having sent a message, Dave turned back onto his belly—and Mark resumed slapping his feet.

The rivals exited Kailua Bay together mere seconds behind the leader, German swim specialist Wolfgang Dittrich. They ran side by side to the changing room, and from there they hustled in lockstep to their bikes, which awaited them in adjacent slots in the bike racks. They straddled their machines, and each struggled to get his first shoe clipped into a pedal so he could jump onto the saddle and clip in the other shoe while already moving. Dave lost his balance, veering to the right toward Mark, who simultaneously lost his balance and veered left toward Dave. They collided, and Mark sprawled into the nearby snow fencing, whose presence was fortuitous because without it Grip would have gone all the way to the ground. Scrambling to right himself, Mark shot Dave a look that said, *Dude, what the hell?* Dave ignored him and rode off. Mark chased.

Dave chose not to capture the lead early on the bike, as Mark expected, but instead fell into a comparatively leisurely tempo that allowed some of the slower swimmers, including the dangerous Scott Tinley, to catch up. Mark began to feel antsy, and fought back the temptation to take a flier. Suddenly a gusher erupted from his nose. He had to ease up to beg a roaming medic for some gauze to staunch the blood, now figuring it was just as well that Dave wasn't pushing the pace.

Mark's appetite had almost disappeared in the three days before the race. Half a sandwich filled him up. He tried to dismiss the sudden disappearance of his hunger, which he had never experienced before, as a benign effect of nerves. In fact, he had been poisoned by some bad sushi eaten a couple of days earlier and was now bleeding internally. Mark would not find out until after the race that his bloody nose was connected to the undiagnosed situation in his gut.

The lead pack of riders was well on its way back from Hawi when Dave finally put the hammer down, and by then Mark, dried blood smeared across his face, was ready. He quickly bridged the gap Dave had opened and with him pulled steadily away from the pretenders. As they neared Kailua Mark suddenly vomited. A minute later he chundered a second time. That was worrisome. He had suffered nosebleeds occasionally in training, and they had not seemed to affect his performance. But he had never barfed before. The vomiting brought relief, however, and Mark discovered that he was able to drink again soon afterward.

Dave and Mark started the run side by side, knocking elbows several times in the first mile. They had now made violent bodily contact in all three legs of the race—surely a first in Ironman history. Climbing the steep hill outside the Kona Surf parking lot, Mark felt great. Dave felt awful—as if his blood had turned to water. Mark sensed Dave's weakness and, executing his plan, turned his stride up a notch at the three-mile point of the marathon. Dave had no choice but to let him go. Over the next thirteen miles, Mark built a lead of five minutes. He began to mentally rehearse his victory speech.

The turnaround point on the out-and-back run course stood about sixteen miles from the bike-run transition, ten miles from the finish line, and just over one mile beyond Keahole Airport on the Queen K. A twenty-foot inflated Bud Light can marked the spot, taunting athletes with an optical illusion that made it seem closer than it was. This part of the race was always critical for the leaders because they met each other head-on as runners who had already made the turn passed runners still approaching it. These moments gave them a chance to measure time gaps with precision and assess each other's appearance. Dave and Mark would later discuss this crucial moment of the 1987 Ironman at a rare event in 2002, a meeting of the Los Angeles Triathlon Club in which the paired legends reviewed the full history of their singular rivalry.

"When you pass your toughest competitor, you want to look as good as you possibly can," Mark said, waggishly taking the tone of a grade school teacher.

"Very true," Dave confirmed with a knowing smile.

"So, out of the corner of my eye," Mark continued, then remarked parenthetically, "(because you also don't want to let them know you're looking, even though they know you are)."

Dave interrupted Mark. "I saw you looking," he teased. "You were nervous. You took two looks, actually. Two long, long looks, and your jaw was dropping."

Playing along, Mark pantomimed pointing a finger and dropping his jaw in awe and wonder. Then he said, "And the thought hit me: *He does not look good at all.*"

"Nor did he," Dave interjected, no longer smiling.

"I knew he was looking as good as he possibly could," Mark continued, as though he had not heard his former rival, "and I thought, *I have this thing sewn up.*"

After meeting Mark head-on, Dave, who wore no watch, counted how long it took him to reach the turnaround—about two and a half minutes. He did a quick mental calculation and learned that he would have to outrun Mark by thirty seconds per mile over the remaining distance to nip him at the finish line. It wasn't looking good. Dave resolved to make the best game he could of the last ten miles. *At least make him earn it*, he told himself.

Fortunes can turn with shocking suddenness in an eight-and-a-half-hour race. At the Bud Light can Mark felt strong and confident. At mile seventeen, a pair of trapdoors opened in the soles of his feet, and his energy poured into the underworld with the instantaneousness of a vacuum flush. Trying to maintain composure, Mark walked through the next aid station so he could eat and drink a little more than usual. He might as well have eaten sawdust and drunk air. He resumed running but could not regain his earlier pace. Another mile down the road, at the next aid station, he pulled up and walked again. The downward spiral continued. The stretches of jogging became shorter as the walk breaks lengthened. Mark began to feel a troubling tightness in his stomach and intestines. Assuming he had to pee, he tried to go as he walked but could not urinate. Meanwhile, the time-gap reports brought ever-worsening news.

Dave was coming. And somewhere, perhaps, Madam Pele was laughing.

A single motorcycle bearing an ABC cameraman accompanied Mark as he struggled along the interminable "homestretch" toward Kailua. Behind him the Man chased him inside a cocoon of media and official race vehicles, a symbol of the respect he had earned through past heroic wins. As Mark approached the twenty-four-mile point, still leading Ironman with barely two miles to go, a slow tide of these vehicles crept upon him from behind. Among them was a decrepit-looking white van with a camera crew inside. It pulled even with Mark, paused momentarily, and then drifted ahead.

Dave Scott was on the other side of that van—and for good reason. Dave himself was on the verge of collapse at this point. He had carved himself hollow in the effort to catch Mark, and as he claimed his reward for that effort, he did so in fear that if Mark was able to muster any kind of response, any answer at all, Dave would crumble to sand. So when he saw the opportunity presented by the van's obstruction, he darted to its far side and passed Mark invisibly.

You again.

According to the lore of Ironman, Mark never saw him. But he says he did. He told the LA Triathlon Club, "On the other side of that camera van, I was able to sneak a look around. And, as I was walking and he was running, I thought, *Damn, he looks really good now!*"

That line drew a good laugh, and Mark laughed too. But he wasn't laughing when it happened. In fact, he cried. Grief and accumulated frustration overcame him as his personal bogeyman disappeared ahead of him, yet again.

Then the real trouble started. Mark ducked into a portable toilet to relieve himself and pissed blood. Now he had a new reason to get to the finish line as quickly as possible. Upon finishing—still in second place, remarkably—Mark reported his condition to the medical staff and was rushed to the hospital, where tubes were snaked down into his stomach via his throat and water was flushed through in an effort to stop the bleeding. A surgeon told Mark he would have to slice him open if it didn't work. Mercifully, it did. But nothing could be done about the pain in Mark's spirit, which was searing. Like a heartbroken lover, he could not take his mind off his loss, his thoughts returning to it again and again with magnetic force, no matter how many times he pulled them away. Getting over it seemed impossible. The only relief he could imagine was falling asleep and never waking up.

What could I have done differently? Mark asked himself. *How could I have trained any harder than I did? What could possibly be missing in my strategy?*

Shortly after Mark woke up in his hospital bed the morning after Ironman, a nurse brought him a copy of the local paper. He read the account of the race. In it Dave Scott, who may or may not have known of Mark's medical emergency, complained about how Mark had ridden his wake and slapped his feet in the swim. Mark was dumbstruck—and incensed. Talk about kicking a man when he was down.

The struggle between Dave and Mark had crossed a line. It was personal now. Grip continued to brood over his tormentor's provocation through a week of convalescence on Kauai following his release from the hospital. He spent most of his time there sitting on the beach, dictating the fresh story of his latest Ironman disaster into a tape recorder so that Bob Babbitt could later transcribe the words, polish them up, and plug them into a book that had been conceived to celebrate and cash in on Mark's first Ironman victory. In his wounded frame of mind, Mark could not resist taking a shot at Dave that wound up on the last page of his book.

"Dave felt frustration because it was a hard race," Mark said, affecting a tone of disinterested analysis. "Dave had to deal with his race and his domain slipping away from him and the pain it took to bring it back into his grasp. He wasn't comfortable. He was pushed beyond the point where he was in control of his own race. If you're forced to dig deep in your reserves, you get pissed off. Sometimes after an experience like that, you are forced to look hard at the dark side of yourself. Unfortunately, you might not like what you see."

Sales of Mark's book would be predictably disappointing. Pro-Grain cereal wouldn't last a year.

1988

For several weeks after the '87 Ironman Mark was through with the race forever. He gorged on fast food and drank like a college student, flouting doctor's orders to be gentle with his stomach until he fully recovered. For several more weeks after that, beginning around the time his recurring nausea abated, he vacillated. Then he decided to give it another go. Still not knowing what he could have done differently, he did nothing differently. He skipped Nice a second time. He trained the same way he had the year before. He returned to Kona on another winning binge.

At Thursday afternoon's press conference Mark instinctively scanned the room for Dave. He was not there. Race emcee Mike Plant's first announcement from the podium was that Dave Scott had just officially withdrawn from the race with a knee injury. The news was less than shocking. Dave had already missed his last two scheduled races with a bum knee. Desperate to salvage another disastrous year with another Ironman miracle, he'd come to Hawaii anyway; tested the knee with an easy run Thursday morning; and stopped almost immediately, ready to put his fist through a wall.

Mark furtively looked around at the remaining male contenders. He saw no one who could seriously challenge him. *Oh, well.* He would have liked to claim his first Ironman title by defeating Dave, but he wasn't going to look a gift horse in the mouth.

Madam Pele struck early that year. Mark had just come out of the swim-bike transition and crested Pay-'n'-Save Hill when he suffered a tire puncture. A steady stream of competitors pedaled pitilessly past Grip during the four minutes it took him to install and inflate a fresh tube. He mounted and spurred his steed angrily. By the time he reached Hawi, he had overtaken most of the opportunists. All was not lost.

Then he flatted again.

"I must have hit the only two pieces of glass on the entire 112 miles of the Queen K Highway," he said afterward.

A classic photo, taken by Tracy Frankel, captures a moment soon after Mark's unlikely second flat. His bike is lying on its side in the dirt like a stubborn mule that has quit at the worst possible time. Mark stands over the recalcitrant beast, looking down upon it, wearing an expression that says, *I cannot believe this!* His arms are splayed outward, his palms turned skyward, his fingers curled and separated into claw shapes, as though he is imploring a higher power to account for his undeserved misfortune.

Mark wheeled into the bike-run transition a hopeless eighteen minutes behind the leader and eventual winner, Scott Molina. He ran well, but it hardly mattered. What mattered was that the world's best triathlete everywhere but Hawaii finished fifth in the juiciest opportunity he would probably ever have to steal an Ironman win.

Dave took small satisfaction in watching Mark fail from the back of an ABC camera van. He was galled by how little his withdrawal from the race had affected the pundits' predictions. It seemed they'd already written him off and anointed either Mark Allen, or the fast-rising Mike Pigg, as the next Ironman champion. Dave's anger increased when he saw the latest *Triathlete* magazine readers' poll for the best male triathlete. He was ranked eighth. *Eighth!* Dave flew home hell-bent on punishing every man ahead of him on that list and shaming every last person who had dared to vote for them.

"There are an awful lot of guys who aren't going to like getting beaten by a 35-year-old next year," Dave told a fan before leaving the island. "If you're betting with your buddies on any of the races I'm at, be sure you bet on the right guy."

1989

Yet again Mark resolved to renounce Ironman and focus on shorter, more temperate races. The hours and days immediately following an Ironman race are not the most reliable moments to make final decisions about one's Ironman racing future, however. It's like trying to decide whether to conceive another child in the hours and days after a long and painful labor.

As time passed Mark's attitude evolved. By December he was vacillating once again, and by January he was ready for round seven of the fight of his life. Ultimately the decision to give Ironman another shot came rather easily. All Mark had to do was think through the consequences of *not* going back to the island. He could give up on any other dream, he realized, quit any other chase, and eventually move on. But not Ironman. Abandoning that dream would haunt him for the rest of his days. No matter how many more races he might win in his career as a triathlete, and no matter what dragons he might slay in his life after triathlon, the voice inside that called him a coward would never be silenced if he let go now. Mark did not know if his best possible effort in Kona would be good enough to allow him to beat Dave Scott and win the race. But he knew he hadn't achieved his best possible effort there yet, and he knew he had to keep trying until he did. Only then could he move on. This particular challenge had long since ceased to be about a certain course and a certain rival. It had come to be about *claiming* himself, and his life—about finishing what he'd started when he cleared out his meager savings to buy a bike suitable for his first Ironman six years before.

Having decided to go back, Mark next asked himself what was the message in his pattern of failure in Kona. Not one to believe in coincidence, he knew it was no accident that he had lost the race so many times in so many ways. What was the lesson that the race had been trying to teach him and that he had so far refused to learn? *Just tell me*, Mark implored of the island. *I don't care what it is. I'll do it.*

An answer came. Indeed, the answer, Mark discovered, lay in his very questioning. At last Mark had stopped trying to force himself on Kona and on Ironman and was allowing the island and the race to guide him. And where these spirits guided him was *beyond*—past and through the false limits he had set.

"The island is like truth serum," Mark would reflect after his retirement from triathlon. "It could see that I really wanted to win this race, but I wasn't willing to do it under the terms and conditions of the race. I wanted to win in a certain way—putting in a certain amount of training, going through a certain amount of pain—but what it was going to take was going to a whole different level."

Mark vowed to go to a whole different level in his preparation for the 1989 Ironman. The perfect opportunity to do just that landed in his lap when his frequent training partner Scott Molina, now the defending Ironman winner, invited him and Julie Moss (to whom he had just become engaged) to spend six weeks training with him and his wife, 1987 Ironman winner Erin Baker, a native Kiwi, in New Zealand. Rob Barel, a great Dutch triathlete, and Colleen Cannon, the reigning U.S. women's national champion, also accepted invitations from Molina and Baker. Mark welcomed the rarefied training camp as a chance to completely eliminate all of life's distractions and to focus exclusively on training and get his mind right for Kona. The group convened in the middle of March. Mark and Julie rented a house in the coastal village of Sumner, five miles from their hosts' home in the Christchurch suburb of Lyttleton.

There was nothing to do, and nothing Mark wished to do, but train, eat, and sleep. He slept nine hours a night and napped for an hour or two in the afternoons. He ate hearty meals of stir-fried vegetables, fruit salads, pasta, and other high-octane fare prepared by Colleen's husband, Howard Kaushansky, an excellent cook and the only nonathlete in the group. Almost every remaining minute of each day was spent swimming, riding, and running.

Molina saw the difference in Mark's mind-set straightaway. When they'd trained together in the past, it had always been Molina who'd wanted to go the extra mile. Now the roles were reversed. However far Molina, known as the hardest-working man in the sport, wanted to go, Mark wanted to go that far plus a mile.

Until that point in his career Mark had never trained longer than six hours in a single day. In New Zealand he routinely packed in seven or more hours of exercise between sunup and sundown. Each day the group challenged itself to do something more ridiculous than the day before. In one three-day stretch they rode 110 miles from Lyttleton to Hanmer Springs, stayed overnight and trained in Hanmer the next day, and then rode five and a half hours back to Lyttleton. On another occasion the group ran for two and a half hours, from the base to the summit of Mt. Herbert, gaining 3,000 feet of elevation, and back down.

It was from none other than Dave Scott that Mark borrowed the notion of challenging himself with training days whose duration more closely matched that of Ironman. Mark had seen many interviews in which Dave had talked about how different an eight-plus-hour race was from a six-hour race, contending that Ironman becomes all mental after six hours and never failing to point out that although any fast fellow can win a six-hour race, a special mental toughness is required to win Ironman.

"I think I have the mental perseverance to outendure anyone in this race," Dave told ABC in 1983. "The topography and the terrain are mentally stifling. I think that most people lose their concentration after about five hours. They give up. It's not physical; it's the mental concentration. If you're used to having a partner to train with, or a nice pretty setting to work out in, you come over here to Kona, it's like training on the moon."

Mark had previously dismissed such remarks as digs at himself—attempts to belittle his wins at the Nice Triathlon, which happened to be a six-hour race. But now, scarred and smarter, he realized that although Dave undoubtedly was needling him, he was also speaking the truth. Surviving beyond six hours really was more a mental than a physical challenge, and to meet that challenge he needed more practice in facing it than he got from Ironman itself.

Grip got that practice in New Zealand, and he noticed an immediate payoff. He survived workouts he never would have imagined he could have done before, and his confidence soared. Nor did he merely survive. The harder he trained, the stronger he became. The training was like a code that unlocked a secret door to a whole new level of fitness.

While in New Zealand Mark also took a long, hard look at himself and admitted that fear, above all, had held him back in Hawaii. He recalled the 1987 Ironman, when he had stepped off the plane in Kona into a blast of incredible heat and recoiled, intimidated both physically and spiritually. He recalled the 1984 Ironman, when fear of Dave Scott had impelled him to sprint recklessly ahead of the Man out of the swim-bike transition, only to implode in the marathon.

"I realized the race was intimidating to me," Mark said in a 2002 interview. "I didn't like the wind. I didn't like the heat. I didn't like the humidity. And the race was just a little bit too long. And I was afraid of Dave Scott. Aside from all of that, I loved it."

Ironman was the only race on earth—and Dave Scott the only athlete—that still made Mark feel like the choker he'd been as a young swimmer. Mark had almost completely conquered his feeble former self. Almost. Ironman and Dave Scott had become symbols of unfinished business, jeering voices in his mind, pushing him to just accept that he was and always would be a coward. There was nothing Mark Allen desired more than *not* to be a coward. So he chose to face those fears squarely.

To face his fear of Ironman's elements Mark imagined that the bleak, sun-browned hills of New Zealand's South Island were the baked black lava fields of Hawaii's Big Island, which was not a difficult thing to do. He went out of his way to ride against headwinds and waited for the hottest part of the day to run.

To face his fear of Dave, and his own fearfulness in general, Mark performed regular "prayer-like meditations," as he described them, in which he psychoanalyzed himself, digging up the roots of his fears in the hope of killing them by exposure. This may have been the hardest thing of all.

IN MID-APRIL MARK FLEW to the sultry Caribbean Island of St. Croix to get his first real taste of the fruits of his New Zealand training. The America's Paradise Triathlon was a traditional season-opening event of roughly half the Ironman distance that always attracted a number of top Kona contenders. Scott Molina traveled there with Mark. Mike Pigg, second at Ironman the year before, and Ken Glah, third, were also present. Dave Scott was there as well. But chance thwarted Mark's anxious wish to measure himself against Dave when Dave suffered a flat tire that took him forever to fix, allowing Mark to win easily. Dave did, however, salvage the moral victory of recording the fastest run of the race, besting Mark's time by nineteen seconds.

The rivals had not squared off for more than a year before that day, and they met again just one week later, at the World Cup Triathlon, a race of roughly three-quarters the Ironman distance, in Gold Coast, Australia. This time Mark flatted, and although he was quick with his tire change, he wheeled into transition one minute forty-one seconds behind Dave, who was gleefully attempting to drive the last nail into the coffin of Mark's race with an aggressive running pace up the road. If Dave sustained that pace— and he would—Mark would have to produce the single greatest run in the history of triathlon to win. And he did.

Face disfigured by his notorious rictus grin, Mark pursued Dave Scott through the smoothly paved streets of Gold Coast with the cold relentlessness of a killer robot and with a newfound swiftness that came to him with god-like ease, shocking even to himself. Ahead of him, proudly clicking off 5:45 miles and aware of Mark's misfortune on the bike, Dave knew he had the race's massive (by triathlon standards) $20,000 first-place prize sewn up. Except he didn't. Mark caught Dave just 12 kilometers into the 30-kilometer run.

You again.

Mark paused momentarily at Dave's shoulder and then, seeming almost disappointed by Dave's inability to counter, eased away from his flabbergasted, redlining rival. Mark completed the run in 1:41:26, having averaged an astonishing pace of 5:26 per mile. He'd outrun Dave by nearly six minutes to beat him by four.

Mark had defeated Dave many times before, and Dave never did his best racing in April. But this kind of ass-kicking could not be shrugged off. Dave would have considered what Mark had just done to be impossible for anyone—and he still considered it to be beyond his own capacity. Dave would have been thrilled with his own run split, in fact, had Mark's not so grandly outstripped it.

Confidence is important in all sports, but in endurance sports it's everything. An athlete can go no faster than he thinks he can. Dave understood this better than anyone. Confidence building had always been the explicit, overarching objective of his training. He did not plan his training by science or logic, and certainly not by precedent. Instead, he simply asked himself what sorts of experiences he needed to have in training to arrive on the start line in Kona feeling invincible. Then he executed whatever answer his intuition gave him, no matter how outlandish. This had been his way since 1980, when he had performed his epic, 127-mile Ironman rehearsal, which had left him feeling so euphorically ready that he shouted out to his friends like a streaking wassailer in the street as he ran his last mile.

Dave was now further from that state of self-belief than he had ever been before. Mark's run in Gold Coast had shattered Dave's confidence in his ability to beat Mark where it mattered most: in Hawaii. In the past, confidence building had been entirely within Dave's control. To arrive on the start line in Kona feeling unbeatable, he needed only to do more or better than he had already in his preparations. But it was different this time. Dave knew there was little chance he could match what Mark had just done with any amount of training. He somehow had to restore his confidence before October, or he was screwed. Mark had raised the bar; Dave had to raise it even higher.

Yet why should he care? Dave had already won Ironman six times, beaten Mark five times. He was 35 years old. What more did he have to prove?

In a word: everything. Dave was acutely conscious of having established triathlon as a legitimate athletic endeavor. But that achievement meant nothing in his own reckoning unless he validated it by remaining at the top of the sport until it reached full maturity. With each passing year triathlon became more competitive. Dave's greatest fear was that the sport would leave him behind, and he would be remembered as the guy who had won only before the "real" athletes appeared. Already the sport seemed on the brink of passing him by as Mike Pigg and other younger racers had relegated Dave to second-tier status in shorter races, and as injuries and periods of apathy had taken him away from competition for long stretches. Dave was determined to defer his retirement until triathlon was full grown and to win at least one more Ironman while the competition was as good as it would ever be. Four years younger, Mark Allen represented that next generation hell-bent on surpassing Dave and (as he saw it) tarnishing his legacy—a legacy that was already very much in jeopardy, in his view, because he had not won a single race since the 1987 Ironman. Dave knew Mark's best day at Ironman was yet to come, and he needed to defeat Mark on that day. His very name depended on it.

The morning after the World Cup Triathlon, Mark frolicked on the beach and surfed with Scott Tinley, Mike Pigg, and Julie Moss, who'd won the women's race and $20,000 to match his own. Later, over breakfast, the friends checked out the coverage of the previous day's race in the local papers and laughed over the gossipy sidebars about Mark's recently announced engagement to Julie. Meanwhile, Dave put in a hard day of training alone, steaming, plotting his revenge.

DAVE WASTED NO TIME in starting the process of restoring his confidence. Two weeks after his stinging defeat in Australia, he raced at the Phoenix stop of the USTS. Also there was Scott Molina, a four-time USTS champion who specialized at that distance. Little was expected from Dave, who was viewed as too slow to win such short events now that the new breed of short-course specialists like Molina had taken over—and perhaps as too old, lately, as well. But Dave defiantly spanked Molina and the rest of the field on the strength of a dominating bike leg. Afterward *Triathlete* editor CJ Olivares asked Dave to respond to the circulating talk about his perhaps being past his prime.

"I think I've still got it," Dave spat. "I'll quit when I want to quit. I don't want people to bury me before my time."

Uncharacteristically, Dave raced yet again the very next week—another USTS event, this one in Miami. He won again, beating by two minutes and change a 17-year-old pro with unparalleled cycling ability named Lance Armstrong.

Dave's photograph appeared on the cover of the October issue of *Triathlete* next to the slug line "DAVE SCOTT: THE MAN IS BACK."

While Dave was on a roll, Mark was on a tear, winning more races (nine) and bigger races (including the first official triathlon world championship recognized by the International Olympic Committee) than his rival. "Anything you can do, I can do better," Mark seemed to taunt through his performances.

Dave had to do more.

As the summer season wound down, Dave was left with one last chance to raise the bar before Kona. At the end of July he traveled to Japan for that country's Ironman in a dangerous frame of mind—the sort that often preceded a descent into one of his dark periods. Dave had almost canceled his flight twice: first when he'd developed a pain in his left knee that had hampered his training and again when a typhoon had forced race officials to postpone the event one week, placing it just days ahead of the expected arrival of his and Anna's first child, and a mere nine weeks before Hawaii. It was always a sense of being overwhelmed that sent Dave into a tailspin, and he was at the edge of the precipice.

Dave was never one to taper his training much before a race, feeling that the freshness he gained from putting up his feet was not worth the cabin-fever agitation he suffered without his customary quota of kinetic release. But there's not tapering, and then there's *not tapering*. Three days before the race Dave set out on what was intended to be a two-hour ride in the Japanese countryside with his old youth swimming nemesis Murphy Reinschreiber, became horribly lost, and wound up riding for five hours. The day before the race, figuring he might as well see this madness through all the way, Dave completed a hard two-mile swim, wearing hand paddles for extra resistance; rode forty-five miles; and ran seven and a half. That's about the equivalent of devouring a sixteen-ounce steak on the way to a hot-dog-eating contest. But there was a strange logic in Dave's outwardly foolish behavior. It was necessary, he perceived unconsciously, to do the irrational to prepare to attempt the impossible.

On race morning, in the same rash spirit, Dave did not even bother to fasten a spare inner tube to his bike's seat post because he wanted to save weight. If he flatted, he was done. His pacing strategy was equally reckless. Dave decided to start the swim at a near sprint and hold the pedal to the metal throughout the race until he crossed the finish line or expired. His strategy was to go faster than he'd ever thought he could for as long as he could, because a mere win and a merely excellent finish time would not give him what he needed. Better to die trying to raise the bar than to achieve excellence by current standards.

A quarter mile into the swim, Dave had a twenty-yard lead. He completed the swim in 48:25, one of the fastest Ironman swim times ever. He was on his bike before anyone else had even left the water. Rolling out of transition, Dave immediately shifted into his highest gear and stomped on the pedals, daring his bad knee to give out. It did not, so he kept stomping. Dave scorched the bike course in 4:27:31—the fastest Ironman bike time ever. At the second transition he cast aside his bike, pulled on his racing flats, and dived headlong into the marathon, pushing himself as if closely chased even though his nearest competitors, Scott Tinley and Ray Browning, were insuperably far behind him. But Dave was not racing Scott Tinley and Ray Browning. He completed the run in 2:45:36—the fastest Ironman run time ever. His total time of 8:01:32 was also a record, by a vast margin. Ray and Tinley were in another postal code when Dave broke the tape.

Julie Moss, who had come to Japan without Mark, won the women's race. After finishing ninety minutes behind Dave, she bumped into him as he was getting a rubdown in the massage area and congratulated him on his incredible performance.

"Mark is going to *shit* when he hears about this," she said.

Dave could not suppress a smile. He was counting on it.

The bar had been raised.

DAVE CONTINUED to turn the screws on Mark's mind in the last month before the "SHOWDOWN ON THE KONA COAST," as the October issue of *Competitor* billed the titanic two-man battle that the whole triathlon world now anticipated. In one magazine article the Man confidently predicted that, given the right weather conditions, he could clock 8:11 in Kona (whose course and conditions were more challenging than Japan's), a time that seemed possible to him now but that Mark, he trusted, would probably deem hopelessly out of reach for himself.

As race day drew closer, Dave's predictions became more aggressive.

"I think, on a good day, 8:09 is in sight in Hawaii," Dave said in an interview for Ironman's race preview press release in late September.

Sure, he believed it. But that wasn't why he kept repeating it to anyone with a microphone.

Mark knew as well as Dave that the outcome of the showdown would be decided in his own mind. While Dave manipulated the press in an effort to soften Mark's mental game before he finished it off in the lava fields, Mark worked hard to get his head straight. He recognized that a big part of this effort would necessarily entail overcoming his fear of the island and the hellish conditions of the race—the bullying winds, the torturing heat, the threatening black lava fields. Somehow he had to make peace with the island—to find a way to feel at home there. But how?

Mark was still searching for a way when he went for a run on the day before his flight to Hawaii. Leaving from his home in Cardiff-by-the-Sea, twenty miles north of downtown San Diego, he made his way down the coast a mile or two and caught a trailhead that led him into San Elijo Lagoon. He followed the soft singletrack as it wound through the soggy marshlands close by the ocean and into drier heath deeper inland. An inviolate blue sky smiled upon him from high above. Gentle autumnal sunlight warmed his exposed skin, which was massaged by a cool ocean breeze. The fragrance of sagebrush sweetened the fresh air that he drew into his powerful lungs. Birds chirped happy songs; insects buzzed.

Ironman was close enough that Mark's mind stayed locked on the coming race as he ran, but he was not brooding or worrying. In fact, he felt great—serene and comfortable in his bodily exertion and in his environment. He became suddenly conscious of these feelings, and the way to make himself at home at Ironman—or at least a way to try—opened up to him.

Every time I run here I feel great, he thought. *I have to have this feeling when I go to Kona. I have to capture this moment and take it with me.*

Mark stopped running and yanked up a handful of the marsh grasses growing along the water's edge. Upon returning home he stuffed the weeds into a suitcase, making a mental note to lie when he filled out his U.S. Department of Agriculture form on the flight into Kona.

Two days later, without Mark's knowledge, his stepmother did some-thing quite similar. Toot and Space had recently returned to the mainland from Guam and unpacked the possessions that had sat in storage through-out the period of Mark's travails in Hawaii. Out came that gorgeous, for-gotten bit of lava she had taken from Mauna Kea twelve years before. Toot looked at the glittering rock and reflected on Mark's struggles. She stuffed the stolen jewel into a suitcase before leaving for the airport with Mark's father to catch a flight to Kona, where she would return Pele's possession and perhaps thereby lift her curse.

CHAPTER 6

DIG ME BEACH

There is no terror in the bang;
only in the anticipation of it.

— ALFRED HITCHCOCK

K ona's airport lies smack in the middle of a lava field. Its lone runway appears to be helplessly floating in, perhaps sinking into, a bubbling tar pit when viewed from the perspective of a descending aircraft like the one Mark Allen stared down from on the afternoon of Thursday, October 6, 1989, nine days before the greatest race ever run.

This bleak aerial panorama could not have been better contrived to intimidate athletes arriving to compete in the Ironman World Championship, all aware that they are looking at the racecourse. The Queen K Highway passes right by the airport, through the tar pit. The bird's-eye perspective on this crucial section of the race's cycling and running routes is particularly daunting to athletes who have experienced Ironman and know what that lava field *feels* like, and is especially threatening for those who, like Mark Allen, have come undone there.

Bad memories threatened to creep into Grip's consciousness as he took in the severe vista below. He pressed them back by reminding himself of his new attitude of embracing the island and its harsh elements. He remembered the reeds he had pulled from San Elijo Lagoon and stashed in his suitcase, which now lay in the plane's hold.

The big jet landed, taxied, and stopped. Mark and his soon-to-be bride, Julie Moss, stepped from the air-conditioned cabin into the equatorial heat of the Kona afternoon as they followed other passengers down a portable stairway and onto the tarmac.

Keahole (as it was known until 1993) is an outdoor airport. The waiting areas at the gates are outdoors. The ticketing area is ceilinged but unwalled. The baggage claim also is shaded but otherwise unprotected from the elements. Mark and Julie sweated through their light, loose travel clothes as they waited for their suitcases and cumbersome bike boxes. Mark again reminded himself of his new attitude.

They packed their belongings into a rental van and left the airport by a narrow two-lane access road that led to the Queen K Highway. At the intersection they made a right turn onto the thoroughfare that accounted for almost 100 miles of the Ironman racecourse. A few minutes down the road they reached the spot where, heading in the same direction, Mark had been forced to begin walking in the '87 Ironman. Another few minutes brought them to the place where, walking in the opposite direction, Mark had been passed by Dave Scott in the '84 Ironman.

The corridor was filled with ghosts of Ironmans past.

Seven miles from the airport they came to the base of Palani Hill, a long, shallow incline that led toward the highway's intersection with Palani Road, marking the edge of Kailua town proper and the starting point of the race's last mile. As they began to ascend the rise, Mark thought, *It could happen here.* He pictured himself running next to Dave in the race's final moments and considered that, in such a scenario, this spot represented his last best chance to make a winning move.

"It could happen here," Mark said.

Although these words were spoken apropos of nothing, Julie knew exactly what he was talking about.

"It could," Julie agreed. "But only if you stay with him."

She meant "stay with him" in the sense of resisting the temptation to break away earlier, a strategy that had yielded such cataclysmic results in '84 and '87. But after the phrase left her mouth, she realized it could also be taken to mean "if Dave doesn't drop you earlier," as the Man had done in '82, '83, and '86. She judged it best to leave this ambiguity hanging in the air, but Mark caught her intended meaning.

"I've learned my lesson," he said. "I can be patient. I *will* be patient."

Julie already knew the strategy Mark had settled on for the race. So did most of the triathlon public, as Mark had made no secret of his plan to shadow Dave through the whole swim leg, the entire bike leg, and most of the run, then try to get away from him at the very end. Even Dave knew about it and had expressed his candid opinion of the strategy in print.

"If I were coaching him I'd tell him to do his own thing," Dave said in *Competitor*. "I think following me would be a big mistake."

Easy for him to say, but following Dave was really the only strategy that made any sense for Mark, considering everything. Dave never screwed up at Ironman—he had never walked a single step of the marathon in seven races. He was certain to be either in the lead or approaching it in the last miles of the marathon. There simply was no better place to be than with Dave Scott at that point in the race. *Ahead of him* had once seemed a better position. But Mark had tried to put himself ahead of Dave in the past, and that tactic hadn't worked out.

Grip knew he was a better uphill runner than Dave, so the plan of sitting behind him all day and kicking past him on the last climb was almost a no-brainer. It might not be the most daring way to win, but it was the most likely way, and it would still take everything he had. Plus no bad luck.

Mark and Julie crested the hill, floated down the gentle descent on its back side, and came to the Palani Road intersection. Instead of making a right turn and rolling into downtown Kailua-Kona, where the race would start and finish, they continued along the Queen K for another six miles in a mostly inland and upward direction. When at last they turned right onto King Kamehameha III Road, they were 500 feet above and 3 miles away from the glassy ocean, which lay majestically before them.

The view gradually diminished in grandeur until it vanished altogether as they cruised down toward the water. After two miles they crossed what is now Ali'i Highway (then still part of Ali'i Drive), at the one-mile point of the Ironman run course, and continued another three-quarters of a mile steeply downward through an upscale residential neighborhood ending at a cul-de-sac. They passed through the gated entrance to the Kanaloa resort, an upscale condominium community where they had rented a two-bedroom unit for two weeks. Mark valued the Kanaloa for its lush, arboreal setting; its seclusion seven miles from the madness of downtown Kailua; its ocean-view balconies, chirping tropical birds, and flitting bright butterflies; and its guarded gate and security staff patrolling the grounds in golf carts. It wasn't cheap, but it provided the tranquillity and solitude Mark required during "Iron Week," and that made it worth every nickel.

Mark liked to arrive in Kona early so he could acclimate and train in peace for a few days before the masses flocked in on the Monday and Tuesday before Saturday's race. By the time of this, his seventh Ironman, Mark's Iron Week routine was a perfected ritual. Every detail was planned and (with the exception of a few carefully selected experiments) familiar. This regimented approach not only served a practical purpose but also gave him comfort through its very familiarity. Mark knew exactly where, when, and how he would train and what he would eat over the next nine days. His inner circle would handle all the details that he couldn't or wouldn't handle himself. His agent, Charlie Graves, with help from his assistant, Brian Hughes, would come soon to buffer him from the race organizers, his sponsors, and the media. Mark's brother Gary, now a 21-year-old professional bike mechanic also living in San Diego, would get his bike race-ready with assistance from some of the best wrenches in the sport. His training and nutrition adviser, Phil Maffetone, and his massage therapist, Mike Rubano, would do more or less the same to Mark's body. Julie would run interference between him and his divided family, with his dad and stepmother, Space and Toot, on one side and his mom, Sharon, on the other, and prevent them from siphoning too much of his energy, as they had been known to do in the past.

Mark and Julie picked up their keys from the management office and moved in.

DAVE SCOTT ARRIVED in Kona the next day. Like Mark, he traveled with his wife. Unlike Mark, he had a second traveling companion: his 2-month-old son, Ryan, who had been born four days after Dave's crucial triumph at Ironman Japan. The eight weeks between that race and his departure for Hawaii had been among the best of his entire career. His record-smashing performance in the land of the rising sun had been a great balm to his frustrated spirit and had given him the confidence he needed for his showdown with Mark Allen. Then came fatherhood, which brought a delirium of a completely different kind. The stork's timing was perhaps not ideal, for suddenly Dave had a big new responsibility to manage just when he was taking on his heaviest training workload in preparation for Hawaii. But the sense of purpose he got from his new son more than made up for the lost sleep.

The sore knee that had bothered Dave before Japan remained tender through August and September, but he was able to train effectively despite the discomfort. He recorded career-best times on the bike and run routes he used to set his Ironman expectations. Even Dave's swim performance reached new heights. His recent times in certain benchmark sets were even better than his old college marks.

Dave and Anna collected their luggage, Dave's bike case, and Ryan's stroller and car seat from baggage claim (Dave's body drinking in the moist heat of his favorite place to exercise), rented a truck, and headed for town. They cruised up the same hill on which, twenty-four hours earlier, Mark had imagined himself making a decisive move. As they came down the hill's back side toward Palani Road, Dave thought, *It could happen here.*

Dave was well aware of Mark's plan to shadow him through the race and break him in the late going. While he would do everything in his power to shake Mark before the closing miles of the marathon, he had to be prepared for Grip hanging tough. And if Mark did hang tough, Dave knew, the negative grade approaching Palani Road represented his last best chance to get away; he was a better downhill runner than Mark but an inferior sprinter. He could not afford to let Mark hang around any farther than there.

When they reached the stop sign at Palani Road, the Scotts did not continue straight on the Queen K, as Mark and Julie had, but turned right and drove three long blocks downhill toward the water. After Palani Road crossed Kuakini Highway, it changed its name to Ali'i Drive and skirted the King Kamehameha Hotel on the right before bending left to run along the coast. All was quiet at the King Kam now, but in a few days its rooms would be stuffed with triathletes and their traveling companions and its ground floor crammed with Ironman expo booths, and the tiny beach and the large pier outside would be swarming with activity.

Iron Week is like nothing else in sports. It's an intensely charged festival of hype—like Super Bowl week in whichever city happens to be host in a given year—but its atmosphere of anticipation is even more potently concentrated. The Super Bowl may be the biggest thing happening in its host city, but Ironman is the *only* thing happening in Kailua-Kona during the week surrounding October's full moon. Kailua is a small city tucked in a corner of a tiny island in the remote South Pacific. As such, it supports a seamless illusion that Ironman is the focus of the whole world, the culmination by consensus of the yearly calendar, during those magical six days when it is overrun by people who, for that week, care about one thing only. Every hotel is booked full of athletes competing in the race, friends and relations of those athletes, people connected with the operation of the event, and professionals in the triathlon industry. Every conversation on the sidewalks and in the restaurants and shops of Kailua village is about the race. Every face radiates an inner sense of being precisely Where It's At.

Ground zero of Iron Week is Dig Me Beach, a minuscule patch of sand wedged close to Kailua Pier where athletes wade into the ocean to approach the Ironman start line on race morning. Before the race it is the place where the athletes and their retinues engage in a little practice swimming and a lot of seeing and being seen (or "digging" and being "dug"). Dig Me Beach is not an official name; it is the name the spot acquired after Ironman arrived in 1981. Every spectator is also a star and every star a spectator in the show that is staged there for six days each year. Those who qualify to compete in Ironman represent the best in the world in the various age and gender categories. So intoxicated are they by their part in this scene that they imagine themselves, as they descend the five stone steps from the pier to the sand, being recognized and whispered about like movie actors at Spago in Beverly Hills. The top elite athletes try to avoid the peak morning hours at Dig Me Beach, when hundreds of gawkers take up perches on the sea wall to enjoy the scene. There are enough pro sightings, however, to sustain the fantasy of celebrity that the rest entertain, and in truth, in 1989, everyone there at least knew someone who knew Scott Tinley.

After passing by Dig Me Beach Dave and his passengers rode through Kailua-Kona's charming central village and continued a mile and a half beyond it until they saw a sign on the ocean side of the road with the words "Sea Village Resort" painted on it. They turned into the parking lot and stopped. Before them stood a trio of three-story buildings around a pleasant grass courtyard. The vacation rental rooms inside were nothing special—two and a half stars, officially—but Dave liked Sea Village because it lay close to the action without being smack in the middle of the action, and because he could climb over a lava beach behind it and swim the Ironman swim course backward without making a stir by appearing at the pier (which he did once each year anyway because it was important to rehearse the real thing). A few years before, Dave had bumped into none other than Mark Allen on that lava beach. The two men had unwittingly checked into the same resort. Mark had moved to new lodgings the following year. Now the only people Dave worried about bumping into at Sea Village were the female groupies who sometimes stalked him in the hope of winning a wink and a smile from the Elvis of triathlon.

Dave would have the weekend to settle into island life with his wife and son and to train in relative solitude. Then the entourage would come. Verne and Dot would check into the King Kam downtown. Dave's old friend and Ironman factotum, Pat Feeney, would take up residence in an extra bedroom in Dave's own condo unit because the Man wanted him close. Pals Mike Norton and John Reganold and sister Jane would stay in an adjacent unit.

This was essentially the same team that had surrounded Dave since his first Ironman victory in 1980. They were Dave's family and his closest friends, but in this context they were something more. They were his circle of confidence.

A LOW-PRESSURE SYSTEM hit the Kona coast on the Monday of race week. The air was unusually cool. Harsh winds riled the waters of Kailua Bay into an ornery chop. Monday is the first major arrival day for Ironman competitors, and dozens among the freshly landed tried gamely to enjoy Dig Me Beach as it was meant to be enjoyed, despite the poor conditions. Monday is also the day when things turn serious for the contenders. Friends and family begin to arrive and demand attention. The usual Iron Week schedule of media interviews, sponsor obligations, and appearances at official Ironman events gets rolling. All of these time sucks must be squeezed into the daylight hours alongside the meticulously planned meals, workouts, massages, bike adjustments, and other preparations the athletes would rather focus on.

Both Dave and Mark woke early that morning to make time for it all. Dave consumed a colossal breakfast of fruit, shredded wheat, yogurt, toast, and rice cakes and then performed his standard Monday-before-Ironman workout sequence. He walked gingerly over the lava beach behind his condo complex and waded into the warm Pacific to swim two miles. His workout included a couple of long surges at sixty-eight seconds per 100 yards, slightly exceeding his planned race pace. He dried off, grabbed a snack, and threw on cycling clothes. Braving the day's wild winds, he rode for two hours, ratcheting his speed up to roughly 24.5 miles per hour—race speed—for forty minutes in the middle. Upon returning to Sea Village, he grabbed another snack, chucked Ryan's chin, and changed into running clothes. He then ran nine miles, moving at a rate of six minutes per mile over the last four.

The afternoon did not belong to Dave, or to Mark. ABC had scheduled interviews with all of the main contenders in a two-hour window, casting-call style. The camera, lights, and backdrop were set up at the sprawling Kona Surf Hotel in Keauhou, seven miles south of Dig Me Beach and the site of Ironman's bike-run transition. Given the format, there was always a chance that Dave and Mark would encounter each other—something neither man particularly wanted. It had happened in 1987. When Mark showed up for his interview, Dave had just sat down for his turn in front of the camera. As Dave silently gazed toward the lens, calmly waiting for those behind it to complete some technical preparations, Mark stole a good long look at his rival—the man who had come to represent Mark's inability to finally overcome the choker he had once been. Feeling watched, Dave shifted his glance in Mark's direction, and their eyes dueled.

No such faceoff occurred at the Kona Surf this year. Conducting the interviews for ABC was Sam Posey, a retired open-wheel race-car driver now enjoying a second career as a sports broadcaster. He asked Dave what Ironman meant to him.

"I look at this event, really, as war with myself," Dave said in the tone of a confession. "I feel as though, once I'm out there, there's no other race that draws out my physical talents as this one does."

When Mark took his turn on the hot seat, Sam asked him simply what his goal was for the race.

"My main goal is, one, to win," Mark said. "But in doing that, I want to race the entire race—to feel like I'm in control of what's going on inside of my body. I don't want to have the course defeat me, and that's what I feel has happened in the past. This year that's what I would like to defeat."

TUESDAY MORNING Dave did his Tuesday before-Ironman workouts—the workouts he simply had to do four days before Ironman because they provided precisely the stimulus he believed his body needed at that time—and because they were the workouts he always did on that day and hence were a comfort to him. He wheeled out of Sea Village on his bike and climbed nearly 2,000 feet toward the High Road, or Route 190, as the maps called it. As he scaled the seemingly endless ramp-like incline toward the center of the island, he periodically got out of the saddle and pedaled for five minutes in a standing posture, as he would do during tactical surges on important hills during the race. After completing the ascent he U-turned, bombed back down to the Queen K, and noodled around on that until he had ridden for three hours. Back at the condo, he refueled and put on his running shoes. He ran six miles, covering the last four in a little more than twenty-five minutes. Finally, he negotiated the lava rocks and swam the full Ironman swim course backward.

Mark started his morning with a swim and then ran from the Kanaloa toward town on Ali'i Drive. As he came close to the Royal Sea Cliff Resort, where his father and stepmother were staying, he saw Space and Toot walking together ahead. He crept up behind them and slowed to a walk. Toot felt his presence and turned, startled. Mark put a finger to his lips, and she smiled. Disguising his voice, he said, "Hey, are you Mark Allen's dad?"

Space whipped around, saw his son, and laughed. This was a regular joke between them, but one with an edge. Mark knew Space relished basking in his son's reflected glory. It was really what he came here for. And Mark couldn't resist calling him on it, under the veil of teasing.

During the forty-five-mile ride that completed his day's training, Mark encountered a minor mechanical problem with his bike, and he returned to Kanaloa in a hurry to fix it. Gary had not yet arrived from the mainland, so after showering and changing Mark looked up the number for one of the two local bike shops, B & L Marine Bike & Sport. George Goldstine, a mechanic Mark knew and trusted, answered. Mark explained his quandary.

"Come on down," George said. "We'll take care of it."

Mark went next door and knocked. Mike Rubano, his massage therapist, answered.

"I'm heading into town to B & L," Mark said. "Want to come?"

"Sure," Mike said, happy to go but having no choice. He knew Mark wanted a buffer against energy-sapping encounters with fans now that the village was teeming with athletes.

They drove seven miles to the store, which was hidden on the far side of Kailua-Kona in a warehouse district. Mark and Mike slunk in with Mark's bike as invisibly as they could and made a furtive search for George. Along the way they might have passed a stack of fresh copies of the new *Competitor*, the pre-Ironman issue featuring Dave Scott and Mark Allen on the cover with the headline "SHOWDOWN ON THE KONA COAST." If they did, Mark likely recoiled on seeing it, as though it were an FBI "Wanted" poster bearing an image of his face.

They found George tied up with another customer, so Mark folded his arms and settled in to wait. As he had feared, the store was inundated with other athletes taking care of last-minute equipment matters, and Mark was subjected to numerous double-takes and sideways stares. One starry-eyed age-group triathlete proved bolder than the rest and approached Grip.

"Hey, Mark!" the fan said, forgetting in his excitement to use his indoor voice. "Do you think this is your year?"

Mark ignored the fellow as completely as if the slightest acknowledgment of his existence would have turned him into a pillar of salt. The fan's face fell by degrees. Reflexively he shifted his eyes toward Mike in mute appeal, but he discerned from Mike's hanging jaw and flushed skin that Mark's friend was equally shocked.

Half an hour later Mike fixed Mark with a sideways stare of his own as they walked away from the bike shop. He half expected Mark to volunteer some kind of explanation for his behavior, but Mark said nothing. Perhaps, in the privacy of his own thoughts, Mark was reminding himself of the permission given to him by his favorite self-help guru, David K. Reynolds: "Feeling pressured by others, by time, by circumstances is just another feeling. The feeling causes you trouble when you believe you must respond to it or fight it or remove it. Just feel the pressure and continue doing what you need to do." Perhaps he needed no reminder.

Back at the Kanaloa, Mark ate a hearty lunch, possibly one of his favorites: tortillas stuffed with beans, tofu, salsa, avocado, onions, tomatoes, cottage cheese, and spices. It contained more fat than anything Dave Scott would have eaten. Grip supplemented the repast with a meal-replacement shake made by Exceed, Ironman's and Mark's sports nutrition sponsor, also high in fat. Months earlier, when mulling over the question of why he always performed well in the Nice Triathlon and poorly at Ironman, Mark had noted that, like any sensible visitor to France, he nibbled a lot of cheese in the days before the Nice race. Phil Maffetone advocated a relatively high-fat diet for endurance athletes. Influenced by Phil's beliefs, Mark speculated that the fat content of the delicious *fromage* he ate before the Nice Triathlon gave him an endurance boost in that race, which he had never lost. So he had developed a plan to duplicate the nutritional advantage in Hawaii.

Desperation had delivered Mark to a place of looking for and exploiting every conceivable way to enhance his Ironman performance, no matter how small. He could not take risks, however. Most of the things he did in the week before the 1989 Ironman would necessarily be the same things he did every year: train lightly, visualize a successful race, load up on high-carbohydrate foods in the last three days before the competition, and so forth. But, since these standard practices alone had not been sufficient to lift him to Ironman victory in past years, he carefully selected a small handful of new measures to try, and eating more fat was one.

Before he took the first bite of a tortilla, Mark doused it with salt. A few months earlier he had traveled to Duke University in North Carolina to undergo physiological testing in the laboratory of exercise scientists Doug Hiller and Mary O'Toole. He had ridden a stationary bike for more than four hours in simulated Kona conditions—90-degree heat and 90 percent humidity. Then he'd jumped off the bike and onto a treadmill to run for a couple hours more in the same conditions. Doug and Mary had collected and analyzed Mark's sweat and found that it was unusually salty. They informed Mark that he lost more sodium in his perspiration than most athletes and that this abnormality might have contributed to his poor showings at Ironman. They advised him to consume extra salt before and during the race. He had added this item to his short list of new things to try.

Another item arrived with a rap on the door later in the afternoon, after Mark woke from his daily nap. Grip answered the knock, and a slight, middle-aged man with a smooth face and prematurely white hair entered the condo. It was Phil Maffetone himself. His right hand clasped the handle of a carry-on-sized, soft-walled suitcase. After exchanging greetings with Mark, and with Julie and Mike Rubano, who were also present, Phil got down to business.

He opened the case and pulled out what would have looked very much like a body bag but for its cheerful red color and flattened it out on the carpet. A small electric generator also emerged. Phil found a wall socket and plugged it in. He attached a length of hose to the generator at one end and to a valve in the bag at the other end. He instructed Mark to remove his shirt, strap on a heart rate monitor, and climb inside the bag.

Phil sealed the bag with a zipper and flipped a switch on the generator, which began to buzz. The body bag with Mark inside inflated. Julie burst out laughing.

"It looks like a giant hot dog!" she said.

"You're right! It does!" Mike Rubano said, laughing too.

"Don't eat me!" Mark called out from inside the bag.

Now everyone laughed. Mike's and Julie's eyes met. *Mark made a joke. He's loose. This is good.*

Grip lay for forty-five minutes inside what Julie would thereafter call the Big Red Wiener while Phil periodically checked his heart rate. Phil knew better than to meddle in the details of Mark's training, but Mark trusted him enough to try couldn't-hurt experiments such as this one. As Mark lay there, Mike sat watching, amazed for the second time that day by what his friend was willing to do to win Ironman.

Phil departed with his portable hyperbaric chamber, which, he claimed, loaded the muscle cells with oxygen for later use during exercise. Mike Pigg had the next appointment with the chamber. Mark had encouraged Mike, his good friend and fiercest short-course rival, to hook up with Phil, less to help a rival than to win a convert to the spiritual, natural-health approach to triathlon Mark shared with Phil. Mark followed his massage therapist, also a stones-and-herbs kind of guy, next door to receive his daily rubdown, and Mike kneaded Mark's flesh for an hour and a quarter.

Ninety minutes of lying in bed, napping. Forty-five minutes of lying in a giant inflated hot dog. Seventy-five minutes of lying on a massage table, being kneaded. Just another busy Iron Week afternoon for Mark Allen.

BY WEDNESDAY THE WEATHER in Kailua-Kona was almost back to normal. The winds had calmed, and the temperature had risen. On that day Dave Scott finally reduced his training to a level that any mortal triathlete would consider necessary to be sure the body was adequately rested for race day. He started his morning with a four-mile run along Ali'i Drive. Although he made no special effort to push the pace, he felt so strong that his tempo increased steadily as he went along.

In his final training block after Ironman Japan, Dave had run six-minute miles until he could almost run them in his sleep. He believed that a 2:37 marathon—or a thirty-seconds-per-mile improvement on his Ironman run course record of 2:49, set in 1987—was possible for him. It might even be *necessary* to win the race, because Mark's superhuman run in April's World Cup Triathlon suggested it might be possible for him too.

Dave was cruising past Kahalu'u Beach Park, a popular snorkeling and turtle-watching spot, at his familiar goal pace when *Triathlete* editor CJ Olivares drove by in the opposite direction. CJ recognized the Man's familiar duck-like running style before he recognized the body. Dave looked like a *runner*—taut and almost dangerously lean. He barely resembled the puffy, top-heavy swimmer who had won Ironman in 1980. A slow metamorphosis had begun immediately thereafter, yet Dave scarcely even resembled the athlete CJ had last seen just a few months earlier at USTS Phoenix. A highway map of engorged green veins under vellum-thin skin was visible in Dave's legs even from across the road.

In consideration of how Mark Allen had performed in his spring and summer races, CJ had come to Kona with a hunch that Grip would finally win. But now, seeing Dave's thoroughbred physique and the bullying confidence written on his face, he reconsidered. *Flip a coin*, he now thought.

CJ quickly pulled off the road and dug out his notepad. He scribbled a few key phrases that would serve to jog his memory when he later sat down to write his race report. Among them was this sentence: "Dave looks ready to *run!*"

Dave followed up his short run with an easy, fifty-minute ride and then made his one foray to Dig Me Beach to navigate the swim course in the proper direction. His appearance there, as always, caused a sensation. Dave was not mobbed as, say, Joe Montana would have been by football fans at a shopping mall. Instead, with that unique Iron Week fantasy of celebrity in their heads, Dave's fellow triathletes played it cool, or so they fancied, thrusting their right hands at the Man in ones and twos as he passed, blurting out the credentials that qualified them as his peers, delineating their 2 degrees of separation while they had his attention.

"My cousin John Smith was at your triathlon camp in Boulder last year."

"My sister's husband works for one of your sponsors. The name John Smith ring a bell?"

"Hi, Dave. John Smith. We met at USTS San Diego in '85."

Dave rolled with it, having budgeted glad-handing time into the mission and being constitutionally incapable of blowing off his admirers. It always took him an hour to cross a room in Kona.

LATER THAT SAME AFTERNOON Mark Roberts, one of Dave's former water polo teammates at UC-Davis and now a cardiologist practicing in San Diego, walked past Dig Me Beach toward the front entrance to the King Kamehameha Hotel. Roberts had followed Dave into the sport of triathlon, albeit as an amateur, and would compete in his first Ironman Saturday. Athlete registration had opened at race headquarters inside the hotel, and Roberts was on his way to pick up a packet containing his race numbers, transition and special-needs bags, and other essential paraphernalia.

Roberts followed the sidewalk past the beach and then along the edge of a small lawn shaded by a huge banyan tree. This tree, which was clearly visible from the swim turnaround point a mile and a quarter away, would be used as a landmark by Ironman competitors as they swam back toward shore on Saturday. Next to the tree Roberts spotted another landmark: a giant inflated plastic likeness of Scott Tinley that stood at this spot every October to promote Tinley's signature line of performance apparel. Next to it a triathlete posed proudly for a photograph. Hundreds of others would do likewise before Saturday. Though Tinley's best days as an athlete were already behind him, he remained one of the most popular figures in the sport. A visit to the inflated figure was a rite of the Ironman pilgrimage, like kissing the Wailing Wall.

Upon entering the hotel's Kamakahonu Ballroom, Roberts encountered a hive of activity. Scores of other athletes were already there, some standing quietly in lines, others standing in circles of animated talk and laughter. Race officials pointed the disoriented ones this way and that. Sponsors' signs competed for attention. As he got his bearings, Roberts noticed that several of the big-name pros were seated at small tables, where they appeared to be signing autographs for fans. There was Dave Scott, looking supremely healthy, as always, behind his centrally placed table. And there was Mark Allen, whom Roberts knew a bit from the San Diego scene, at a table just far enough from Dave's to avoid awkwardness, with Tinley between them.

Roberts was surprised to see that dozens of excited-looking athletes were lined up waiting for Dave's signature, but only a handful stood at Mark's table. As much as Roberts favored his old teammate, this disparity was no reflection, he knew, of the relative statures of the two men in the sport. Sure, this was Ironman, and Dave was a six-time winner of the race, while Mark was a perennial bridesmaid. Thus, Dave deserved and was expected to be the most popular man on the island. But the score should not have been 80 to 4, as it seemed to be. After all, Grip had won many more total races than Dave, was universally considered the best all-around triathlete in the world, and got just as much press as Dave did.

Closer study revealed the true reason for the disparity. Dave was having fun. He engaged each fan in lively conversation and showed not a trace of impatience to keep the line moving. He did not half listen, as most celebrities do in such situations; instead he seemed to truly want to hear about his admirers' backgrounds and goals and to impart a bit of helpful advice if he could. It was the coach and teacher in him coming out.

Dave also unabashedly relished being the Man. He enjoyed being fawned over and admired. Early in his career he had unashamedly expressed his desire to be remembered as a legend. In excess, this kind of hullabaloo drained him, as it would anyone, but in modest doses it energized him, and there was no better time to absorb such energy than three days before the race he personified.

By contrast, Mark was pleasant enough in his interactions with those who dared approach him, but his body language discouraged engagement. While Dave absorbed energy from his admirers, Mark felt that fans stole his energy. Like many spiritual people, Grip had a mystical understanding of energy. For him, energy wasn't just the adenosine triphosphate molecules packed inside muscle cells whose breakdown fueled muscle contractions. It was also an intangible force that moved between people and existed as a resource in different environments. Knowing this, Scott Tinley had once jokingly waved his arms around Mark to "disrupt his aura" right before the start of a race. Mark not only found no humor in the prank but was angered by it because, from his perspective, Tinley really *had* disrupted his energy aura.

At no time was energy hoarding more important to Mark than during the last few days before Ironman.

Disregarding Mark's "leave me alone" signals, Roberts walked up to the table and said hello. Grip seemed almost not to recognize Roberts, despite having frequently shared a lane with him at masters swim workouts in San Diego. The conversation was awkward (on Roberts's end—Mark seldom showed awkwardness) and brief. Roberts then made his way over toward Dave. He had no wish to wait in line for a word with his besieged friend, but he wanted to connect, so he bum-rushed Dave's table from the side, apologized to the fan whose experience he was interrupting, and offered Dave his hand.

"Hey, Mark!" Dave said. "Fancy seeing you here. Are you racing?"

The line of dozens was instantly forgotten. Roberts had Dave's full attention. Dave's nonverbal cues suggested to Roberts that he could chat with his old teammate all day if he wanted to. But Roberts had things to do, and he didn't want to be rude to those waiting, so he kept the tête-à-tête short, then moved on to pick up his race packet.

After the autograph session wrapped up, Dave made a couple of appearances at the expo booths of his sponsors. This was an obligation Mark had also borne for his own sponsors until 1987, when a long autograph session at the Kellogg's Pro-Grain booth had left him traumatized. Mark had staggered away from the nightmare of meeting and greeting as though each fan in turn had sunk a pair of fangs into his jugular vein and sucked out a pint of blood. He had vowed never to do the expo thing again. With today's duties fulfilled, Mark was relieved to have the chance to hurry back to the Kanaloa.

DAVE HOSTED A GATHERING at his condo that evening. The whole circle of confidence attended: Verne, Dot, Jane, Pat Feeney, John Reganold, Mike Norton, and baby Ryan, who had no choice. Anna cooked a big pot of pasta, and there was spirited talk as everyone ate. This was a yearly ritual. Dave liked to bring everyone together when the race was close, but not *too* close, to create a happy atmosphere and make a plan for spectating and support on race day.

Pat presided over the meeting. Affecting the bearing of a war-room commander, he told his attentive troops where he wanted them to be to supply Dave with encouragement and information, and how they would get there. This year, he said, Anna and Verne would ride along in his car, which they would pile into right after the swim and spur to Waikoloa Resort, where they would see Dave at the twenty-four- and eighty-mile points of the bike leg. Mike and John would cannonball farther out in a separate vehicle, to Kawaihae, where they would see Dave at thirty-three and seventy-one miles.

As Pat issued his orders, he couldn't help but notice that Dave seemed preoccupied. Pat stopped speaking in midsentence, his eyes lingering on Dave as he waited for instructions.

"I want to see Ryan," Dave said.

Both the athlete and the father were speaking. Dave wanted the competitive advantage he would derive from the emotional lift of that moment. But orchestrating that moment would be no small feat for Pat. On the one hand, Anna was determined to get out on the course and see Dave at multiple points in the bike and run legs. On the other hand, dragging Ryan along on that mission would be disruptive to the baby's routine. What to do?

The women took over. Pat held his peace while Dot, Jane, and Anna went back and forth with various ideas until they settled on a plan to leave Ryan and a supply of pumped breast milk with Dot on race morning. Anna would watch the swim and catch Dave at a couple of spots on the bike leg with Pat and Verne. At the end of the bike leg Anna would race back to Sea Village, give Ryan a quick feeding, and take him outside to see his dad run past, six miles into the marathon. Then she would leave the baby with Dot once more and get back out on the course.

All eyes turned back to Dave for his approval.

"As long as I see him," he said.

Dave did not discuss his personal race plan with the full assembly of guests. After everyone else had left, Pat alone was clued in to those details.

"Do you think Mark's really going to try and sit on you all day?" Pat asked him.

Dave told Pat he did not think Mark was bluffing.

"So what are you going to do about it?" Pat asked.

"I'll try to get away from him."

"When?"

"In the swim."

Pat lifted his eyebrows in surprise.

"Do you think you can?"

"Maybe; maybe not. I'm swimming well. But even if I don't, I'll make him work harder than he wants to."

"And the bike?"

"Same thing."

"And if he's still with you in the run?"

Dave told Pat that, in the very unlikely event that they were still together coming into town, he would break away from Mark on the descending half of Palani Hill, with about a mile to go.

THURSDAY MORNING Dave and Mark saw each other again, in closer quarters than they had during the previous day's autograph session, at the professional athletes' race meeting held at the King Kamehameha Hotel. Before the session formally convened, Tinley, like the free spirit in biology class, made a show of pulling items of equipment from his transition bags as though they were magic sacks. Out came a cycling shoe. He widened his eyes, mouthed, "Wow!" and showed the clever invention around the room.

Out next came a bike helmet. Tinley licked an index finger, touched it to the skid lid, and made a sizzling sound.

For the next ninety minutes Tinley and his peers racing in the men's and women's elite divisions slouched in folding chairs while Marshals Director Dennis Haserot, Swim Director Jan War, Bike Director Nick Rott, Transition Coordinators Joe and Sharron Ackles, and a few others took turns holding forth on the most important race rules. The dominant theme of the presentations was outside assistance to athletes during the race from friends, family, supporters, and spectators, which was forbidden in all forms. None of the race officials was heard to utter the word "crackdown," but that was what many of the gathered athletes understood—that the officials had agreed to crack down this year on the illegal provision of nutritional, equipment-related, and even informational aid from race watchers.

Brian Hughes, fresh-faced assistant to Mark's agent, Charlie Graves, who had chaperoned Mark to the meeting, listened to the harping with consternation. Before leaving the mainland Brian had bought a small American flag at a Hallmark store, having hatched a plan to hand the symbol to Mark near the end of the race in the event that he won. Brian thought the gesture would be good for Mark's image. But he now saw that it might be very bad for Mark's chances of avoiding disqualification. In any case, Mark had received the idea tepidly, perhaps out of superstition. Grip had counted his chickens before they'd hatched before—and wound up with egg on his face.

At the end of the meeting the athletes handed in their numbered transition bags—the bags of cycling clothes that would await them in the swim-bike transition area on the pier and the bags of running clothes that would await them in the bike-run transition area in the parking lot of the Kona Surf Hotel.

Outside the King Kam, preparations for the race were moving apace. The finish-line arch was under construction smack in the middle of Ali'i Drive. A complex network of fencing and partitions was being erected on the pier. These images sent swarms of butterflies fluttering through Dave's and Mark's stomachs as they walked their separate ways. It was getting close.

Dave had almost escaped the triathlete-packed area unmolested when a giant man with a bushy beard lumbered toward him, shouting his name.

"Hi, Dave! I'm John Boyer!" the big man boomed, towering over the six-foot-one-inch legend.

"Nice to meet you," Dave said, shaking the man's hand while trying to remember the name or face.

Boyer read the lack of recognition in Dave's eyes.

"The Mad Triathlete?" he prompted.

Dave continued to smile uncertainly.

"Did you get the tape?" Boyer tried.

"Tape?"

"Yeah, there was supposed to be a tape in your race packet," Boyer said, straining to maintain his original tone of enthusiasm through rising disappointment. "'When Dave Came to Town'? By John Boyer, a.k.a. the Mad Triathlete?"

"Oh, right!" Dave said.

"Did you like it?'

"Yeah, that was great," said Dave, who still had not heard the song but faintly recalled seeing the tape in his race bag. Valerie Silk, a friend of Boyer, had placed it there personally as a favor to the fervent fan of the Man. Truth was, Dave had little interest in music outside his own piano playing. "Thanks."

Boyer let Dave go, thrilled by the apparent success of the encounter.

Dave's workouts that day served to groove his race tempo in each of the three disciplines and nothing more. On the bike, between a short warm-up and a cooldown, he rode three times three minutes at 25 mph. He ran three miles, going easy except for three half-mile surges at six-minutes-per-mile pace. He dived into the ocean and swam one mile, accelerating to race speed several times. He felt fitter and faster than ever before.

While Dave swam, Mark relaxed at the Kanaloa, having decided not to train at all that day. His body throbbed with that familiar two-days-before-Ironman feeling. A massive reservoir of hoarded energy churned inside him. He felt almost able to open the door to the balcony, step outside, and take flight, swooping back and forth over the pool-blue ocean like Peter Pan. Mark always relished the sensation of supreme latent power he experienced in that brief window of time when a state of peak fitness overlapped with a condition of optimum rest.

Mark's mother had left a magazine on the coffee table during a visit to the condo the previous day. It was the current issue of *Yoga Journal*. The cover story was titled "If Buddha Had Been a Shrink: The Link Between Psychotherapy and Spirituality." An illustration showed Buddha scribbling on a notepad while a man reclined on a sofa and talked. Needing something to take his mind off the race, Mark grabbed the periodical and began flipping through it idly. He was too nervous to actually read. He just scanned and turned pages, scanned and turned. An advertisement near the front of the magazine caught his attention. Not the advertisement itself but a small black-and-white photograph it contained, depicting a very old man, Native American in appearance. His leathery face, framed by a floppy sombrero, wore a broad, toothless smile. Something about that smile arrested Mark. It somehow communicated lasting happiness instead of the momentary joy expressed by most smiles. The old man seemed to embody pure peace. He was a shaman, apparently, who, along with another man pictured next to him, was hosting an upcoming spiritual retreat in Mexico. Mark let his eyes linger on the face, the smile, a few moments longer and turned the page.

AT THREE O'CLOCK in the afternoon Dave and Mark were forced to see each other yet again, and in even closer quarters than at the morning pro meeting. The Ironman press conference was held in a meeting room at the Kona Surf Hotel. Dave and Mark were seated inches apart in chairs set behind a long table with only a handful of the other big stars, including Scott Tinley and the defending women's champion, Paula Newby-Fraser, before a gaggle of reporters. All eyes were on Dave and Mark. The room held the tension of a title fight weigh-in between boxers harboring genuine mutual loathing. Every athlete besides Dave and Mark might as well have been invisible. What reporter in his right mind was going to waste his questions on anyone else? Mark was evasive and tight-lipped in his answers. Dave spoke concisely but with characteristic pugnacity.

"What's it going to take to win this year?" one reporter asked everyone at the table.

Tinley, Mike Pigg, Ken Glah, and Grip passed the question like a hot potato. Dave grabbed it and took a big bite.

"Eight-ten," he said. "If the conditions are good, I think that's certainly possible."

Tinley rolled his eyes at Dave's right-in-character bravado but did not doubt the prediction, which, if borne out, he knew, would make him a loser by no less than twenty minutes. Mike Pigg made an effort to doubt the prediction and then, having failed in that effort, made an effort to imagine himself capable of the same feat. Everyone else present, athletes and reporters, understood Dave's prediction as a direct challenge to Mark Allen.

Dave might as well have stood up from his chair, put his snarling mug right in Mark's face, and shouted, "I'm going to make you *cry tears of blood* this year, you little jellyfish!"

Among those in attendance, whistling under his breath, was Mike Reilly, a publisher of race event listings who was present at Ironman for the first time as an announcer. A total geek for the sport and a speechless admirer of Dave and Mark, he studied the two men throughout the conference. Everyone else seemed to stop paying attention when it was adjourned amid a cacophony of scuffing chairs, but Mike kept his eyes glued on the rivals. Naively, he was waiting to see if they would shake hands. Instead, they scrambled out of their seats as though they were practicing a fire drill and left the room in opposite directions. Mike was now twice as excited for the race as he had been already.

At six thirty that evening the Exceed Carbo Loading Party and Mandatory Pre-Race Meeting took place in the parking lot of the King Kam. A stage had been set up at one end of the lot, and round tables with eight place settings each filled the middle. Hundreds of athletes and scores of their friends and family who had purchased tickets feasted on pasta, rolls, and salad while Mike Plant hosted a program of entertainment that included a three-song set from John Boyer, the Mad Triathlete, who sang while accompanying himself on acoustic guitar. His last number was the world premiere of "When Dave Came to Town," sung to the tune of the B. B. King and U2 collaboration "When Love Comes to Town" that had been a hit earlier that year.

> *I heard that he was injured, yeah I wouldn't see his face.*
> *With David Scott at home, I would surely win this race.*
> *I'm a humble kind of guy and I really hate to brag,*
> *But you know I got the Ironman right here in the bag.*
>
> *But when Dave came to town, I just sat there and cried.*
> *When Dave came to town I should've stayed inside.*
> *Maybe I was wrong to put the word around,*
> *But I said what I said before Dave came to town.*

As he left the stage, the Mad Triathlete was heckled by a bunch of drunk Australian athletes. Dave wasn't even there.

ON FRIDAY MORNING Dave and Mark had time for one last spin on their bikes before they were required to check them in at the pier, where the machines would remain under guard overnight in their number-designated transition spaces, along with 1,284 other bikes. Ironman's pro racers were given their own bike check-in window that was separate from that for the unwashed masses. Since the procedure involved all of the sport's biggest stars trickling onto a single public stage within a small span of time, a crowd formed at the approach to the pier to make true theater of what was already an inherently theatrical affair. It was triathlon's version of a Hollywood red-carpet walk. The marquee athletes promenaded one by one into the transition area, their multithousand-dollar two-wheelers drawing the sorts of oohs and ahs that starlets' dresses attract on Oscar night.

There was Kenny Souza, rocking his Guns N' Roses hair, with his Nishiki Altron. Kenny liked to race duathlons in nothing but a bodybuilder's posing suit (basically, naked). Close behind him came Mike Pigg, a sticker reading "Pigg Power" affixed to his bike. Pigg was ogled with the respect due the last man to have defeated Mark Allen in any race besides Ironman.

Dave cruised in with his bike ahead of Mark. As far as the triathlon public knew, it was a Centurion Ironman Dave Scott signature model, but in fact the frame was designed by a boutique northern California bike maker named Albert Eisentraut and painted to look like the model Dave endorsed but never actually rode himself because he didn't like it. Mark, always the less punctual of the two, came in later with his "Schwinn," which was really a Kestrel. The bicycle had not been overlooked in Mark's efforts to find every little advantage for the race. Unlike Dave's frame, which comprised several steel pieces welded together, Mark's was an advanced prototype made from a single piece of carbon fiber—lighter, stiffer, and more aerodynamic than the Eisentraut. Mark's Scott-brand aerobar was also superior to Dave's Profile aerobar. It was among the first that positioned the gear shifters right at the fingertips instead of leaving them on the downtube of the frame, where Dave's remained, requiring the rider to break his aerodynamic tuck for every gear change.

Luddite that he was, Dave probably knew nothing about Mark's technological advantage, and if he did, it cost him no sleep. Let Mark scurry around for small benefits. The Man would rely on the same single big advantage that he brought to Kona every year.

"I had this idea that if I trained more than anyone else, I was bound to succeed," Dave said in 1987. "If I found out that Scott Tinley or Mark Allen was working out fifty hours a week, I'd work out fifty-one."

Dave Scott did not stretch, as Mark did. He did not get massages or monitor his heart rate or submit to physiological testing or mentally rehearse his races or fuss over his bike, as Mark did. He just made sure he outworked Mark—and everyone else.

SHORTLY AFTER LUNCHTIME USTS cofounder Jim Curl, who would compete in his first Ironman the next day, stopped by the Sea Village Resort to visit a friend. Jim's host mentioned that Dave Scott was staying in the unit directly underneath his. Dave had been Jim's first swim coach in 1980, and he also knew Verne, Dot, and Dave's sisters from his time in Davis. So he decided to drop by on his way out.

Jim was just raising a fist to knock on the door to Dave's unit when he heard a burst of uproarious laughter from within. When he was admitted, Jim encountered Dave's entire family (minus sister Patti), and a few other people whom he didn't know. Every face was glowing with good humor. Apparently Dave had just spilled a smoothie all over himself and was being roundly ragged on for his klutziness. Dave himself joined in the mockery, pretending to spill and knock over everything in sight.

In eighteen hours Dave would compete in a race that meant everything to him, and more than ever before. He bore a burden of crushing pressure, initiated both internally and externally. Yet here he was, cutting up as if he didn't have a care in the world. Until this moment Jim had never seen the slightest hint that Dave had a goofy side, and he was letting it out now, of all times.

Jim hung out for fifteen light and relaxed minutes, then left. He heard another wave of laughter behind him as he walked away. *There's no way he can lose*, Jim thought.

AT ABOUT FOUR O'CLOCK Mark left the Kanaloa with Julie. They climbed into their van and drove a couple of miles toward town on Ali'i Drive. They parked on the inland side of the road just past Pahoehoe Beach Park and crossed to the ocean side on foot. The crazy weather of a few days ago had all but vanished. The late-afternoon air was not quite hot but warmer than it had been all week and disturbed by only the gentlest of breezes. Thick clouds hung over the high inland hilltops, but overhead the sky was blue. The sinking sun hung 15 degrees above the horizon straight off the west-facing shore.

Mark and Julie descended three concrete steps accessible through a gap in the guardrail and entered a grassy, leafy bower. Passing a tall palm tree to the left and a squat banyan to the right, they followed a short path through an opening in a low stone wall and paused briefly, facing one of the most curious bits of architecture on the entire island. The structure looked like a clapboard colonial church that had been magically miniaturized to one-third of its original magnitude—not a very small church but a *shrunken* one. A simple rectangle, it had room for twelve pews and not one more. Its steeple came to a point scarcely twenty-five feet above the neatly trimmed lawn below. The immaculate white paint job, with bright blue trim and matching tin roof, heightened its dollhouse appearance. Quaint lettering above the blue double door in front identified the edifice as St. Peter's by-the-Sea Catholic Church, but everyone called it the Little Blue Church.

The wall that one crossed to enter the church grounds wrapped all the way around it in an irregular shape. Beyond it lay a jumbled field of rough stones that had obviously provided the material for the man-made boundary. And beyond that, the sea.

This was one of Mark's favorite spots in Hawaii—one of very few places where he felt as comfortable as he did in San Elijo Lagoon at home.

A small sign next to the church's entrance read, "Mass Sat Only 7:30," but when Mark tried the door, it opened. The couple peered inside and saw a lone woman sitting in a middle pew, her head bowed in prayer. They shut the door and left her in peace. This wasn't their true destination anyway.

Immediately north of the church, just beyond a thin line of trees, and made from the same stones as the church's surrounding wall, lay the foundation of an ancient temple, or heiau, known as Kuemanu. A thatched-wood shrine and carved wooden images of gods once stood upon it. These were destroyed or allowed to decay after King Kamehameha II renounced the traditional Hawaiian religion in 1819. St. Peter's was built next door a few decades later as an unsubtle symbol of Christianity's usurpation, but native Hawaiians still came to what was left of Kuemanu Heiau to make offerings. And so did Mark Allen, on the eve of the greatest race ever run.

Mark and Julie made the short walk to the heiau and gingerly stepped onto the lumpy foundation of large stones, spanning 100 feet in length and 50 in width. Leaving Julie's side, Mark stepped forward and laid the grasses pulled from San Elijo Lagoon on an altar made from four long sticks stuck into the ground at the corners of a small square, with a crude shelf of twigs and grasses connecting them at shoulder height. As the soft light of late afternoon fell upon his face, Mark spoke.

"Hey, just let me be here with my strength," he said. "Let me just feel good as who I am and somehow find power and strength on the race-course—find those things I've been missing."

The prayer seemed to have some immediate effect, as Mark felt a sense of peace wash over him. He closed his eyes and held a meditative silence. Images began to form inside his mind. Humanoid figures coalesced. He recognized them as the island's great healers, or kahunas. In a single voice they spoke to him as in a dream.

"Yes, you can race as you hope to," he heard. "But first you must show courage. You have to be brave."

Mark knew he could be brave. He left the heiau with Julie feeling more confident and relaxed than he had ever felt in Kona.

Later, as the golden sun melted into the sea, Mark ate his last solid meal before the race on his balcony with Mike Rubano and Julie. Glorious sunsets are commonplace on the Kona Coast, but this one was better than glorious. It was perfect. Not the slightest change in the air temperature or wind direction or anything else could have made it better. Then it did get better. In the ocean below them a pod of dolphins began to jump in formation. It was like a private show, compliments of the island.

"Mark, this is a really good sign," Mike said, believing it.

Mark smiled his Mona Lisa smile and said nothing.

CHAPTER 7

IRON WILL

To win Ironman, you have to have physical and mental strength. And everyone has physical strength.

— WOLFGANG DITTRICH

It is one minute before three o'clock on the afternoon of October 14, 1989, and Dave Scott and Mark Allen are sprinting shoulder to shoulder through a lava field on the Kona Coast of Hawaii. Meanwhile, Samuele Marcora is studying for the classes he's taking as a physical education student at the University of Milan, Italy, and feeling a little sore from the hits he took in a game of American football that he played earlier in the day as a linebacker for the semiprofessional Frogs of Busto Arsizio.

Years later, his football days behind him, Sam will develop a novel, brain-centered scientific model of endurance performance. Using this model, Sam will be able to explain that Dave and Mark are three miles ahead of their closest competitor on the Queen K Highway not for the heart-lung-and-muscle reasons Sam's fellow exercise physiologists would give but instead for the very reason that Dave and Mark themselves would give: because they are mentally stronger. In fact, Sam will be able to look at an image of the human brain and point out exactly where the superior strength sits in the minds of Dave and Mark.

IT WAS AMERICA that drew Samuele Marcora away from his originally planned career path of owning a gym and onto the laboratory-centered path he walks today. Sam loved not only the most American sport but American culture generally, and spending time in the United States was high on his bucket list. His twin brother, Eduardo, had gone to Boulder, Colorado, to pursue doctoral studies in biology. Sam wished to further his study of exercise science for the sake of his future work as a fitness industry entrepreneur but discovered that graduate programs in that discipline did not exist in his native country, whereas America had the best programs in the world. Altogether, he really had no choice but to leave his *cara madre* and go west.

Sam selected the University of Wisconsin-Lacrosse for his master's studies in exercise science because it was the cheapest among the best-respected programs. During his two years there Sam fell in love with research and decided he wanted to go all the way. Still unable to earn a terminal degree in his field of passion in Italy, he accepted an offer from Bangor University in Wales.

Exercise science is studied not only for the sake of learning more about the benefits of exercise and discovering ways to help athletes perform better; it also teaches us about how the human body works. Physical exercise accelerates or intensifies the normal operations of many of the body's systems—metabolic, endocrinal, neuromuscular, and cardiorespiratory, in particular—and stresses those systems in ways that stimulate adaptive responses. Studying a system in a state of stress is often the most fruitful way to figure out how it functions normally. Sociologists obsess over deviance and revolution, for example, because these exceptions elucidate the rule of order in society. Similarly, looking at the body as it responds and adapts to the stress of physical exercise sheds light on how it works generally, yielding knowledge with both athletic and clinical (that is, life-enhancing) applications.

At Bangor Sam became interested in a particular clinical application of exercise science. As everyone knows, exercise builds the muscles. Certain diseases have the opposite effect. Sam wrote his dissertation on the effects of exercise on disease-related muscle wasting. He had a special motivation: His mother had been diagnosed with a rare kidney disease that caused muscle wasting. He wanted to find a way to help his *cara madre* and others in her sad situation.

Possessing not only a sympathetic heart but also a keen mind with a special gift for perceiving the obvious thing that others miss, Sam focused his attention on a particular aspect of muscle-wasting disease that previously had been given zero attention.

"Working with these patients," he says, "and also with my mom, I noticed that what bothered them was not so much the muscle wasting itself as the fatigue that came with it."

In his efforts to gain an understanding of disease-related fatigue, Sam spent time with patients suffering from systemic lupus erythematosus, an autoimmune disease characterized by pervasive fatigue. Sam observed a curious feature in the fatigue associated with this particular illness: It fluctuated drastically from day to day. Although the tissue inflammation that supposedly caused the fatigue changed very slowly, becoming only slightly worse day by day, a patient might experience her bodily fatigue as paralyzing one day, barely noticeable the next, and halfway between those extremes the day after that.

Sam asked himself what inside the body could possibly change quickly enough to explain such rapid fluctuations, knowing that the inflamed organs themselves could not. There was only one possibility: the brain.

To test his hunch that disease-related fatigue is somehow regulated by the brain, Sam designed an eyebrow-raising experiment in which he subjected a group of breast cancer patients to a maximal exercise test immediately before and after chemotherapy treatments, which are known to cause disease-like muscle fatigue. As anyone would have expected, he found that the women had a much lower exercise capacity after chemotherapy. However, measurements of heart rate, oxygen consumption, and so forth revealed no changes in any of the physiological parameters typically associated with exercise capacity. From the neck down, the women seemed capable of working just as hard as they had before their treatments. Yet they could not. Sam suspected that a toxic effect of the drugs on the central nervous system caused the patients to *feel* more fatigued by the same level of physiological stress and thereby reduced their exercise performance. But this could be true only if *the feeling of fatigue itself*, not the body's actual physiological capacity, determined the limits of exercise performance—a heretical idea.

Throughout the previous century and into the present one, the prevailing model of exercise fatigue has been the so-called catastrophe model. According to this model, fatigue is an involuntary drop in performance caused by the loss of homeostasis (or balance) somewhere in the body. For example, lactic acid builds up in the muscles and makes them too acidic to function properly. Or the muscles become depleted of glycogen (their primary, carbohydrate-based fuel), so there's no longer enough energy available to sustain performance. This model associates fatigue with a "catastrophic" functional breakdown in the muscles. In this model the brain is understood to have no influence whatsoever on exercise fatigue; it is merely along for the ride. But Sam's observation of the effect of chemotherapy on exercise performance gave him a different idea—that the brain may in fact be the true source of limits on exercise capacity.

As he pondered this idea Sam could not help but consider its relevance to endurance sports, since he was then serving as a scientific adviser to the now defunct Mapei professional cycling team. Could it be, he wondered, that the barriers to performance that cyclists, runners, triathletes, and others fight against day after day exist not in their muscles, blood, or hearts but inside their heads?

Sam found a simple way to test his hypothesis. To pull it off he needed subjects who knew how to suffer. So he approached the Bangor University rugby team and asked for ten volunteers. One by one the willing athletes visited Sam's exercise lab, where they were placed on a stationary bike equipped with a power meter and subjected to a grueling three-part test. First, the athletes were instructed to pedal as hard as they could for just five seconds. On average they were able to produce 1,075 watts in this brief all-out effort—an impressive number, as was to be expected from strong, well-trained athletes. Next, after a rest period, they were required to pedal at a fixed wattage as long as they possibly could, stopping only when they felt they could not complete a single additional pedal stroke at that power level. The fixed wattage was high but submaximal—something the athletes could sustain for ten to fifteen minutes before reaching exhaustion. On average the subjects were able to sustain only 242 watts for approximately twelve minutes in this second part of the test. Finally, as soon as the athletes quit part two and before they had any chance to recover, they were asked to repeat the original five-second all-out effort.

What Sam was interested in was the difference in the amount of power the rugby players were able to put out in the first five-second maximal effort, when their legs were fresh, and the last, when their legs were tired. He knew the catastrophe model would predict a massive difference. Remember, according to this model exhaustion occurs when a functional breakdown occurs in the muscles. An athlete slows down involuntarily at the point of exhaustion because he physically cannot sustain the desired pace, his muscles having run up against some sort of hard physical limit such as lactic acid buildup. It's like a car running out of gas. In the case of this study, proponents of the catastrophe model would say that the athletes stopped pedaling their bikes after roughly twelve minutes during the second part of the test because their muscles no longer had enough "gas" to sustain a power output of 242 watts (in the average case). Therefore, the catastrophe model would predict that in the second five-second maximal effort that immediately followed their capitulation, the volunteers would be able to produce no more than 242 watts. After all, how could anybody possibly produce more than 242 watts when a functional breakdown in his muscles has just forced him to stop pedaling at that very power level? It would be like a car driving without fuel.

This was not what Sam expected, however. Sam expected that the athletes would quit the second part of the test not because they actually ran out of gas but because the suffering required to continue pedaling at the required intensity would become unbearable, causing them to quit voluntarily. Although the athletes would *feel* as if they had run out of gas, in fact their muscles would be perfectly capable of continuing—not forever, of course, but for some time. The voluntary nature of their quitting would be revealed (Sam anticipated) when the athletes discovered they were able to crank out significantly more than 242 watts for five seconds in the third and final part of the test.

Any triathlete familiar with the phenomenon of the finishing kick would probably make the same prediction. It happens all the time in races. An athlete starts to tire and slow down inexorably in the closing miles of the run leg of a race, only to find that he is able to unleash a full sprint to the finish line in the final 100 yards or so. Mark Allen was the victim of such a finishing kick in the 1988 USTS championship race at Hilton Head, South Carolina. Young Mike Pigg, the strongest cyclist the sport had ever seen, got off the bike with a three-minute lead on Mark. Knowing Grip was coming at him from behind "like a bullet," as he later described it, Pigg ran as hard as he could, but in the last mile he began to falter. Mark nearly caught him with half a mile to go. But Pigg dug deep and sprinted ahead of Mark in the homestretch to take the victory. According to the catastrophe model, that should have been impossible. If Mike had begun to slow with a mile to go because he was running out of gas—if his slowing was completely physical and involuntary—then he simply could not have increased his speed again. Yet he did.

And guess what? In their second five-second bike sprint, the subjects of Sam's experiment managed to crank out 731 watts, on average—more than three times the power they had felt unable to sustain a second longer immediately prior to that sprint.

Those five seconds unraveled 100 years of exercise science doctrine. The catastrophe model was dead, just like that. A car cannot drive without fuel, and a rugby player who has stopped pedaling his bike at 242 watts after twelve minutes because his muscles have broken down cannot immediately thereafter produce 731 watts for five seconds. The only reasonable explanation for this rebound was that the subjects of Sam's experiment did not, in fact, break down in the middle part of the test; *they gave up.* They quit the sustained submaximal effort after twelve minutes because they could not bear the open-ended suffering anymore. Sure, they were physically able to persist a little longer, but their misery was great and was only going to become greater, and they had to draw a line somewhere. They were then able, for five seconds, to blast out three times more power than the amount they supposedly could no longer sustain because, well, it was only five seconds. It would hurt, but only briefly, so without a thought the athletes tapped into the reserve capacity that they had hidden from themselves just moments earlier.

In his published report on this study, Sam proposed that fatigue in endurance exercise is *always* voluntary and always occurs as a response to an intolerable level of suffering, or what exercise scientists call perceived effort. The problem is never lactic acid buildup or muscle glycogen depletion or any other form of running out of gas. These things happen, but they never become so extreme that they directly stop the muscles from working. They merely force the brain to make a greater and greater effort to keep the muscles working at a desired level until this effort becomes so unpleasant that continuing no longer seems worth the agony.

Sam calls this idea the psychobiological model of exercise tolerance. It is based on an old and simple psychological construct called motivational intensity theory, which understands persistence in challenging tasks as being determined by a weighing of cost and reward. As long as the reward remains attainable and outweighs the cost, we persist. When the reward comes to seem unattainable, or the cost becomes more significant than the reward, we quit.

In endurance exercise the cost is suffering, or perceived effort. The potential rewards are many and vary between individuals, but the satisfaction of proving one's toughness seems to be almost universal among these rewards. The more meaningful the rewards are, the more motivated the athlete will be to tolerate suffering. Perceived effort increases slowly and steadily throughout a race, whereas the motivation level is fixed before the race begins. If the increasing burden of perceived effort eclipses the fixed weight of motivation before the finish line is reached, the athlete raises a white flag, one way or another. He either quits or slows down. Defeat is never death but always surrender.

In reality, quitting is rare because endurance athletes learn through experience, by feel, how to start each race at a pace that, if held steadily all the way through (with small adjustments along the way), will cause their perception of effort to reach the maximal tolerable level just when they reach the finish line. This perception-based art of pacing is how endurance athletes finish races in the shortest time possible. But even the athlete who masters this art must fight against a desire to quit in the last part of each race. If you don't want to quit, you're not doing it right.

MOST EXERCISE PHYSIOLOGISTS don't like Sam's model, but they're having a hard time disproving it, even though he has told them exactly how to do so. Sam enjoys issuing the following challenge to his many doubters:

"If you can show me a treatment that can change performance without changing either perception of effort or motivation, I will say that my psychobiological model is wrong."

So far, nothing. Meanwhile, researchers have identified a variety of "treatments" that enhance endurance performance by changing perception of effort and without affecting any part of the body except the brain, which is something else that is not possible according to the catastrophe model. For example, a team of English scientists has shown that both cycling and running performance are improved when athletes periodically swish a sports drink around their mouths and *spit it out*. The carbohydrates in the drink never enter their bloodstream to provide energy to the muscles. Instead they stimulate receptors on the tongue that in turn activate a "pleasure center" in the brain, reducing perceived effort—that is, causing exercise to feel easier.

It's not only Sam's professional peers who greet his model with skepticism. The relatively few endurance athletes who know something about it do too. They hate being called quitters. Nor do they feel like quitters. When an endurance athlete experiences exhaustion in a workout or race, he certainly feels as though his body has broken down and that his slowing is completely involuntary. But perceptions frequently deceive. Look no further than the Bangor University rugby team, whose mentally tough members felt certain they had held 242 watts as long as they possibly could, only to betray the illusoriness of this feeling by tripling that power output immediately after having given up in seeming total exhaustion.

Another source of the skepticism with which athletes greet Sam's explanation of endurance fatigue is less experiential and more conceptual and can be expressed in the following question: If fatigue is caused by a mere perception, why can't athletes simply override it by an act of will?

This objection reflects a common misunderstanding about the nature of mental phenomena. Intuitively, most people regard perceptions as nonphysical and therefore as lacking the power to exert deterministic control over physical functions. But perceptions *are* physical—they are specific patterns of electrical and chemical activity in the brain—and they have as much causal power as a punch to the gut. The drug addict's need for drugs and the starving man's hunger are perceptions against which the force of will may be impotent. Exercise fatigue is much the same. We certainly have some power to push through suffering—some of us more than others, all of us in some moments more than in others—but even the Dave Scotts and Mark Allens among us have only so much capacity to suffer.

When people think "voluntary," they think "conscious," but a behavior can be voluntary without being conscious. For example, it has been demonstrated that baseball players "decide" to swing at good pitches before they are consciously aware of the speed and direction of the pitch at which they are aiming. The act of swinging is voluntary, but it is initiated unconsciously. Exercise fatigue is like that. A marathon runner who begins to lose pace after mile twenty-two despite trying his best to hang on is not consciously slowing down. But he *is* slowing down voluntarily, as we could easily demonstrate if we were to place a false finish line at the twenty-three-mile mark, upon seeing which the runner would suddenly find himself able to sprint. Fiendish, but it makes the point.

But why would nature choose to make a species incapable of approaching its true physical limits in sustained exertion? What sort of survival advantage could possibly be conferred by experiencing sustained exertion as so unpleasant that the animal gives up while its muscles remain capable of continuing?

"The reason perception of effort evolved is to limit energy expenditure," Sam says. "Forty thousand years ago it was very difficult to find food. So you didn't want people running around and wasting energy for no reason. Perception of effort evolved to make us avoid spending energy unnecessarily. We run around only if we have a very strong motivation to do so. People exert effort only when they believe that effort is worthwhile. It's also why most people don't exercise at all."

Not every athlete is skeptical of Sam's theory. Interestingly, the very best endurance athletes—including Dave Scott and Mark Allen—have always believed that performance limitations are more psychological than physiological.

"I have the ability to concentrate on the task at hand," Dave said concerning his Ironman dominance in 1984. "I just don't think some contestants out there have developed the ability to concentrate for that race."

Dave was often asked *how he did it*, and he always, in one way or another, pointed at his head.

MUCH IS KNOWN about the perceptions of pain and hunger. Not much is known about perception of effort. Neither psychologists nor exercise physiologists had seriously studied perceived effort before Samuele Marcora became interested in the phenomenon.

Some researchers have proposed that feedback signals sent to the brain from the muscles and other organs during exercise are responsible for perception of effort. Sam believes otherwise. He thinks it all happens inside the brain, and he is able to adduce some compelling evidence against a role for feedback from the body. For example, researchers at the University of Zurich measured the effect of injections that interrupted the transmission of somatosensory signals from the legs to the brains of cyclists engaging in a simulated five-kilometer time trial. In plain English, the subjects could not feel their legs while they pedaled. If the brain depended on this type of feedback to perceive effort, then the injections should have sharply reduced their ratings of perceived effort compared to a control trial. They did not.

Sam also points out that perceived effort during exercise is not affected by heart transplantation. The brain has no nerve connections to a transplanted heart. If the brain relied on somatosensory awareness of heart rate to perceive effort, as some have proposed, then heart transplant patients would exhibit a reduced perception of effort. Again, not so.

Instead of arising from sensory feedback from the body to the brain, Sam argues, perception of effort arises from the brain's own activity level in two key areas. The first area is the motor cortex, whose job is to generate the electrical signals that make the muscles contract. The motor cortex is connected to the muscles through nerves that snake through the spinal cord. It also has direct links to the brain's sensory cortex, where conscious perceptions are produced. Because of these dual links, the more active the motor cortex becomes, the harder the muscles work *and* the more effort is consciously perceived.

The second area of the brain involved in perception of effort is the anterior cingulate cortex (ACC), a collar-shaped area deep inside the forebrain whose function during exercise is more complex and nuanced. Brain imaging studies have shown that the ACC becomes intensely active when a person is performing mental tasks that require sustained attention and involve *conflict resolution* and *response inhibition*. The classic example is the Stroop Test. In this test a person is presented with a series of words, all of which are names of colors. The words are also presented in a variety of colors. The Stroop Test subject is required to simply (but quickly) name the color in which the word is printed. This is very easy to do when the meaning of the word and the color of the text match but surprisingly difficult when they diverge. There is a reflexive impulse to just read whatever word one is looking at, which the test taker must inhibit while making a conscious effort to speak the name of the color in which the word is presented. To perform well in a Stroop Test, one must sustain focused attention, resist impulses, and resolve cognitive conflicts. This combination of tasks is the specialty of the ACC, so this part of the brain becomes intensely active during a Stroop Test.

The ACC also becomes highly active during physical exercise. One reason it does so is that it has a role in regulating heart rate, breathing, and other autonomic responses to exercise. Another reason, Samuele Marcora believes, is that exercise is "cognitively demanding" in a way that is very similar to the Stroop Test. Exercise, by activating the motor cortex, generates a perception of effort that is unpleasant. This discomfort, in turn, gives rise to an impulse to stop. To keep going the exerciser must continuously resist this impulse and resolve the conflict between the desire to quit and the desire to continue in favor of the latter. Ironically, this cognitive challenge itself adds to the perception of effort by activating the ACC, which, like the motor cortex, has direct links to the sensory cortex, where conscious perceptions are produced.

So perception of effort during exercise has two components. The first is the feeling produced by activity in the brain's motor cortex, which drives the muscles directly. The second is the feeling produced by the cognitive effort (centered in the ACC) required to resist the impulse to quit exercising.

Exercise is generally not recognized as a cognitively demanding activity. Samuele Marcora argues that not only is exercise cognitively demanding but its cognitively demanding nature is one of the main reasons exercise feels hard and ends in exhaustion.

In 2008 Sam conducted an ingenious study proving that exercise is, in fact, cognitively demanding. He began with the premise that if endurance exercise is truly cognitively demanding, then athletes should give up more quickly in exercise tests that they start in a mentally fatigued state than they do in exercise tests that they start when mentally fresh. Sam recruited sixteen subjects and asked them to pedal stationary bikes to exhaustion at a fixed high intensity on two occasions: once after performing cognitively demanding mental tasks, similar to a Stroop Test, on a computer for ninety minutes to induce mental fatigue (and, in particular, fatigue in the ACC) and once after watching "emotionally neutral" documentaries for ninety minutes as a nonfatiguing control scenario. Incredibly, the mental task reduced performance in the subsequent ride to exhaustion by 15 percent compared to the control condition. On average, the subjects lasted for twelve minutes, thirty-three seconds on the bike after watching documentaries. After playing the brain-draining video games, they gave up after only ten minutes, thirty-nine seconds.

Physical fatigue was obviously not a factor. The mental task imposed only brain-centered fatigue, especially in the ACC. The study thus proved that exercise is cognitively demanding, for if it were not, preexisting mental fatigue would not have affected physical performance. The study also proved that the effect of mental fatigue on exercise performance is mediated by perception of effort. The subjects quit at the same maximal level of perceived effort in both exercise trials, but they started the post-video-game trial at a higher level of perceived effort, which was why they did not last as long.

Of the two sources of perceived effort in exercise—activity in the motor cortex, which drives the muscles directly, and activity in the ACC, which resists the impulse to quit—the motor cortex is most influential in shorter, higher-intensity exercise bouts, and the ACC is most influential in longer efforts. The reason may be that, whereas perception of effort is linked equally to the *intensity* and *duration* of activity in the motor cortex, it is linked mainly to the *duration* of activity in the ACC. A short race lasting, say, ten minutes will certainly leave an athlete feeling exhausted, but that feeling will arise mostly from the intense activity in the motor cortex that is required to drive the legs as hard as they can be driven for a mere ten minutes. The cognitive challenge of sustaining mental focus (that is, resisting the desire to quit) through a ten-minute race is comparatively smaller. When the duration of a race extends beyond minutes to hours, however, perception of effort comes increasingly from the strain of sustaining mental focus on the task.

This difference explains why most experienced triathletes feel that Ironman racing is more psychologically challenging than competing in shorter races. In 2002 Dave and Mark were asked if they would like to see an Ironman triathlon included in the Olympic Games alongside the shorter triathlon that was already an Olympic event. Both men said they would— and for the same reason.

"The shorter races are a little more physical," Mark said. "Once you get into the longer races, it becomes more a test of *you as a person* on top of a test of you as an athlete."

"I agree with Mark," Dave said. "A race that comes down to a 10K run is quite different from the mental game that goes on in an Ironman."

Ironman racing is extremely physical, of course. It pays to have the greatest physical capacity you can possibly achieve. But the reason it pays is that the greater your physical capacity is, the farther and faster you can go before you reach the maximum level of suffering you can tolerate. No matter how great your physical capacity, it is this tolerance that ultimately determines your performance limits. Given two athletes of equal physical fitness, the one who tolerates the most suffering will prevail. And at the Ironman distance small differences in suffering tolerance are magnified.

THE TYPICAL ENDURANCE ATHLETE thinks of training strictly as a process of strengthening the body so that it can go faster and farther before it runs out of gas. And that's certainly how most exercise scientists think of training.

Not Dave Scott and Mark Allen. The two guys who were able to go faster and farther than anyone else thought of training primarily as a process of cultivating a greater tolerance for the suffering of extreme fatigue. They pursued this objective in a commonsense way: by repeatedly exposing themselves to extremely high levels of fatigue-related suffering in workouts. Intuition told them that, as friction builds calluses that protect the skin against friction, so suffering in exercise must develop mental strength that increases the mind's tolerance for suffering in exercise. So Dave and Mark both consciously sought out misery in workouts the way other athletes seek to cover a certain number of miles at a particular pace.

"You're out there in a race, and it hurts—it's uncomfortable," Mark once explained. "You say to yourself, 'Hey, what am I doing? I don't want to go this hard or be in this much pain or be this hot.' But if you have trained so that you have experienced these feelings before, then it isn't so foreign—you'll be able to work through it."

Dave too approached workouts as opportunities to practice suffering. He thought about this practice differently, though—as another dimension of the game-playing that always structured his exercise experience.

"In workouts, when I'm by myself riding for four hours, I play mental games," Dave told Bob Babbitt in 1996. "I go through periods where I feel like I'm going to collapse, and I pull myself out of it. When I put that into a race, it seems to pay off."

Dave did not distinguish races from workouts to the same degree that most triathletes do. In races and workouts alike, his intention was "to see what he could do"—to test, define, and redefine his limits. Dave understood that his ability to manage and tolerate suffering, or perceived effort, was always the primary barrier to extending his capacities. The games he played were ways of motivating himself to absorb more suffering and thereby go faster or farther than he would be able to go otherwise.

One of Dave's favorite swim workouts was a set of seven 500-yard intervals with a short rest period after each. As he worked his way through the set, Dave swam faster and faster. But he also made the rest periods shorter and shorter. Plenty of other swimmers would do one or the other—either increase the tempo of the intervals or reduce the rest periods between them. Dave did both. He thought it was a good idea to practically cripple himself with fatigue before attempting his fastest efforts.

A reporter watched Dave perform this workout at the Civic Center Pool in Davis on a winter night in 1983. Earlier that same day the reporter had driven a car alongside Dave as he completed a long ride in frigid temperatures and howling winds.

"I feel terrible," Dave told the reporter as he pedaled up a tough one-and-a-half-mile climb known locally as Cardiac Hill. He was smiling as he spoke these words.

Dave took a special satisfaction in trying hardest when he felt most unable. He relished and even looked forward to those days in training when his body felt defeated. Instead of taking it easy on those days, he would seize them as opportunities to go even harder.

"I can go to workouts totally haggard and whipped and feeling like I've got an anvil on my back, and I can still press the 'will it' button," he once said. "I have the capacity to persevere, and I like doing it—I love doing it. It doesn't matter when it is. I don't have to pick the perfect scenario. 'Okay, I'm going to go really hard today because I feel really rested and ready. I had my guava juice and I feel great.' I just wake up and say, 'Okay, I can do it.' So I do it."

Mark's style of suffering was starkly different. Instead of piling on work and never giving himself a break, he picked his spots. He suffered just as intensely as Dave in workouts, but not as often. If Dave differed from other elite triathletes in pushing hardest when he was weakest, Mark differed from his peers in precisely the opposite way, through his habit of storing strength and waiting patiently until he was absolutely ready to challenge his limits.

"Mark has the ability to contain and absorb energy, to use it when he needs it," Mike Rubano, Mark's massage therapist, told *Outside*. "To hold it, hold it, hold it, and then *explode*."

Each year, between January 1, when he resumed training after a post-Ironman break, and April 1, Mark never allowed his heart rate to exceed the Phil Maffetone-imposed limit of 155 beats per minute. This was a period of absorbing energy for later use. There were temptations to stray from this wise and patient approach, but Mark was wise and patient enough not to give in to them.

"You come back a little out of shape, you start working out, you get an ache and a pain here or there, and you see people who have been working out straight through, and you think, *Man, I shouldn't have taken time off,*" Mark said in a 1985 interview. "But that doesn't last long. After about a month you can feel the energy coming back into your body—there's a transition from someone who's just working out to someone who's feeling really strong."

Come April, Mark finally added high-intensity efforts to his training mix. By this time his body contained so much stored potential that he positively exploded into these hard sessions, which in turn catapulted his fitness to a whole new level. The training partners who were leaving Mark behind in January were now left far behind him.

Athletes who got their first exposure to Mark in the winter faced a rude awakening in the spring. One such athlete was Jürgen Zäck, a German triathlete several years younger than Mark with exceptional cycling ability. One January Mark and Jürgen climbed to the top of Palomar Mountain—the toughest climb in San Diego County—on their bikes. Jürgen dropped his famous and accomplished new training partner easily. When Mark finally reached the summit, ten minutes behind, he found the German riding in circles, waiting, gloating.

A few weeks later they repeated the workout, and again Jürgen was turning circles at the top when Mark got there. But this time Mark was only five minutes behind. A few more weeks went by, and they did it again. Mark finished right behind Jürgen, who had no chance to turn circles on this occasion. On their fourth trip up Palomar Mountain, Mark dropped Jürgen. When he reached the top, five minutes behind, Jürgen found Mark turning circles, waiting, gloating.

DAVE SCOTT AND MARK ALLEN were not the only triathletes of their generation who suffered like sled dogs in training. Scott Molina, Scott Tinley, and Mike Pigg, among others, also punished themselves famously. Yet Tinley and Pigg were among the group of also-rans who found themselves struggling more than three miles behind Dave and Mark on the Queen K in the final stretch of the 1989 Ironman, and Molina would have been among them too if he'd done the race. It would seem, then, that other factors besides repeated suffering in training contribute to the magnitude of an elite triathlete's capacity to tolerate suffering in races.

One look at Dave Scott tells you this mental capacity must be at least partly hardwired—genetic. Dave was always the last to quit in any contest he cared about from his earliest years.

"I hadn't been born with the natural ability to swim, but I wanted to be the best at it, anyway, so I swam until it hurt, then went back for more," Dave wrote of his first days in the pool as a young boy.

Some people are born with big feet. Others are born with exceptionally good eyesight. Perhaps Dave was born with a crazily overdeveloped ACC—a hidden suborgan of extraordinary capacity to tolerate suffering lurking deep inside his forebrain.

Before Dave was even 10 years old his father wrote checks for the household bills once a month, stuffed them into envelopes, and sent his son out to deliver them directly to their addressees by bicycle to save postage. Dave, of course, made a game of it, seeking to complete his rounds faster each month. Verne had meant to build discipline in his young son by forcing him to perform a productive task he did not enjoy. But Dave loved it.

By age 13 Dave was racing the bus more than five miles to school on his bike. He did not learn such behavior from anyone; it came naturally from within. Whenever Dave spoke of this capacity, he seemed amazed by it himself and acknowledged that it was not something he controlled. It was just there.

"I've always felt that, as the race lingers on, the psychological part of it becomes a huge factor," he said in a *Competitor* interview. "I seem to thrive on that, even though I'm feeling fatigued just as everyone else is."

Dave not only thrived on the challenge of feeling fatigued in races but was compelled to confront that challenge in every single workout. Some mysterious inner force coerced him to go hard every day without respite. The price of a few missed workouts was essentially the world's worst case of cabin fever—a miserable sense of confinement. Complicating matters, this mysterious inner force nourished Dave's sense of self, cultivated an image of himself as the last man to quit. So it wasn't just fear of cabin fever but also fear of failing to live up to his own perfect standard that drove Dave, and ironically drove him so hard that he sometimes broke down and suffered the torture of an unsatisfied need to move.

In Mark Allen, it's apparent that the will to resist the impulse to quit must be at least partly nurtured—that the ACC you're born with is not necessarily the ACC you die with. As a young swimmer, Mark did not have much mental stamina. As a mature triathlete, he did. Mark might not have developed this capacity if the wounds he carried away from his boyhood had not ultimately affected him in accordance with the principle that whatever does not kill us makes us stronger.

Behind how many great male athletes is a lousy father? Mark Allen. Lance Armstrong. Haile Gebrselassie. Michael Phelps. History's greatest triathlete, cyclist, runner, and swimmer all had difficult relationships with their dads in one way or another. Coincidence? Not bloody likely.

Mark Allen sometimes speaks to this point—in general terms, scrupulously avoiding self-references—in interviews.

"If you dig deep enough into the life of any of the top athletes who are pushing their bodies to the absolute limits, you're going to find a story," he once said. "You're going to find something that those athletes are trying to make up for that they didn't get when they were younger. Something that hurt them."

This is a purely motivational explanation, and undoubtedly a valid one. But Samuele Marcora believes that the brains of such athletes are also physically transformed by their early experiences. He believes that living in a difficult family environment may in fact strengthen the ACC in its own way.

"There is now some evidence that chronic exposure to situations requiring self-regulation (in other words, the exertion of effort to control your own behavior) improves self-regulation in completely different situations," he wrote in an e-mail message. "Chronic exertion of cognitive effort required to control your own emotions and deal with difficult family situations may induce neurocognitive adaptations that will translate into a competitive advantage during endurance competitions later on in life. I don't have experimental data to back this up. But, according to my endurance performance model based on current psychobiological research, this transfer is certainly plausible."

This idea might raise eyebrows among those who are aware of other research demonstrating that early childhood trauma, including physical and emotional abuse, compromises brain development. Numerous studies have shown that the stress of a difficult family environment alters the developing brain's functioning for the worse, not for the better. However, this is not the effect in every case. Psychologists recognize a phenomenon they call "resilience," whereby certain relatively fortunate victims of abuse are essentially made stronger—at least in some ways—by what doesn't kill them.

Psychologists have identified a few factors that seem to be associated with resilience. Among them are "external interests and affiliations" and "early temperament and behavior." Mark had both of these factors working in his favor. His swimming outlet may have saved him from much of the developmental damage that he might otherwise have suffered as the son of his father. And his self-reliant temperament may also have helped him cope with the stress of his upbringing in ways most children cannot.

Mark's emotionally withdrawn adult personality shows strong evidence of childhood training in self-control. He seldom expresses extreme highs or lows, and he almost never shows anger in face-to-face confrontation. But it's there.

"Mark doesn't take shit from anyone," Phil Maffetone says. "He doesn't really confront things head-on, but if you say something bad about him, he won't forget it."

Julie Moss used to wonder if Mark ever felt anger. She had been with him for years before she saw him explode. But then he did. They were riding their bikes together when a driver cut in front of Julie, coming within inches of sending her flying off the road. Julie's field of awareness collapsed around her as she swerved out of harm's way, then was restored. By then Mark was gone, screaming invective as he chased the motorist for blocks at 30 mph until the offender, lucky to have the greater horsepower, escaped.

The incident was completely out of character for Mark, yet his rage was so authentic and extreme that Julie realized it must always be there, deep inside him. Some might claim that such emotional containment is unhealthy. If so, it was a hang-up with a collateral benefit. For it seems as if Mark's unbending efforts to keep that rage—as well as most other strong emotions—locked away served to hone a tremendous capacity to resist other physical urges, such as the urge to slow down when races became painful.

AS THEY RUN TOGETHER down the middle of the Queen K Highway, Dave Scott and Mark Allen are, in a manner of speaking, not fighting a fair fight. Neither man has appreciably more physical talent than the competitors quarreling over third place far behind them. But disparate accidents have gifted Dave and Mark with a clear advantage in mental stamina that is rooted in the depths of their brains. Dave got his overactive ACC from nature—his genes. Mark got his from nurture (an ironic word in this instance)—a lousy father.

Dave's extraordinary power to persevere has come at the cost of an unremitting drive to keep moving, and moving toward perfection. He's like a man who cannot sleep until sleeplessness almost kills him, who delightedly gets a lot more done than anyone else until he suddenly feels awful and collapses into a deep coma while the world passes him by. Then wakes and does it all again.

Mark's mental grip of death, his ruthless strength of will, has come at the cost of an extraordinary walling-off of natural affect, a channeling of all the rage and hurt of the proverbial unblessed son into an unbending pursuit of redeeming achievement.

To an observer unfamiliar with the unique makeup of endurance athletes, Dave and Mark might seem somewhat psychologically unbalanced. But in the context of their competition, they are just a little crazier than the rest of us, in particular ways that happen to strengthen a tiny, collar-shaped part of the brain that renders them capable of enduring the suffering of extreme fatigue like no one else. And that's why no one else stands a chance.

CHAPTER 8

SHOT OUT
OF A CANNON

Before you embark on a journey of revenge,
dig two graves.

— CONFUCIUS

A t last the day has come. A cheap digital alarm clock resting on the nightstand in Dave Scott's bedroom at the Sea Village Resort displays a time of three fifty-nine a.m. Dawn remains a distant prospect. The time flips to four o'clock, and the alarm sounds. Dave is already awake. Much less than the apprehension of racing Ironman is needed to keep the insomniac Dave from getting a good night's sleep.

He is alone. Anna slept in Verne and Dot's lodgings at the King Kamehameha Hotel with Ryan, whose presence would have further reduced the Man's already slim chances for uninterrupted slumber. He climbs out of bed, stretches a bit, and puts on a set of running clothes that he laid out neatly last night.

Pat Feeney's backup alarm buzzes in the next bedroom. You can't be too careful. Wake-up mishaps are surprisingly common at Ironman.

Pat steps out of his bedroom, ready to take over. He will do everything for Dave short of spoon-feeding him and wiping his bottom from now until the race starts. The logistics of the last two hours of getting ready for Ironman are almost expeditionary in scope. Racing suit, swim goggles, backup goggles, swim cap, bike bottles, solid nutrition, tire pump, sunscreen, body lube—one small oversight could spell disaster. Dave puts it all on Pat so he can relax—sort of—and focus on the few things his friend cannot do for him.

"How are you feeling?" Pat asks.

"Not bad," Dave says. "I think I could exercise a little."

Pat knows Dave well enough to understand that his friend is telling him he feels terrific. If he felt merely good, he would have said, "Gosh, I'm old."

Dave heads to the kitchen, puts two slices of bread in the toaster, and scarfs down a banana. He eats the toast dry. Pre-race nerves have given him cottonmouth, so it goes down with some difficulty, even with water. Dave puts one more slice in the toaster and eats a second banana while he waits. After dispatching the next round of toast, he eats a third banana. It's a small breakfast by his standards, but he dares not eat more for fear of starting the race with a full stomach.

While Pat fiddles with drink bottles, Dave leaves the condo. He negotiates his way through the darkness toward the parking-lot entrance and then eases into a jog, heading south on Ali'i Drive, away from Dig Me Beach. It is already warm—warmer than seems right in such darkness. A light breeze floats in off the water.

As Dave shuffles along, his heart races ahead of his effort. Inside him a tug-of-war is being fought between a delicious aliveness, an instinct to capture and hold on to every sensory detail of this once-a-year (and how many more times ever?) moment, and a burning eagerness. He can't wait to race. And he's in no hurry. A nonspecific fear further throttles Dave's heart, but he enjoys this as well, as an indispensible piece of the thing he lives for: the chance to see what he can do.

It is the best morning of his life.

Back inside the condo, Pat is joined by Mike Norton, John Reganold, and Dave's sister Jane from next door.

"Warming up?" John asks Pat, noting Dave's absence.

"Warming up," Pat says.

The two men trade smiles and shakes of the head. After all these years, they still can't quite understand why Dave feels he needs to exercise before eight-plus hours of exercise. He's an odd one. But that's why they love him.

Dave cruises along for half a mile before turning around, enjoying the loosening feeling in his muscles as they slough off the stiffness of sleep. By the time he returns to Sea Village, something else has begun to loosen up. This is the true object of his early-morning ritual—to facilitate the single most important pre-race act.

AT FIVE O'CLOCK race announcer Mike Plant fires up the public address system from his perch atop the finish-line tower on Ali'i Drive. He speaks gentle words of welcome and orientation for the benefit of the few athletes arriving at the start area far earlier than they should. Bustling around them, and far outnumbering the athletes for now, are scores of race volunteers wearing pale pink or blue T-shirts.

"In case anyone somehow has been on another planet the last couple of days," Mike says, "the race will start at seven a.m. this morning."

Mike's voice is muted, as befits the somnolent mood of the moment, and as it must be if he is to have any chance of being able to speak at all when the last finisher of the race passes under his tower at midnight.

Darkness still reigns, though a perfect full moon casts a soft glow over Kailua-Kona, and event lighting creates stark visibility on and around the pier. The stone seawall bordering the sidewalk on the bay side of Ali'i Drive is already crowded with spectators. They began arriving hours ago to claim coveted parcels of the best real estate from which to watch the start. Many lie with towels underneath them, some fast asleep. By the time the cannon fires, all will be standing and crowded together with dozens of opportunistic latecomers, like Tokyo subway passengers awaiting a rush-hour train.

AS MIKE PLANT'S FIRST WORDS of the morning boom through the loudspeakers at Dig Me Beach, Mark Allen is just waking, seven miles away, at the Kanaloa resort. A big sleeper, Mark likes to set his alarm as late as he possibly can without leaving himself unduly rushed before the race. Like Dave, he is alone in bed. Julie slept in the second bedroom so she would not unwittingly siphon his energy during the night.

While hardly the insomniac that Dave is, Mark always has trouble sleeping in Kona before Ironman. He becomes afraid of the dark in Hawaii and has nightmares about people breaking into the condo and attacking him. Last night, however, Mark was spared such awful visions. His subconscious did no worse than conjure up a version of his usual Ironman-eve dream of (what else?) oversleeping and arriving at the start line late, already too far behind Dave Scott to catch him.

Mark moves about the condo in total silence, taking frozen water bottles from the freezer, drinking a liquid breakfast of Exceed meal replacement (his stomach being too knotted up to handle solid food), gathering his stuff together. He does not bid good-morning to Julie, who, also racing today, is similarly occupied. Julie respects but does not share her fiancé's preference for silence. Early in their relationship she turned on some psych-up music on the morning of a race. Without a word Mark walked over to the source of the noise and silenced it, not in a dramatic display of annoyance but matter-of-factly, as though it had somehow turned itself on.

Mark's silence is not evidence that he is more nervous than triathletes who do talk before races. He is, however, nervous. It is impossible not to be anxious when facing hours of guaranteed intense suffering. Every athlete is prone to feel some anxiety over what's at stake in a major competition and what the outcome will be, but for the Ironman triathlete, this disquiet is rooted in a fear of imminent, prolonged agony.

As she stares without appetite at an egg she just scrambled, Julie thinks the same thought she thinks every year: *This is the worst morning of my life.*

At another hotel in Kona Rob Mackle is so traumatized by the suffering at hand that he's weeping. Rob is a strapping young man, exceptionally strong and muscular for an elite triathlete, and no crybaby. A former scholarship swimmer at Indiana University, he has a good chance of leading the race through the end of the swim and into the start of the bike leg later this morning. Technically an age-group competitor, not a professional, Rob knows he cannot run well enough to win, place, or show, and his highest hope is to claim the last spot on the fifteen-deep podium. So he does not bear a heavy burden of competitive pressure on his broad shoulders. But he raced his first Ironman last year, and he remembers what it felt like. He knows he's about to feel the same misery again. It is the worst morning of his life. And that's why he's crying.

Mike Rubano knocks on Mark and Julie's door at a quarter past five and is quietly admitted. He does little more than take a seat and observe while the betrothed athletes complete their rituals of preparation. Mike is just about the only person who never sucks energy from Mark. Their energies pulsate at the same frequency.

Fifteen minutes later Charlie Graves and Brian Hughes arrive.

"Ready?" Charlie asks.

Mark nods. Charlie and Brian lead Mark and Julie out to a rented Jeep. Mike returns to his bed to get another forty-five minutes of shut-eye before heading into town to catch the start. Charlie steers the Jeep through the front gate and then the snoozing neighborhoods surrounding the Kanaloa. He turns left onto Ali'i Drive, blindly tracing the early miles of the marathon course that Mark—barring catastrophe—will start upon at approximately twelve thirty this afternoon under blinding sun and in 90-degree heat.

As they cruise along in the warm darkness, wind tousling their hair, Julie watches Mark out of the corner of her eye, wondering, as she often does, and as everyone who knows Mark often does, what is happening inside his mind, behind the silence.

Mark is probably thinking about an article he read in a triathlon trade publication a few days ago. Its author was handicapping the top contenders for today's race. The same writer had predicted that Mark would win past Ironmans. This time, however, he demoted Grip to dark horse on the grounds that, over the past several years, Mark had proven himself all but fated never to win the only race that really matters. It hit Mark like a slap in the face. *No one had ever told him he couldn't win Ironman before.* A lifetime's worth of other reasons for wanting to win were instantly replaced with a somehow even more intense desire to win *only to make this guy eat his words.* He's been brooding over payback ever since. Mark wants to mentally rehearse the coming race right now. But a subconscious part of him keeps changing the channel back to this grudge. This consuming need to prove he *can* to one who says he *can't* speaks to Mark's deepest reason for wanting to win.

The closer they come to town, the thicker the traffic becomes. Most of the 1,286 athletes competing in the race slept somewhere along Ali'i Drive last night, making for a weird predawn rush hour along a stretch of road that is normally calm even at midday. Not a single word is spoken inside the vehicle for the full twenty minutes it takes to reach a VIP parking area near the finish line, right next to the official Ironman T-shirt booth and across from the local dive shop. Charlie finds a spot and kills the ignition. Just as everyone puts a hand on a door handle, Mark breaks the silence.

"Let's do it," he says.

For Charlie, these three words change the meaning of everything that came before. Mark sounds calm and ready, whereas his silence had seemed fearful. In fact, like everyone else racing today, Mark *is* fearful—but he is also calm and ready. And a little angry.

The scene at Dig Me Beach has transformed in the hour since Mike Plant first picked up his microphone. At that time his greetings and instructions and sponsor plugs were spoken over a soundtrack of mellow music played at modest volume. Volunteers, many of them swim-course safety crew members carrying surfboards, were then streaming in, athletes trickling. The roads were still open, and the last bits of race signage were going up.

Now the music is louder and more up-tempo. Athletes come thickly, slowly, silently walking in from two directions, Ali'i and Palani. Most have been dropped off a few blocks away by family or friends. Some wear warm-ups, others just their swimsuits or triathlon racing suits. Many carry bicycle tire pumps. The sidewalk along Ali'i Drive is a crush. Restive lines have formed at the portable toilets. First light appears above Hualalai Volcano on the left shoulder of the bay, like the gap beneath a rising curtain.

"Once your body has been marked, you can proceed to the pier," Mike Plant announces, continuing his helpful stream of consciousness. "You can check your bike, make those last-minute adjustments, get your water bottles in, pump your tires up, and get ready to go."

Veterans Mark and Julie have no need for this guidance, but they behave as if they are heeding it anyway. After parting from Charlie and Brian, the couple walks toward the pier and joins the line for body marking. When Grip reaches the front, a volunteer wielding a Marks-A-Lot marker asks him what his race number is and then draws a "5" on his upper arms and lower thighs. This figure matches the number on paper bibs affixed to his bike jersey and his running singlet and represents his finishing place in last year's Ironman, thanks to Pele's curse and two flat tires. An "X" is inked on his left calf, indicating that he is racing in the professional division. Age-group racers have their age written on that spot. Julie gets the number 53 and an X of her own.

Access to the pier is constricted and controlled. Athletes push toward the pinched entry point in a dense herd. Two of the more menacing-looking race staffers check for body markings before allowing admittance to the athletes-only zone. Once inside the transition area, Mark and Julie hug and separate. Julie knows Mark needs total isolation now. It's just the way he is—or has become.

Leaving Mark at his racked bike, Julie moves toward hers, stomach twisted in worry, but not for herself. She has told Mark often that she believes he can win this race. But in her private thoughts she is not nearly so certain. She has seen too many things go wrong too many times.

Eyes crawl all over Mark as he wades through the crowd of nervous triathletes, one after another of whom is briefly distracted from his or her own fear by recognizing Grip's iconic chestnut curls and green-eyed stare. Although he does not return their smiles, Mark does not avoid their looks, and so begins his last pre-race experiment. Mark decided this year to withdraw and isolate himself from his fellow humans so completely in the last days of Iron Week that a part of him welcomes this fleeting contact with dozens in the final moments of the countdown. The idea was that instead of taking his energy, the people would feed him energy. It's working.

When Mark gets to his bike he sees Dave already busy at his own machine farther along the same rack. Dave looks sharp in a white Brooks tracksuit with black accents. Having missed last year's race, Dave has been given the number 23, which he takes as an insult even though he knows numbers are distributed through an impartial formula. His bike is accordingly racked in the twenty-third slot from the end of the row allotted to male professional racers. It feels like a ghetto in contrast to his familiar number-1 slot. Charlie Graves and Brian Hughes have taken up a position in the spectator zone of the pier and look on as Dave and Mark consciously ignore each other, concentrating more intently than necessary on inflating their bike tires and placing fluid bottles in their cages.

Mark is assisted in these tasks by his brother Gary, who has leveraged his status as a bike mechanic for several of Ironman's top racers to score a pink Ironman volunteer T-shirt that gives him access to the bike racks before and during the race. Soon the brothers are joined by Space and Toot, who are similarly attired. Although they lack technical skills, they volunteer for the race each year as a way to feel and be more involved in the Ironman experience. Knowing Mark's preferences, they say little. But Toot's heart is full, and there is a message that she feels compelled to share with Mark.

"You're going to be all right this time," she says, gently placing a hand on her son-in-law's forearm. "I have a feeling."

Yesterday Toot made her own secret visit to the Little Blue Church, arriving there a scant few hours before Mark and Julie poked their heads in on their way to the neighboring heiau. She told Space she was going for a run and set out from the Royal Sea Cliff Resort, heading south on Ali'i Drive. She carried a plastic bag containing an unopened jug of Tanqueray gin (Pele's brand of choice, she was told) and a piece of lava rock shaped like a wave and sparkling with golden flecks. As she jogged along the shore side of the road, she passed a small field of flowers and pulled up a bunch with her free hand.

Toot had a healthy sweat going by the time she entered the church, two and a half miles from her starting point. She placed a few of her flowers on the altar and prayed.

"Blessed Virgin Mary," she said, "please watch over Mark and give him a helping hand tomorrow."

Still carrying the heavy plastic bag, Toot left the church and walked over to Kuemanu Heiau. There she dug a hole in the earth and buried the gin and the lava rock, placed the remaining flowers on top of them, and hid the offerings under a layer of soil. Then she spoke to the kahunas.

"If you have any relationship with my God," she said, "please get together with him and help Mark get this monkey off his back."

Finally she addressed Madam Pele, with two words: "Bug off."

While hurrying back to the Royal Sea Cliff, knowing Space would be worried about her long absence, Toot said her rosary. Instantly she was filled with a warm feeling of assurance, not unlike the sensation Mark carried away from the same place a few hours later.

It is this good feeling that she has just shared with Mark.

Chores completed, Mark sneaks off toward the far end of the pier, the most isolated place available to him, while Dave starts to make his way over to the spectator area, where Jane, Pat, John, and Mike are waiting for him. He doesn't get far before an ABC camera crew buttonholes him. Donna de Varona, a former Olympic swimmer, sidles up next to him with a stick mike. Her cameraman centers the pair in the frame, and another guy shines a blinding light in Dave's and Donna's eyes. Dave's been through this many times and submits without protest. Actually, he loves it.

"Dave, it seems all the talk has been about a showdown between you and Mark Allen," Donna says. "Do you think he has the best chance of anyone to dethrone you?"

"Well, Donna, I don't have a crystal ball," Dave says, expressing some irritation at Donna's choice of question. "But I know this: If Mark beats me, I'll make sure it's the most painful thing he's ever done."

The crew releases the six-time Ironman champion to complete his search for his circle, whom he finds on the pier at the water's edge. In the final minutes before battle, Dave likes to talk and to have people around him as much as Mark wants to be silent and alone. The conversation among the five is serious yet natural. This is not anyone's first rodeo.

"Boy, I'm going to be anaerobic in those first 400 meters," Dave says as he stares into the water, punctuating his remark with a low chuckle.

He's referring to his plan to start the race hard and perhaps, with any luck, shake Mark early.

"I'm glad it's you and not me!" John says, trying to imagine the depths of suffering his friend will endure before the next time he sees him.

The group is joined by Dave's father and wife, who have arrived by way of a twenty-second elevator ride and a two-minute walk from Verne and Dot's room in the King Kam. They've left Ryan behind with Dot. The conversation expands to include Verne and Anna as light stretches across the sky overhead.

Dave, who does not wear a watch, has instructed Pat to tell him when it's time to start his warm-up swim, and Pat now gives the signal. Anna gets the last moment with Dave.

"Get out there and do it!" she says. "I love you."

Dave could slip into the water from the very spot on the pier where he now stands, but he does not. He knows Mark is probably spying on him, as he has done in past years, waiting to see where Dave lines up at the start so he can draw close beside him and easily fall into his slipstream after the cannon fires. This parasitical tactic has become a serious bone of contention, and Mark intends to make the most of it. But Dave has his own two-part plan to thwart it. Part one entails sneaking over to the lightly trafficked north side of the pier and wading into the bay there. He will warm up by swimming around the pier and then melt into the huddle of heads masked in identical yellow swim caps floating behind the start line. Having escaped detection, Dave will execute the second part of the plan, turning Mark's own tactics against him and using his better-than-ever swim form to latch on to the feet of a faster swimmer, maybe Chris Hinshaw or Wolfgang Dittrich, and shake Mark straight out of the gate.

Dave slinks off, feeling clever. Meanwhile, Mark sits on a small bleacher positioned at the very end of the pier, alone, head down. Inside him a quiet battle is taking place between his fears and his chosen self.

Dave looks fitter than ever. Those veins!

So what? He's no god.

It's going to be a hot one. I can tell already.

And? It's always hot.

As this internal dialogue continues, secondary race announcer Mike Reilly approaches the bleacher from the left on his way toward the spot on the pier where the start cannon, a surprisingly small toy cannon, rests, to help oversee its firing. He sees a shadowy figure sitting at the right edge of the second bench from the bottom, head down. Not another soul is nearby. Reilly comes nearer and recognizes Mark Allen. He slows to give Mark time to notice him before he passes by. Although he fears it may be a breach of protocol, Reilly can't resist the temptation to wish Mark good luck before the race. But Mark seems oblivious to his approach, if not insensible to the whole frenetic scene behind him, if not on another plane of existence entirely. So Reilly forces it.

"Good luck, Mark," he says.

Mark hears a voice, but his concentration is so deep that there's a delay before he recognizes the voice and a further delay before he understands what has been said. Seeing no sign that he's been heard, Reilly continues walking, feeling like an idiot. He is three paces beyond the bleacher when he hears a single word spoken softly behind him.

"Thanks."

Moments later Dave Scott swims around the end of the pier, right underneath Mark. So much for that plan.

Bon Jovi's "Living on a Prayer," or some other crowd-stirring rock anthem, is now blasting over the loudspeakers. It seems to come from heaven and to fill the entire earth with sound. The atmosphere is electric. Dawn has passed; day has arrived. Some of the younger spectators, now standing on the seawall, pump their fists to the thundering beat of the music. Others sip coffee and let their enchanted eyes play about the large and variegated spectacle. Everyone, athletes and spectators alike, has been caught up in a quivering field of social energy. Mike Plant orders the athletes into the water, and the voltage is cranked up another notch.

The last quarter hour before the start of Ironman is charged with a jittery anticipation that no other sporting event can match. The stakes— the sheer magnitude of the challenges facing the athletes—seem to transcend sport. The awesome setting—the limitless sea and sky, the looming Hawaiian volcanoes, so recently revealed by the transition from night to day—lend a sense of almost cosmic importance to what is about to begin.

ABOVE: Mark and his Mona Lisa smile.

RIGHT: Dave became the first two-time Ironman winner in October 1982.

Mark exited the swim-bike transition of the October 1982 Ironman a minute behind Dave.

Dave fell ten minutes behind Mark during the bike leg of the 1983 Nice Triathlon. Then Mark blacked out during the run. He held on to win but was left in a stupor, and he still hadn't fully recovered his legs by October at Ironman.

LEFT: Scott Tinley came up just thirty-three seconds short of catching Dave in the 1983 Ironman.

BELOW: Dave had a few more witnesses for his third Ironman win in 1983 than he'd had for his first in 1980.

ABOVE: Dave erased a deficit of almost twelve minutes to pass Mark halfway through the marathon at the 1984 Ironman.

RIGHT: Pat Feeney and Anna Scott were all smiles after Dave consummated his 1984 Ironman victory.

By 1984 the Ironman start was already a spectacle like no other in sports.

BELOW LEFT: Dave watched Scott Tinley break his Ironman course record from this seat in 1985.

BELOW RIGHT: As owner of the event, Valerie Silk, shown in 1984, shepherded Ironman from its origins as a cult sideshow to status as a first-class world championship.

ABOVE: Mark felt that his victory in the 1986 Nice Triathlon came too easily. This feeling strengthened his desire to finally win Ironman.

BELOW: By the time he won the Nice Triathlon for the fifth time in 1986, Mark was a hero in France. (It didn't hurt that he delivered half of his victory speech in French.)

ABOVE: Dave snarled his way to his fifth win and another course record in the 1986 Ironman.

BELOW: The "curse of Pele" culminated in Mark's suffering two flat tires in the 1988 Ironman.

But the kicker is the fact that nobody knows exactly when the race will start. Officially it starts at seven o'clock; however, it never actually starts at seven on the dot, and there is no countdown. This system is needed because it would be easy for one or more deliriously amped athletes to jump a predictable start, like a defensive lineman timing a quarterback's snap count. It would take only a few such miscreants to launch the entire field prematurely, and there would be no way to cram that genie back inside the bottle. The surprise start format makes the athletes' eagerness even more difficult to contain. Race staff in kayaks and on surfboards beat the racers back behind the start line, which stretches across the water some fifty feet from shore, and Mike Plant shouts threats and admonitions over the loudspeakers.

The athletes' faces wear alarmed expressions as they descend the five stone steps to the sand of Dig Me Beach and enter the water. Some who have not yet strapped on their goggles have red-rimmed eyes, like Rob Mackle's. Others are bug-eyed, lips pursed with undisguised terror. The Catholics cross themselves. A few of the women seem to struggle for breath. A few of the men smile and squint menacingly, as though ready to bite someone. They are the most terrified of all.

The music stops. An ABC television helicopter swoops over the bay. A local kahuna recites an invocation, and the national anthem is sung. It can't be long now. But several dozen athletes continue to warm up in front of the start line, confident the rocket won't launch until they're on board.

Mark Allen completes his warm-up swim and finds Dave Scott on the start line. It isn't hard. The pros always start at the front, and the fastest swimmers among the pros always congregate about twenty feet from the pier. Dave has to be there, and Mark knows it, and the Man's trademark mustache makes him hard to miss. Dave's goggles are currently on his forehead, not over his eyes, rendering him especially easy to find.

Mark has rehearsed this moment in his mind again and again for months. He has mentally practiced feeling no fear or intimidation and bowling Dave over with his own confidence and strength. He has imagined himself saying, "I hope you have your best race today, Dave, because I'm going to beat you!" The time is here.

"Good luck, Dave," Mark says.

Oh, well. It wouldn't have come out as he'd imagined it anyway. Dave merely nods in acknowledgment of Mark's offering.

On the pier, race owner Valerie Silk and race director Debbie Baker stand behind the cannon. With them is John Waihee, governor of Hawaii, today's honorary race starter. Mike Reilly is also there. Valerie has shown Governor Waihee what he needs to do and instructed him to wait for her signal. The race might not start at any particular time, but it does start when Valerie decides. Mike Reilly can't help but notice that the governor seems distracted, almost irritable, as though he would rather be somewhere else.

In front of this group, almost directly in the cannon's line of innocuous fire, *Triathlete* photographer Gary Newkirk is poised on the edge of the pier with his legs dangling over the start line below. He likes to capture an image of the start as it happens, which requires that he hold the camera in front of his face beginning about two minutes before the cannon fires and use his instinctive flinch at the weapon's report to activate the shutter. Once Mike Plant finally succeeds in getting almost everyone back behind the start line, Gary knows to assume his position. But a good fifty athletes are currently swimming toward the start line from the far side, so Gary's camera rests idly on his lap.

Boom!

Governor Waihee has decided he can do whatever the hell he wants. Valerie Silk's jaw drops. The woman widely regarded as the gentlest soul in Hawaii might brain the son of a bitch if she had a frying pan handy.

Meanwhile, chaos—more than the usual chaos.

Taken unawares, Dave Scott frantically pulls his goggles over his eyes and starts swimming before a thousand of his greatest admirers swim over him. His plan to lose Mark straight out of the gate has possibly been ruined before he can take a single stroke.

Mark's plan to follow Dave is no less compromised. Although he was somewhat readier for the cannon and is able to respond to its firing more quickly, he feels strangely flummoxed to find himself swimming ahead of Dave when he had no intention or expectation of doing so. His confusion saps a bit of the power from his typical all-out start—or perhaps instinct tells him to wait for Dave so he can salvage Plan A.

The unhappiest swimmers are the fifty who were swimming in the wrong direction, toward the other 1,200, when the cannon fired. They have become victims of a watery stampede. Try as they might to swiftly about-face and race ahead of the coming swarm, the very fastest swimmers are at the front of that swarm, so the fifty victims are doomed to be slapped, elbowed, and pushed under.

Even some of the safety volunteers, paddling prone on surfboards, are brutally engulfed, having also been surprised by the premature firing of the field piece and having failed to respect the barracuda speed of the swimmers off the front.

It's not much better for the fastest swimmers themselves, who want nothing more than to get out ahead of the aquatic mosh pit and into clean water so they can enjoy a swift and unmolested swim.

The view from the pier and the seawall is spectacular. Flailing arms and thrashing legs churn the bay into a frenzy of whitewater, as though eager piranhas have congregated in a bid for the most cattle carcasses devoured in ninety seconds. Inside the frenzy, goggles and sports watches are being ripped off, heads are being dunked, esophagus-searing salt water is being inhaled, and worse. It's not uncommon for an athlete or two to not even get beyond the pier before grabbing hold of a surfboard and calling it a day.

ABC's Sam Posey stands on the pier with this savagery behind him, a television camera focused on his upper half. Wearing a blue polo shirt and holding a bulbous microphone, he delivers his opening lines for the one-hour Ironman show that will be broadcast several weeks later. Although it is not live, he'll get only one take because his dramatic sea-of-humanity backdrop will soon flow out of frame.

"And so the thirteenth Ironman Triathlon is under way!" he enunciates. "The Ironman: quite possibly the toughest, most demanding single-day sporting event anywhere in the world. Consider what's ahead: 2.4 miles of swimming, 112 miles of riding a bike, and 26.2 miles of running–a full marathon. Now, when the Ironman was first held back in 1978, it was a struggle just to survive and to finish. Today, despite the brutal distances involved, the Ironman is very much a race."

As these words are spoken, the man who made Ironman a race, Dave Scott, is sprinting in total abandonment toward the front of the melee, angry enough to kill. He loves to race angry. He always races angry. It takes little to flip the switch of fury inside his mind at the start of a race. But his bad start today is one of the most incensing setbacks he has experienced in any triathlon, and he has seized upon it as an opportunity to stoke his rage and save his original plan for the swim. He torpedoes ahead of nearly everyone who got out in front of him and soon enough catches and passes Mark, who, with relief, tucks in behind him. Dave does not relent but continues to stroke as hard as he can in an effort to dislodge the parasite.

Grip is not the only swimmer to hitch a ride. A massive pack of nearly twenty men forms behind the Man. This is not 1982, and Dave and Mark are no longer in a class by themselves in the water. Dave senses the scope of his company, and his animus expands to encompass the whole lot. His efforts in this early part of the race are as much a message to the others as a matter of personal performance.

This is how hard I am willing to go. This is how much I am willing to suffer. You want to stay with me? Then get ready for an extremely unpleasant experience that will not end well for you.

The most threatening men in the group besides Mark are Mike Pigg and Ken Glah, last year's second- and third-place finishers. Pigg has been a dominating force since turning pro three years ago and is the reigning Triathlete of the Year. A scrapper, Pigg has been compared to Pete Rose, who usually played well but *always* got his uniform dirty. Glah, a Pennsylvanian, is known as the Beast of the East, so novel is the phenomenon of an East Coaster among Ironman's top echelon. Only 25 years old, like Pigg, the mustached redhead is strong in all three disciplines.

Behind Dave's pack the field strings out quickly, elongating from a roundish blob to a stretched-out teardrop in a matter of minutes. While the swim is by far the shortest leg of the race in distance and duration, it is also the discipline in which the greatest disparities in speed are manifest. The leader will cover the 2.4-mile out-and-back course in forty-eight minutes. Forty-eight minutes after that, athletes will still be staggering in droves up the swim exit ramp.

AS THE FAT BACK END of the teardrop drifts away from the pier, a strange and colorful detritus is left behind in the beach's shallow waters: hundreds of abandoned flip-flops of various hues. Over the course of Iron Week the prickly sea urchins carpeting the ocean floor off Dig Me Beach caused a run on flip-flops at Whalers General Store across the street, and at other vendors.

The entire swim course lies in water clear and shallow enough to sight bottom. If they care to look, swimmers can see craggy blue coral on the ocean floor and schools of small tropical fish in flaming colors darting about in tidy formations. A group of manta rays glides gently underneath the lead swimmers as they pass beyond the pier.

Close to shore, crosscurrents sweep the athletes sideways, first to the left, then to the right, then left again. The surface is placid closer to the beach, but the swimmers face gently rolling swells once they pass beyond the protection of the pier. Some years are rougher than others. This year the sea is virtually a mirror.

At the tip of the still-lengthening teardrop of swimmers, having taken no time to separate themselves from the rest, are Rob Mackle, no longer scared now that he's moving, and Wolfgang Dittrich, a West German who qualified for his country's Olympic trials in swimming in 1984 and who posted the fastest swim time of the day in his first Ironman in 1987. Rob and Wolfgang know each other from the pool at the University of California–San Diego, where Rob does most of his swimming and where Wolfgang swims when he's in town. Knowing they have no other match in the water, they talked before the race about cooperating to ensure that one or the other of them earns the $1,500 swim prime awarded to the first racer out of the water, and they started the race side by side to facilitate that cooperation. Now they are well clear of the rest of the field less than half a mile into the race. Wolfgang is the stronger man today, and Rob follows in his wake. A race staffer paddling a kayak pilots Wolfgang along an arrow-straight line just to the left of the orange guide buoys toward the *Captain Beans*, a party boat anchored at the turnaround, sparing him the chore of sighting.

The two men are in a class by themselves, churning through the water at a steady sixty-eight seconds per 100 yards, faster than most serious recreational swimmers can sprint 100 yards in a pool. Their strokes are beautiful to behold. The arms cycle with perfect left-right symmetry and in metronomic rhythm. A relaxed scissoring of the legs is exquisitely syncopated with the churning arms, which contort underwater to form stiff paddles that create tremendous thrusting pressure—as if they are grabbing invisible rungs and yanking their bodies forward. They slice so swiftly through the water that a bow wave is visible at the crown of each man's head.

Their gap on Dave and the other top contenders grows from ten seconds to twenty, from thirty seconds to a minute, and beyond. Long gone are the days when Dave could post the fastest split times in all three legs of Ironman. The sport has grown, drawing in swimmers of a caliber that Dave and Mark never had to face at their NAIA and NCAA Division III universities.

Rob's and Wolfgang's strategy in relation to the rest of the field is similar to Dave's in relation to Mark. To gain as much distance as possible. To inflict suffering. To make their competitors second-guess themselves and possibly even give up.

Both men are strong cyclists too. If they can build a big enough gap on the very best cyclists in the race—beginning with Dave and Mark—by the end of the swim, they can keep the race interesting in an unexpected way for hours to come.

Swimming all alone in third place, in an undesirable no-man's-land, is Bill Penn, a 37-year-old age grouper from Olympia, Washington, who is not a strong cyclist or runner and will fade to 474th place before he reaches the finish line. Nine years from now, after completing Ironman Canada, Bill will announce, "An Ironman is just too long to race," and quit the pursuit, wishing he'd figured it out sooner.

Next behind Bill is Patrick Bateman, former star swimmer of the Roanoke Valley Aquatic Association and a legitimate top-twenty contender in today's race. Chasing him is Chris Hinshaw, who had his finest Ironman moment in the 1985 boycott year, when he finished second behind Scott Tinley, and is racing on tired legs after taking second place behind Ray Browning at Ironman Canada just a few weeks ago.

Right on Chris's heels and using 15 percent less energy to swim the same speed, thanks to the draft effect, is West German pro Joachim Zemke. A frustrating ten or twelve seconds adrift of Joachim is Kentuckian Don Livingston, another age grouper who has managed to swim his way through most of the pros toward the front of the race but who will see most of those same pros reclaim their positions on the bike.

Then comes the first big pack, containing more than a dozen athletes, including most of the real contenders, and headed by Dave Scott, who much prefers the psychological control of pulling others to the physiological advantage of letting others pull him. Mark Allen is equally comfortable leading and chasing, but in this race he sees every advantage in shadowing Dave. Approaching the midpoint of the swim, Grip remains close enough to touch his rival. Dave's effort to shake him has failed, and he knows it has failed because once every minute or so Mark slaps Dave's foot to let him know he's still there.

It is normal for some accidental slapping to occur when one swimmer drafts off another, but after a couple of slaps a chaser following race etiquette will slip a few inches farther back to prevent additional violence without losing the advantage of the slipstream. But the slapping now continues, as it did throughout the swim in the 1987 Ironman. Dave feels strongly tempted to flip onto his back and glare at Mark, reenacting his response of two years ago, but decides against it, remembering how little difference it made then.

Instead he tries something else. Each time Dave feels another slap, he kicks violently in the hope of striking a painful counterblow. That doesn't work very well either, but in any case Mark is not taking Dave out of his game by pissing him off. The angrier Dave gets, the faster he goes.

On shore, nobody has any idea what's happening. The cannon fired, the athletes swam away, and now the spectators wait. Mike Plant puts the rock 'n' roll back on to keep the energy from flagging and finds a remarkable number of things to talk about. He plugs sponsors, reviews some of the race's top story lines, and passes on what little real information about the progress of the swim he can get, which comes from an ABC camera crew on a small boat and a race official on the *Captain Beans* who notes race numbers as the athletes come around and reports them back to shore. In the fifty minutes it takes the big names to complete the swim, Mike will be able to tell the crowd little more than that Wolfgang Dittrich and Rob Mackle have a huge lead; Dave and Mark and several other top competitors are in the lead chase pack; and Wendy Ingraham is the top woman, only seconds behind Dave's group.

Bob Babbitt watches the swim from the pier with Ironman elite athlete liaison Bob Bright.

"What does Mark have to do to win?" Babbitt asks Bright, not so much in his editor's capacity as out of pure curiosity.

"He's got to do what's been most difficult for him," Bright says. "He's got to get off the bike alongside Dave Scott and then run with him all the way. Breathe on him, bump him, maybe spit on him. But stay off the front. He can't do anything flamboyant."

Mark has gotten a good start on the bumping part.

WOLFGANG DITTRICH and Rob Mackle have made the turn and are now swimming back toward shore, still guided by the lead kayak. Their lead over Dave's pack has ballooned to nearly two minutes. Dave is accustomed to losing no more than a few seconds to the swim leader. He'll have something else to stoke his rage when he completes the swim and finds out how far behind he is—not that it matters as long as Mark is behind him.

On shore, Charlie Graves and Brian Hughes, who have been joined by Mike Rubano and Brian's friend John Martin, watch the approaching disturbance of the water in a state of mild apprehension, as do Space and Toot, separately, and Sharon Allen, alone. It is said that you can't win Ironman in the swim, but you can lose it. Mark Allen's supporters will be able to relax just a bit when they see that he has not lost the race in the swim. Then they can begin to worry about broken derailleurs, nosebleeds, and flat tires on the bike.

Dave Scott's circle looks on as a single group. Pat Feeney squints into the watery distance with particular purpose, looking for the Man's distinctive stroke pattern and well able to spot it 100 yards out. This ability says as much about Dave's freestyle technique as it does about Pat's knowledge of Dave, who is a violent swimmer, and especially violent for such a good swimmer. Freestyle swimming is a technique-dependent discipline, and generally there is a strong correlation between gracefulness of movement and speed in the water. But Dave muscles through the sea, seeming to overcome inefficiency through sheer will. He whips his arm out to the side in the recovery phase of the stroke instead of coming over the top, and he slaps the surface of the water with his hand at the entry point of the stroke instead of piercing it with his fingertips, creating a splash that is visible at some distance.

Pat is not surprised to find that Dave's ugly stroke is missing from the lead pair of swimmers now discernible in the distance. But he is momentarily troubled by the vastness of the gap between this pair and the splashing of the first chase pack, in which he trusts he will eventually spot Dave's stroke. Then he remembers that all that really matters is Mark's position relative to Dave.

The leaders raise their heads to check on their progress toward shore every four to eight strokes. At first the beach doesn't seem to get any closer. But, almost imperceptibly, the big banyan tree in front of the King Kam grows taller, and mashed-together flecks of color on the pier separate into individual people. Then, suddenly, they hear Mike Plant's voice drifting across the water, and the sound affects them as the ringing of the bell at the start of the last lap affects track runners. The lead kayaker peels off. Wolfgang begins a final surge. Rob swings out to the right and commits the full capacity of his considerable musculature to stealing the swim prime from Wolfgang in the literal last minute. The German sees him sneaking up on his right shoulder and finds just enough extra power to hold him off through the final strokes.

The swim exit is a boat-launch ramp on the north side of the pier—the side opposite the starting line. Wolfgang continues swimming until his hand touches the ramp, as he can swim much faster than he can run in water that is more than knee deep. He rises somewhat dizzily and comes out of the ocean in three big bounds. Rob is on him like a knapsack. The official swim course finish line is located at the top of the ramp. Wolfgang reaches it at 48:13, the second-fastest time ever. Rob crosses the line eight-tenths of a second later. This is going to be no ordinary Ironman.

Mark's brother Gary stands on the pier next to Mark's bike, waiting to hand it to him when he arrives. As Wolfgang and Rob charge into the transition area, Gary hears a loud *pop!* followed by a menacing *hissssss.* He wheels around and sees that the front tire of Mark's bike has spontaneously burst.

"Oh, shit!" he shouts.

Every once in a while the warming atmosphere on race morning causes the highly pressurized air inside a tire to expand just enough to blow a tube on a waiting bike in the transition area. It's just the kind of rare disaster that commonly befalls Mark at Ironman. With a stab of panic Gary realizes he has about two minutes to flawlessly change the flat, or else Mark will have to stand around and wait for his bike while Dave gets away. Two minutes is about the minimum amount of time it takes an experienced wrench to change a flat bike tire even without the incredible pressure under which Gary must now change this one. He frantically removes the wheel from the front fork and kneads the tire with both hands like a masseuse to break up the glue seal between tire and wheel rim. His palms are wet with panic sweat, and it seems to take forever. With a single violent yank he rips the blown tire off the rim and grabs one of Mark's two spares off the back of the saddle, leaving him with only one. As he fits the fresh tire onto the wheel, other swimmers begin to trickle in, increasing Gary's heart-gripping sense of urgency.

Bill Penn charges up the ramp with his arms upraised, contracting his chest muscles and biceps like a steroid-addled bodybuilder and screaming like a man being eaten alive by a grizzly bear. He has completely lost his mind to his five seconds of fame. That's just as well, given what the next ten hours hold in store for him.

As Dave's pack approaches the shore, more than a dozen men fight for position in the final sprint. Dave puts everything he has into a late effort to separate himself from Mark, if only by a few seconds, but because of the drafting advantage it's just not possible. Jeff Cuddeback, a 31-year-old pro from Florida, and Dirk Aschmoneit, yet another West German, show the best closing speed and hit the ramp at the vanguard of the group.

Dave bursts out of the water in eleventh place overall. Just behind him is his old water polo teammate Mark Roberts, who was able to hold on to the lead pack the whole way and squeeze between Mark Allen and Dave in the mad dash for the finish. Roberts does not know it's Dave he shadows until his old friend, flailing like a bleeding one-ton bull amid a pack of wispy matadors, smacks him full force in the cheek with an errant elbow.

Holy shit: That's Dave Scott's elbow! Roberts realizes, having taken more elbows to the face from Dave than he can remember back in their water polo days. He would know that blow anywhere. Roberts is briefly stunned but manages to keep his feet and quickly regains his forward momentum.

He is fortunate. The accidental hit could have fractured his cheekbone and taken him out of the race. Mark Allen too is lucky, although he doesn't know it. His brother has managed to stretch a new tire around the front wheel, inflate it with a couple of dozen ferocious pumps, and lock the wheel back in place between the blades of the front fork just as Mark scuttles up the swim exit ramp one step behind Dave. For a moment it seemed as if Madam Pele had defeated Mark yet again.

Dave Scott and Mark Allen have completed the swim, and neither man has lost the race, although both came close—Dave with his late start and Mark with his blown tire. Dave's official time is 51:17; Mark's, 51:18. They have been separated by no more than a body length since the cannon fired.

CHAPTER 9

BURNING MATCHES

Invincibility lies in the defense;
the possibility of victory in the attack.

— SUN TZU, *THE ART OF WAR*

Dave Scott launches out of the ocean, tearing the swim cap and goggles off his head and casting them aside in the water to save the single second it would take him to remove his headgear in the transition area. He scampers up the swim exit ramp on the balls of his bare feet, loosening the tie on his swim brief to save the two seconds it would take him to do so in transition. Hands free, Dave needlessly brushes away the race officials and spectators who form a tunnel of noise along a narrow, fenced-off gangway and hurries ahead onto the pier. Mark Allen is right behind him.

Neither man pauses under the makeshift freshwater shower that has been set up at the entrance to the transition area for their comfort and convenience. Instead they charge straight through and into a space containing row upon row of plastic transition bags marked with race numbers hanging from long metal racks. Grabbing their bags on the fly, they enter a semiprivate changing area where, in company with others from their swim pack, they pull off their swim briefs and suit up in cycling clothes. Dave's kit is white and lime. Mark dons a white jersey with rainbow striping and black shorts. Dave gets his wardrobe together first and mounts his bike before Mark, who loses five seconds fastening a heart rate monitor strap around his chest. Mark receives his bike from Gary–flushed and sweaty from his just-completed tire repair–and throws a leg over the machine, one eye on what he's doing and the other on Dave, who's now pedaling away ahead of him.

The Ironman bike course begins, as it should in the world's toughest triathlon, with a grueling hill climb: notorious Pay-'n'-Save Hill. The transition area spits the athletes onto Ali'i Drive just at the point where it bends away from the coast and heads inland–which on the Big Island, as on most islands, means up–becoming Palani Road. From the perspective of cyclists at its base, the road looks something like a three-quarters-of-a-mile-long, 300-foot-high water slide, forming three distinct undulations as it drops steeply from the top at its intersection with the Queen K highway, levels out briefly at the traffic light that allows access to the Pay-'n'-Save supermarket on the north side and to another shopping center standing opposite, tilts downward again to the intersection at Kuakini Highway, and there flattens again briefly before dropping once more toward the King Kam and the pier.

Dave Scott scorches up the hill, face ugly with exertion, bouncing on his pedals, leaning far over the handlebar like a ski jumper over his skis and rocking his bike from side to side to squeeze out that extra dram of power. His strategy here, already evident, is the same as it was in the swim: to start hard enough to make Mark feel real discomfort and perhaps second-guess his own strategy of shadowing Dave regardless of what Dave does. To send a message: *So, you're going to let me dictate the pace, Mark? Okay, then, how about* this *pace?*

Before the race Dave told Pat Feeney that when he started the bike leg, he would pretend it was not 112 miles long but only 25 miles, the standard USTS distance, and would ride the first 20 miles at his usual short-course speed. Dave knows that he has only a couple of speeds, so the plan's not quite as crazy as it would be for another athlete. But still, it's a gamble.

And it works rather well, initially, as Mark, in his urgency to check Dave's escape, struggles to get his feet into his bike shoes, which, unlike Dave, he preclipped onto his pedals so that he wouldn't have to run from the changing room to his bike in the shoes–always an awkward maneuver given the clunky knob under the ball of the foot. Mark loses precious starting momentum in the first segment of the climb as he fumbles with his footwear. Strapped in at last, he stands on his pedals and launches into a full sprint, holding nothing back in his effort to shrink Dave's dangerous early advantage. Just ahead of him Ken Glah does the same. Ken knows as well as Mark that at Ironman, the race is wherever Dave Scott is—so he's damned if he's going to let Dave get away.

A scene of awful carnage plays out on Pay-'n'-Save Hill as several members of the lead swim pack fail to maintain contact with Dave in his rocketing ascent. Some of the greatest long-distance triathletes in the world are among the casualties, including three-time European champion (and one of Mark's New Zealand training partners) Rob Barel of the Netherlands and recent Ironman Canada winner Ray Browning. A few of them judge Dave's speed suicidal, for themselves if not for him, and willingly let him go. Others try to stay with him but can't. All of them know they're watching any hope they had of winning disappear up the road with Dave, who, judging by precedent, will not be caught from behind later in the day.

By the time he reaches the Queen K, Dave has already passed a couple of the ten athletes who finished the swim ahead of him, among them Dirk Aschmoneit, who came down with an ill-timed flu earlier in the week and now puts up no fight, and defending European champion Yves Cordier, who counters by leaping out of his seat and stomping on his pedals. Yves has come here to win.

Turning left onto the highway, Dave drops his butt onto the seat at last and rests his forearms on the aerobars, hunkering down for the long haul. Yves continues his standing sprint until he's established contact with Dave. Ken Glah makes the turn next and continues to shovel coal into the fire until he's locked on to Dave and Yves, towing Mark behind him. Mike Pigg now sweeps around the corner and puts all his chips into joining the group, latching on as it crests Palani Hill and prepares to drop into the lava fields below.

The vista that greets them there is deathly, Dantean—perfectly constituted to terrify the triathlete who faces it one or two hours into a nine-, eleven-, or fourteen-hour day. Coal-like rock sprawls for miles ahead on the vast expanse below. In the far distance mountains tower, offering a dubious reprieve from the magma pits the athletes must traverse to reach them.

Dave sees the colorful dots of other competitors spaced out on the vanishing ribbon of road ahead. Automatically he sets his sights on the nearest. Chasing fast swimmers who can't ride for shit is always a good game, and in this case it's a game that dovetails nicely with Dave's strategy of making Mark hurt. So torrid is Dave's tempo that Ken Glah and Mike Pigg, both of whom know they need a lead off the bike to have any chance of winning the race, follow him without even a thought of attempting a pass. They're like boxers pressed against the ropes with their forearms raised as shields, warding off a furious barrage of blows from an opponent intent on a first-round knockout, hoping for nothing more than to survive to the bell, saving all plans for a counterattack for some wished-for future round. Yves Cordier, who, with a stab of panic, has discovered a problem with his gear shifters, checks his speedometer, which reads 44 kph. *C'est de la folie*, he thinks. *This is insanity.*

It is said that each athlete starts Ironman with a book of matches. If at any time he puts out an effort that exceeds the maximum effort he could sustain evenly from start to finish, he burns a match. There are only so many matches to burn, and when they're gone the athlete himself flames out. Dave burned a match right away climbing Pay-'n'-Save Hill, and he's already burning another as he mows down the dwindling number of riders ahead of him, one by one, and forces Mark to burn a few of his own matches, hoping his nemesis started with one fewer.

The chugging five-man, ten-wheel train catches and drops Joachim Zemke, sixth man out of the water. Patrick Bateman, fourth, is chewed up and excreted minutes later. The next victim is Chris Hinshaw, fifth in the swim. But Chris gamely increases his effort and hitches a ride on the back of the train, becoming its sixth car—the caboose.

Civilization drops away behind the convoy along with its few discarded quasi rivals. Frowning with exertion, the six lowered heads roll through an unsightly warehouse district on the town's outskirts. Massive metal electrical poles lining the inland side of the road complete the industrial wasteland aesthetic. A passenger jet rises ahead, silent from this distance, as the group churns toward the airport eight miles outside town. The riders pass the city dump on the right, its great heaps of garbage plainly visible, and all too plainly smelled, from the road.

Then nothing. Nothing but oily black lava rock spreading in all directions. A natural disaster frozen—if that's the word—in time. Some lava patches still look fresh, soft, and hot.

There is life, though. Tufts of golden fountain grass sprout through gaps in the sooty ground. Here and there stands a tall hibiscus bush festooned with magenta flowers, their prettiness augmented by their deathly backdrop. Luminous white pumice rocks, which seem almost living in context, dot the landscape. Most of those close to the road have been gathered to form messages. Some are for those who made them: "David ♥ Jessica." Others are for today only: "Go Rick!"

The sun chases Dave Scott, Mark Allen, Ken Glah, Mike Pigg, Yves Cordier, and Chris Hinshaw from behind while they pursue the only men left ahead of them, Wolfgang Dittrich and Rob Mackle. As Apollo drives his burning chariot ever higher above them, the air warms steadily, whisking any remaining salt water from their skin and leaching sweat from their bodies. The athletes suck greedily on the two or even three squeeze bottles they carry in cages on their bike frames: one on the downtube, a second on the seat tube, and perhaps a third behind the seat. These will be emptied and replaced multiple times in the next four hours.

Each man has his own special formula. This is still the Wild West era of ultraendurance nutrition. Everyone's experimenting. Mike Pigg drinks a sort of fruit smoothie from his bottle. Mark Allen sucks on a meal replacement shake diluted with extra water and spiked with added salt, as indicated by his recent testing at Duke University. Dave Scott carries a couple of bananas in his jersey pocket.

A mile up the road Wolfgang is drinking baby food and pulling away from Rob. The two men are well-matched cyclists, but whereas Rob is cautious, fearful of overextending himself in only his second Ironman, Wolfgang just wants to be left alone in the lead. He hates having other athletes around him on the bike. They are annoying. Their presence exerts an insidious pull that threatens to yank him out of his ideal rhythm.

Rob reads the interior signals of his body and concludes that although he could stay with Wolfgang, he'd better not. He lets the German drift ahead. After shaking off his tagalong companion of the past seventy-five minutes, Wolfgang pulls a Twix candy bar out of his jersey pocket and shoves it down his gullet.

With Rob now behind him, Wolfgang is left solitary. Here he is, the leader of the most important triathlon in the world, yet there is not a single race official present to guide him (not that he could possibly get lost on this simple out-and-back route) or a journalist to document his exploits. Meanwhile, a pod of media and official race vehicles—ABC cameras in vans, course marshals on mopeds, still photographers on motorcycles, print journalists in cars—has formed around Dave's group. There is a total consensus among them that Wolfgang Dittrich is a plucky but ultimately defenseless sheep straying helplessly toward the looming shadow of the slaughterhouse. He'll be dragged in soon enough. No need to go looking.

Cathy Plant, wife of race announcer Mike Plant, is working as a spotter and riding in the backseat of a convertible with three other Ironman officials. Her job is to repeatedly leapfrog ahead of the leader, whoever it may be, order the driver to pull over, start a watch when the leader passes, stop it when the chasers follow by, and then report the time gap back to her husband at the finish line and to the chasing cyclists themselves after her car catches them again. She stops at the twenty-mile point of the bike leg and notes a gap of 2:20, down from 3:00 at the start.

The slaughterhouse looms.

It doesn't take long for the gang of six to catch Rob Mackle and become seven. Rob does not lament his envelopment. Like everyone else, he knows that wherever Dave Scott is, that's where the race is. Although Dave's group is riding at least as fast as Wolfgang, whose pace Rob judged unsafe for himself, he doesn't want to fall any farther back than he has already, so he lifts his tempo and latches on. Unlike Wolfgang, Rob would much rather ride with a group, especially the group with all the cameras around it, than alone.

All six riders behind Dave are careful to stay at least seven meters off the back wheel of the next bike ahead, as the race's antidrafting rules require. Some believe there is nevertheless an advantage to being at the back of such a paceline. Not Dave. He steadfastly refuses to allow any of the other riders to get ahead of him, for he experiences an intolerable psychosomatic enervation whenever another athlete creeps in front of him. Nor does he covet the much-whined-about advantage of riding directly behind media vehicles, whose noxious exhaust he'd rather not inhale.

Mark shows no interest in leading the pack as the group burrows into the heart of the bike leg. He stays near the back as resolutely as Dave holds the front. While Dave snarls and gestures trucks out of his path, Mark keeps his eyes downcast. He seems almost tuned out, like a teenager at church or—almost the opposite—as one witness observes, as though he is praying. But it's really just a continuation of the silent withdrawal Mark retreated into in the days before the race. His efforts, or antiefforts, to conserve energy seem nearly superstitious in their absoluteness. One could imagine Mark catching himself holding too much tension in his fingers and consciously relaxing their hold on the bar ends, reminding himself that such waste could cost him the race. If he could ride with his eyes closed, he would. He appears very nearly unconscious as he is.

At twenty-four miles, the bike train and its hovering pod pass Waikoloa Beach Resort, a verdant oasis in the charred surrounding landscape. They are cheered by a smattering of spectators who have managed to

cannonball there from Kailua-Kona on the High Road, the Queen K being closed to normal vehicle traffic. With Dave setting a nearly vehicular
tempo of 27 mph, and with the route to this point via the High Road being
a few miles longer than the direct way on the Queen K, it takes good planning and vigorous driving to arrive ahead of the lead cyclists after watching the swim, and few fans bother trying, save the most interested. Among
those who took the chance and succeeded are half of Dave's circle of confidence: Verne and Anna Scott and Pat Feeney. Also present is Mark's entourage—Charlie Graves, Mike Rubano, Brian Hughes, and John Martin. These
men are fortunate to possess a VIP course pass and have been following
directly behind Mark and the others in their Jeep. A few minutes ago they
decided to shoot ahead and stop at Waikoloa to cheer, not realizing Dave's
people had already staked it out. The rival camps stand awkwardly apart,
shouting at their respective champions as they pass. The riders are within
earshot for all of fifteen seconds. Then they're gone. Forty minutes of dangerous driving for that.

Having no chance of beating the bikes via the High Road to Kawaihae, where Dave and his followers will turn onto a part of the course that
is inaccessible to nonofficial vehicles, Verne's group settles in to await the
athletes' return in a couple of hours. Mark's people, with their VIP placard,
could continue to follow the cyclists on the Queen K as far as Kawaihae,
but they decide to kill time with a swim at nearby Waikoloa Beach instead.
It's a long day.

BACK AT KAILUA PIER, a barrel-chested 49-year-old man is lifting his
rigid, emaciated 27-year-old son out of an inflated rubber raft. Dick Hoyt
swim-towed the raft, with 125-pound Rick Hoyt inside it, behind him in the
water for 2.4 miles. With an ABC camera aimed at him, Dick carries Rick
up the swim exit ramp and through the labyrinthine transition area, then
carefully sets him down in a forward-facing, hammock-like passenger seat
at the front of a specially made three-wheel bicycle.

Rick Hoyt was born with cerebral palsy. When he was an infant, a
specialist told Dick and his wife, Judy, "Forget about the boy. Put him in an
institution. He's going to be nothing but a vegetable the rest of his life."

They couldn't bear to do it. But they could scarcely bear the alternative of raising him.

"At first I wanted him to die," Judy admitted in an ABC interview, "so
I wouldn't have to deal with it."

By the time Rick was a toddler his parents had figured out that although he could not move or speak, the boy was no vegetable—there was absolutely nothing wrong with his mind. They had him outfitted with a computer that he could use to communicate, and with it he communicated perfectly well. The young Bostonian's first words were "Go, Bruins!"

The family struggled along until, at age 16, Rick asked his father to push him though a local 5K charity running race. Dick was not a runner, but he did it. Something magical happened over those three miles. Rick spoke to his father through the computer as soon as they got home. "When we were running, it felt like my disability disappeared," he said.

Dick felt it too. As strange a thing as it was to push his nearly grown boy through a running race, it seemed right—almost predestined. So he did it again, but went farther this time. And again, farther still. The father-son team quickly worked up to running full marathons. They not only went the distance but finished well toward the front of each race. Though he had the build of a plumber, Dick turned out to be a fine endurance athlete. Yet he had no interest in seeing what he could do alone and unburdened and swore he was faster with Rick than without him, anyway.

The Hoyts' exploits at the Boston Marathon and elsewhere garnered them heaps of press attention, which they never shied away from, and eventually they made the predictable move of establishing their own charitable foundation. But there was no end game. All they really wanted was to be able to keep running, because it gave Rick a life and Dick a stronger relationship with his child.

The mood of the two men is serious yet quietly celebratory as they prepare to hit the bike course. They have a long way to go. But they survived the swim, completing it with twenty minutes to spare before the cutoff time after having failed to make it in their first Ironman last year and having been forced to withdraw from the race. Valerie Silk has made a special rules exception to allow the pair to participate, but all other rules apply. Rick may receive no assistance (except medical help) from anyone other than his father, and, like everyone else in the race, the duo must reach the finish line by midnight or they will be pulled off the course once again. Dick shifts anxiously back and forth on his feet as he waits for a nurse to remove a catheter from his son's penis.

"Come on, come on!" he mutters, wearing an expression much like Dave Scott's twenty-eight miles up the road.

APPROACHING THIRTY MILES into the bike leg, Wolfgang still has not been caught. A course marshal decides he'd better scoot ahead to check on him. Minutes later the lone but not lonely German sees a motor scooter pull alongside him. The course marshal shouts something that he doesn't catch.

"What?" he shouts back.

"Don't draft!" the marshal repeats.

Wolfgang stares at him a moment, processing the words. He turns his head to look at the empty road in front of him. Then he looks at the marshal again.

Are you fucking kidding me?

He thinks these words but knows better than to say them. The retort would go over about as well as the same words spoken to a highway patrolman during a traffic stop.

At thirty-one miles Dave's group comes upon a Shimano Technical Support station set up at the roadside. Yves pulls himself out of the paceline and stops. He needs to get his shifters fixed before he starts the climb toward Hawi. He wouldn't have survived Dave's tempo much longer anyway. The lead chase group is thus reduced to six.

The landscape changes. As Dave's group draws near the hills crowding the northwest point of the Big Island, black and gold give way to brown and green; hardened lava spills are replaced by fields of low, dry grass. Already the terrain has become more undulant. The Queen K section of the Ironman bike course is considered the flat part, but it's only flat relative to the climb to Hawi. The thirty-two-mile stretch of pavement between Kailua-Kona and Kawaihae is in fact consistently rolling, thwarting racers' wish to hold a steady rhythm.

Dave now leads the pack up a bitch of a hill approaching the Route 270 intersection at Kawaihae, where, he knows, the other half of his circle of confidence awaits. He stands out of the saddle, forcing everyone else to do the same—everyone except Mark, who almost never stands to climb.

As Dave thrashes his way up the incline, Mark glides. The two men's riding styles contrast in more or less the same way their personalities do. While Mark rides with a quiet posture, in harmony with his machine, Dave wrestles his bike, lashes it along as though continuously punishing it for not going fast enough.

Chris Hinshaw cracks. He's been redlining ever since he latched on to this train, and now he's over the line and exploding. Each year at

Ironman Chris affixes a printout of the split times he hopes to hit at various points of the bike course to the top tube of his bike. When the group passed the twenty-five-mile point, they were seven minutes ahead of his schedule. He tore the printout off his bike and tossed it into the wind, knowing he was doomed. Lungs heaving, he now falls behind the other five like a sinking stone. With the climb toward Hawi approaching, it's only going to get worse. Chris will finish the bike leg sixteen minutes behind Dave and Mark. Next year the 1985 Ironman runner-up will quit the sport, having decided it's left him behind.

As he climbs Dave is struck by the thought that he has not actually seen Mark since the transition area. But he knows he's there. He can feel him. Mark has been as good as his promise to shadow his nemesis. Clearly he wants Dave to sense but not see him, as in the swim. He wants to be outside Dave's vision and inside his head.

If Dave were to suddenly lose his mind and launch into a full sprint less than halfway through the bike leg, and sustain it until he keeled over in exhaustion, taking himself out of the race, Mark would too.

If Dave were to stop dead in the middle of the road and refuse to continue unless Mark went before him, the two men would remain at that spot forever.

At least that's what Mark wants Dave to believe, and Dave almost believes it.

The group tops the hill and hits the Route 270 intersection, at thirty-three miles. Mike Norton and John Reganold are there. John cheers. Mike shouts out a time gap.

"One forty!" he calls.

Dave winces. They've pulled only forty seconds closer to Wolfgang in the past nine miles. Dave is galled by how little progress he's made despite almost dangerous efforts.

Immediately after the turn onto Route 270, the road drops steeply toward the Port of Kawaihae. The five men stop pedaling and crouch into their most aerodynamic positions, letting gravity drag them to speeds nearing 45 mph. At the base of the hill they bear right to stay on 270, and the road turns upward. The eighteen-mile climb to the turnaround point at Hawi has begun.

Dave stays seated but pushes the pedals with impatient force, aiming for a tempo that is slightly faster than Wolfgang's up the road. He figures catching Wolfgang before Hawi is a good game for the moment.

Heart rates climb; breathing deepens. Another match is lit, albeit a slow burner this time.

The ABC crew members are growing restless. They decide to send forward a woodie station wagon containing a cameraman and Mike Adamle, a broadcaster who used to play football and will later achieve his greatest fame as the host of *American Gladiators*, to get some footage of the surprising upstart, figuring Wolfgang has earned it.

On any given day mumuku winds roar through this part of the island. They come in violent, unpredictable gusts from the ocean, shoving riders left to right across the road as they climb toward Hawi and right to left during their subsequent descent. At a minimum, the mumuku are a nuisance, forcing athletes to pedal with tension held in every muscle as they brace for the next invisible shove. At worst, they are deadly. Cyclists are routinely blown clear off their bikes by sudden 60-mph gusts. In more than one instance riders have been forced to lean so far to one side to stay upright that a wheel edge has scraped the road, stripping the tire from the rim.

Today, however, the mumuku are unusually quiet. Only soft breezes blow in from the water. This happens twice a month or so—or once in every fifteen Ironmans. Mike Adamle has been told about the legendary mumuku and notices their absence as his van catches up with Wolfgang six miles into the climb.

"Not too much wind today, huh?" he shouts through an open window.

Conversation between athletes and reporters during competition is unthinkable in most sporting events, but at Ironman it has a rich tradition. It's a long day, and in a way everyone's in it together.

"No wind," Wolfgang answers. "It's all right. Maybe in two hours. We will see."

It's not only the language barrier that forces Wolfgang to speak like a caveman. He's climbing a tough hill at an aggressive tempo, standing out of the saddle and mashing on the pedals, pushing a massive gear at a low, diesel cadence of sixty revolutions per minute. But with the camera on him, he will spare what breath he can.

"How's your stamina at this point?" Adamle persists. "Pretty good?"

"Yeah," Wolfgang answers. "It's very good today. Good swim. Not *very* good, but good. Bike is okay."

"Are you aware of how close Dave Scott and Mark Allen are behind you?"

"How far?" Wolfgang asks, not sure he's understood the question.

"Yes. Are you aware?"

"Nah. It doesn't matter. I will make my race, and we will see."

The terrain that surrounds Wolfgang is nothing like the arid coastal plain he traveled through along the Queen K. He now pedals through fertile tropical highlands. Whereas the ride through the lava fields was totally exposed, the road here is intermittently banked on either side by hedges, earth mounds, and rock formations. Squat trees grow close to the roadway. Grassy hills rise into the distance on the inland side. Here and there a small pack of cattle or a solitary horse grazes on a hill. Wooden fences along the roadside mark the boundaries of ranches and are virtually the only signs of civilization. The ocean is intermittently visible to the left, falling farther below with each reappearance. Sunlight sparkles on the rippled surface of the sea. On any other day those ripples would be bearded with white foam, a warning to competitors to fear the mumuku on the way down.

The climb starts at sea level at the Port of Kawaihae and tops out at almost 700 feet of elevation in Hawi. There is a three-mile reprieve from the ascent roughly halfway up, where the road turns gently rolling before bending consistently upward again. If not for this break from the fight against gravity, 190-pound Rob Mackle would be in trouble. Climbing is not his forte, and he burns matches like a pyromaniacal 7-year-old through the heart of the climb. The reprieve affords him just enough recovery to stay in contact with the group, usurping Mark's place at the back of the caravan, all the way to the top.

Unable to resist, Dave sneaks a look back at Mark as they ascend. Mark quickly lowers his head so Dave can't see his face.

So that's how it's going to be, eh?

Fifty miles—the distance between Kailua-Kona and Hawi—is a long way, especially on an island as small as Hawaii. Hawi is a place unto itself, with no connection to Ironman's host city. Yet it's close enough for intervillage resentment. Hawi locals complain that, despite the event organizers' assurances, Ironman is not, in fact, good for business. Sure, a fair crowd assembles in Hawi on race day to see the bikes come through, but then the roads are closed to vehicle traffic and not a single new customer blows in after early morning. It's not as if the athletes pause to shop.

Hawi is tiny—little more than a main street with craft shops, boutiques, and homey restaurants packed into the space of a few blocks and serving a clientele that is almost exclusively tourists. There are other streets tucked behind the main, but the chamber of commerce prefers that they not be seen. Most of the town's residents, many of whom are mainlanders who moved here to "get away from it all," live in shacks; some in veritable shanties. Times have been hard in Hawi since the sugar industry went bust in the 1970s. Even the structures on the commercial strip show long neglect. Faded paint and sagging eaves add sad character to much of the nineteenth-century western colonial architecture.

Hawi is the sort of village where you're sure to see a mangy dog running loose in the middle of a street if you stay longer than fifteen minutes.

Wolfgang Dittrich's blue-and-green kit becomes visible at the edge of town. Now back in the aero position, he grinds toward a banner floating above the road and marking the turnaround point of the bike course. A few dozen spectators and an almost equal number of volunteers wearing light blue T-shirts greet his arrival. Closely following the scooter-riding course marshal who warned him against drafting, Wolfgang makes a hard left turn at a traffic cone onto a paved cul-de-sac that passes through a tiny park and dumps him back on Route 270 heading back the way he just came. He grabs a squeeze bottle from one volunteer but does not avail himself of the portable toilets. Like the other top contenders, he will urinate on the fly.

A full three minutes pass before Dave Scott's group follows, having seen Wolfgang making his way down. Wolfgang will later claim that he did not see Dave and the others approaching, so thick was the swarm of race and press vehicles around them, but that is a memory of convenience. In fact, all press vehicles except ABC's are stopped at Kawaihae and prevented from climbing to Hawi because the road is so narrow.

Dave winces anew when he makes the turn and learns that, far from erasing Wolfgang's remaining 1:40 advantage on the climb, he's allowed Wolfgang to nearly double it. Dave's blood boils, as though the leader has gone back on an earlier promise to cooperate.

The five riders in Dave's group grab their special-needs bags from volunteers. Each has his own chosen Ironman feast waiting for him. Rob's consists of two peanut-butter-and-guava-jelly sandwiches, a can of tomato juice, and a fruit smoothie. He takes both hands off the handlebars, sits up, and forces it all down as fast as he can.

The human body was not really designed to absorb food during exercise, but in an Ironman race the body must defy its nature and absorb food anyway. Completing an Ironman is a 10,000-calorie task. Without refueling on the go, it could be done only at a crawl. Some bodies absorb food energy during exercise better than others, and in Ironman this ability is almost as important as speed and endurance. Many a successful short-course triathlete has failed to make the jump to Ironman because his gastrointestinal system wasn't up to the challenge, even though his lungs and muscles were.

Mike Pigg's GI system works just fine, normally. Back in April, however, on his way to the America's Paradise Triathlon in St. Croix, he stopped in Texas to undergo some physiological testing and, while there, ate a bad hamburger. The intestinal parasite he acquired from the tainted meat has left him largely unable to absorb carbohydrates during exercise so that he now suffers from "runner's trots" whenever he tries to eat during long workouts and races. Lately Mike has had to plan routes for his long training runs around bathroom opportunities. He's doing okay so far, but he looks ahead to the run, where things usually get dicey, with dread.

Ken Glah has a different concern. He knows he can't run with Dave and Mark. To have any chance of winning, he has to get off the bike several minutes ahead of them. Although he doesn't look it, being tall and lanky like Mark, Ken is a power cyclist, a big-gear guy, stronger going down than up. The descent from Hawi to Kawaihae is therefore tactically his best chance to make a move. He puts himself in position by leading the train through the turnaround and hurriedly scarfing the contents of his special-needs bag. The moment the road turns downward, he gears up, lowers his head, and punches the accelerator. A gap opens. Mike makes the most serious effort to counter the move, as he too is a power rider and knows he must finish the bike leg ahead of Dave and Mark to win. Last year, in fact, Mike caught Ken from behind on the descent from Hawi. But today Ken is stronger, or more willing to burn matches, and he gets away. Some proper mumuku winds would help his cause, but he'll work with what he has.

Ken's best hope is to catch Wolfgang alone so the two of them can work together to reach transition ahead of Dave, Mark, Rob, and Mike. He won't know if his effort is succeeding until he gets a time-gap update when he turns back onto the Queen K, but he is indeed cutting into Wolfgang's advantage as he barrels toward Kawaihae at speeds exceeding 40 mph on the steeper declines. Unfortunately for Ken, his chasers are also pulling closer to Wolfgang, having silently agreed to work hard enough to keep Ken's margin in check.

Several media vehicles have sat parked on the dirt shoulder of the road at the Port of Kawaihae as their occupants waited for the race leaders to climb to Hawi and return. Now they see Ken Glah come screaming down the last descent and merge back onto the port access section of Highway 270. Among those who stopped and waited was *Triathlete*'s CJ Olivares, who has been a passenger on the back of a motorcycle with a bulky camera slung around his neck. Seeing Ken fly by, CJ leaps back into the saddle and taps the driver's back. The driver pulls out blindly and is immediately sideswiped by the station wagon carrying Mike Adamle. The Harley fishtails as it rebounds back onto the dirt shoulder, and it's all the driver can do to keep it upright.

This kind of thing can happen at any time, not just to journalists but also to racers, whose awareness of such ever-present danger causes them to ride in an uninterrupted state of low-grade mental stress. Later today Lisa Laiti, a top female pro, will collide with a car on her bike and break her neck.

Ken starts up the nasty hill from the Port of Kawaihae to the Queen K just fifteen seconds ahead of his chasers—not enough, given his relative weakness as a climber. By the time he reaches the top, he has been swallowed up.

"Two thirty!" Mike Norton shouts at Dave as the re-formed group passes. Wolfgang's up-and-down lead is coming down again.

As soon as they've completed the turn onto the Queen K, Mike Pigg moves to the front and ratchets up the tempo. Mike is as gutsy as any athlete in the sport, and although he doesn't feel great, he's still racing to win. The weakest runner in the group besides the behemoth Rob Mackle, he has to take his shot now. And he has the chops to do it. There isn't a triathlete in the world who can match Mike's top-end speed on the bike. In April 1988 he rode perhaps the greatest bike leg in the history of the sport, outsplitting all rivals, including Dave, Mark, and even Lance Armstrong, by more than seven minutes on the grueling 58-mile course in St. Croix, which includes a hill known as the Beast.

Mike pulls hard for a few miles, but he's unable to achieve any separation. Dave refuses to let him go, Mark refuses to let Dave go, and Rob and Ken are just hanging on. Like Mark, Mike wears a heart rate monitor. His Ironman heart rate is 165 beats per minute. If he goes any higher, he's burning matches. Mike checks his monitor and sees he's lighting matches by twos and threes, and to no avail. He eases up, and Dave moves back to the front of the train.

Rising heat ripples the air above the road in front of the group. It's almost eleven o'clock. The sun has moved high overhead. The day continues to heat up—80 degrees and climbing.

By this time most of the other athletes in the race have passed Dave's train coming the opposite way. There now approaches a strange bike with three wheels bearing a young man whose body is locked and twisted and who wears an openmouthed grin, catching a ride on a hammock-like seat in front of a barrel-chested pedaler.

Dave and Mark and the others watch the Hoyts with mild interest as they pass. The father-son team will not finish until well after dark, but they will finish. Dick's total lack of desire to race except as his son's workhorse is a world away from Dave's consuming need to see what his body can do and to prove himself able to outlast anyone. Dick's utterly selfless support of his son's brave but pitiable athletic ambitions is a world away from Ken Allen's neglect of his son and subsequent efforts to hitch his wagon to Mark's star. Yet here they are, in the same race, all belonging equally in their own ways, each getting what he alone needs from the challenge.

WOLFGANG'S PURSUERS have now ridden seventy-five miles. If anyone in this group is going to make a move that has a meaningful effect on the race, it must happen soon. But Ken and Mike have already given their best shots and failed to escape. It's obvious that Mark will not initiate anything. Nothing is expected of Rob, who after all started the bike leg three minutes ahead of the other four. It's all on Dave. Either he goes or no one does. Meanwhile, Wolfgang continues to ride frequently out of sight ahead, although easily tracked from behind by the helicopter floating above him.

At eighty miles the group returns to the Waikoloa Road intersection. Dave's supporters are still there. Pat Feeney started a watch when Wolfgang passed and now shouts out the gap: "Three minutes!"

Golly! Dave thinks. *This is ridiculous. Who the heck does that crazy Euro think he is?* Underneath his anger, Dave knows it doesn't matter. Wolfgang won't survive long on the run even with a three-minute lead off the bike. But still.

The hills of the Queen K are bigger on the way back to Kailua-Kona than on the way out. At least they feel bigger. A slow leak of fatigue has sprung in all five members of Dave's pack. Exhaustion is still many miles away, but none feels as fresh as he did charging up Pay-'n'-Save Hill. Every turn of the pedals is now experienced as something like the sixth repetition in a set of ten machine leg extensions. But all perceptions are relative, and Dave feels fantastic relative to this point in past Ironmans. He has matches to burn, and his confidence inflates as he fingers them in his pocket.

The biggest hill on the Queen K section of the course comes at eighty-four miles. It ascends more than 250 feet at a steady grade of 7 percent. When Dave reaches the base of the climb, he jumps out of the saddle and launches. It's a serious move, requiring the others to show their cards. Mark is ready and counters with apparent ease. Mike and Ken lose ground initially but are able to hang on. Rob, his meaty butt still in the saddle, teeters at the brink of freefall at the back. Dave sees none of this, and doesn't need to see. He can assess the damage later. Right now he needs to inflict it.

As he reaches the summit of the hill, Ken cranes his neck to the left and vomits. Throwing up is never done more nonchalantly than in an Ironman. Stomach emptied, Ken calmly returns to his aero position and chases after Dave and Mark. A mile farther down the road, and another match poorer, he regains contact. Mike and, eventually, Rob follow.

Ninety miles into the bike leg the five men in Dave's group can't wait to get it over with, including the two—Mike and Rob—who dread the run. Their butts are killing them. No matter how often they ride 100 miles in training, athletes' bodies never fully adapt to passing four or five hours hunched in a near-fetal posture, with 60 percent of their body weight supported by a three-inch strip of tender flesh between the private parts and the butt crack, so that the perineum and low back scream always for relief in the final miles of such a journey. Rob is especially uncomfortable. He has spondylosis, degenerative arthritis in his L3 vertebra, and must stand and stretch frequently to slow the steady intensification of pain in his low back.

The last big hill comes at ninety-six miles, about eight miles outside town, just before the airport. As Dave leads the approach toward the base of the 200-foot rise, the four men behind him are asking themselves, *Will he do It again?*

He does. As abruptly as a stalking cat pounces at an unsuspecting field mouse, Dave leaps out of the saddle and crushes his pedals. This is his last chance to soften up Mark before the run, and he's going to make the most of it. Ken cracks almost immediately; he leans over and barfs a second time. Pigg tells his heart rate monitor to go to hell and chases with everything he has. Given the choice between staying within his known physiological limits and staying in the race, he will always choose to risk all and fight.

Despite his abandonment of all caution, Pigg loses ground. Rob lifts his tempo enough to prevent a cataclysmic time hemorrhage but stops short of crossing the red line, knowing he'll be left behind on the run soon enough anyway. Dave and Mark have been together all morning, but for the first time in this race they are *alone* together as they pull away from their longtime traveling partners.

CJ Olivares, none the worse for his recent collision with Mike Adamle's station wagon, observes the moment from the back of his motorcycle and appreciates its significance.

Here we go!

Again Dave does not see the immediate effect of his surge, but he senses that one and only one rider has been able to respond, and he knows it's Mark. He can't fool himself any longer. He wishes to hell he could see the guy and assess his status. If only he could observe Mark's body language. Is he starting to rock from side to side? Are there any soft spots in his pedal stroke? Is he coasting at any point because he's tired or his low back hurts? If any of these things is happening, it would be helpful to Dave to know it. If not, it's just as well that he doesn't know.

Dave can't help himself. He looks back. Mark lowers his head.

No chance, Dave.

Ahead, Wolfgang has also started to struggle. His ascent of the same hill minutes ago brought his supply of matches critically low. He has made the dreadful discovery that, through a combination of being alone, off the front, inexperienced, under the spotlight, and naturally aggressive, he rode just a little—maybe 1 percent—too hard. And now he's carrying an anvil on his back, pedaling in squares, pumping his torso in rhythm with his legs to compensate for their loss of power. Adding insult to injury, the winds have finally picked up and are coming stiffly from the south—straight into Wolfgang's face. His lead is coming down again, and this time there's no chance of a rebound. The last twelve miles to the Kona Surf Hotel will be an eternity for him.

At the top of the hill, Dave dials back the intensity just a bit. He's done what he can do. It's going to come down to the run. But he still feels strong, and there's no reason to make it easy for anyone else. Mike Pigg continues to execute his strategy of staying with the leaders as long as possible, which, given his present state of depletion, amounts to clinging to a ten-second deficit like driftwood behind Dave and Mark. Rob is another ten seconds back and grateful that the last big hill is behind him. Ken vomits one more time for good measure after topping the hill last of the five.

Dave and Mark pass a sign marking the ninety-nine-mile point of the bike leg. It sits at the base of Palani Hill, at the very spot Mark has chosen to break Dave in the marathon should they reach that place together three hours from now. As he whizzes past it, Mark cannot help but cast his mind ahead to that possible moment, as he has done dozens of times already in the preceding days.

The hill tops out some 300 yards from Palani Road and then descends gently toward the intersection. This is where Dave plans to pull away from Mark in the marathon, if it comes to that—if he can't somehow finish Mark off sooner.

But the bike course does not go there. Instead, just beyond the ninety-nine-mile sign, Dave and his followers turn right onto Kaiwi Street, which takes them into the heart of the warehouse district on the outskirts of town and past B & L, the shop where Mark got his bike fixed on Tuesday. Three blocks down they turn left onto Kuakini Highway. Moments later they zip through the intersection at Palani Road, just one block above the pier, where it all started. A sizable crowd of spectators—the first since Hawi—is gathered there and makes a joyful noise as they pass. Three blocks farther on, Dave and Mark lean hard to the right and turn onto Hualalai Road, in the heart of town. More alley than avenue, it drops them quickly down to Ali'i Drive and the Hot Corner. The crowd is massive and raucous, having been expertly fomented by rookie secondary race announcer Mike Reilly, and by libations in the case of many. The mob, which for a long time had little to entertain it besides thumping music and Mike's infrequent race updates from the field, was primed to fever pitch by Wolfgang's passage through a little more than two minutes ago. Now, as the two titans of Ironman come into sight, everyone goes berserk. The noise is so great that it pains the ears of its chief objects as they accelerate savagely from the top of the block, brake just enough, and then lean hard left to make the turn onto Ali'i Drive.

Dave and Mark now head south through the most urban portion of the bike course, blazing between two-story wooden buildings containing restaurants, jewelry shops, clothing boutiques, and knickknack stores. Spectators line the street thickly for a few blocks, but their presence dwindles as Dave and Mark move swiftly away from the village center. They pass through an area of resort hotels and condominiums, including Sea Village, where Dave woke up seven hours ago, and then into more residential and vegetated surroundings.

As they approach one house on the water side, Dave's eyes alight on a man lying faceup on a fully reclined lounge chair. He is shirtless, and his exposed, freshly sunburned belly is distended like a bullfrog's throat pouch. A pile of empty beer cans surrounds him.

The commotion of Dave and Mark's advance seems to wake the man from a drunken slumber. His head snaps up. His eyes bulge as they work to focus. Dave makes a mental note that he will see this character again a couple of miles into the run.

The last hill climb on the Ironman bike course falls between 110 and 111 miles, as Ali'i Drive veers away from the water. It is short but very steep. Wolfgang's legs burn terribly as he climbs it with atrocious form, flopping all over his bike in an effort to find unused muscles to take him the rest of the way. At the top he follows Ali'i as it bends right to run along a ridge above the water. He passes the Kona Country Club, half of its green holes to his left, half to his right, and then turns right onto Ehukai Street. He plunges down a hill that is the mirror image of the climb that burned the last match he had left for this segment of the race and sweeps into the vast parking lot of the Kona Surf Hotel. A race official hastens to meet him at the bike dismount line and holds his handlebar steady as he shakily climbs off. A race clock positioned there displays the cumulative race time: 5:27:17.

Two legs down, one to go. Wolfgang Dittrich still leads the 1989 Ironman World Championship.

A large, party-minded crowd has gathered at the bike-run transition area, creating a scene and an energy not unlike those of a Tour de France stage finish. Wolfgang receives a nice welcome, but the crowd explodes when Dave Scott and Mark Allen race in together one minute fifty-one seconds later.

Mark's bike split is 4:37:52, third fastest in the history of the race.

Dave's bike split is 4:37:53.

Mike Pigg comes in ten seconds behind them, Rob Mackle eleven seconds after Mike, and a somewhat recovered and refueled Ken Glah forty-nine seconds after Rob.

Mike Plant has come down from the finish-line tower to lead the celebration. His steady microphone chatter trails off as he watches Dave and Mark tear into the transition area almost on top of each other. He can feel what's coming.

CHAPTER 10

VISION QUEST

Success is counted sweetest
by those who never succeed.

— EMILY DICKINSON

D ave Scott and Mark Allen are stark naked, in close proximity, for the second time today.

Upon dismounting from their bikes a moment ago, Dave just ahead of Mark, the two men dashed inside the Keauhou IV Conference Room of the Kona Surf Hotel's detached convention center building, which has been requisitioned to serve as the men's bike run transition changing room. It is everything that the racecourse they've just left and will soon return to is not. gloomily lit, softly carpeted, air conditioned. As race volunteers wheeled their bikes over to racks set up to accommodate more than a thousand bikes in the multiacre hotel parking lot, Dave and Mark ripped off their cycling clothes (Mark also removing his heart rate monitor strap, which he does not wear for the run), their movements frantic, as though the race were certain to be decided by tenths of a second.

They now tear open their transition bags and pull on their running shorts, shoes, singlets, and headwear. (Dave dons a visor, Mark a cap.) Mark is first to burst out of the refrigerated semidarkness of Keauhou IV and reenter the stifling heat and midday glare of the island day. He runs like a fugitive through a gauntlet of clamoring spectators besieging a roped-off path that cuts across the parking lot. Dave emerges seconds later and accelerates to a near sprint, panicked by Mark's novel position ahead of him. As Mark reaches out to grab a cup of Exceed sports drink from a volunteer at an aid station located within the confines of the parking lot, Dave nearly clips Mark's opposite elbow with his own in passing him—whether accidentally or intentionally, only he knows.

Having overtaken Mark, Dave does not relax but persists at a pace that seems certain to leave him completely out of gas within a couple of miles if he keeps it up. Mark watches Dave pull away and finds himself momentarily paralyzed in disbelief. Gathering his wits, Mark begins hauling after him. By the time they escape the hotel grounds onto Ehukai Street, the pair is shoulder to shoulder and locked in a rash game of back-and-forth speed one-upping. Grip has cast aside the gamesmanship of following Dave on the bike and now refuses to let Dave nose ahead, no matter how reckless his tempo. The most knowledgeable spectators among the roaring hundreds lining the road on both sides wonder if the rivals have lost their minds. Their pace is unsustainable by a long shot.

Have Dave and Mark become so lost in their lust to destroy each other that they now risk destroying themselves?

Not quite. They know what they're doing—or at least what they're feeling. As they tear through the first quarter mile of the marathon, both men are gauging the status of their legs. It is a moment of truth. After four and a half hours of hard cycling, a triathlete's legs will inevitably be sore, stiff, and heavy, causing the transition to running to lack coordination; nonetheless, he can feel right away whether he's going to have a bad run or a good one. With a surge of confidence, Mark discovers that his legs feel better than they ever have after the Ironman bike leg. This realization gives him the courage to match Dave's crazy tempo. Beside him, Dave detects the same sensations in his own legs, and so, with a kind of sadistic delight, he forges ahead with his pre-race plan to terrify Mark into mentally imploding with a vicious early run pace. Mark is, in fact, astonished and alarmed by what Dave is doing, but he would sooner die than let him go.

Just like the bike leg, the run leg begins with a demoralizing climb—an eighth of a mile at a 9 percent grade up Ehukai Street, from the Kona Surf parking lot to Ali'i Drive. Yet Dave and Mark seem to flatten the hill as they stampede heavenward with huge, ballistic strides, thwarting the course designers' malicious aims. The spectators clap and holler with special fervor, a glint of rapture in their faces. The stunning velocity of the running, the naked ferocity of the struggle, the mythical status of the men—all of this against the backdrop of their singular rivalry: It is almost too perfect. More than a few watchers find themselves laughing with delight.

"Dad, it's like a movie!" says one 12-year-old boy as the runners pass.

At the top of the hill the warriors turn left onto Ali'i, retracing the route by which they arrived at the Kona Surf on their bikes a short time ago. An escort forms around them as they cut due north along a ridge some 200 feet above the water. Leading it is the station wagon carrying Mike Adamle and his ABC crew, which is followed by a white Ford flatbed truck bearing photographers and writers. Immediately in front of Dave and Mark are a scooter carrying a course marshal and a convertible bearing four race officials, including Mike Plant's wife, Cathy, who continues her work as a spotter. Behind the runners is a white Jeep with Mark's support crew—Charlie Graves, Brian Hughes, Mike Rubano, and John Martin. And, hanging at the very back of the escort, as inconspicuously as possible, are two men on mopeds: Dave's pals John Reganold and Mike Norton.

Cathy Plant checked her stopwatch at the start of the marathon, and she checks it again now to get a split for the first mile: 5:55. She communicates the split to her husband, who remains back at the Kona Surf parking lot, by two-way radio.

"You mean 6:55," he corrects.

After all, this was Scott Molina's average pace for the marathon in his winning effort last year.

"No, 5:55."

"Holy smokes! And they're running side by side?"

"Side by side."

"Wow. Fantastic."

"Mike . . ." She pauses, groping for the right words. "I wish you could see this."

The tone of Cathy's voice sends a shiver down Mike's spine. Mike shares the information with the crowd, which is briefly hushed by the report. They sense it too.

By now Dave and Mark have shaken off their cycling legs and found their normal running strides, which are as unalike as almost everything else about them. Mark's, as always, looks fluid and efficient. He scuttles lightly forward with minimal vertical displacement, like a Jesus lizard on water. Dave runs with fists clenched, chest protruding, low back arched, butt sticking out, knees splayed wide, and feet flared. His form is as gangly and unorthodox as Mark's is graceful and textbook. But he goes just as fast.

There's a lovely view of the Pacific Ocean over the two men's left shoulders. But their eyes are focused on the aid station they're approaching on the west side of the road. Running at Mark's left shoulder, Dave has easier access to the cups. Mark, on the other hand, must slow down and merge left to get his. Having slaked his thirst, he must then surge to catch Dave. It's a sequence that wastes only a small amount of energy in a single instance but could become a decisive drain if repeated every mile or so throughout the marathon.

Both runners slow down as little as possible for these exchanges, each preferring to risk missing a pass or sending a cup flying to the ground than to sacrifice an inch to the other. Fortunately, the aid stations are long—about fifty yards—and well staffed, with redundant numbers of volunteers at each, allowing Dave and Mark more than one opportunity to grab a cup. Some are filled with Exceed and others with water, which they alternately gulp and pour over their heads. There are also specially designed plastic bottles of decarbonated Coca-Cola.

It's impossible to breathe and drink at the same time. Dave and Mark are breathing hard enough that even briefly halting their respiration to swallow some liquid causes them to gasp through several breath cycles afterward as their lungs scramble to catch up with the backlog of demand for oxygen. Despite the hassle and the discomfort, both men grab as many cups as they can in those fifty yards—four and five apiece.

A quarter mile past the aid station the road turns sharply to the left and immediately plunges precipitously toward the shore, sending Dave and Mark hurtling down a hill very much like the one they climbed a mile earlier, leaving the Kona Surf. Running downhill is infinitely worse than running uphill in these circumstances. Each foot strike sends a sharp jolt of pain through the quadriceps muscles, which worked as prime movers for four and a half hours on the bike and now, on the run, serve as the body's primary shock absorbers, accommodating forces equal to seven or eight times Dave's and Mark's individual body weights as they barrel down the decline at 14 mph.

Something about Dave's odd stride gives him a preternatural gift for downhill running, and he steamrolls ahead of Mark by a few paces as they drop toward shore level and then make a hard right to begin a five-mile journey into downtown Kailua-Kona along the coast. But within 100 yards of the road's flattening out, Mark is again hip to hip with his rival.

They pass the Kona Surf and Racquet Club, a large complex of condominiums and townhomes that is a popular choice for Iron Week accommodations because of its twenty-five-meter outdoor pool. A crowd of friends and family members of racers staying there erupts as the heroes pass at a breathtaking pace with their escort.

They pass the Outrigger Hotel, a multistory luxury hotel for those with a little more money to spend. Another small crowd of spectators is left with hands on mouths.

The runners pass a white sign with a big red "2" printed upon it. Mark checks his stopwatch, sees they have run another mile in less than six minutes, and thinks, *Whatever.* Dave wears no watch and is pacing himself completely by feel.

Just ahead on the left, Dave spies the shirtless, beer-swilling dude he saw sprawled out on a reclining lawn chair earlier. He is now perilously awake and standing at the edge of his driveway, shouting nonsense at the cyclists (lesser male pros) trickling through in the opposite direction. The commotion of Dave and Mark's motorcade behind him grabs his attention. He turns, blinks twice, and a look of recognition seizes his face, then a look of inspiration. As the runners pass him, the barefoot drunk breaks from the curb and gives thundering chase. Arms pumping wildly, he draws up beside Dave and bellows, "Come on, guys! Pick it up!" There is no one to stop him—no security detail among the course officials and journalists and friends of Dave and Mark in the convoy. Their only way of escaping their tormentor is to outrun him, which, fortunately, they need all of ten seconds to do.

"Where's the fire?" is his parting shot.

As it wends its way toward town, Ali'i Drive curves gently left and right along the contours of the coast, undulates up and down, and is closely bordered by lush vegetation on both sides. The view ahead is thus usually limited to a couple of hundred yards. But there comes a moment when the street straightens and flattens out enough to reveal Wolfgang Dittrich, the race leader for almost six hours, ahead.

Blood in the water.

Dave instinctively, needlessly presses even harder. He cannot help himself. A runner ahead is like a terrible itch that can be relieved only by a quick overtaking. Mark surges smoothly with him, thinking, *If I go down, let me take him with me.*

Approaching another aid station, Mark makes a surprising and clearly calculated move. Instead of easing behind Dave and merging left to take his drinks, he bolts ahead and cuts across, stealing the inside position for this and subsequent aid stations on Ali'i Drive. Dave briefly considers trying to wrest it back at the next opportunity but decides not to waste his energy on such small tactics. He has been granting Mark the little advantages all day—allowing him to ride his wake in the swim, to hide out on the bike—trusting that the race will be decided by one big advantage in his favor: a stronger will. No reason to change his mind about that now. *Go ahead, Mark. Knock yourself out.*

Between three and four miles, Dave and Mark pull close enough behind Wolfgang that their scooter escort and the ABC camera car must leapfrog the leader to clear the gap for the coming pass. Upon seeing these vehicles join his own escort, Wolfgang looks back and spots his chasers. *Already?* The German knew he would be passed eventually, but he did not anticipate losing his two-minute lead in less than four miles.

Dave and Mark blow by Wolfgang. He's running well by his standards, but the brutal swiftness of his eclipse leaves him feeling deflated. It's as if he has been removed not only from first place but from the race itself—forced to turn in his race number and catch a ride back to the pier in the backseat of a police cruiser as the crowds lining the street hurl taunts. Running a full 2 mph faster than Wolfgang, Dave and Mark leave him behind as quickly as a window shopper leaves behind a dropped scarf.

Cathy Plant again radios her husband.

"Dave and Mark just took the lead."

"Still side by side?"

"Still side by side."

"Man, oh, man!"

The new race leaders now run past Pahoehoe Beach Park, the site where CJ Olivares saw Dave running on Wednesday morning and was inspired to change his race prediction. More park than beach, it consists of a manicured lawn shaded by a few palm trees fronting a lava-rock beach that is hidden on the far side of a knee-high stone wall. Children are playing in the park, oblivious to their near brush with history in the making.

The occasional mongoose skitters across the road in front of the runners. Life goes on.

DAVE CONTINUES TO PRESS a torrid pace. Worry creeps into Mark's mind. He still feels decent, but it won't be long before this mad effort begins to exact an awful toll. Reason tells him Dave will have to pay the same price, so surely he will relent. But another voice says, *Maybe not. Maybe not.*

One of the larger hills on Ali'i leads the pair to the six-mile point. As they blast upward, Mark becomes conscious of an incipient hot spot on the ball of his right foot—an area of throbbing warmth caused by friction between his wet sock and the sole of his shoe. With twenty miles left to run, this hot spot is almost certain to become a gory, excruciating blister. His worry deepens.

The Sea Village Resort stands at the top of the hill on the left. Among the smattering of spectators standing before it is a young woman with straight blond hair who wears bright yellow running shorts and holds an infant in her arms. Anna hoists Ryan toward his father as Dave passes.

"'Go, Daddy! Go, Daddy!'" she shouts on Ryan's behalf as she hops up and down like a first grader at a parade.

Mark Allen notices almost nothing peripheral when he races. (He will, for example, retain no memory of the drunken local running along-side him and shouting in his ear.) But he notices this. In the intensity of the moment it seems as if the child's head is bouncing on its delicate neck like a bobblehead. Without a second's premeditation, Mark turns to Dave and says the only words either man will speak to the other all day.

"Hey, that's not fair!" he jokes.

The surprise of hearing Mark's voice causes Dave to reflexively turn his head in the other man's direction, but he catches himself quickly and reverses the movement without uttering a syllable in reply. Behind the silent treatment Dave secretly analyzes his foe's unexpected outburst. What information can he extract from it? On the one hand, the fact that Mark would not only speak but crack a joke tells him that Mark feels strong, per-haps so strong that he can't keep a poker face. On the other hand, the sheer frivolousness of the remark tells Dave he's perhaps dealing with the same goofy "kid brother" who asked if he wanted to go for a run after the bike ride in the moment of their first meeting in the October 1982 Ironman. If so, then Mark remains vulnerable in the same way he was then, and has been ever since, in this particular race. Dave knows how to humble Mark on this island.

Not a minute after Dave receives his wife's encouragement, Julie Moss zips by in the other direction on her bike. She is currently in third place in the women's race, ten minutes behind two-time and defending champion Paula Newby-Fraser.

"Go, Mark!" she shouts, her heart leaping in hope and fear, for few sights could be more simultaneously hopeful and fear-provoking than that of Mark sharing the lead with Dave Scott at this point in the race.

Mark says nothing.

Just beyond the seven-mile point Dave and Mark return to the Hot Corner, the intersection of Ali'i Drive and Hualalai Road. The massive crowd there has been thrown into a state of fevered anticipation by Mike Reilly's announcement of the recent lead change, and it detonates as the two enemies make the right turn and shoot up the hill toward Kuakini Highway.

"Here are your new race leaders!" Reilly booms over the loudspeakers. "Dave Scott and Mark Allen! This could be a race for the ages!"

A traffic cop who is supposed to be controlling the crowd, keeping motor vehicles off the course, and pointing athletes in the right direction completely forgets himself, jumping up and down and hollering like a Pentecostal overcome by the Holy Ghost. As a result of his dereliction, the crowd presses within inches of Dave and Mark on both sides as they bank through the corner, their clothes visibly dripping with sweat and water. The short hill to Kuakini Highway does little to slow them. Their heels nearly strike their butts with each swing-through as they ascend, like milers kicking on the final straight.

Two minutes pass before Wolfgang appears. Mike Pigg trudges through next, looking like he needs a toilet. Closing quickly behind him is Ken Glah, who has received regular updates on his time deficit from spectators and, after overcoming his initial disbelief, has resigned himself to racing for third place.

At Kuakini Highway, Dave and Mark turn left and, still soaking up the shouts and applause of the thick downtown crowds, run three blocks to Palani Road. There they turn right and rumble up Pay-'n'-Save Hill, pressed as tightly together as runners in a three-legged race, despite the generous width of the street. Standing at the eight-mile point near the top of the hill is Pat Feeney, who arrived from the Kona Surf, where he last saw Dave, with little time to spare despite his mechanical advantage. He presses the lap button on the watch he started back at the second transition. 58:24. Like most physicists, Pat is good with figures, and he quickly does the math: 5:48 per mile through the first eight miles of the marathon. *Jesus.*

As the runners turn left onto the Queen K and head for the lava fields, Dave finally gears down. Slightly. Mark gratefully does the same. Dave's bid to blow Mark's mind, or legs, or whatever in the first third of the marathon has failed. He must now consolidate his remaining resources and wait for the right moment to make his next big move. Their pace slips toward 6:15 per mile, which is still faster than the best average pace ever run at Ironman and still more than thirty seconds per mile faster than anyone behind them is running.

The road now leads the two men up the gentle ramp of Palani Hill, at the top of which they are given the same gut-punching view of the lava fields below that hit them this morning before they descended into the inferno on their bikes. It is now approaching one thirty in the afternoon—the hottest time of day. The mercury has risen to 88 degrees. A ceiling of clouds has begun to creep over the inland hilltops and toward the coast. Dave and Mark are sweating a liter of fluid every half hour. Their core body temperatures have climbed to 103 degrees.

Eighteen years from this day, the Chicago Marathon will be canceled midrace when the temperature soars into the mid-80s. Pandemonium will break out as runners collapse left and right. But here, now, at Ironman, in even more severe weather conditions, Dave and Mark just deal with it. As do those behind them. Only 55 of the race's 1,286 starters will fail to finish. It's all about expectations—hell's a bit more bearable when you always knew you were going there.

The aid stations on this section of the course sit on the right side of the road, whereas on Ali'i they sat on the left. At the base of Palani Hill, Dave and Mark hit another aid station, and Mark craftily cuts across again to reclaim the inside position. Dave again lets him have it, dropping behind Mark and merging right to take drinks from the outstretched hands of volunteers.

All Ironman volunteers undergo a day of training before the race. Those assigned to drink stations are taught that there are two effective ways to hand drinks to passing runners. One is to stand still and hold the cup under the base by the fingertips, leaving almost the entire surface area of the container available for the athlete to wrap his hand around. The other is to start running in the same direction the athlete is traveling, just before he reaches you, so that the pass from hand to hand can be made at a relative speed of zero, as in a track-and-field relay baton pass. For whatever reason, only a minority of volunteers manages to get it right. And the odds of a bad pass are greatest for the race leaders, because they arrive at each aid station before the volunteers have had a single opportunity to practice their technique—and also because volunteers become awestruck and forget their jobs.

It's even worse for Dave, as Mark, being the first man through, steals the attention of the volunteers, leaving them even less ready for the second man. Dave has gotten precious little to drink at a couple of aid stations already, thanks to botched handoffs, so he chooses to assert himself at this one.

"Run with me!" he shouts at a woman volunteer standing ten yards ahead of him who represents his last chance to get a cup at this aid station.

She flinches like a student startled out of a daydream but remains otherwise motionless, having failed to understand Dave's command.

Too late. He's now upon her and forced to do what he didn't want to do—attempt to snatch the cup from her unmoving hand, which is wrapped around the container in a vise grip. Sure enough, the cup sails to the ground and skitters along the hot pavement.

"Come on, lady, run with me!" Dave yells back at the woman, who still holds a cup in her other hand, as he speeds away without even a suggestion of easing up.

The volunteer snaps to attention and sprints after Dave, whose only effort to help her help him is to reach back toward her outstretched arm like God reaching toward David on the ceiling of the Sistine Chapel. When Dave catches a glimpse of her footwear—pumps—he knows it's hopeless. Moments later the woman flags and quits, looking for a hole in the ground, conscious of having failed to sustain for thirty yards the pace Dave has held for eleven miles *after* five and a half hours of prior high-intensity exercise. Dave turns his attention to catching Mark, cursing his burning thirst.

Mark is beginning to have problems of his own. Despite the settling of the pace, he is becoming increasingly uncomfortable. The whole hard day is catching up with him. They have passed through the ugly industrial area on the outskirts of town and plunged into the dark heart of the lava sprawl. Like a living thing, this landscape threatens Mark—reminding him of all the pain and heartbreak it has caused him in past years. He feels as helpless in the face of its terrible power as a dreamer inside a nightmare. The hot black rock floor seems to scoff at Mark's offering at Heiau Kuemanu. Suddenly Mark realizes nothing has changed. He was fooling himself. He has no quarter here. He's doomed. At the same time Mark feels a new strength emanating from Dave. He can feel his opponent's will, and it feels like a wall.

They pass the midpoint of the marathon. To the right loom the reeking garbage piles of the town dump. Bad thoughts enter Mark's mind. The old voice of doubt, the hated tape loop of fear.

He's too strong.

He'll never crack.

Thirteen miles to go, and I'm already dying.

It's only going to get worse.

I've lost again.

I don't have what it takes to win this race.

I will never win this race!

A downward spiral has begun. Mark is abruptly aware that he is boiling inside. *Was it this hot a minute ago?* His legs have turned to lead. He's light-headed. The noxious stench of the dump assaults his nostrils and somehow intensifies his vertigo. Energy drains from his body like blood from a knife gash. A flu-like weakness has overtaken him from head to toe. His blistering right foot is on fire. It feels as though the skin has been peeled off and his foot has been dipped in a vinegar bath. His thoughts are scrambled. The taunting voice in his head stops making sense, then falls silent. He now lacks the energy to think a single thought. Mark is conscious only of suffering and the desire to suffer no more. He is a zombie, a shackled man in a burning prison.

Suddenly Mark catches a glimpse of something out of the corner of his right eye. Appearing first as a blur of color, the image coalesces to form a vitreous face hovering above the lava field. The vision does not shock him. His weary mind occupies the dream state of awareness that is surprised by nothing. He recognizes the face of the elderly shaman he saw in a magazine two days ago. It wears the same beatific expression that arrested him then, an expression that communicates pure happiness and unspoiled inner peace.

Mark rotates his head to get a square look at the face, but when he does, it vanishes. He turns his eyes back to the road ahead, and the image instantly returns in his peripheral vision.

Somehow, despite Mark's incredible suffering and despair, he feels his spirit absorbing the joy and acceptance that emanate from the shaman's countenance. At first Mark merely discerns what the old man is feeling; then he feels it himself. A sense of peace washes over him, not displacing his pain but enabling him to accept it. A new monologue enters his mind.

How cool is this?

I'm leading Ironman with Dave Scott with twelve miles to go!

Win or lose, this is an amazing experience.

Anyone else in the race would kill to be where I am now, so what the hell am I complaining about?

I'm going to enjoy this moment as best I can.

Yes, I'm hurting, but Dave is too. I can still win.

And if I don't, so be it.

There's more to life.

No sooner has Mark given up, in a sense, than he begins to feel his energy return—some of it, anyway. That verge-of-fainting feeling dissipates. A bit of strength, perhaps just enough, is restored to his legs. Hope seeps back into his spirit.

Second winds happen all the time in triathlon. Athletes routinely overcome bad patches. Traditional exercise science, with its exclusion of the brain, cannot explain the phenomenon, which is obviously brain-based, if not completely psychological. But the source of the second wind is almost never a phantasmagoric spiritual vision.

"A penny for their thoughts," Mike Adamle says to his ABC crewmates at about this time, as the camera rolls inside his station wagon.

THE TWENTY-FOOT INFLATED Bud Light can marking the turn-around point at sixteen miles appears in the distance. As always, the approach seems to take three times longer than it should. Dave and Mark are not there yet when John Boyer, the Mad Triathlete himself, comes cruising toward them on his bike. Boyer is stunned to see the race leaders approaching the marathon turnaround before he has even reached the 100-mile point of the bike leg.

As he draws closer, Boyer perceives an incredible will in both men's faces, and he thinks, *Neither one of these men could possibly lose this race.* Yet their energies, he notices, are completely different. Dave huffs, blows, spits, and grimaces—stopping just short of breathing fire. Through these and other, ineffable signs he emanates pure aggression. He is the predator. In contrast, Mark seems sealed inside himself behind that unreadable rictus grin. It's as if he's holding his breath until Dave suffocates.

At last they reach the Bud Light can. Dave focuses on the digital race clock and notes that the time it displays is about fourteen minutes less than his best previous time to this point in the race. He realizes that his predicted 8:10 finish time is within reach. Although Dave still has Mark Allen to worry about, his primary Ironman goal has always been to go faster, to redefine his own limits—so the discovery excites him and feeds his motivation to do what he was already planning to do next.

They round the turn. Ten miles to go. *Bang!* It's as if a second start cannon has fired. Dave hits the gas. His acceleration is so sudden and extreme that it is plainly visible to onlookers. But Mark is ready and responds, well knowing Dave's passion for the final big push, for pounding it out at the end. Tactics are pretty much out the window now. Dave is running as hard as he thinks he can without exploding into a million bits of shrapnel before he reaches the finish line. Mark has no idea if he can hold this pace—and no choice but to try.

They scream past the airport for the fourth and final time today and arrive at the start of a long, negative false flat. Dave calls upon his special gift for downhill running and accelerates even more.

Cathy Plant catches the split time between seventeen and eighteen miles.

"Mike!" she shouts through the radio. "They just ran mile eighteen in 5:40!"

There is no immediate reply. Mike feels a wave of emotion rising in his chest as he absorbs this impossible information. He wishes he could climb down from the finish-line tower and dash out to the Queen K to see what has never happened before and surely will never happen again.

"How close are they?" he croaks.

"Mike . . ." Cathy is overcome by her own emotion. "They're practically touching."

It is no longer a battle to survive. It is a bona fide two-man footrace. For the first time in the history of this event, the winner will not outlast the runner-up—he will have to outrun him.

Their entourage is growing. Word of the titanic battle has spread, drawing photographers, writers, race marshals, spotters, support crew, and VIPs on scooters and motorcycles and in four-wheel vehicles, as well as spectators on bikes, away from the women's race leader, Paula Newby-Fraser, and elsewhere on the course, causing a miscellaneous train nearly half a furlong long to form behind the gladiators. Its passengers watch in reverential silence, of which all are hyperconscious, so incongruous is the soundlessness of the procession in relation to its image. The low throbbing of motorcycle engines and the distant hum of ABC's helicopter hovering high overhead create a low sonic backdrop to no greater noise than the occasional shout of encouragement from a roadside spectator or aid-station volunteer, the rhythmic huffing of the athletes' exhalations, and the soft slapping of their feet against the pavement.

The runners' shirtfronts are discolored with spilled Exceed and Coke. It looks like blood. It might as well be blood.

Dave's number bib is missing. He tore it off a few miles back. It was irritating him. It's of little consequence; this contest of wills has transcended the formal event, like a boxing match that continues as a brawl outside the ring.

The nonpartisans among those watching squirm with anticipation. They know that before long one of these men is going to strike a death blow. But who? And when? And exactly how? Those with some skin in the game—namely John Reganold and Mike Norton on their mopeds and Mark's group of Charlie Graves, Brian Hughes, Mike Rubano, and John Martin, now riding in their Jeep right behind the action—can barely watch.

As Dave and Mark reach the bottom of the false flat, Ken Glah, having passed a fading Mike Pigg for third place, strides by in the opposite direction. The next-best Ironman triathlete in the world is two full miles behind the leaders and falling ever farther back at a steady rate of fifty yards per minute. For ten seconds Ken is no longer in the race but just another awestruck spectator. More than twenty years later this moment will be his only clear memory of the day.

The road turns upward now, and in ascending it Mark notices that it's not as hard to keep up with Dave as it was on the recently completed descent. Instinctively Grip eases up just slightly to hide his strength as he thinks ahead to the last climb of the race: Palani Hill, the place he pointed out to Julie upon their arrival in Kona.

I have to make my move there if I possibly can.

They crest the present hill and begin another gentle downgrade. Dave turns the screws even tighter. Instantly Mark is back on the ropes. Blood has visibly soaked through the upper of Mark's shoe. The foes are now running faster than they have since their initial burst out of transition, and Mark seems to be barely hanging on—Dave is that much stronger when the road bends down. Sensing his advantage, Dave thinks ahead to the last descent of the race, the back side of Palani Hill, the place he discussed with Pat Feeney earlier in the week.

I have to make my move there if I possibly can.

They draw closer and closer to town, and the closer they get, the faster they run.

JULIE MOSS CONTINUES to have a pretty good race. She got off the bike behind only two other women and has lost just three spots in the first ten miles of the run. But her mind is not focused on her own performance. Since turning onto the Queen K at eight miles, she has been watching for Mark—and wondering whether she will see him before or after Dave. At last, yet much sooner than expected (for she has never seen the returning men's leader this early on the outbound portion of the run), she spots a massive procession of vehicles drifting toward her in the distance, a helicopter hanging above. The press truck and other official vehicles at the front end of the convoy obstruct whoever the leader is until the parade has come very near. Then she sees—not him but them! They're still together. *Oh, God.*

In the blink of an eye they are gone, and Julie is alone again on the simmering highway. The encounter has left her shaken, a single echoing question dominating her thoughts: *What will happen?*

The suffering of racing an Ironman is tolerable only if you are totally focused on your race, and even then it is not always tolerable. Right now Julie cares a lot more about the outcome of Mark's fight with Dave than about her own struggle.

Well, I guess I'll know soon enough, she thinks. *But will I? No. I have to see this. It's too important.*

A man on a motorcycle is coming her way in the southbound lane, another spectator drawn toward Dave and Mark by the spreading news. Julie darts in front of him and waves her arms above her head like a marooned sailor. The astonished biker comes to a stop face to face with her. He notes her race number, 53, indicating an elite female. He notes that her position is well toward the front of the women's race and that she appears neither ill nor injured.

"Julie Moss," she says, knowing she need say no more. "I have to see what happens."

"Hop on."

Julie passed her fiancé at the twenty-one-mile point of his race. As she climbs onto the back of a Kawasaki, Dave and Mark approach mile twenty-two. Anna stands in the dead center of the highway there.

"Come on, Dave!" she screams, pouring her entire soul into her plea. "You can do it!"

Anna raises her right hand. Dave presses his hand against hers. He's so damn tired it feels like he's yanked an emergency break. But he relishes the contact and even lets his arm stretch behind him so his hand can linger in his wife's as he forces his body onward.

Approaching the next aid station, Mark pulls a small plastic film canister out of his shorts, opens it, and drops the last salt tablet into his palm. After casting the empty canister to the side of the road, he reaches out for a bottle of decarbonated Coke, drops the tablet into that, and drinks. The captain of this particular aid station happens to see the blur of the flying canister and, suspicious, fetches it. Recalling this year's crackdown on outside assistance to racers, he decides to report *Dave's* canister to Marshals Director Dennis Haserot, almost hoping a rule has been broken.

Dave again falls behind Mark and merges right for refreshments. But something happens. Maybe he slows down a little more. Maybe Mark doesn't slow down as much. Whatever the case, Dave emerges from the feed zone fifteen feet behind Grip. Reflexively he moves to close the gap and with a flash of panic he discovers that he can't. Or rather, he *could*, but it would be the last thing he did. His body knows it. Lifting his tempo to catch Mark feels three times harder than it would have felt just a mile back and would now require a dangerous, likely terminal dedication of resources. The dozen or more gap-closing surges Dave has executed already—on top of everything else—seem to have zapped his legs. To his great relief, however, it becomes apparent that Mark is either unable or unwilling to press the advantage. Even so, Dave knows he must catch Mark before he reaches the base of Palani Hill or his last best chance to win will be lost. Dave heeds a guiding intuition that tells him to be patient and shrink the deficit literally inch by inch, to burn as little energy as possible in making the catch.

Mike Norton and John Reganold, having leapfrogged the action and dismounted from their mopeds, stand just beyond the aid station and are alarmed by the gap, small and static though it is.

"Come on, Dave!" Mike shouts. "Crush him!"

I'm trying, Dave answers in his mind.

This is how things stand when the motorcycle bearing Julie Moss catches up with the white Ford flatbed truck carrying photographers and writers. She negotiates with the driver, who pulls wide and slows to allow her to leap off the Kawasaki and execute a train-hopper's boarding of the truck. Among those lending a helping hand is *Sports Illustrated* writer Kenny Moore, who cannot believe his good fortune. He pulls out his notebook and prepares to write down everything Julie says.

With its new passenger safely aboard, the press truck pulls back in front of the racers. Soon thereafter a barely perceptible lifting of Mark's chin indicates that he has noticed Julie's presence. She shoots him a thumbs-up.

"This next hill," she tells Kenny. "He plans to do it on this hill."

Dave catches Mark 100 yards from the base of that next—and last—hill. Palani.

Another journalist in the convoy notes the time on the race clock at this moment: 7:58:02. The start cannon fired at one minute after seven this morning. It is one minute before three o'clock on the afternoon of October 14, 1989.

AS DAVE PULLS EVEN with Mark, he shakes out his arms to relax. He is prepared to whip out his saber, as it were, and chop off Mark's head at the summit. Their final opportunity to refuel is coming up—an aid station at the very base of the hill. Both men move toward the reaching arms of the volunteers stationed there. Mark is just about to grab a cup when a voice in his mind shouts, *Go now!* Startled, Mark instantly withdraws his arm, veers back to the middle of the lane, and surges. Caught off guard, Dave hurriedly tosses away the cup he's claimed and counters the move. This time he puts everything he has into the chase, knowing he must. Mark's saber has come out first, and it's at his throat.

Try as he might, Dave cannot haul Mark back. Sensing this, Mark turns his head just enough to ascertain from Dave's absence in the margin of his vision that his rival is struggling. Then he really punches the gas, rocketing ahead of Dave as though a towline between them has snapped. Dave runs after Mark with the same degree of purpose with which a burning man rolls around on the ground, but his desperate effort to respond seems to serve only to precipitate a sudden and spectacular disintegration of his stride. His head begins to bob and his knees lock, leaving him to run on disjointed stilts. The abrupt loss of coordination suggests that he has held it together by will and will alone for some time.

Showing not a shred of mercy for Dave or himself, Mark throws his body into the hill. He knows that the last mile of the race is basically all downhill—all to Dave's advantage—and he is therefore determined to put himself out of reach by the top of the incline, no matter the cost. His lead stretches ever wider.

"You're doing it!" Julie shouts. But she still isn't sure. She has seen him doing it before, only to come undone.

"Stay within yourself!" she calls. Then adds, "You never have to do this again!"

"It's over," says a photographer.

"It's never over," Julie says. "If he cramps, Dave will be on him."

Dave is thinking the same thing. Although he is absolutely dying of fatigue, he concedes nothing more than the present hill. If he can just keep Mark within range, within ten or fifteen seconds, he can reel him in on the shallow descent to Palani Road, and if not there, then on the steeper drop down Pay-'n'-Save Hill.

Mark's lead is thirty seconds at the top of the hill. He does not relent but now hurls himself headlong down the back side, spurring himself onward by picturing Dave coming after him. As he makes the right turn onto Palani, Mark hazards a glance back along the Queen K. Dave is 200 yards behind him. Mark continues to press. The density of spectators and the volume of their noise increase exponentially as Mark flies down Pay-'n'-Save Hill. He reaches Kuakini Highway and uses the opportunity of the left turn he makes there to steal another glance back. Dave has not even come off the Queen K.

Suddenly Mark stops dead in his tracks. Julie's heart leaps into her throat. *What? No!* But her fright is short-lived. Mark balls both fists, extends his arms skyward, and drives his elbows into his sides, shouting, "Yes!" Then he's running again.

No sooner has Mark completed the left turn onto Kuakini Highway than a young man bolts from the curb and begins to run alongside him, at a respectful distance. It is Brian Hughes.

"Mark!" he shouts. "John Martin is at the next corner. He has the flag. He'll give it to you."

This is the solution Brian has come up with to the conflict between his desire to see Mark cross the finish line with a star-spangled banner in his hand and Ironman's crackdown on outside assistance to racers. Brian is Mark's official representative, but his friend is just an innocent bystander. Brian hopes this makes a difference in the judgment of any Ironman official who might witness the transfer. Mark couldn't care less.

"Where's Dave?" he shouts back. "How close is he?"

Nonplussed, Brian looks back toward Palani Road.

"I can't even see him," Brian says, now struggling for breath. "Mark, you won."

Brian stops, and Mark continues. The cheering crescendos as he runs down Kuakini toward the next-to-last turn of the race, at Hualalai Road. At the corner, as promised, stands John Martin. As Mark reaches him, John thrusts the flag into Grip's right hand.

The roar of the fans rises as Mark approaches the Hot Corner once more and turns—to the right this time—onto Ali'i Drive. Cathy Plant's last report to her husband from the field was garbled by the rising din on his side, allowing him to announce only that *someone* had broken away, leaving the crowd in a state of almost unbearable anticipation for four minutes. Mark's arrival hits the crowd like news of enemy surrender from the front line of a long and costly war. A bedlam of celebration erupts as Mark embarks on the final stretch. He has finally done it, and good God, what it took! The people know the story—enough of it anyway—and they rejoice in full appreciation of his overcoming.

THE VICTOR'S RUN down Ali'i Drive: This is the dream of every triathlete gifted enough to dare. Not breaking the tape at the finish line but running that iconic final stretch. Mark has dreamed this dream a thousand times and more, and the reality is exactly like his dream in every detail, just a little more vivid and a whole lot louder. The central village of Kailua-Kona has a quaint dreamscape quality that makes the ultimate triathlon experience even more surreal, or unreal, than it would otherwise be. The way the street snakes left and right to hide the finish banner until you're almost underneath it; the way the shops and restaurants, all with second-story balconies, press in on the street from both sides; something vaguely Candyland, with a South Pacific twist, about the zoning and architecture—Mark floats through it all, six inches above the ground, now in a soundless vacuum, in slow motion, seeing every shouting mouth and every pumping fist, dreaming with his eyes wide open.

His pace does not slacken. Mark continues to run swiftly as he approaches the banner stretched across the finish line at belly level by two race officials. He does not so much wave the flag gripped tightly in his right hand as beat the air with it in convulsive stabs, the sort of unconscious "take that" gesture that is often seen in moments of hard-won victory, but a little different here. Through a clench-toothed grin he tries and fails to restrain his sobs. The moment he breaks the tape—his total time an unimaginable 8:09:15, his marathon split (minus the bike-run transition) an unbelievable 2:38:49—he gives up all restraint and breaks into unashamed weeping.

Mark Allen does not weep like a ferociously competitive athlete who has won the most important event in his sport after years of maddening frustration. He weeps like a man who has overcome something much deeper, older, and more personal. His whole life Mark has dreamed of doing something that makes people look and say, "That's incredible." Since discovering triathlon Mark has done many things that are incredible in the eyes of others. But until now, no victory has exactly represented what he meant when he first articulated his dream as a young boy. Nothing has filled the emptiness that inflated that dream. Now Mark has finally done something incredible in his own eyes. He has filled the emptiness, and it is indescribably good.

Will the feeling last? Will the fullness remain? Hush. These are questions for tomorrow.

Julie dashes forward and throws her arms around Mark, who crumples into her embrace in a mixed expression of exhaustion and emotional release. Gary, of whose earlier heroics Mark will soon learn, pats his big brother on the back and fixes him with a huge grin and sparkling eyes that communicate both worshipful pride and concern over Mark's unaccustomed tearful outpouring. Sharon squeezes herself between her sons.

"Oh, Mark, you did it," she moans in tones that could only ever be heard in mother-to-child speech. "You finally did it. Oh, Mark."

Space is caught on the back side of the family scrum and must wait to stake his claim to the new champion of Ironman.

The massive crowd erupts anew as Dave comes to the finish line, fifty-eight seconds behind Mark. So great is the roar of appreciation that the man who carried this race on his back toward this pivotal moment for ten years is compelled to acknowledge the people with a small gesture of his left hand. Not even a decibel quieter than Mark's ovation, Dave's reception communicates a clear message: *You did not lose this race. Not really.* And the crowd is right. The enduring image of the greatest race ever run will not be Mark breaking the tape alone at the finish line but Dave and Mark together, still together, less than two miles from the finish line, at one minute before three o'clock on the afternoon of October 14, 1989.

CHAPTER 11

BREAKING POINT

How can you think and hit at the same time?

— YOGI BERRA

I t is three o'clock on the afternoon of October 14, 1989, and Mark Allen is running away from Dave Scott on Palani Hill in Kailua-Kona, Hawaii. Meanwhile, 22-year-old Stephen McGregor is hanging out with fellow students at Tri-State University (since renamed Trine University) in Angola, Indiana. A triathlete himself, Steve is aware that the race is happening on this day, but since there is no live coverage of any kind, he will not learn the result until some time afterward. Partial to Dave Scott, he will be disappointed to find out that Dave has been unable to respond to Mark's last surge.

Two decades later Steve will develop innovative tools in his work as an exercise physiologist that will yield surprising discoveries about the human running stride. Among these tools will be an esoteric statistic called *control entropy*, which can be used to precisely measure a runner's fatigue level as well as to quantify how hard a runner is trying to resist the fatigue he's feeling. The concept of control entropy will also provide a compelling explanation of what happens in the critical moment of the greatest race ever run, when Dave's legs fail him, and will expose the remarkable achievement hidden in his failure. Specifically, Steve's analysis will lead him to conclude that in the last ten minutes of the race, Dave Scott fights as hard against total physical exhaustion as any athlete ever has for as long as human beings have raced.

AN ONLY CHILD, Stephen McGregor spent the first ten years of his life in the small town of St. Thomas, Ontario, Canada. His father, Jim, worked as a factory manager and made a better living than most men who lack a college education. On weekends Jim pursued the uncommon hobby of racing dragsters and achieved no small measure of success, winning a Canadian Top Fuel Championship and holding his nation's speed record for a time. Steve looked up to him, as any son of a race-car driver would, and inherited his love of the adrenaline rush. His mother, Patricia, who had completed one year of college, taught first grade.

In 1977 Jim's work took the family to Indiana. Steve joined the middle school football team and found another valuable role model in its coach, Tom Saylor, who would have a lifelong influence on the undersized cornerback. Steve still remembers Coach Saylor's favorite slogan: "Effort is everything."

In 1980 Jim and Patricia divorced, and Steve moved back to St. Thomas with his mom. In high school Steve played soccer and ran track. He also took up the guitar and made a little money gigging in local bars with rock and country bands.

When Steve was 20 and in his first year at the University of Windsor, located near Detroit, Patricia died of brain cancer. Steve did his first triathlon soon thereafter, finding a healthy release for his grief in the prolonged suffering of endurance training. In 1989 he switched to bike racing, preferring it, as he would tell others, because the sport seemed even more sadomasochistic than triathlon.

By this time Steve had resumed his college studies, having transferred his credits to Tri-State University. He started a major in physical education and then moved to a dual major in biology and chemistry. He developed a passion for science and saw his future career in it, so he took the next step and entered a master's program in microbiology at the University of Toledo. As these studies progressed, Steve's passion for cycling continued to grow. After receiving his degree, he chose to defer life in the real world in favor of racing his bike full time, rambling across North America from race to race with a few fellow "bike bums," as they called themselves. They slept on floors, packed light, ate cheap, and used whatever bit of money they had gotten from the last race to put gas in the car and get to the next one.

At Toledo Steve had fallen in love with a local girl named Christy Frankowski. There came a time when he had to choose between her and his bike, and he wisely chose her. But he did not want to leave the world of athletics entirely, so he returned to Toledo to study for a PhD in exercise physiology. Steve was fortunate enough to score a job at Eastern Michigan University while the ink of his dissertation on muscle injury was still drying, and he's been there ever since.

In his first few years at EMU Steve concentrated on developing mathematical tools to quantify training workloads in cyclists, using data collected from bicycle power meters. He decided the logical next step would be to develop similar tools for runners, but he immediately hit an obstacle in the nonexistence of running power meters. He settled on accelerometers as the next best thing. An accelerometer measures changes in the speed and direction of its own movement (or in the movement of whatever it may be attached to). Steve's efforts to quantify running workloads with accelerometer data were not unsuccessful, but after playing with the instruments for a while he became far more interested in using them to quantify various characteristics of the running stride and in using these measurements to answer such interesting questions as: How does the running stride change through years of training? What are the truly meaningful differences between the strides of gifted and average runners? What happens to the stride when a runner gets tired?

ACCELEROMETERS ARE BUILT into a variety of consumer speed-and-distance devices that runners affix to or insert in a shoe to track their pace and distance traveled in real time as they run. These simple accelerometers capture data in a single plane of movement: anterior-posterior, or forward-backward. Steve uses fancier accelerometers that capture data in all three planes of movement and at much higher resolution than the consumer units. They are able to measure the tiniest changes in a runner's forward, vertical, and lateral movements.

One of several surprising discoveries Steve has made with the help of these devices is that lateral and vertical movements are not all that important. Although running coaches often instruct athletes to minimize "wasteful bouncing" in their strides, it turns out that the most efficient runners are not the least bouncy—rather, they fall somewhere in the middle of the vertical displacement spectrum. Less experienced runners are just as likely to bounce too little as too much, and in any case Steve's research has demonstrated that overall stride efficiency is typically not much spoiled either by too much or by too little bouncing.

Only accelerations in the anterior-posterior (AP) plane are strongly associated with running economy. The runners with the smallest accelerations in this plane are the most efficient, regardless of their degree of bounciness or whatever else is going on with their stride. This makes sense when you consider that a runner who exhibits large accelerations in the AP plane is a runner who slows down and speeds up quite a bit from stride to stride, even while trying to hold a steady pace. The greatest source of energy waste in running is the braking that occurs when a foot makes contact with the ground. Those runners who brake the least when a foot lands spend the least energy trying to get back up to speed when pushing off the ground. Steve found that highly trained runners exhibit much smaller accelerations than nonrunners in the AP axis. He also found that, within a population of highly trained runners, those who exhibited the smallest accelerations in the AP plane were the most economical.

The most surprising discoveries in Steve's research on the running stride came after he began to apply a more arcane mathematical analysis to his data with the help of Erik Bollt, an expert on nonlinear mathematics at Clarkson University. Erik worked out a way to measure the control entropy of a runner's stride at any given moment. Control entropy refers to the variability or unpredictability of the behavior of a physical system. It can be any physical system, from something as simple as a few gas molecules bouncing around inside a sphere to—well, a runner's stride. Each system is subject to certain constraints. The looser the constraints are, the more unpredictable the system's behavior is and the more entropy is said to exist in the system. The tighter the constraints are, the more predictable the system's behavior becomes and the less entropy is said to exist in the system. For example, suppose a sphere with gas molecules bouncing around inside it shrinks. In systemic terms, this means the constraint represented by the volume of space that the molecules have to move around in has been tightened. Consequently, the total number of possible states in which the system can exist—that is, the total number of different positions the gas molecules can occupy in a frozen moment—decreases. The result is that the system is now more predictable; it has less entropy.

In running, a stride pattern exhibits low entropy when each individual stride looks almost exactly like the preceding one and the next. A stride pattern exhibits more entropy when each stride looks a little different from the one before and the one after. These variations are not typically visible to the naked eye, but the accelerometers can pick up very subtle differences.

One of the first things Steve wanted to look at through the lens of control entropy was the relationship between entropy and fatigue. So he slapped accelerometers on a bunch of subjects and had them walk and then run at incrementally increasing speeds on a treadmill until they quit in exhaustion.

Steve expected to find that entropy increased near the point of exhaustion. This hypothesis was intuitive. Entropy can be thought of as disorder, or chaos. No great feat of imagination is required to conceptualize fatigue in running as a falling apart, or disintegration, of the stride. But Steve found the opposite of what he expected. Control entropy in the strides of his subjects *decreased* with fatigue. Instead of falling apart, their strides became more locked into a particular pattern—robotic, if you will.

In retrospect, Steve realized he should have anticipated this finding. A constraint suggests a limit. It is clear that exhaustion in running occurs when the body (which, of course, includes the brain) encounters a performance limit. Regardless of where that limit originates, it has to be mediated through the stride, because that's all running is. An exhausted runner must, therefore, exhibit a constrained stride, or a stride with low entropy.

To give an unrealistically simple example, suppose a certain muscle in a runner's leg gives out toward the end of one of Steve's dreadful incremental treadmill runs to exhaustion. Unable to use this muscle any longer, the runner will have to adjust his stride, coming up with altered movement patterns that allow him to sustain the same speed. That one muscle, normally preferred but now useless, will act as a constraint on the stride going forward, making the adjusted stride more rigid and robotic—less entropic— than the runner's normal, nonfatigued stride.

Steve was also interested in comparing control entropy in the strides of nonrunners and experienced runners. He found that entropy tended to be greater in the strides of advanced runners at all speeds. This finding was to be expected, as research in the field of motor learning has long shown that beginners always exhibit less variation in motor skills than practiced experts. Beginners are locked into a certain way of tossing a Frisbee or shuffling cards, whereas experts have acquired a certain amount of freedom, or play, in their movements. They are less constrained by limits on their coordination.

There's a twist, however, where things get really interesting. While the strides of all runners, novice and advanced, become more robotic, or less entropic, as fatigue increases, and while the strides of experienced runners generally exhibit more entropy, or freedom, advanced runners are usually more constrained, more locked up, than beginners at the point of exhaustion. What does this mean?

The answer lies in a crucial difference between the running stride and our prior example of a constrained physical system—gas molecules bouncing around inside a sphere. Gas molecules move around constantly because that's just what they do in obedience to the laws of physics. But the act of running is different; running happens because a mind wills it to happen. A fall in entropy therefore indicates more than just the constraining effect of fatigue on a runner's stride. It also indicates a mental effort to push through that fatigue. As soon as a tiring runner gives up and slows down or stops, entropy skyrockets. The stride is no longer constrained because the runner is no longer pushing against a constraint—no longer trying.

It makes sense that the only way to become really, really fatigued in running is to refuse to slow down despite fatigue. You simply can't experience extreme fatigue without having exerted extreme efforts to resist fatigue. Fatigue and the fight against it are two facets of a single thing, and control entropy highlights their connectedness. A runner who exhibits an extremely low level of entropy at the point of exhaustion is a runner who has pushed his body deeper into the misery of muscle fatigue than a runner who abandons the treadmill before becoming quite so robotic.

In a strange but real way, then, control entropy allows us to begin to quantify the mental toughness of a runner in action. When subjects raise the proverbial white flag in Steve's terrible treadmill tests, they always *look* and *feel* exhausted. But the control entropy readings that emerge a day or two later, after the numbers have been crunched, lay bare the truth. They reveal who really carved himself hollow and who wimped out. The lower the entropy, the greater the mental toughness. And it happens that experienced runners are generally willing and able to suffer more—in a running task, anyway—than nonrunners. That's why they exhibit lower levels of entropy at exhaustion even though, by dint of their experience, they start with higher levels of entropy.

It is interesting that low entropy is indicative of inexperience in running, on the one hand, and of extreme fatigue and extreme efforts to resist fatigue, on the other. The link between these two correlations becomes clear if you think of entropy as an indicator of how much a runner's stride is being mentally *forced.* Nonrunners have to apply a lot of mental energy to their running, even before they get tired, because they have not practiced the skill much. They're like a kid taking his first drum lesson, who's mentally exhausted after two minutes spent trying to tap quarter notes with his left hand and half notes with his right. Experienced runners are able to run with a much quieter brain because repetition has made their stride movements almost automatic. They're like a professional drummer who can play with all four limbs simultaneously while also singing and feel virtually no mental strain. Advanced runners don't have to force their stride as much with their minds, and control entropy registers this quiescence of the brain as a certain looseness in the stride.

The more fatigued the muscles become, however, the more mental energy nonrunners and advanced runners alike must apply to their strides. Tired muscles are less responsive to the brain's whip, so the brain must whip the muscles harder to get the same amount of work from them. Also, the more fatigued a runner becomes, the more suffering he experiences. Thus, an additional amount of "forcing it" is required to resist the psychological temptation to quit—to shout down that old devil on the left shoulder. Control entropy captures this intense application of mental resources by marking an increased rigidity in the stride.

The upshot is that a runner's brain must be as inactive as possible to turn out the best possible performance. The stride must not be forced any more than necessary. But when approaching the breaking point, a runner wants to have the capacity to force it more than the next guy.

THE FIRST QUESTION any runner will ask when presented with these ideas is how they might be exploited for practical benefit. If the critical characteristics of a superior stride are less braking when the foot hits the ground and looser, less forced movement patterns, then the performance-seeking runner will want to know the best way to develop a freer stride with less braking. A coach as well as a scientist, Stephen McGregor wants to answer this question too. He still has a lot of work to do before it's been answered fully, but he's making progress.

Actually, the question was halfway answered before Steve even started to address it formally. After all, one of his earliest studies with accelerometers showed that experienced runners exhibited more entropy and less braking than nonrunners, and the salient difference between nonrunners and experienced runners is, obviously, running experience. That alone is pretty strong evidence that simply running a lot over a long period of time makes the stride more efficient. It is an unconscious, automatic evolution.

Some running coaches try to improve their runners' strides the same way golf instructors teach swings and strokes: by defining correct technique and encouraging (or forcing) their athletes to consciously emulate it. In fact, technique instruction has become quite a vogue in running within the past decade. However, scientific testing of these techniques has consistently shown that making conscious changes to one's natural stride actually reduces efficiency. It makes no difference what the specific change is. Steve's work with control entropy explains why. When you make a conscious change to your stride, your brain becomes more actively focused on your running. Your body wants to do what's natural, but your brain *forces it* to do otherwise. And forcing it always reduces control entropy.

Steve believes, on the basis of his work, that there is no such thing as correct running form. Yes, there are some general differences, visible to the naked eye, between the strides of nonrunners and those of advanced runners. "But within the population of trained runners," he says, "there is nothing you can capture on a camera and put on a billboard and advertise as good running form. The runners on our team at Eastern Michigan that we've tested all train in a similar way, but they have different running styles. I look at some of them and say, 'Wow, that person has really horrible form,' and they actually do very well in our testing."

The reason for the great variety of running styles observed in high-level runners is straightforward, according to Steve. It's merely a reflection of the great variety in the structure of runners' bodies. Two runners with disparate physiques cannot be expected to maximize their individual running economies with precisely the same stride. Efficient running is like a puzzle that each body must solve for itself. And that puzzle cannot be solved consciously. A runner cannot, for example, determine that if his height is X, his inseam Y, and his thigh circumference Z, his optimal stride cadence is therefore 168 steps per minute. The refinement of running form must instead be left to unfold through unconscious trial and error. In much the same way that a species of life figures out how to survive in a changing environment by evolving blindly through random mutation and natural selection, the running stride evolves through repeatedly confronting speed and endurance limits—through crises that challenge the neuromuscular system to come up with novel movement patterns that yield more speed and endurance. You just have to run hard, without thinking about it, and let the process happen. Consciously fiddling with your stride in the hope of accelerating its evolution toward greater efficiency not only can't help but is almost guaranteed to hurt.

Which is not to say the process can't be accelerated by other means. Steve has seen some evidence to suggest that runners who train in groups and runners who train at relatively high intensities have better strides than runners of equal experience who train alone and runners who train at lower intensities. He thinks it's possible that simply *trying harder* day after day may accelerate stride improvement. Runners who habitually push themselves to keep up with teammates or training partners, or who chase after challenging time standards, raise the stakes on their bodies, pressuring their bodies to figure things out faster. Just as species evolve fastest in a rapidly changing environment that threatens extinction, the running stride may improve most quickly when a runner exacerbates the cost of his stride's current constraints by pushing against those limits over and over again.

THE EXERCISE SCIENCE laboratory at Eastern Michigan University is located in Room 248 of the Warner Building. It makes an intimidating first impression on the subjects of Stephen McGregor's grueling running tests. The space looks more like a laboratory than a gym, and in this context the giant Woodward treadmill on which the accelerometer testing is performed looks more like a torture device than a piece of exercise machinery. About forty feet deep and fifteen feet wide, Steve's lab is stuffed with all manner of equipment, some items identifiably exercise-related, others not. Half of the stuff appears to be in use and the other half in storage, yet it is difficult to discern which is which. A homemade sign is plainly visible on a wall near the treadmill:

CALL 911 FOR ALL MEDICAL EMERGENCIES

That's for the subject's benefit should something bad happen during his running test.

A couple of posters displaying guidelines for rating perceived effort are also taped to the walls. Most of the test subjects Steve works with are very familiar with the Borg scale. Steve's subjects either know coming in or quickly learn that the test they are about to start will not end until they rate their effort as *very, very hard.*

VERY, VERY LIGHT	6
	7
	8
VERY LIGHT	9
	10
	11
FAIRLY LIGHT	12
	13
	14
SOMEWHAT HARD	15
	16
	17
VERY HARD	18
	19
VERY, VERY HARD	20

Not everyone who comes to Room 248 to run is intimidated. One day, during a period when Steve was testing Eastern Michigan's current crop of cross-country runners, a tall, bony kid walked into the lab munching on a giant chicken burrito. Steve looked at him incredulously.

"Are you getting tested?" he asked.

"Yeah."

"And you're eating a burrito?"

"Grand opening at the new Chipotle," the young man answered. "They're giving them away free."

The hungry runner was Curtis Vollmar, a local guy and one of the best performers on coach John Goodridge's team that season. He finished his burrito and submitted to the ministrations of Steve's assistants, who taped accelerometers to his low back and wrists and stuck a breathing mask over his face. Curtis stepped onto the treadmill and was led through the standard protocol, running at increasing speeds until he felt he could not take another step, at which point he quit, dripping sweat and gasping for air. The whole thing lasted about twenty-two minutes.

Steve analyzed the results and was astonished. Curtis was unique in almost every measurement. His aerobic capacity, or VO_2max, was pitifully small for a runner performing at his level. His oxygen consumption peaked at sixty milliliters per kilogram of body weight per minute, a value that was 25 percent lower than the numbers posted by some of his teammates whom Curtis regularly beat in races. He was also the most economical runner Steve had seen. Indeed, he had to be, to run as well as he did with such a small aerobic engine. Curtis practically floated above the treadmill, scarcely braking at all when his feet touched the belt. Moreover, the control entropy reading at the end of Curtis's test was the lowest in the history of the protocol. To top it all off, no runner had ever continued running as long after reaching his maximal rate of oxygen consumption. Curtis survived for four and a half minutes and two speed increases after he'd completely tapped out his ability to draw more oxygen from the environment.

"Tell me about Vollmar," Steve requested of the young harrier's coach at the first opportunity.

John Goodridge rolled his eyes and smiled, as if to say, "Where do I even begin?"

"Well, he's not the most talented kid," John said. "But boy, does he know how to suffer."

Goosebumps rose on Steve's forearms. This was exactly what the test had told him.

John explained to Steve that Curtis tortured himself to stay at the front of every race and every workout. He never mailed in a run, as even the best runners sometimes do, but always turned himself inside out to compete, regardless of how much more talented those he was competing against were, or how unimportant the race or workout might be, or how tired he was from his most recent effort to hang on or die trying.

Curtis had started running in high school. Before that, in middle school, he'd played football. His coach sometimes made the team run as punishment for making mistakes or showing lack of effort. It was almost half a mile to the baseball field backstop and back. Curtis always finished way ahead of everyone else. It was his favorite part of football practice.

Smart enough to realize there was another sport whose athletes did exclusively what football players did only as punishment, Curtis left his pads behind in the ninth grade and took up cross country and track. He quickly discovered that outrunning middle school football players is one thing; outrunning high school distance runners is another. Despite high expectations, Curtis failed to make varsity selection as a freshman. Two years later, however, he was the top runner on the team.

Curtis's remarkable improvement was fueled by a purely psychological factor: a gigantic passion to compete. He loved to test himself against other runners. He loved it so much that racing was all he ever wanted to do, and he was impatient with training. The concept of running without the intent to win made no sense to him. Running alone made even less sense. Curtis saw no reason to run except to race.

In college, Curtis's attitude was the same. Unlike some of the prima donnas on John Goodridge's team, who wanted to be held out of early-season meets and who chafed against being asked to run multiple events, Curtis would have gladly raced fifty-two Saturdays a year and as many Wednesdays. But when he was on his own over the summer, his training was inconsistent, at best, and he always arrived back on campus in August in poor shape.

Coach Goodridge, in his thirty years of coaching, had never seen a runner quite like Curtis Vollmar. It struck him as more than a little strange that Curtis wanted every run to be a race and had no interest in running aside from racing. Yet he couldn't deny that the kid's eccentricity seemed to serve him well, overall. Throughout his college years Curtis routinely beat runners he had no business beating in championship races, based on their respective best times. He ran above himself.

"I think running is 90 percent mental," Curtis once told his coach. "Lots of runners are great in training, but they can't really race."

Curtis was never intimidated by other runners, no matter what they had accomplished, for the simple reason that he was utterly oblivious to others' accomplishments. Curtis paid no attention to his sport except to do it. He just showed up at the starting line, licking the burrito grease off his fingers, and when the gun fired, he went all out.

Some runners are running geeks. They frequent running websites, acquire knowledge about the art and science of training, and generally spend a lot of time thinking and talking about running when they are not actually running. Others don't. Curtis was not a running geek.

Several months after Curtis had completed his last season of NCAA eligibility at Eastern Michigan, he appeared unexpectedly at his former coach's office.

"I was wondering if maybe I could train with some of the guys," he suggested.

Goodridge was dumbstruck. He had always assumed that Curtis would be one of those runners who never ran again after completing their last relay in an Eastern Michigan singlet. But Curtis missed the competition desperately. It wasn't running itself or being fit that he missed. If that had been the case, he could have jogged on his own. It was racing, testing his limits, that he craved. So Curtis set a goal to break four minutes in the mile (his best was 4:07) and got Goodridge's permission to work out with some of the current university runners and other young alumni.

One day, when Curtis was only a few weeks into his comeback and still regaining lost fitness, Stephen McGregor watched him perform an indoor track workout. Coach Goodridge had prescribed a tough session of 300-meter intervals on short rest periods. Curtis's partners for the workout were steeplechasers Jordan Desilets and Corey Nowtizke, both Olympic Trials finalists, and Ethiopian Terefe Ejigu, the team's current best runner.

All three were more gifted than Curtis, and he knew it—and that was exactly why he'd chosen to run with them.

The runners set off together under Goodridge's watchful eye. The first thing that struck Steve, who had tested all four of the runners individually, was the stark individuality of their running styles. Jordan's legs seemed to move in perfect circles, as though he were pedaling a bike. Corey was more of a grinder, with a high back kick. Terefe ran ballistically, like a sprinter. And Curtis ran like he was inside a phone booth: quiet and compact. Studying these contrasts, Steve decided that he would not want to be the coach who had to deal with the consequences of trying to force all four men to run with the same technique.

Around and around they went. Curtis refused to fall farther back than second position in the group of four. Yet he was the first to show obvious signs of strain, and those signs intensified steadily with each successive interval. By the halfway point of the workout, Curtis's face was mutilated with hurt. Just watching him caused Steve to grimace empathically. Curtis never backed off, though, and finished the last interval ahead of the two near-Olympians and right behind the East African with a VO_2 max of 75.

"And you say he's always like this?" Steve asked Coach Goodridge.

"Every time," he said.

IF STEVE'S RESEARCH makes an experimental case that hard running is the key to a better stride, then Curtis Vollmar is real-world Exhibit A. Another surprise finding of Steve's research supports this notion in a different way. Steve's accelerometer data revealed that faster runners tend to be less economical than slower runners at slower paces and more economical at faster paces. Steve reasoned that since faster runners seldom experience much fatigue at slower paces, there is little pressure for their strides to become more economical in those lower gears. They can afford to waste energy when jogging, so, without being aware of it, they do.

This finding reminded Steve of one of the oldest mysteries in his field: the widely reported observation that the runners with the highest aerobic capacities are almost never the most economical. It's usually the Curtis Vollmar types, the aerobically disadvantaged, who exhibit off-the-charts economy. Steve realized he could now explain this curious phenomenon. His research suggested that struggling to keep up with naturally faster runners is one of the most powerful ways to improve running economy. But, by its very nature, this method is not one that the best born runners can exploit. Runners gifted with mighty aerobic engines simply cannot experience the same physiological pressure to keep up with other runners that the Curtis Vollmars do. They never have to pay the same price for inefficiency, so their strides don't become as efficient. They can always afford to get away with just a bit more waste, and waste in the running stride is diminished only to the degree that it must be.

Runners with smaller aerobic engines are not always more economical, however. There are plenty of runners who are aerobically weak *and* uneconomical. Only the ones who "really know how to suffer"—whose brains support an especially high tolerance for the agony of endurance fatigue—are able to take advantage of the opportunity presented by more talented training partners. And that's another talent altogether.

The most mind-bending implication of all this science is that the repeated application of will, or mental toughness, changes the body over time. The purely psychological act of trying harder day after day transforms the purely physical patterns of brain and muscle activity that produce a running stride, in ways that save energy—and in ways that a lifetime of conscious tinkering could never duplicate.

One month after Stephen McGregor watched Curtis Vollmar practically give his own life to an indoor track workout, Curtis beat reigning Olympic 1,500-meter silver medalist Nick Willis in an indoor half-mile race. He caught the New Zealander in a vulnerable moment, weakened from having run a mile race earlier the same evening. But Nick was still one of the best middle-distance runners in the world, not to mention a ferocious competitor. Curtis, however, had only a vague idea who the hell Nick was and went straight after him. The most talented athlete does not always win the race.

THROUGHOUT HIS CAREER Dave Scott was known for, and was sometimes thought to be limited by, his ungainly running style. Self-critical perfectionist that he was, Dave was not oblivious to his condition.

"Look at my form," he said in a 2000 interview. "I'm a horrible runner. I'm terrible. I've got the worst form of anyone alive. I see the videotape—my feet are turned, my arms are all weird. And then you look at [some of the top triathletes] today. Their form is just beautiful. I think, *What beautiful form. If God would only give me a piece of it.* But the other part is, I've just run like a dog. And I beat them."

Like others in the sport, Dave assumed that the visible awkwardness of his running style was evidence of poor economy. But, as Steve's research has shown, ugly runners are sometimes very efficient. You can't judge that book by its cover. Steve has also shown that there is no such thing as a proper way to run, and so the parts of his stride that Dave thought were wrong probably were not wrong at all. Rather, like any athlete who acquires as much running experience and pushes as hard as he did, Dave probably found the best possible running style for his body, or something close to it.

Dave never made any conscious effort to change his running style. But his stride changed nevertheless. When he started running, before he did his first triathlon, he noticed that his running shoes showed signs of wear at the back of the heel after he'd used them for a while. It indicated that he landed on the back of his heel when he ran. Beginners and slower runners often exhibit this biomechanical pattern, which exerts a tremendous braking effect. But Dave overcame it. Over time he started landing farther forward on the foot, and the heel wear went away.

Dave's running improved enormously between the time he raced his first triathlon in 1976 and the time he ran what still stands as the second-fastest marathon in Ironman history in 1989. This progress was largely the result of improvement in his movement efficiency, as his aerobic engine was already well developed when he started running. But Dave's running economy did not improve by means of any conscious meddling with his stride. Intuitively, he must have known better than to make that mistake. Instead, Dave's stride improved because, as he said himself, he ran like a dog.

Although he seldom ran in groups, Dave ran hard. With his time-based games, he pushed himself to the point of discomfort, at the very least, every time he laced up his shoes, and he frequently drove himself to the point of near collapse.

"I keep the intensity high," Dave told one interviewer. "Even if I'm doing a longer run, I make a huge part of that run hard, if not the whole thing."

All great endurance athletes train extraordinarily hard. Not merely a lot, but *hard*. And that's really the only thing that all great endurance athletes do. The details of their training methods are surprisingly varied, which suggests that these details are not terribly important. Dave Scott and Mark Allen understood what was important and what wasn't.

"The ingredients to proper training aren't a secret, and no one has the proper recipe anyway," Mark said early in his career.

Many triathlon coaches and experts try to make the recipe more complicated than it really is. "Run like this." "Keep your blood lactate level between here and here." Stephen McGregor would tell you it's all bullshit—or window dressing, anyway. The true keys to greatness—as the athletes themselves demonstrate on the proving grounds, and as Steve reaffirms in his lab—are contained in the baldest clichés. No pain, no gain. Effort is everything. Just do it. Run like a dog.

Few members of triathlon's first generation were guilty of overthinking the sport. These athletes shared a pioneer's mind-set, which is very different from the geek's attitude. There were plenty of geeks around in the 1980s, but they remained swimmers, cyclists, and runners. It was the more adventurous athletes who became triathletes. Having few proven methods or qualified coaches to direct their training, they leaned on gut instinct instead.

In Mark's view, any second spent thinking or talking about training was a minute of life wasted. Paul Huddle, who trained with Mark for several years, can count on one hand the number of technical conversations about training they ever had. Mark's book, *Mark Allen's Total Triathlete*, was a huge disappointment to fans who bought it in search of practical training information.

"Several people have beaten me to the punch on books about training and racing techniques and theories," Mark wrote in the preface. "Enough great information is already available on those subjects."

In truth, Mark could never have filled a book with his own training and racing techniques and theories because he trained with a simple logic. The goal was to win races. To win races, you had to beat everyone else in the race. So Mark used his training to measure himself against his regular training partners, who were also the best triathletes in the world besides himself (except Dave Scott) and therefore the athletes most likely to challenge him in races. If he could beat those guys in the workouts that mattered most, he could win races. The only sophistication to Mark's training method was that he didn't try to beat his training partners every day.

If Mark trained simply, Dave trained more simply still. The goal was to get faster. So Dave timed his workouts and tried to go faster. He knew no better.

"When I began training, my practical knowledge base was very limited," Dave wrote for Active.com. "I had a limited understanding of all of the nuances, including technology. Looking back, this was probably an as set for me."

The less athletes think, the better they perform. Stephen McGregor's research with accelerometers in running is not the only proof of this law. Studies involving the use of EEG to measure brain activity in golfers, for example, have shown that those who exhibit the least brain activity when hitting putts are the most accurate putters. Mindless performance may be especially helpful in endurance sports because of the supreme importance of the capacity to suffer. The more science and technical detail an athlete incorporates into the training process, the more distracted he becomes from the only thing that really matters: getting out the door and going hard.

Mark Allen routinely practiced the skill of clearing his consciousness during hard workouts and races. When he succeeded, he said, he felt his mind emptying into his bike or his legs. Once that happened, his body became relaxed and efficient.

A stranger once asked Dave what he thought about while training for hours and hours.

"My rhythms," he said. "And lunch."

Around the time Dave Scott and Mark Allen completed their last Ironmans in the mid-1990s, the geeks invaded. A new wave of coaches came along and published influential books detailing training formulas that required a master's degree to understand and apply. These systems, with their cycles and phases and zones, were later complemented by computer programs that made the correct way to train even more dazzlingly complicated. There are now well-paid experts who specialize in adjusting the positioning of triathletes on their bikes. That's it. And, of course, there are other experts who do nothing but videotape athletes running and teach them how to run more correctly.

Despite all of this, or perhaps in some measure because of it, nobody today is racing Ironmans any faster than Dave Scott and Mark Allen did in 1989. And those who race best at Ironman and elsewhere today are those who, like Curtis Vollmer, approach their sport intuitively, with a hunger to win and a capacity to suffer that enable them to seemingly transcend their physical capacities in ways the geeks and coaches can't explain.

MARK'S SURGE CATCHES DAVE by surprise. It is sudden, explosive, and decisive, creating an instant gap that cannot be closed. It is now clear which of the two men is physically stronger on this day. Mark has always had more physical Ironman potential than his nemesis, but not until today has he been able to actualize his inborn advantage. What made the difference? Those seven-hour training days in New Zealand? Mark's patient new race strategy? His willingness to finally, fully face the fears that defeated him in past Ironmans? The extra fat he consumed before the race and the extra sodium during? His offering to the island spirits? His stepmother's appeasement of Madam Pele? The anger provoked by the writer who predicted that Mark would never win Ironman? His vision in the lava fields? Some combination of these things? Informed persons will forever disagree.

Dave recognizes Mark's advantage, but he still believes in his bones that his will can trump another's talent—at least here, in *his* race. So Dave does the only thing he knows—he tries harder, wills his legs to accelerate, understanding that he must answer Mark's move immediately or the race is lost. But something strange happens. He seems to lose control of his body. He cannot attain the speed he needs in the normal way, by simply getting up on his toes a little more, lifting his knees, and driving his arms. His body seems incapable of doing these familiar things. He's like an orator who is forced to deliver a speech after several Novocain shots and must come up with a whole new way of making words come out of his mouth, on the fly, before an audience of thousands. More literally, the preferred muscle fibers in Dave's legs that he has been using all day are now so damaged and depleted and otherwise compromised that they cannot respond to his brain's command to work harder. This physical mutiny is communicated back to Dave's brain, which scrambles to stimulate the muscles in alternative ways.

The result is a terrible transfiguration of Dave's stride. His knees lock. He begins hurling his rigid legs forward like a rusted Tin Man. His torso twists from side to side. His shoulders cinch up toward his ears. The effort is total, but Dave makes up no ground. At one point he looks down at his legs, as though asking them what the hell is going on. This is, in fact, exactly what he's doing, as he will later report. Dave is stunned by his body's insubordination. Nothing like it has ever happened before. Upon finishing, Dave will be heard to utter repeatedly, to no one in particular, in a tone of dazed disbelief, "I couldn't do it. I couldn't do it." Meaning *I can't believe I couldn't do it.*

Endurance athletes call it "tying up" because that's what it looks like. It's as if the runner has been roped with multiple lassos and is gamely trying to run through his bondage. Stephen McGregor's research has shown that the effect of fatigue on the stride is very much like running in bonds. Control entropy plummets, meaning the stride becomes rigid, robotic, constrained.

Usually, however, the changes are not plainly visible. Accelerometers capture them, but the naked eye does not. The grotesque distortion of Dave's stride therefore suggests an extraordinary drop in control entropy, an almost superhuman effort to resist unimaginable fatigue. Further evidence in support of this conjecture comes from Dave's pace over the final 1.7 miles of the race. He covers this agonizing final stretch of the contest, already knowing he has lost, in 10:13, which works out to precisely six minutes per mile—slightly *faster* than his average pace for the entire marathon.

One of the reasons Steve never sees a runner's form fall apart in his lab as spectacularly as Dave's does now is that there is no possibility of slowing down in his treadmill test. If the subject feels he cannot sustain his current pace, he must stop. There is no middle option. Even in races, over-the-top episodes of tying up are fairly uncommon. When they do happen, they are almost always associated with a dramatic loss of speed. A sort of three-quarter quitting occurs, and as the runner's speed comes down, his control entropy increases because he is no longer forcing it so much, although his form may remain goofy because his muscles remain damaged, depleted, and compromised. The sustained *increase* in speed Dave manages despite his horrific tying up is the rarest of rarities—truly a one-in-a-billion exhibition of will in sports. If Dave Scott were wearing accelerometers, he might set a never-to-be-broken record for low control entropy. That is, for mental toughness.

Dave Scott's mission in life has been to see what his body can do. Fulfilling this purpose has required that he first cultivate his body's capabilities to the highest possible level and then, on the right day, try harder than it has ever been known possible to try. As Mark Allen drifts away in front of him on Palani Hill, Dave has finally found what his body can do. And what it can't.

The premature cannon shot that started the 1989 Ironman caught many racers—most notably Dave Scott—off guard.

ABOVE: Dave was accompanied by Rob Mackle, Mark, Mike Pigg, and Ken Glah (not pictured) through most of the bike leg.

BELOW: Dave and Mark climbed the tough hill leading out of the bike–run transition side by side.

ABOVE LEFT: Mark claimed inside position at aid stations, forcing Dave to drop back for his drinks.

ABOVE RIGHT: Dave surged hard at the run turnaround (marked by the tall inflatable Bud Light can visible in the distance) with ten miles to go. By then a long caravan of spectators on wheels was following Dave and Mark.

RIGHT: Mark's brother Gary and father, Ken, seemed almost as happy as Mark after he won.

ABOVE: Mark chased Greg Welch through the early miles of the 1992 Ironman, which Grip won in course-record time (8:09:08).

BELOW: Mark turned in a career-best Ironman bike split of 4:29:00 on his way to winning the 1993 Ironman.

ABOVE LEFT: Dave expected to swim better than he did in the 1994 Ironman, despite being 40 years old and not having competed in the event since Iron War.

ABOVE RIGHT: In 1996, at age 42, Dave ran a 2:45:20 marathon to move up from twenty-sixth place at the bike–run transition to fifth at the finish line.

RIGHT: Dave enjoyed a happy moment with sons Drew and Ryan and wife Anna after taking second place at Ironman in 1994.

ABOVE LEFT: Mark took a year off from Ironman in 1994 to start a family with Julie Moss.

ABOVE RIGHT: Mark smiled the smile of a satisfied man after winning his sixth and final Ironman at age 37 in 1995.

A high-tech Nike skin suit helped Mark stay close to defending champion Greg Welch in Grip's 1995 Ironman swan song.

ABOVE: Today Mark has a succesful online coaching business, and draws both fans and accomplished athletes to his in–person triathlon clinics.

RIGHT: Shaman Brant Secunda has had a big effect on Mark's life.

ABOVE: When Dave talks Ironman, as he did in Kona before the 2008 race, people listen.

LEFT: Dave's father, Verne, made his own mark on triathlon as the cofounder and leader of its first governing body. In 2009 Verne was inducted into the USA Triathlon Hall of Fame.

CHAPTER 12

THE MAN'S SEARCH FOR MEANING

What is to give light must endure burning.

— VIKTOR FRANKL

hree weeks after finishing second in the 1989 Ironman, Dave Scott
traveled to New Braunfels, Texas, to host a weekend triathlon camp.
Assisting him were fellow professional triathletes Paula Newby-
Fraser and Ray Browning as well as 1981 Ironman winner John Howard,
now retired, and celebrity bike mechanic Dan Rock. That Sunday happened
to be the day on which ABC's coverage of the recent Ironman was broadcast. Dan and Ray watched the show together in the room they shared on
the second floor of a major-chain business hotel. Dave watched it alone in
his ground-floor room. Forty-five minutes into the program, Ray stood up.

"I'm going to check on Dave," he announced.

"Okay," Dan said with a knowing smile. "I'm going to stay here and
see what happens."

Both men not only knew what had happened but were among the first
to have known, having competed in the race themselves.

Ray entered Dave's room at the precise moment when, on the nineteen-
inch screen Dave was watching, Mark was breaking away from him on
Palani Hill.

"Hey, Dave, what's going on?" Ray said.

Dave's eyes continued to bore holes into the television screen as he delivered his full-throated reply: *"I'm losing!"*

NEVER HAS AN ATHLETE lost so well. The sheer valiance of Dave's Iron War defeat was as magnificent as any victory. Refusing to accept his vanquishment until it was an irreversible fait accompli, if even then, the Man ran as hard as he could all the way to the finish line, though there was no real cause to do so and though the cost in agony was immense. The race was over the moment Dave lost contact with Mark at the base of Palani Hill, with 1.7 miles left to go. From there Mark flew ever farther ahead of his nemesis on the giddy wings of assured victory. Meanwhile, the next guy behind Dave, Ken Glah (who would be passed by Greg Welch less than a mile from the finish), was so far back that Dave could literally have walked the rest of the way and still beaten him.

But he did not walk. Instead he fought for every second over the remaining distance, because anything could happen—and even if the race was lost, a great finish time was not. The competitor in him had been mortally wounded, but Dave still had a chance to break 8:10, and he still cared.

Dave ran like a man with a bullet in his chest. It was ugly. Yet his determined death sprint was also beautiful as an expression of his incredible, pointless unwillingness to relent. Among the witnesses was Jim Curl, who had last seen Dave at his condo, relaxed and ready, on the eve of the race. Jim was having a tough day, walking up Pay-'n'-Save Hill as Dave came down it like an avalanche in futile yet unyielding pursuit of Mark.

Thank you, triathlon gods, Jim said to himself as he carried this humbling image of perseverance—of carrying on despite everything—through the remaining nineteen miles of his own race—and, after that, through the rest of his life.

In triathlon today, it is customary for race winners to purposely dog the homestretch, high-fiving fans along the barricades, mugging for cameras, hoisting their children, and all but turning cartwheels in a show of savoring their triumph. Such behavior drives Dave nuts, not because he sees it as showing up those finishing behind the winner but because it demonstrates a lack of respect for the clock. How can these kids, today's so-called professional racers, allow their precious finish times to bloat by ten, twenty, even thirty seconds while gamboling like simpletons for the mere sake of extending their winning moments?

"It's a race!" he raves. "You're supposed to finish it as fast as you can!"

So deeply time-obsessed was Dave, and so terrific was the second-place time he achieved in the 1989 Ironman (8:10:13), that, as much as he hated to lose, he was not as immediately disappointed by his defeat as one might have expected. But his satisfaction did not last long.

Dave had not even caught his breath when he saw Carol Hogan standing before him. The local reporter who in 1980 had asked Dave if he was going to retire after he won his first Ironman still worshipped the ground he walked on. A diminutive woman, she looked up at her vanquished hero with tears streaming down her cheeks.

"Dave," she cried, "you lost!"

"I know," Dave said with a sigh. "I had a great race. Mark had a fabulous race."

Carol's disappointment made Dave feel suddenly defensive about his feeling that he had in fact had a great race. But it was another post-race incident that really took the wind out of his sails.

Anna pushed her way to her husband scant seconds after he crossed the finish line—teetering with exhaustion, his face cadaverous—and threw her arms around him. Insofar as his brain was working well enough to expect anything, he expected her to say, "You did great, Dave," or "Better luck next time, honey." But instead she whispered something about a suspicious canister that Dave was believed to have discarded during the marathon. Anna warned her disoriented and uncomprehending husband that the race officials were buzzing about it and that he should expect to be interrogated.

"What?" Dave mumbled, barely above a whisper. "A canister? What kind of canister?"

"I don't know. A film canister, I think."

Then he remembered that he had seen an item like that tucked into Mark's running shorts. Apparently Mark had tossed it away at some point, and a race official had picked it up, wrongly assuming that it was Dave who had dropped it and that the canister—whatever it had contained; probably something innocuous like salt tablets—must have been given to him illegally by a friend or supporter earlier in the race.

Sure enough, a race official soon found Dave and pulled him aside to ask about the canister. Dave told the man what little he knew. The official then left him, whether to question Mark or to deliver his findings he would never know, as the matter never again came to Dave's attention. Most likely the officials prudently decided against ruining the greatest race ever run by disqualifying either of its heroes over an unproven minor infraction. Nevertheless, that arbitrary and accusatory intrusion on Dave's immediate emotional processing of the race's outcome spoiled whatever satisfaction in his performance he might otherwise have enjoyed.

At the awards ceremony the next night Valerie Silk broke from tradition and allowed Dave to say a few words before the winner spoke. Dave took the gesture of respect as his due and stayed resolute in his refusal to forgive the previous day's insult.

I'll show them. Wait till next time.

Dave did not sleep well the night after the race, or the night after that. As he lay awake, the Man (was he still the Man?) seared his memories of the great fight he had narrowly lost into the tender tissues of his brain with the hot iron of voluntary recall. In the hours, days, and weeks that followed the race, Dave replayed it obsessively in his mind, trying to figure out how he could make it come out differently. And he succeeded in that effort.

Dave recognized that he'd made a few small, tactical errors, such as letting Mark take the inside position at the marathon aid stations as they ran side by side through all but the last 1.7 miles. Identifying such errors afforded him some relief because it meant he could have beaten Mark—and if he could have beaten Mark, then he still might. Next time.

After a short off-season break, Dave resumed training with great optimism and ample motivation, confident he could come up with the fifty-nine seconds he would need to turn the tables on Mark in the 1990 Ironman. Little did he know that he would never get his chance to exact vengeance on Mark Allen—not in 1990; not ever. An ankle injury kept Dave out of his first rematch opportunity, which Mark won, and also the 1991 Ironman, where Mark collected his third title. The following year, still recovering, Dave allowed the responsibilities of fatherhood (he and Anna had a second son, Drew, by then) and an expanding coaching business to distract him from his still smoldering desire to return to Kona, where Mark won yet again.

There were several "beanbag-chair" periods in those years, precipitated by the mutiny of Dave's body, stress from his side business, fear of aging and its effects on the physical powers that had always been the pride of his life, and the slow unraveling of his marriage—sometimes individually and sometimes in combination.

Ray Browning witnessed a number of these downswings from his vantage point as a partner in Dave's training-camp business. He always saw them coming, like storm clouds on the horizon. First Dave would become irritable—everything was a hassle. Then he would just disappear. Phone calls would not be returned. Ray became worried enough about Dave on some occasions to contact other friends and acquaintances and ask if they had seen him. Usually nobody had.

In 1992, at age 38, Dave formally announced his retirement from professional racing. It was an emotionally driven gesture of frustration and largely self-directed disgust precipitated by another nagging knee injury. Dave had not exercised in ten days when *Outside* writer John Brant came to Boulder—where Dave and his family were staying with his sister Jane, who had recently moved there—to follow Dave around for a couple of days and gather material for a profile to mark the end of Dave's legendary career. Ironically, John's visit was just the sort of thing that was guaranteed to pull Dave off the couch; he had always rallied under a spotlight.

Sure enough, on the first morning of John's visit, Dave proposed that John follow along in his rental car while Dave rode his bike for a few hours. They met at Jane's house. John was led through the living room, where Legos, Babar books, an inflatable whale, and other children's belongings were scattered about, and seated at the kitchen table, from which vantage point he quietly observed the family dynamics while Dave got ready.

"Look at these hairy legs," said Dave, who had stopped shaving them when he had stopped training. "I'll be the laughingstock of every triathlete in Boulder."

"So go ahead and shave them," Jane said. "Anyway, who's going to challenge you?"

Dave smiled boyishly at his sister's not-so-subtle flattery before taking another dig at himself.

"I couldn't do that," he said. "If I shaved my legs, everyone would see that I don't have any muscles down there."

Anna now spoke to John directly. "My husband," she said, "has more problems with body image than a 15-year-old."

Ready at last, Dave clomped outside in his cycling shoes and mounted a road bike. John took the wheel of his car and followed Dave out the driveway. An eighth of a mile down the road, Dave pointed out a house to John: Mark Allen's summer house. Dave did not stop to see whether Mark, currently training toward his fourth straight Ironman victory, cared to come along.

Dave rode first through the flats east of Boulder and then into the hills. The workout ended abruptly at the top of the famous Left Hand Canyon climb when an approaching storm forced Dave to pull over, throw his bike into the back of John's car, and hitch a ride home.

"That was fun," Dave said, beaming like a child, after settling into the passenger seat.

They rode in silence for a minute or two, watching the storm gather.

"The funny thing is," Dave said eventually, "now that I've decided to stop racing, my knee feels better than it has in three years."

Again silence filled the vehicle.

"You start working out," Dave said, unprompted, "you start getting ideas."

By the time John Brant's article about Dave's retirement was published, its subject was already out of retirement, at least privately. His training became increasingly consistent and intensive over the next several months. Although he was healthy, Dave held himself out of the 1993 Ironman, feeling that he was not yet fit enough to achieve a performance worthy of his name. Instead he watched Mark claim his fifth consecutive Ironman title.

Dave Scott was 40 years old and had been almost completely absent from competition for nearly five years when he committed to race the 1994 Ironman, which, as fate would have it, Mark Allen skipped, citing burnout. Dave knew that no athlete in any endurance sport had ever returned from pasture at his age to win a major championship. In light of this lack of precedent, he wondered, what should his goal be for his return to Ironman? What could he expect?

Screw precedent.

"The only level that I could do Ironman, contrary to what I might have said at the time, was to do well again," Dave said afterward. "And well is not sixth place."

He had to win.

But first he needed confidence that he could. He sought that confidence at the Gulf Coast Triathlon, a half-Ironman held in Panama City, Florida, in May. Having lost his bike sponsor during his long layoff and needing the support of a new one, Dave unwisely competed on a bike he had never ridden before, which was shipped to the race site by a prospective new sponsor. Its geometry was just different enough from what Dave was used to, and perhaps his aging body had lost just enough of its former adaptability, to leave him standing next to the bike some 40 miles into the 56-mile cycling leg, trying desperately to stretch out vicious cramps in his hamstrings.

By the time he rolled into the transition area, the pro bike rack was already filled with his opponents' machines—a sight Dave had never seen before. And it was about to get a whole lot worse. The moment he dismounted from his ill-fitting bike, the entire back side of his body seized up, and he flopped to the ground as though he had been Tasered. This happened just as the race announcer, already embarrassed for Dave on account of his tardy return from the bike course, was drawing the crowd's attention to the great legend's presence. Medics rushed to his aid. Humiliated, he waved them off, scrambled for and painfully laced up his running shoes, and hobbled onto the run course, as much to escape the pitying attention of the crowd as to continue the race.

Dave heard the chatter afterward.

He's washed up.

Why is he doing this to himself?

He's tarnishing his legacy.

Just what a man who trained and raced best with a chip on his shoulder needed. As Dave trained through the summer in Boulder, where he now lived full time with his family, he savored fantasies of the shock and regret his doubters would express when he won Ironman despite his disastrous rust-buster in Panama City. He came to Kona even leaner than he'd been in 1989. Having shaved his trademark mustache, he looked about 28, or the age at which he'd told Linda Buchanan that he intended to be fitter at 40 than he was then. And so he was.

Nevertheless, the doubters seemed halfway vindicated when Dave exited the swim eighteenth, nearly a minute and a half behind pre-race favorite Greg Welch, the very man who'd finished a galactically distant third behind Dave and Mark in '89. But on the bike Dave performed like his old—or young—self. Anger plainly written on his grimacing, clean-shaven face, the Man mowed down all seventeen athletes ahead of him and snatched the lead from Greg at forty miles.

Mark Allen, working for NBC Sports (ABC had given up rights to broadcast the race in 1990), witnessed the moment from inside a VIP vehicle. The producer of that year's Ironman special, Lisa Lax, sat next to him in the backseat of the convertible, trying to guess what he was thinking. Was he nostalgically rooting for the old-timer? Sickened by the very idea of Dave winning yet another Ironman? Desperately wishing he was in the race to squash Dave's return to glory? She would never know, as Mark said nothing.

The 1994 Ironman scarcely resembled Dave's first Ironman. In 1980 the swimmer from Davis who'd believed he could "pound it out with anyone at the end" had competed against 107 mostly ill-prepared Californian endurance misfits on inadequate bikes. Now he faced more than 1,500 superbly trained qualifiers from all over the world riding multithousand-dollar machines whose materials and components had not even existed at the time of Dave's first Ironman. But one thing had not changed in fourteen years: the man leading the race halfway through the bike leg.

At eighty-five miles, Dave found himself in a lead pack with Greg Welch, Ken Glah, Jürgen Zäck, and Peter Kropko. A flag marking the Timex Bike Prime—a $1,500 prize awarded to the race leader at that point of the race—appeared ahead. Jürgen and Peter took off after it. Greg made to follow, not so much for the sake of the prime as to mark the others. But Dave called out to him.

"Let it go, Welchy," he said. "That's not the race. The race is here."

Greg took Dave's advice and let the others get away. Later he wondered why Dave had given the free counsel. Since his last Ironman in 1989, Dave had drifted back into his coaching roots. He had even coached Greg himself, informally, over the summer. Perhaps Dave just couldn't help himself at this stage of his life—couldn't help being a good coach even at his own expense as an athlete.

Dave and Greg quickly dispatched Jürgen and company at the start of the marathon. Peter Kropko was last seen stumbling into a dolphin-shaped mailbox and tearing it out of the ground by the post as he fell over, clinging to it like a life preserver. Greg pulled twenty seconds ahead of Dave over the first half of the run. Dave surged, classically, on a long downhill stretch with ten miles to go and drew within eleven seconds of regaining the lead. Reports of the dramatic chase, radioed from the lava fields back to the finish area, sent the crowd into a frenzy. Although Dave liked to focus on his doubters, he had fifty believers for every hater.

The Man had played his last card, however. The miracle was not to be. As Dave folded, Greg went all in and stretched his lead to four minutes over the last miles. Dave held on for second place and put the exclamation point on the statement he'd sought to make. His finish time of 8:24:32 was better than any of his winning times at Ironman, and obliterated the men's 40-plus age-group record by thirty-five minutes.

"That race proved to me that it wasn't about age," Dave said later. "Age was the biggest hurdle, deterrent, and handicap that everyone else put on me, and I recognized it, but at 40 I didn't really think I was old."

A confident, hungry Dave Scott left the island already thinking ahead to his next opportunity.

Fit and ready for a final showdown with Mark Allen at the 1995 Ironman, which Grip, now 37, had decided would be his last, Dave dropped a dumbbell on his foot before the race, breaking a toe. With Dave watching, Mark won his sixth title, matching Dave's career haul.

Well, that was disappointing. But another year of consistent training in Boulder's moderate altitude, which seemed to agree with Dave, more than made up for any physical decline wrought by another year of aging, and when he arrived back in Kona in October 1996, now 42, he believed in his heart that he could win number seven and thus surpass Mark in his absence, although he kept this belief to himself for fear of being socially straitjacketed.

No matter. He was whispered about anyway, ridiculed in some quarters for daring to compete in a professional division dominated by men whom he might have babysat a quarter century earlier. Cameron Widoff, a brash and rising young pro who had placed twelfth at Ironman the previous year, had caught sight of Dave in Kona a few days before the race and elbowed *Triathlete* editor T. J. Murphy in the ribs.

"What the hell is *he* doing here?" he'd sneered.

Dave certainly looked out of place. He still wore no sports watch or heart rate monitor, even though he was now sponsored by heart rate monitor manufacturer Polar. His bike was an anachronism. No power meter, no mileage counter, nothing.

Just give me a water bottle and get out of my way.

Dave felt as out of place as he looked for the first five hours of the race. He had an unaccountably terrible swim. Worse, although he had ridden better than ever in his summer training, his legs betrayed him on the bike. It seemed as if the mighty red fibers of his thighs and shanks had been scooped out and replaced with vanilla pudding. Dave had been greedy in the last month before the race, pushing himself more and more in training as the fumes of his simmering fitness had gone to his head, and now he was paying the price. As a parade of young pros and even age groupers whizzed by him like Manhattan pedestrians overtaking an octogenarian with a walker, he was, for the first time in ten tries, seriously tempted to quit Ironman.

Tempted.

At eighty-five miles, Dave decided to stop feeling sorry for himself. Knowing from experience that an atrocious ride can sometimes inexplicably be followed by a great run, he mentally flushed his horrendous bike leg and decided to let it all hang out in the marathon.

Dave reached the bike-run transition in twenty-sixth place, farther back by a long shot than he had ever been in Hawaii. He burst onto the run course as if he'd stepped on a hornet's nest and almost immediately began to pass other runners. It became a classic Dave Scott game, a kind of kinetic outdoor cousin of Pac-Man. Five thousand morale points per pass, as it were. Having accepted the race as an unsalvageable disaster, Dave still wanted to see what he could do.

A few miles into the marathon, Dave began to receive accurate information on his position from tuned-in spectators, and the game became even more exciting.

"You're in sixteenth place!" he heard.

Dave had never been in sixteenth place before. He should have been ashamed. Instead he was exhilarated. *Here I go!* he told himself. *I'm in sixteenth place! This is terrific! Let me get to tenth!* Dave caught the tenth man at about mile thirteen, a scenario he would have considered nightmarish before the race but which now felt more like *waking* from a nightmare. He had never had so much fun.

Among those Dave passed as he approached the top ten was Cameron Widoff. Cam What-the-Heck-Is-He-Doing-Here Widoff.

Dave did not stop there. With four miles left in the race, 42-year-old Dave Scott moved into fifth place. As he sprinted the final stretch on Ali'i Drive, Ironman race announcer Mike Reilly, who had taken over Mike Plant's job in 1991, recognized the Man's distinctive duck-like stride from his perch above the finish line. He nearly swallowed his tongue.

"Here comes Dave Scott in fifth place!" he hollered into his microphone. It wasn't quite his "The band is on the field!" moment, but it was pretty darn close.

As he crossed the finish line, Dave pumped his fist in grim satisfaction.

"No one would introduce me as Dave Scott, six-time Ironman champion, and oh, by the way, he got fifth in 1996," Dave said in a 2010 interview. "That's a real blight on my résumé. But for mental fortitude and tenacity, it was one of my best races ever, if not *the* best."

Dave knew winning as well as any athlete, yet he would ultimately rank two losses—1996 and Iron War—as his favorite racing memories.

Dave walked away from the finish line of the 1996 Ironman with an obvious limp, leaning on Anna, who with her free arm held the couple's third child, Kara, as Ryan and Drew gallivanted proudly ahead of their parents. Dave had hurt his knee during the run. That same knee was still bothering him when he started his next Ironman in 2001, racing in the pro division once more at age 47 (and deservedly, having run a 1:15 half-marathon in the Vineman Triathlon earlier in the season). Dave dropped out forty-five miles into the bike leg, his knee on fire. For the first time in ten tries, he quit Ironman. Afterward Dave announced—as he had five years before—that he'd raced his last race in Kona. But he soon discovered that he couldn't live with failing to reach the finish line of his final Ironman. On top of that, he couldn't live without Ironman.

In 2002, the year after his unprecedented DNF, Dave got permission from Ironman to access the racecourse in a car, which he shared with *Competitor* publisher Bob Babbitt. Dave insisted on driving and followed the men's professional race so closely that he practically seemed to be *in* the race. Dave and Bob were cruising next to first-timer Chris McCormack when Chris took the lead on the bike.

"What should I do?" he shouted at Dave. Chris had been an adoring Dave Scott fan long before he met him.

"Go for it!" Dave bellowed.

When Dave and Bob reached the barricade barring access to the narrow section of the bike course between Kawaihae and Hawi, Dave argued his way past it, very nearly pulling the "Do you know who I am?" card.

Dave spoke almost without pause through the entire day, more to himself than to Bob, analyzing every move, volunteering what he would be doing if he were in the race.

"What the hell are they doing?" Dave said as the lead cyclists made what he considered a rather timid descent from Hawi. "There's practically no wind! These guys should be flying!"

Dave's eyes met Bob's; that mad gleam was still there. For an instant Bob was convinced that Dave was going to pull over, haul a bike out of the trunk, and show the young punks how it was done. He did not—perhaps only because there was no bike in the trunk.

IN 2003 DAVE SCOTT was recruited to participate in a charity event called Ironman Revisited, in which athletes were invited to swim, bike, and run the original Ironman course on Oahu. More or less healthy, although only "80 percent fit," as he told anyone who would listen, Dave agreed to ride the bike course as part of a relay with challenged athletes Rudy Garcia-Tolson, who would swim, and "One-Arm" Willie Stewart, who would run. Shortly before the race, Dave was talked into doing the swim, too, as a guide to 15-year-old Rudy, a two-leg amputee. Having completed the bike leg in first place, Dave jumped into a car—again with Bob Babbitt—and followed Willie as he ran. A steady stream of tensely voiced encouragement issued from Dave's wide-open window toward Willie, who clung to a two-minute lead over David Lourens, the top individual racer. With thirteen miles to go, Willie weakened, and his lead shrank. Dave stopped the car, scrambled out, and ran with Willie through the final thirteen miles of the race, to victory.

Dave returned to Ironman Revisited each year thereafter. In 2007 he raced it as part of a relay team with sons Ryan and Drew, now 17 and 15 years old and showing a strong interest in the family business. The trio took second place. Dave felt stronger and more sound of body than he had in years. Perhaps this perception was not strictly physical in origin but was an effect of doing the thing he loved most with two of the most important people in his life. In any case, Dave flew home with his boys fixated on the idea of returning to Ironman—the real Ironman—now that his children, including 11-year-old daughter Kara, were old enough to really appreciate it, and while he still had the ability to do it well, by his standard.

Dave's form did not come around in time for the 2008 Ironman, but by February 2009 the Man was divulging to those in his circle of confidence that he was thinking about returning to the Kona start line in October. His plan was to throw himself into his training for six weeks in May and June, see where that left him, and then make a formal decision. Dave made an *in*formal decision midway through that training block, during a fifty-six-mile solo ride on Sunday, May 17. He rode hard and felt great, and when he returned to the Boulder outskirts he calculated that his total time for the ride, including the ten minutes it would take him to cruise through town to his front door, would be about 2:23. Solid.

As he rolled westward along Broadway toward his home in North Boulder, Dave began to run some numbers in his head. His swim pace in recent workouts was only two seconds per 100 yards slower than it had been in his prime. He figured he could go 0:52, maybe 0:51 in the Ironman swim. With five months to build on his current cycling fitness, an Ironman bike split of 4:45 seemed realistic. On a great day, perhaps 4:41 would be possible; on a lousy day, he would surely ride no worse than 4:51. The run was more of a mystery. He had not done enough running lately to know exactly where he stood, but 6:30 miles still felt pretty easy. A sub-three-hour marathon in Kona was thus a conservative hope. Tallying his estimates, Dave came up with a projected finish time of roughly 8:40. That time would have placed him twelfth in the previous year's Ironman and represented a sixty-seven-minute improvement on the existing course record for the men's 55 to 59 age group.

Dave knew better than to go public with such an estimate. It would be much doubted. But he had no reason to second-guess his projection. Dave had correctly predicted that he would lop more than an hour off the Ironman course record on his first try in 1980. He had rightly predicted that it would take about an 8:10 to win the race in 1989, when the existing course record was 8:28. Nobody was better able to estimate his Ironman performance capacity at any given moment than Dave Scott. He'd been doing it every day for thirty years. Not a single rotation of planet Earth was completed, not once, without Dave's being able to accurately guess how fast he could finish Ironman at his present fitness level. It was as routine as checking his appearance in the bathroom mirror.

In high spirits, Dave turned right off Broadway onto Poplar Avenue. Immediately he noticed a beige BMW X5 sport utility truck stopped in the middle of the right lane ahead of him. Dave assumed the driver must be looking for someone or something. The driver, 61-year-old Ramona Sands, was in fact looking for an open house. As Dave approached the vehicle from behind, wondering if he'd been seen in the rearview mirror, the BMW began moving. Dave continued to ride at a steady 24 mph as the accelerating truck pulled away.

A few hundred yards later the driver stopped again, in the middle of the road, without signaling. Dave's antenna went up. Thirty years of cycling experience had taught him the warning signs of a bike-blind motorist.

Again Dave drew closer to the BMW from behind, and once more it began moving before he could overtake it. He saw the truck reach a stop sign ahead and turn left onto Wonderland Hill Avenue, the same direction he was going. The vehicle disappeared from Dave's sight until he completed the turn, and then it reappeared above him on a long hill that he now began to climb. The truck stopped at the top of the hill and remained stationary almost long enough for Dave to catch up to it. He was just deciding whether to pass it on the right or the left when it took off yet again, accelerating down the back side of the hill. A quarter mile later, at the bottom, the driver veered onto the right shoulder, no signal, and stopped just behind two parked cars. This was a popular area for dog walking. Dave supposed the motorist had at last found her destination.

Nevertheless, he remained alert. As he came down the hill behind the SUV, Dave was prepared to swerve wide to the left if the driver suddenly swung back onto the road and began moving forward. What he was not prepared for was an abrupt U-turn, and that was exactly what happened. At the worst possible moment during Dave's approach from the driver's rear, Ramona pulled onto the road without signaling or looking behind her. Dave knew instantly that he was going to hit the truck broadside, and hard.

"Hey! Hey! Hey!" he shouted as he clenched his brakes.

Ramona heard the shouts, but it was too late. Dave plowed into the side of the vehicle at full speed and dropped to the ground like a sandbag. The double impact of Dave's body striking first the car and then the ground shattered his left wrist into several pieces; fractured and dislocated his left ring finger, leaving a bone projecting through the skin; fractured his left wrist; crushed his left shoulder blade; and caused a bone-deep bruise to his right thigh and multiple cuts and abrasions.

Ramona scrambled out of her vehicle and stood over Dave, who had not lost consciousness.

"Call 911," he croaked.

The pain in his shoulder was searing. He knew his leg was in bad shape too. He lay faceup, biting his lip as Ramona made the emergency call. Moments later he heard a familiar voice. It was Lars Finanger, a local triathlete who was out for a ride when he happened upon the scene.

"Dave, what can I do?" Lars asked, looming above him. "Can I call someone?"

Dave asked Lars to call his sister Jane and his daughter, Kara, and have them meet him at the hospital. A police car pulled up while Lars was on the phone with Jane. An ambulance arrived a moment later.

As he lay in the street under his bike, knowing he'd been badly hurt, a number of worries traveled through Dave's mind.

Will I ever be whole again?

How long will I be unable to travel for my business?

And at least one other worry.

"I knew there was a finality to my exercise regimen and any thoughts of racing," Dave told a reporter afterward. "I was very aware of that even when I was lying on the ground."

Nothing had changed. A week without a workout remained for Dave like a week without water or sunlight for a vegetable garden. Endorphin junkies are a dime a dozen. Dave Scott had become a self-described *endorphin lunatic.*

"If I don't get it," he said, referring to exercise, "it just makes me go haywire. It rules my life. It's a powerful drug for me. It's huge. It's gigantic."

Too big, Anna had finally decided. Dave and Anna separated in 2000 and divorced five years later. During their separation Dave just *had* to get a workout one day when Kara, born in 1996, was in his care. He put her on a little bike and instructed her to ride along behind him while he ran, which turned out to be not nearly as much fun for the child as he had imagined. Later Kara tearfully reported the incident to her mother. Anna knew that Dave would never have exposed his child to any real risk, but the situation was symbolic of the couple's irreconcilable differences.

On Father's Day 2003 Dave's three children had given him a hand-made card that read, "Dear Dad, you can do anything you want for Father's Day except swim, bike, or run."

Dave Scott is, by all accounts, as good a father to Ryan, Drew, and Kara as Verne was to him. But it wasn't always easy to live under the same roof as the Man, given the "drop too much" that nature had given him.

"When I'm on," Dave confessed in one interview, "and when I feel good about my exercise and I've been on a good wave, I feel invincible. I can handle any kind of hurdle and I can meet any kind of challenge head-on. And when I don't have it, when I don't have that morphine-like endorphin feeling that resonates throughout my body, it affects everything. It affects my personality, it affects my confidence, it affects my ability to interact with other people."

And so, even in 2009, as the paramedics gingerly loaded him onto a stretcher, Dave foresaw in his coming period of postaccident immobility his own personal hell, an experience far more terrible than the same situation would be for most people. Upon learning of his accident, Dave's family and friends feared for his mind as much as they did for his body, and rightly so. They knew he was likely to do desperate things for a fix while he recovered, and his doctors and therapists were duly warned.

Dave was taken by ambulance from the site of the accident to Boulder Community Hospital, where he was stabilized and spent one night before being transferred to the famous Steadman Clinic in Vail for surgery on his shoulder. On her first visit there Jane pulled aside his orthopedic surgeon, Randy Viola, and delivered a warning in the form of a story. Many years ago, she told him, Dave had been hospitalized after another bike wreck. Early one morning his doctor had entered Dave's room during his rounds and found him lying on the floor, bench-pressing his own bed.

Randy soon discovered that time had not mellowed his patient. Dave tested the limits any way he could, to the point where the staff had to assign nurses to keep a close watch on him, to protect him—from himself.

The doctors at the Steadman Clinic had found a blood clot in Dave's lung. He was told he must avoid any kind of exercise until the clot was broken up with anticoagulants. Knowing the chance he was taking, Dave took it anyway. A fate worse than death awaited him, he felt, if he obeyed doctors' orders and went stir-crazy like never before.

Walking was the first form of exercise Dave was actually allowed to do after the blood clot had dispersed. Running was forbidden, but Dave tried it anyway, convincing himself that he was not disobeying doctors' orders if he renamed the activity "quick steps."

One afternoon Dave was joined on a walk by Peyman Razifard, a member of Dave's Wednesday-morning running group. Before they started Peyman joked, "This is the first time I'll be able to beat you."

Big mistake. Dave said nothing, but when the pair reached the base of a long hill, Dave began to quick-step, and soon his challenger was left in his dust.

Dave was able to swim with one arm before he could swim with both, so, naturally, he did. One morning Mirinda Carfrae, who would win Ironman the following year, arrived at the Flatiron Athletic Club pool in Boulder to find Dave swimming with fins on his feet and his left arm pinned against his side.

"What are you doing today?" Dave asked her.

"Oh, just some 200s," she said, already knowing where this was going.

"Mind if I join you?"

Sure enough, Dave did not merely join Mirinda but tried to egg her into competition. Possessed of her own competitive nature and an impish sense of humor, Mirinda swam just hard enough to nip Dave at the wall on each interval. But the wounded old man put everything he had into the final 200 and outreached her by a hair's breadth.

"Only the last one counts," he deadpanned.

ON A SATURDAY MORNING in June 2010, a little more than a year after his accident, Dave Scott drove to Boulder Reservoir with his 19-year-old-son, Drew, who was home for the summer from Montana State University, where he competed on the Nordic ski team. They were drawn there by an open-water swim competition organized by Jane. Dave was out of town most weekends leading triathlon clinics, at which he typically found little time to train. He planned to take advantage of being home this particular weekend to work out to his heart's content.

As they were preparing to leave the house, Drew had emerged from his bedroom with a triathlon wetsuit slung over a shoulder.

"What are you doing?" Dave said, scowling.

"I'm bringing my wetsuit," Drew said, defensive.

"No, you're not. The water's 70 degrees. You'll get a better workout without it. You'll see the truth—the truth of how your swimming is now."

With an adolescent groan, Drew turned around and put the wetsuit back in his room. As they drove toward the reservoir, Dave completed his sermon.

"You can't always take the easy way, Drew," he said. "Sometimes it's okay. If your ego needs a boost, go ahead, wear a wetsuit. But other times, take the windy road. *See what you can do.*"

Drew absorbed the speech without comment.

At the reservoir, Dave and Drew wove through the gathering crowd of swimmers and found Jane, who was checking off names on a clipboard and handing out swim caps to competitors.

"How are you?" Dave asked her quietly, looking deeply into her eyes as though that was where he expected to find the true answer, regardless of what her mouth said.

This encounter was more than an ordinary meeting of the siblings, who saw each other a few times a week. Jane had learned four days earlier that she had uterine cancer. Dave had been coaching a regular Tuesday swim workout at Flatiron Athletic Club, where Jane also coached, when his cell phone rang. He checked the number. It was Jane. His entire body clenched. Jane had already told him that some abnormal cells had been found in a recent Pap smear and that she was having further tests. Dave answered.

"I'm out in the parking lot," Jane whispered. "Please come."

Dave abandoned his swimmers, raced outside, found her car, and climbed in. She told him what he already knew. They broke down together and sobbed in each other's arms. Dave and Jane had been as close as a brother and sister could be for their whole lives. Their entire journey had been shared—every high and every low. They had started swimming together, then built a coaching business together. Jane had cheered Dave through almost all of his Ironmans. They had moved to Boulder together. Now this.

"We've got to have faith," Dave said, gathering himself. "We've got to have faith."

Dave was likely speaking to Jane from precisely the same place from which he spoke to himself when things were looking bad at Ironman.

Now, having received a swim cap from Jane, Dave stripped down to his swimsuit and made small talk on the beach with friends and acquaintances in the minutes before the race started. He still looked damn good in a Speedo. Six firm rectus abdominus muscles were outlined like small loaves of wheat bread under his bronzed skin . His swimmer's chest looked as though it would meet a fist with a satisfyingly deep thudding sound. His thighs retained that bulgingly lean form that makes the legs appear skinny from some angles, massive from others, and is witnessed only in endurance athletes of the highest caliber—an undeceiving outward manifestation of inward ability.

Dave no longer looked younger than his age. Any stranger could see his 56 years in his crow's feet and in the flecks of gray in his close-cropped hair. He just looked like the fittest 56-year-old man in the history of the world. And he probably was, despite everything.

A hub of the Boulder athletic community, Dave knew almost all of the four or five dozen other athletes present and greeted many with his trademark gentle sarcasm.

"Looking kind of pasty, Matt," he told one swimmer, eyeing his luminously white belly, which he correctly judged to be a source of self-consciousness.

Moments before the start, a sinewy woman with hair hanging in shoulder-length coils sidled up to Dave. She was three-time Ironman winner and Ironman world record holder Chrissie Wellington, whom Dave had recently begun to coach. Dave demonstratively eyeballed the wetsuit she wore but said nothing.

"Aw, come on, Dave!" she pleaded with a laugh.

"Okay, this time," he said.

There were 1-mile and 2-mile swim options. Dave, of course, chose the longer alternative. He covered the course in 47:15, finishing three minutes behind Chrissie. Had Dave swum the full 2.4-mile Ironman distance at the same pace, he would have finished in 56:38. Not bad for a 56-year-old man who lacked full range of motion in his left shoulder, could not straighten his left ring finger, and suffered from constricted breathing associated with lingering damage from his bike wreck. But not good enough.

"I used to be an athlete; now I just exist," Dave told a friend with an unconvincing smile as he air-dried on the beach.

Age was his new archnemesis. In 2000, when Dave was 46, a reporter had asked what motivated him to continue working out several hours a day even though he scarcely raced anymore.

"I think it's age—awareness of age," Dave said. "I don't want to lose it. I don't want to start slipping."

While Dave talked with others about their respective swim experiences, he eagerly scanned the water for Drew's familiar stroke. He waited and waited. At last he spied his son's flailing arms. Drew got out of the water at fifty-five minutes and change.

"Your stroke looks terrible," Dave teased.

Father and son walked together to the parking lot to pull bikes out of their truck. Their friend Marek, who falls between them in age, met them there, already dressed to ride. Disdaining the concept of the warm-up as much as his father, Drew hunkered into his aerobars and dropped the hammer before they had even left the reservoir's mile-long access road. Marek held fast at Drew's shoulder, and Dave tucked in behind them.

It was a beautiful day, dry and sunny with temperatures in the low 80s. The trio chose a mostly flat route, heading west and then north along Highway 36. On such terrain, after more than a year of recovery and fitness rebuilding, Dave often felt as strong, or almost as strong, as he had on the day of his accident. He would lock into an effortless rhythm at 23 mph, and it would seem as though he could go forever. Could he get back to 24 in Kona? It seemed possible.

After ninety minutes of comfortable spinning, the three men ventured into the hills, turning off the highway and ascending more than

2,000 feet in Left Hand Canyon, the same climb Dave had made with John Brant during his 1992 retirement. It was every man for himself. Marek fell back first. Dave held on to his son's back wheel for several minutes, but then Drew stood out of the saddle and surged away easily. As Dave's breathing deepened, that all-too-familiar feeling of constriction seized his lungs. This now happened every time he started sucking wind while exercising. He just couldn't draw a belly breath anymore. It was enough to bring tears to his eyes at such moments—the frustration of effectively having a governor on his respiration, limiting him to 80 percent of his normal capacity.

It's over, he thought in these moments. He would never compete at Ironman again. People who encouraged him to do the race just to do it had no clue what it meant to him. Crawling through the race in ten hours at age 56 when he knew he could have finished in 8:40 or 8:50 at age 55, blowing people's minds one more time, would do absolutely nothing for him. Less than nothing.

At the top of the hill, Drew sat up triumphantly and waited for the losers to catch him. Dave rode right past his son and began the descent without even looking at him.

THE NEXT MORNING the group reconvened at Marek's condo for a trail run. Again Drew took off hard from the start. Dave groaned in pain with each landing of his left foot for the first ten minutes, until it went numb or he just got used to the hurt. He'd injured it after the crash in his haste to return to training, and it remained unhealed, in part because he refused to stop running.

They ran for forty minutes and then turned around. Along the way they met several other groups of runners. Dave knew them all, including a pair of older women, members of Dave's Wednesday running group, who came walking in his direction.

"You're supposed to be running, not walking, ladies," Dave admonished as they passed.

"We were, I swear!" one of them said. "We just stopped."

"Yeah, right."

Dave began to tire noticeably with about three miles left to run. Still a better downhill than uphill runner, he fell into a pattern of slipping behind the others on the climbs and then running them down on the back sides. On the last big hill, a long, gentle rise followed by a long, gentle descent, much like Palani Hill in Kona, Dave fell way back. He figured he had seen the last of his workout partners until they regrouped at the finish. But when he crested the hill, Dave looked ahead and saw that Drew had broken away from Marek, who appeared to be struggling.

Blood in the water. Dave went after Marek like a torpedo. He had about a mile in which to make up 200 yards on the little punk: numbers that exactly matched what he'd needed to do to catch Mark in 1989 upon reaching the top of Palani Hill. Perhaps Dave even imagined himself back there, back then, enjoying a second chance to make the greatest race ever run come out differently. His pace dipped under six minutes per mile, just as it had twenty-one years before. The gap steadily closed. Marek felt Dave coming, turned back, and flinched at the sight of the oncoming missile. He sped up, but he didn't stand a chance. Dave shot past Marek in the final fifty yards. He won.

"I thought you were toast," Marek said after he'd caught his breath. "How did you do that?"

"I still like to play the game," Dave said with a smile. "I can push myself as hard as I ever have. Even now, with all my limitations, I can reach down deep into that barrel of discomfort and pull out one single thing that allows me to hang on. I like doing that. I take pride in doing that."

He looked proud.

BETWEEN HIS SECOND AND THIRD workouts of the day—another ride and a swim at Flatiron Athletic Club—Dave returned home with Drew to wash up and refuel. After showering, Dave called his parents, who now lived in Boulder also, to confirm plans for a family meeting at their home. Dave and Jane would drive over separately in the evening. Patti, who lived and still coached swimmers in Sonora, California, would join them by phone. The spoken purpose of the meeting was to discuss Jane's illness and impending emergency surgery. The real purpose of the meeting was to comfort Verne and Dot, who had been hit hard by the news. Both had passed their eightieth birthdays, and they did not want to outlive their youngest child, having made it this far.

Hanging up, Dave blended several batches of smoothies, whipped up a bowl of guacamole, and sat down with Drew to watch World Cup soccer. The United States was playing Ghana. Dave shouted at the television. He drank two full blenders and ate several pieces of whole fruit plus a dinner party's worth of mixed nuts and corn chips with guacamole.

Dave's house is smaller and less sparkling than some might expect the home of a six-time world champion to be. But then, his total prize haul for those six titles was less than $50,000. Throughout Dave's career Verne had urged him to market himself more aggressively to compensate for the sport's dearth of race booty.

"You should be the next Jack LaLanne!" he'd said. "You have to put yourself out there more!"

His advice fell on deaf ears. Dave refused to take a single step to the left or the right of his independently chosen path for an extra dollar. He turned down a sponsorship offer from Timex because it would have required him to wear a watch during races, which he refused to do. He returned a hefty book advance to the publisher because he couldn't make the manuscript meet his standards.

Dave's finances, never as robust as they might have been, were not helped by his divorce from Anna. But he makes little effort to increase his income beyond hanging out a shingle as a triathlon coach. And he doesn't even make as much money in coaching as he could because, although Dave remains very much in demand as a coach, he weeds out athletes.

An athlete has to be a little like Dave Scott in order to be coached by Dave Scott.

"I don't allow any of my athletes, regardless of their age or background, to be mediocre," Dave said in his 2011 USA Triathlon Hall of Fame induction speech. "It drives me crazy."

A few days before he participated in his sister's open-water swim competition, Dave was swimming with his group when he noticed that another swimmer in his lane was taking the easy way through the set by using a pull buoy. When he left it on the deck for a recovery lap, Dave snatched it, swam to the other end of the pool with it, and hurled it ten feet out of reach.

Dave feels a small sting of disappointment when he scares away such athletes—a sting that is not dulled by any amount of repetition. He suffers a fresh disillusionment each time he rediscovers just how few are willing or able to reach deep down inside that barrel of discomfort in every swim, every ride, and every run. But the stakes are much higher with his own children, all now high-performing athletes themselves. His love for them demands that, in certain ways, he cut them a little more slack than he allows others. Yet he owes it to them and to everything sacred to hold them, when it really matters, as unyieldingly as he holds anyone to what he once called his "high, high, high expectations."

While Dave and Drew watched professional soccer together, Kara, then 14 years old, was playing soccer at an out-of-town tournament. She was an outstanding defender for the Boulder County Force, and Dave proudly attended many of her team's games and practices. It was always a bit awkward for him, though, because Dave did not exactly bond with the parents of Kara's teammates. He vexed them. They, in turn, annoyed him. The focus of Dave's annoyance was their pointed discouragement of competitiveness in their daughters, their almost sanctimonious way of telling the girls to "have fun" as they took the field for games. Dave, by contrast, told Kara to give everything she had to win.

"You can still have fun when you push yourself as hard as you can possibly go," he told her. "And if you don't win, you should be satisfied that you did your best. Figure out how you can do better next time, and maybe you can win next time."

If there is a next time.

CHAPTER 13

SHAMAN SURFER

We count them happy who endure.

—JAMES 5:11

I have to find that man.

Mark Allen's mind was a thousand miles away from the barrage of congratulations that was fired at him by an ambush of family, race officials, media people, and others behind the finish line on Ali'i Drive. His thoughts were fixed on that old shaman with the toothless smile who had appeared to him in the lava fields, giving him the strength—or the serenity—to win the race. Mark hungered for more of the peace and acceptance that seemed to emanate from the old man. Intuition urged Mark to seize all that was offered by the venerable native Mexican, whose visitation during his moment of crisis halfway through the marathon was not only a gift, he knew, but also a beckoning. Mark's need to beat Dave Scott and win Ironman had been satisfied. But the manner of that satisfaction had perhaps revealed what he *really* needed.

As soon as he got back to the Kanaloa with Julie, Mark tore the condo apart in search of the journal in which he'd seen the shaman, but it was nowhere to be found. He later obtained another copy only to discover that the advertised ten-day retreat, beginning November 17, fell too close to his and Julie's wedding date of December 10 to permit his attendance. More reluctantly than Julie would have liked, Mark skipped the retreat in favor of keeping his nuptial commitment and made plans to attend the following year's retreat instead.

Mark was initially quiet about his vision and its effect on him, at least publicly. In his speech at the Ironman awards banquet, he referred to a "vision of strength" that had helped him win, but he said nothing about the shaman. With Julie and his closest friends, however, Mark was more open, and not merely open but evangelistic. He gave brochures about the retreat he'd signed up for to Paul Huddle and Kenny Souza. They saw the same photograph of the shaman that Mark had seen before his battle with Dave Scott. He was identified as Don José Matsuwa, a 109-year-old Huichol Indian spiritual leader and healer, renowned and respected throughout central Mexico. Also pictured was a white man, Brant Secunda, who was identified as Don José's adopted grandson and creator of the Dance of the Deer Foundation, the sponsor of the retreat, which the brochure described as a "ten-day intensive seminar at the Pacific Ocean in Mexico."

"What do you think?" Mark asked his friends. "Do you want to go with me?"

Paul and Kenny both tossed their hats into the ring in a why-the-hell-not way. Mark had hoped for something more. Sure enough, when the time came to go, Mark's closest triathlon buddies sheepishly asked to have their hats back.

One night, as the retreat was approaching, Mark woke up with a terrible feeling of foreboding. He scrambled out of bed and began pacing the room while Julie remained sleeping. *Something's wrong*, he thought. *Something's wrong.* As he tried to walk off the mysterious anxiety, Mark was again visited by a vision of the radiant face of Don José. The same feelings of peace and acceptance he had absorbed from that image in his moment of crisis on the Queen K Highway flowed into him a second time. The sense of foreboding that had awakened him dissipated, and he was able to return to sleep.

A few days later Mark was contacted by Brant Secunda. He informed Mark that Don José had recently passed away, but that the retreat would go on. Mark asked Brant when Don José had died. It was the very night of his vision.

At last Mark's opportunity came. On November 30, 1990, fresh off his second Ironman victory, Mark flew from San Diego to Puerto Vallarta. Brant had instructed his guests to meet in a particular location within the airport. Arriving early, Mark hovered off to one side and observed the others as they gathered.

Oh, my God, Mark thought, taking in their clothes, speech, and manners. *I am the only normal person who's going to this workshop.*

Of course, Mark had spent the last eight years in a world where male leg-shaving and five-hour workouts were normal.

Brant showed up, and Mark felt some relief. He had vaguely worried that the first real shaman he would meet would walk around with sparks shooting out of his head and eagles circling over him. But Brant just seemed like a regular guy with an unusually powerful presence. Mark's relief deepened as the group was ferried toward a villa set on a pinch-me-beautiful bluff overlooking the sea. In talking to his fellow initiates Mark discovered that they were, in fact, some of the most interesting and grounded folks he had met in a long time.

At the first evening's welcome dinner, Brant Secunda introduced himself and told his story.

"I grew up in New York City and northern New Jersey in the '50s and '60s," he began, as he always did.

As a teenager, like many other young seekers of the day, Brant had become interested in the books of Carlos Castaneda, the very same anthropologist of Mexican Indian shamanism whose books would captivate Mark Allen at about the same age a few years later. So strong was the spell that Castaneda's stories cast on Brant that, four days after he graduated from high school in June 1970, he hopped aboard a bus and made a cross-continental pilgrimage to central Mexico in search of the great teacher described in Castaneda's books, Don Juan Matus, who, unfortunately for Brant, did not actually exist. Castaneda had fabricated almost everything he'd passed off as real in his work. Starting in the remote village of Ixtlan del Rio, Brant embarked upon what was supposed to be a five-day hike in the Sierra Madre Mountains that would lead him to the home of the invented Don Juan.

On the third day, Brant became hopelessly disoriented, lost under towering oak and Brazil trees and amid thick underbrush. A city kid, 18 years old and utterly lacking in survival skills, he soon lost his grip, surrendering to a state of panic. *I should have gone to college like my friends*, he thought. Brant walked and walked without seeing a single human being, sign of civilization, or orienting clue. Hours passed. A hot sun beat down on the young man, who had long since consumed the two pineapples and the small canteen of water he had packed to sustain him and was now desperately thirsty, hungry, sunburned, and fatigued. He became convinced that he was going to die and even sat down to write a farewell letter to his mother and father. He cursed himself for having attempted such a foolish adventure alone.

Eventually Brant fell unconscious, suffering from severe dehydration and heat exhaustion. Some time later he awoke on his back in the dirt to discover several exotic-looking Indian men standing over him, sprinkling water on his face and gently kicking him to break his slumber. They explained, in Spanish, that the old shaman of their village had dreamed about Brant the previous night and had sent the rescue party that was now saving his life.

The natives led Brant along a narrow path that eventually opened onto a clearing, where a small village of mud huts greeted Brant with the aroma of corn tortillas being cooked over open fires and the laughter of children playing. Brant's rescuers introduced him to their shaman, the venerable Don José Matsuwa, then a sprightly 90-year-old with twenty good years left in him.

Don Juan, Don José, whatever.

Brant stayed. Don José adopted him as his grandson, and over the next twelve years apprenticed him in the traditions, lore, and rituals of Huichol Indian shamanism, which is big on animism (the notion that spirits inhabit physical things), spiritual healing, and peyote.

Typical of one who finds spiritual answers in a tradition outside that of his own people, Brant developed a yearning to take Huichol Indian shamanism back to America. In 1981 he established a foundation for that purpose in Soquel, California, near the surf city of Santa Cruz. Brant divided his time between Soquel and Mexico until Don José's death in 1990.

Brant's story was appealing to Mark, who, over the next several days, learned about Huichol beliefs and healing practices from Brant and from Don José's widow, Doña Josefa Medrano, an ancient woman who smiled as radiantly as her late husband and who costumed herself in bead necklaces, flowing skirts, and head scarves. The simple, practical nature of the wisdom and the penetrating influence of nature on every aspect of the faith were likewise to Mark's taste. He performed sunrise and sunset prayers with the group and hiked with them to "places of power"—mainly hilltops. He did the sacred dance of the deer, after which Brant's foundation was named. He sat in a sweat lodge, which sorely tested his legendary tolerance for suffering. Merely sitting in that heat was as mentally challenging as running with Dave through the lava fields of Kona during the 1989 Ironman had been.

It was all very enjoyable but not quite transformative until sunset on the seventh day. Mark was sitting in a circle with his fellow initiates, listening to the trance-inducing chanting of Brant Secunda, when suddenly he experienced what can only be described as a classic spiritual awakening, like Buddha's enlightenment under the Bodhi tree and Augustine's conversion in his back garden. Mark suddenly felt, with absolute certainty, that he had just found—in the person of Brant and in the tradition he represented—the answer he had been searching for since he was a young boy. Mark had always been drawn to images in movies of wise elders from ancient traditions who utter simple nuggets of wisdom that put everything in perspective. All his life he had searched for someone or something in the real world that would connect him to that type of knowledge and clarity. But try as Mark might to experience his hazy ideal of how life should be lived and to feel something that deeply touched his soul, he always fell just a little short. The many traditions and practices Mark sampled had brought him closer, but never the whole way, to peace and inner happiness.

All of that frustration was forgotten as Mark absorbed Brant's chant. This man was the real deal. He had done what it takes to possess the wisdom that brings peace and inner happiness, and Mark knew he could do the same through him. It was happening already. Through the remainder of the retreat, Mark tasted the reality of the possibility that had been teasingly alluded to in his past spiritual wanderings. He felt as though he had been swallowed up into nature and eternity and was now fundamentally connected to every person and to all other living things. He felt a new joy—not the familiar kind that came from achieving results, but a joy that was already inside him, and that became his jumping-off point for going out into the world.

When he left Mexico Mark was committed to going all the way with Huichol Indian shamanism. Whatever it took, he would learn from Brant Secunda until he was as complete as Brant himself.

Mark came home a different man. Life changed at the summer house in Boulder. The old gang still trained and hung out together, but the dynamics of the relationships shifted subtly toward a new equilibrium. Paul and Kenny and the others got used to Mark interrupting bike rides to put dead birds in his pockets. They got used to him waving burning sage around them and praying for traveling mercies before they boarded airplanes. Mark grew his hair long, and they got used to that.

AFTER BEATING DAVE in 1989, Mark briefly considered putting Ironman behind him forever. *I've done everything that I possibly could have dreamed to do in this sport*, he thought. *I've filled my bucket.* But although the feeling of winning Ironman was wonderful, it was not lasting. No sooner had it worn off than Mark began to crave it anew.

Dave Scott had publicly retired from Ironman after each of his last four victories, only to come back. Mark now understood why. Winning Ironman was so hard and so fulfilling that it was natural to fly home from the island feeling it was enough. But as memories of the pain faded and the afterglow dissipated, returning came to seem just as natural.

Having decided to race Ironman again, Mark set a goal to top himself. He created a five-year plan. The plan centered on a small bag of tricks, or potential performance-boosting measures, that Mark wanted to try, to see if they would enable him to perform even better in Kona. One year he teamed up with bike wizard Steve Hed for extensive testing that yielded a more aerodynamic riding position on his bike. Another year he worked with strength and conditioning coach Diane Buchta to develop a weight lifting program that added several pounds of muscle to his bony frame. And each year he took his spiritual practices a step further.

Mark Allen and Brant Secunda became triathlon's equivalent of Luke Skywalker and Yoda. While Mark's interest in shamanism was completely independent of his pursuit of triathlon, his everyday life was so dominated by the sport that it naturally became the primary field of application for his new spiritual practice. Mark regularly visited Brant in Soquel for healing rituals to fix his frequent overuse injuries. He fell into a routine of traveling with Brant to a place of power such as Mt. Shasta or Alaska each summer, right before he started his big Ironman training ramp-up. During such trips Mark would spend several days neglecting his workouts and getting his mind right, the Huichol way. Brant gave Mark a full indoctrination into the wisdom of his religion and aided him in discovering how to apply it in training and competition.

The result was essentially the perfection of Ironman racing. Grip became unbeatable in Kona as the Man never had. After learning just two weeks before the 1990 Ironman that Dave had withdrawn from the race with an injury, Mark won it by nine minutes over Scott Tinley. The following year, Mark took the race by six minutes over Greg Welch.

While training for the 1992 Ironman, Mark was struck by a car. As he flipped over his handlebars and sailed toward impact with the road, he felt something dense and heavy dislodge from his chest, like a cinder block flying out of his heart. He landed wrong and broke his collarbone.

Mark lived in a kind of trance for the next week. His mind's eye was bombarded with vivid memories of encounters he'd had with his father when he was a child—memories he'd kept locked away in a dank cellar of his soul for almost a quarter-century. Something had indeed been dislodged in that accident, and it wasn't physical. A dark need had been stirring inside him lately, since he and Julie had begun to try to conceive a child together. His brush with death brought that need to the surface and exposed it to daylight. Suddenly Mark understood why winning his first Ironman had not made him feel better about himself or more reconciled to the world, and why the second hadn't either, nor the third. His motivation to win Ironman was partly positive: a reward for testing and improving himself as a whole person. But winning Ironman was also a source of conditional self-approval, and to get where he really needed to go as a human being, Mark recognized, he needed to move beyond that.

Mark promised himself that he would try to take a more positive mind-set into his next Ironman. He would seek victory not to prove his worth but to realize himself.

Mark also decided to confront his father at long last about the hurt Space had caused him. The meeting, which Mark probably dreaded as much as he craved it, took place after that year's Ironman, where Mark met with an unexpected challenge from Chilean newcomer and 2:16 marathoner Christian Bustos but stomped him in the second half of the run to win by seven minutes and set a new course record of 8:09:08.

Two months later Mark and Julie hosted a family gathering for the holidays. Julie's heart was in her throat, as Mark's must have been also, when Mark shut the door to finally have it out with his father. Space showed no surprise when Mark revealed the reason for the conversation. In fact, he said, he'd been expecting it for a long time. Mark told Space about the memories of ill treatment that had lately come back to him with terrible force. Knowing the power of silence, Mark stopped there. The truth was on the table for Space to affirm or deny, own or disown. Space affirmed and owned his harsh behavior. It had happened, and he had done it. He confessed with a steady eye and in plain words. And he stopped there.

Afterward Julie could see that a great burden had been lifted from her husband. He seemed free, in a new way. Not free to start over with his father. Free *of* his father.

In '93, Mark lowered the Ironman record once more, to 8:07:45, beating Finland's Pauli Kiuri for his fifth Ironman title.

Mark decided to skip Ironman the following year. He needed a break. His body was beginning to wear down. But his desire was also flagging. Mark had succeeded in taking more positive motivations into the world's biggest race. Ironically, this success had left him needing Ironman less. He still loved it, but he did not need it as he once did.

"I don't know how many more times I will keep doing this race," Mark said wearily from the stage of the Ironman awards banquet—the stage he had once wanted to stand on more than he wanted anything else in life.

Mark was on the mountaintop. He was outrageously successful, respected, affluent, and more famous than he could sometimes fathom. But he was beginning to covet other summits, and to attain them, he would first have to descend.

AT A PARTY HELD the night after his fifth Ironman victory, Mark found himself talking to Gatorade president Bill Schmidt, who offered him two tickets to the 1994 Super Bowl, which would take place in Atlanta in late January, a couple of weeks after Mark's thirty-seventh birthday. Mark didn't know football from checkers, nor did Julie, but Mike Rubano was a big fan, so Mark invited his friend to make the trip with him. Before leaving, both men rented tuxedos. Bill had said they'd need them.

The night before the game Gatorade hosted a swank party for the rich and famous at the Buckhead Theater. The first person Mark and Mike saw after gaining admittance was Spike Lee. A band was playing for the few hundred special guests. It was the B-52s. The triathlete and his massage therapist were shown to their table, from which they had a good view of a velvet-roped VIP area. Bill Schmidt was sitting inside at a table with Michael Jordan. Muhammad Ali was among those seated at the next table over. Mike observed two empty chairs between Bill and Michael.

"Mark, those seats are for us," Mike said, grabbing Mark's sleeve and leaning into him as he pointed obviously. "That's where we're supposed to be sitting!"

"We can't sit there, Mike," Mark said. "Those seats are probably for President Clinton and Ted Turner."

Mike had already caught Bill's eye. Bill whispered into the ear of a young assistant seated near him, who immediately stood and left the VIP area. Mike gave Mark a significant look. Mark shook his head and laughed helplessly. The assistant approached their table.

"How can I help you gentlemen?" he asked.

"Can we sit at that table?" Mike blurted. "There's no one sitting in those two seats."

"I'm very sorry," the assistant said with studied politeness. "Those chairs are reserved for other guests."

The assistant returned to the VIP area and spoke in his boss's ear. Moments later Bill was waving Mark and Mike in. Mark sat down next to Michael Jordan, who gave him a friendly greeting. They had recently filmed a Gatorade television advertisement together.

Mark Allen's fans would have given much to have listened in on the conversation that now took place between the greatest athletes of all time in two disparate sports. In all likelihood, Michael asked Mark the same questions other team sport jocks typically ask endurance athletes, and made the same remarks.

What do you think about out there all day?

I can't run long distance. It hurts my knees.

Do you really pee on the bike?

As Mark conversed with Michael he noticed that Muhammad Ali was messing with Mike's hair from behind him. The horseplay provoked a conversation between the two men, and before long Muhammad was autographing Muslim brochures for Mike to take home and give to friends, or sell, or whatever.

"Well, I guess I'll be leaving," Michael said to Mark, becoming impossibly tall as he rose from the table. "I don't want to steal the spotlight from Mark Allen."

The line came out sounding less funny and more condescending than intended, but only Mark caught it. Mike was oblivious to all negativity. He was, in fact, in heaven, feasting on every detail of the once-in-a-lifetime experience. Mark, meanwhile, was completely indifferent to the household names surrounding him. Ten years before, he might have been starry-eyed, but not now. He would take one Brant Secunda over fifty Michael Jordans today. Mark was just happy he had made his friend happy.

AFTER THAT NIGHT Mike Rubano began to notice that Mark seemed often to wish he were somewhere else—somewhere other than the top of Triathlon Mountain. His contracts with Nike and Ironman required him to race Ironman one more time. Mark decided to fulfill that obligation in 1995 and then quit, but he remained steadfast in his choice to skip the 1994 race. As fate would have it, that was the year of Dave Scott's first comeback. In an interview published in the September 1994 issue of *Triathlete*, Roy Wallack asked Mark if news of his old rival's return tempted him to change his mind.

"Not really," Mark said, laughing. "The race in '89 was one of those moments in sports that you couldn't orchestrate. He and I each maybe had the best races we'd ever had there. The way we raced each other—I couldn't have picked a better scenario. But to go back when he's going back? I don't think we'd be in the same place in the race. With all respect to him, I think our strategies would be very different. Maybe he'll win the race this year. I don't know. But my decision to not go back is firm, and whatever he does is good for him."

Trash talk has rarely been more artfully bleached. One could almost read Mark's answer as something other than a total dismissal of Dave as a competitive rival. The Mark Allen of 1988 and before would not have dared, or even thought, to say such a thing.

Mark continued to train and compete throughout 1994, but he tried some different stuff. He raced a sprint triathlon series in Australia. He trained for the Berlin Marathon, aiming to qualify for the Olympic Trials by clocking 2:22 or better, but pulled up lame during the race and dropped out. At the same time, he took advantage of the absence of pressure to be Ironman-fit in October to raise his shamanistic explorations a level—or two, or three. Mark subjected himself to sweat-lodge ceremonies that made his first, which he'd barely survived, seem like a sip of chamomile tea. He went off into the wilderness and sat inside a perimeter of stones for four days with only a jug of water to sustain him. Well, that and perhaps a little bit of a certain kind of cactus.

Upon returning to Boulder from one of these vision quests, Mark told Kenny Souza that while he'd sat inside his circle of stones, a deer had approached him and started a conversation.

Wrong guy to confide in. Kenny was, after all, the same impious jokester who liked to rearrange Mark's crystals to annoy him. Kenny broke out laughing.

"Dude!" he said. "No food for four days? What do you expect? A deer *will* talk to you!"

Mark looked at Kenny mournfully and said nothing more. At that moment, Kenny decided to stop teasing Mark about his shamanism thing. At the same time, Mark decided to stop sharing so much of his spiritual journey with his athlete friends.

As ready as Mark was in mind and body to move on from triathlon by this time, he had two strong motivations to race the 1995 Ironman as a career encore. The first of these was a single item that remained in his bag of tricks—one last unused tool that might enable him to reach a little higher yet. Mark had optimized his bicycling aerodynamics. He had mastered his race nutrition. He had gotten stronger with weight lifting. He had done everything he could physically do. Mark's final innovation was to approach Ironman as a spiritual endeavor, a kind of whole-body prayer. His last and, he hoped, greatest performance would be a gesture of gratitude to the universe of which he was a small part for the gifts and opportunities it had given him. After that, he would walk away.

Mark's second motivation to race his twelfth and final Ironman was Dave Scott. Going into 1995, Dave had six Ironman titles. Mark had five. Mark could not walk away in Dave's shadow. Not when he was this close.

Smart as ever in his approach to the sport, Mark recognized that, at age 37, he would have to reduce his training as a concession to the declining capacities of his body. But he wasn't above fretting over this concession. While Mark knew that dialing back his training was the best thing for him, he feared it might also be the best thing for his younger competitors, the fresh-legged kids ten and twelve years his junior who were able to continue training as hard as Mark ever had and who hungered to dethrone him.

The sport had changed since Mark had won Iron War, and had changed even during his year of sabbatical. Greg Welch, seven years behind Mark in age, had taken advantage of Grip's absence to win the 1994 Ironman, and many pundits considered him strong enough to possibly win even with Mark back in the mix. There had also been a full-scale German invasion of Ironman-distance racing while Mark was away. Members of a new breed of marauding Saxon supercyclists were posting stupendous Ironman bike splits and threatening to do what no one had been able to do in the sport's mature age: win Ironman on the bike.

Breaking from his past formula of competing in shorter races over the summer and making Kona his lone Ironman-distance competition,

Mark chose to contest Ironman Japan on June 25 as a rust-buster. He wanted the confidence that a win and a fast time would give him, especially considering how poorly he had performed during his Ironman sabbatical year, losing several shorter races, failing miserably in an attempt to break the eight-hour barrier at Ironman Germany, and dropping out of the Berlin Marathon. Mark needed to silence the inner doubts that echoed others' speculation about whether, after twelve years in the sport, he still had it. Despite suffering some setbacks in the lead-up to the race (including an ankle sprain and a bout of flu), Mark won easily over a weak field in 8:23 flat.

Two weeks later, Ironman Germany took place. Jürgen Zäck, age 30, one of those marauding Saxon supercyclists, won in 8:08:07, blitzing the bike leg in an absurd time of 4:20:28. Right behind Jürgen was 24-year-old Thomas Hellriegel, who rode 4:21:14. A thunderbolt of anxiety shot through Mark's head when he saw these results. He had covered the same bike course more than eleven minutes slower the previous year. Worse, as the summer wore on, Mark wore down. He felt increasingly sluggish and rickety. On the verge of panic, he made an appointment to see his doctor, who ran blood tests. In a follow-up, he delivered the results.

"Your DHEA and testosterone levels are very low," the doctor said.

"So what does that mean?" Mark asked.

"Hormonally, you're about 70 years old."

As soon as he returned home, Mark called Brant Secunda to apprise him of the situation and ask for help. Brant suggested Alaska. In August Mark spent eight full days with his spiritual mentor near Juneau, chanting, drumming, making offerings, and fasting while Greg Welch, Jürgen Zäck, and Thomas Hellriegel were logging six hours of training a day in preparation for Ironman.

After returning to Boulder from Alaska, Mark did as much hard training as his 37-year-old body could handle. He did so without joy. It was evident to Paul and Kenny that their friend was dragging himself through rides and runs with them. His heart just wasn't in it anymore—nor was it as hard to keep up with him as it used to be.

"I hate to say it," Kenny told Paul after one long run that was particularly disastrous for Mark, "but there's no way he can win Ironman."

Mark's situation had not improved by the time he flew to Kona. Phil Maffetone came over to the Kanaloa resort daily to practice manual muscle testing on his longtime client. Phil placed his hands on various meridian points on Mark's body and asked him to resist the pressure he applied. The strength of Mark's resistance told Phil how well the athlete's neuromuscular system was functioning. Mark bombed every test. Never had Phil seen him so out of balance. It seemed as if Mark's body had already retired.

The day before the race Phil came over one last time. He placed his hands on Mark and nearly leaped back in surprise. Mark's body felt completely different. The vitality had returned. His outward energy had changed too. He now gave off an aura of grim determination. Phil understood: Mark was going to will himself through this.

On the evening before the race Mark stopped by the Little Blue Church with Julie and made an offering at Kuemanu Heiau, as he had done each year since Iron War. It was no mere superstitious luck ritual—or not mainly. Mark believed in the island spirits and he feared the consequences of failing to show them proper respect.

On race morning Mark was driven to the pier from the Kanaloa in silence, as always. He went through the same pre-race routine he had gone through eleven times before, getting his body marked, applying waterproof sunscreen, putting air in his tires. He was acutely conscious that he was doing each of these things for the last time.

Mark was no less conscious of his attire. Nike had supplied him with a high-tech, low-drag racing suit that would perhaps cut his swim time fractionally. Its one drawback was that it looked like something he'd pulled out of Julie's side of the closet, and Mark was vain enough to dread showing himself in its girlie splendor. He waited until all of the other competitors were already in the water and NBC's cameras were off filming someone else, then sneaked to the far end of the pier and hastily took off the heavy sweat clothes he'd been hiding under. He was just about to jump into the water when he saw Jürgen Zäck's head bobbing in front of him.

"Mark, Mark, Mark," Jürgen said in mock disappointment.

At least the suit worked. Mark completed the swim near the front of the first pack of top contenders, right on Greg Welch's heels and well ahead of Jürgen Zäck and Thomas Hellriegel, who were not known for their swimming chops. On the bike Mark quickly passed the dozen or so better swimmers who had left transition ahead of him and found himself in the lead earlier than expected. He settled into a groove at a heart rate of 135 beats per minute, comfortably below the 150 bpm limit that represented his maximum sustainable heart rate for 112 miles.

Suddenly Jürgen Zäck zipped by Mark so swiftly and easily that Mark at first mistook him for a race marshal on a motorized scooter. Less than two minutes later Thomas Hellriegel followed, moving even faster. Mark increased his tempo to keep the Germans within range and watched his heart rate climb to 140, then 145, then 150. He was now riding as hard as he dared, and still he was losing ground to the virile young meat machines chugging away ahead of him. Not helping matters were the vicious mumuku crosswinds, which blew harder than Mark had ever experienced, ripping across the Queen K in gusts of 45 mph. They slowed Mark's advance to a frustrating grind, yet his German rivals seemed to slice right through them. Even with his heart rate pinned at 150, Mark could only watch helplessly as they receded out of sight ahead of him. He did some arithmetic. He figured he could spot either man seven or eight minutes at the start of the marathon—*maybe* 10, but that was really pushing it—and still win. So it became his goal to keep his deficit within that margin.

Mark started the run in seventh place, thirteen minutes and thirty-one seconds behind Thomas Hellriegel, who had completed a ride for the ages, besting the next-fastest bike split (Jürgen's) by eleven minutes. No one had ever made up a gap of that size at Ironman.

As he left the Kona Surf Hotel parking lot, Mark tried to tell himself that anything could happen. A roaring, partisan crowd of hundreds cheered him on as he hoofed his way up the steep hill of Ehukai Street leading to Ali'i Drive (now called Ali'i Highway along this stretch) from the hotel. He was nearing the top when his peripheral vision strayed to a group of three older women in the throng.

"Go, Mark!" they screamed.

As he passed, one of the women addressed her friends in a stage whisper that Mark was not meant to overhear: "Oh, my, he doesn't look so good."

The marathon course had been changed since Iron War. Instead of turning left onto Ali'i Drive at the top of Ehukai Street to head toward Kailua-Kona, runners now turned right onto Ali'i Highway and ran down a steep and winding hill dead-ending six-tenths of a mile away in a basin set close against the ocean, with a golf course on one side and a lava field on the other. Only to turn around and come right back.

That lava field was also a burial ground known as Lekeleke. In 1819 a battle had been fought there between a faction of Hawaiians led by the future King Kamehameha II that wished to abandon the island's traditional religion in favor of Christianity and a faction that opposed this sellout to the native people's European conquerors. Three hundred men and women died in the Battle of Kuamo'o, and their bodies were interred in rock cairns on the lava field. Ironman participants nicknamed this morbid basin the Pit, and its inclusion in the marathon course was seen as a gratuitously sadistic move, adding 200 feet of painful downhill and spirit-crushing uphill running to the first mile of the marathon and forcing racers to come to a near dead stop, turn 180 degrees, and struggle to get their momentum going again in a stifling, airless topographical concavity where heat pooled thickly. More than a few corpses of a kind were added to the Lekeleke burial ground during the several years when the Ironman racecourse brushed against it.

By the time Mark made the right turn onto Ali'i Highway to head toward that sweltering rocky crucible, Thomas Hellriegel had already gone through it and returned and was now cruising toward town on Ali'i Drive. Mark carried this demoralizing knowledge with him as he descended into the Pit. When he reached the one-mile point of the marathon, with the burial ground on his right, Mark learned that he had gained only a few seconds on Thomas—not nearly enough. To make matters worse, Greg Welch, who had started the marathon 10 seconds ahead of Mark, remained 10 seconds ahead. A wave of exhaustion swept over him, and he suddenly doubted that he could even finish the race, let alone win.

A door had been opened for another visit from that serpent in the garden, *the voice*, which Mark still heard in almost every race. Right on cue, the familiar tape loop began to play in Mark's head, with a new twist.

I'm too old. I'm too far behind. Screw it. I've won this thing five times. Isn't that enough? It's not worth the pain. Let the young guys have it.

Mark trundled along in a miasma of self-pity for some time before a second voice entered his consciousness. It was not quite the same voice Mark had used to rally himself in races before Iron War. It was the voice of Brant Secunda.

Be fearless in the face of your fears, he said. *Quiet your mind.*

Mark used all the power of concentration he had to imagine his thoughts, good and bad alike, slipping down into his legs, leaving his consciousness empty and free. It didn't happen right away, but it happened. In the moment his mind went quiet, Mark could feel the whole dynamic of the race change.

Greg Welch abruptly stopped to stretch out a muscle cramp, and Mark slid into fourth place. His rictus grin emerged, and his tempo increased. At the top of Palani Hill, now running side by side with Rainer Müller, Mark learned that he had lopped nearly 10 minutes off the leader's advantage. Thomas was not running slowly—his rate of progress was well under a

3-hour marathon pace—but Mark was flying, running faster than he had at any time since his great battle with Dave Scott. At 11 miles Mark dropped Rainer and took over third place. A mile down the road Jürgen Zack went down. He refrained from commenting further on Mark's wardrobe.

The final catch became possible, then likely, then inevitable as Mark gained strength through the lava fields that used to weaken him and as Thomas ultimately faltered. Mark snatched the lead with 3 miles to go. Thomas bravely counterattacked, but Mark parried with a ruthless surge that finished off the youngster. Twenty minutes later Mark consummated the greatest come-from-behind victory in Ironman history, surpassing Dave Scott's performance in 1984, when Mark had given away an advantage of just under twelve minutes. When he broke the finish-line tape, Mark smiled the smile of a satisfied man—a man who had now done all he could do and all he cared to do in his chosen field of endeavor. He went straight to Julie, already retired, who reached toward him with a baby held between her palms. Mark kissed the head of his 11-month-old son, Mats, whose birth had been another motivation for his year away (Mark was determined to do fatherhood differently than his father had), and then he threw up a quart of Gatorade and was dragged to the medical tent.

Mark's body had rallied just in time, held itself together just long enough, and now it fell apart. Always a big sleeper, he would sleep more than ever for the next two years.

As Mark lay shielded from attention on a triage cot with an IV jabbed in his forearm, he experienced a moment that he understood as the matching bookend to that distant moment in November 1982 when he had run along a boardwalk in the south of France on a warm night and seen that it was all in front of him.

It's all behind me, he now thought. *I will never again face this test that has meant so much to me for so long—this test that has made me who I am. It's over now. I will never be this strong again. I've reached the pinnacle, and it's time to go down. Tomorrow my body will be less than it is today, and the next day less still.*

Mark grieved deeply for the passing of his athlete self, but briefly. For he truly was ready to move on. He knew he would not regret quitting, just as he had known he would love swimming before his first lesson, and surfing before his first wave, and triathlon before his first race, and shamanism before his first sweat lodge. He said a tearful good-bye to triathlon and turned his back on it.

THROUGHOUT HIS CAREER Mark had experienced a recurring dream in which he found himself at a post-race awards ceremony where everyone received an award except him. The dream challenged him to be happy anyway. It reminded him that he would not have true peace and wholeness until he no longer needed to win.

Deep down Mark knew that he could never be a happy loser and that he would have to leave the sport to complete his journey toward the inner peace he desired. For a time winning had served him well. The growth and self-discovery it had taken Mark to win—and to beat Dave Scott and win his first Ironman, most particularly—had moved him closer to wholeness than he had been before he had discovered triathlon. But by 1995 Mark recognized that winning could take him no further. To complete his journey, he had to let go.

After his last, triumphant Ironman, Mark never again dreamed his dream of being left out at the awards ceremony.

IN MAY 1999 Mark Allen and Brant Secunda cohosted a four-day retreat called Sport and Spirit in Sedona, Arizona. By this time Mark had moved with Julie Moss and young Mats to Santa Cruz, thus becoming Brant's neighbors, and the two men had gone into business together. These Sport and Spirit retreats had been created to expose athletes to the physical and spiritual secrets of Mark's success.

At the height of a dry, warm Wednesday afternoon, guests trickled into the Sedona Dahn Retreat Center, a cluster of clean-lined, fresh-looking low buildings designed to blend in with their famous red-rock environment, manifesting a sort of adobe-meets-Pier-1 aesthetic that was probably attractive to the thirty spiritually open-minded endurance athletes who assembled for the event. Many of the campers arrived with a certain amount of anxiety in their guts. They admired Mark, respected him, and were prepared to be embarrassed for him. This whole shamanism thing was a bit out there from the perspective of mainstream triathlon culture. News of Sport and Spirit's creation had inspired more than a little joking at Mark's expense in the broader triathlon community.

"Don't let him brainwash you!" teased a training buddy of one Mark Allen fan who'd signed up for the retreat. "Call if you're in trouble. We'll send one of those deprogrammers."

Those who wished the best for Mark could not help but feel some concern that he might be slipping off the deep end in middle age. As the new arrivals shook the hand of their legendary host, having found him at Brant's side in the center's conference building, they reflexively searched his eyes for that ineffable but impossible-to-miss glint of madness. It wasn't there. He looked completely sane.

Mark and Brant's guests would soon discover that their hosts were keenly aware of how they were perceived, and they took pains to prove their normalness. Brant, a man with regular features on a broad, appealing face that was perennially framed by a cowboy hat, then 47 years old, took the first speaking turn after the group had eaten a healthy welcoming dinner.

"I grew up in New York and New Jersey in the '50s and '60s," he began. "Has anyone ever heard of those places?"

Appreciative laughter. Brant then told the story of his adventure in the Sierra Madre Mountains and his entry into Huichol culture, summarizing, "Anyway, that's a little bit of the story of how I came to be here today, except that I flew here from Santa Cruz, where I live."

More laughter. *Growing up in New York and New Jersey, flying from Santa Cruz—that's not weird at all!*

Then things got weird. Drums and rattles were brought out and put to use. Brant began to sing. The thirty gathered athletes of three hours' acquaintance were instructed—and then pressed—to perform the dance of the deer around a candle. Embarrassment invaded the room. Mark and Brant broke the ice by demonstrating the dance. Guests stole frequent glances at Mark as they aped his prancing movements, all thinking the same thought: *I can't believe this is happening.* Yet, as they continued to dance, an amazing thing happened. The embarrassment vanished, and a sublimely atavistic feeling of connection between the music and the movement and something deep and ancient inside each person took its place.

The next morning Mark distributed heart rate monitors to everyone in the group and led them on a forty-five-minute run on dirt roads through the high desert. Mark was careful not to confess that this was about as long as he had run since he had retired. When Mark quit, he *quit*, leaving behind his training as thoroughly as retiring tightrope walkers probably do. While Dave Scott continued to train two to four hours a day through his forties and into his fifties, Mark let his bike slowly rust in the garage and forgot what chlorine smelled like.

In 2002, at one of their rare public appearances together, Dave and Mark were asked who would win a race between them now. Dave pointed a thumb at himself. Mark just smiled.

On the second night of Sport and Spirit Mark's guests found themselves seated on a dirt floor inside a canvas tent, forming four concentric rings around a shallow pit filled with a pile of lava stones. Every few minutes Brant ladled water over the hot stones, which instantly transformed the liquid into a stifling blast of steam that filled the tent with a fog of heat.

Sweat-lodge time.

The glowing stones were the only source of light, illuminating faces like moonscapes in the blackness surrounding them. Brant explained the significance of this ceremony, of whose kind Mark had experienced many. To keep the mood light, Brant tossed the occasional joke into his monologue. To keep it from becoming too light, he made everyone sing Huichol spiritual songs they had learned earlier in the day.

The heat was unbearable. The first-timers tried their best to obey Brant's gentle encouragement to focus on singing and praying instead of their physical misery, but they kept forgetting the words as they submitted to their bodily discomfort's insistence on completely dominating their attention. After a few minutes of such internal warring, a few of the guests felt that they were beginning to gain a bit of mastery over their suffering, but then a fresh ladleful of water was dropped onto the hot stones and they were forced to recognize that they had gained nothing; the tent had merely cooled down a few degrees. And that problem was now corrected.

As they had done the night before, Mark's admiring but bewildered guests stole frequent glances at the six-time Ironman champion. What they saw was a man who was completely unself-conscious, totally absorbed in the moment, singing and praying openheartedly and showing every sign of existing in a state of real connection with the mysterious spirits everyone present was supposed to be connecting with. This was not a celebrity spiritual pose or lark. This was not Madonna's kabbalism. The tenth anniversary of Mark's first Ironman victory—and of Mark's shamanistic vision on the lava fields—was coming up in a few months. It was now apparent that nothing short of a life-changing spiritual transformation had been required for Mark Allen to beat Dave Scott in that race.

Breaking from his normal breviloquence, Mark spoke for hours at a time during those four days away from reality. He spoke about the "go slow to get faster" training philosophy he had relied on over the course of his career. He talked about how all of this spiritual stuff had helped him in his racing.

"Your physical capacities are only part of the big picture," he told the gathering. "If your spirit is happy and strong, then you're stable under pressure."

In the few days they spent hiking in the wilderness, making hilltop sacrifices to nature gods, dancing like deer, sweating like pigs, and singing and praying with Mark and Brant, the campers did not embrace Huichol Indian shamanism as wholly as Mark had on the seventh day of his own first retreat, but most gained a genuine respect for it that they took home with them.

A couple of Sport and Spirit's attendees found themselves on the same flight as Mark from Phoenix to San Diego. When they deplaned at their destination, they were herded like cattle through a confining Jetway and thrust into the chaos of a crowded concourse bustling with harried and disconnected persons—something they had experienced many times but now felt differently.

One man turned to Mark with an expression of shock, bordering on horror.

"Oh, my God!" he said.

"I know," Mark said quietly, smiling his Mona Lisa smile.

MARK ALLEN LIVES a couple of blocks from one of the best surf breaks in Santa Cruz. Each morning he crosses the street with his board and passes a couple of hours riding waves. He still loves everything about surfing. The cold, smelly, living ocean. The rush of the ride, which rewards the labor of paddling and the patience of waiting. The circular purposelessness of it.

Mark returns home to an empty house, where he typically spends the rest of the day in his own company unless Mats is around. Life is less crowded for Mark than it used to be. Retiring from triathlon and moving to Santa Cruz tore him loose from most of his existing friendships, and he now draws companionship mainly from the spiritual community in which he has immersed himself. The major social occasion of Mark's typical week is a Wednesday-night drum circle. He sees Brant almost daily and often exercises with him, slowing way down for his spiritual mentor's sake. Mark also has a few surfing acquaintances, and his mom, Sharon, still lives in Palo Alto, less than an hour's drive away. That's plenty.

In their last years together Julie accompanied Mark on trips to retreats that Brant Secunda hosted at places of power such as the lush and historical island of Crete, where the couple, accompanied by Mats, lodged with fellow pilgrims within earshot of the ocean and traipsed about fragrant fields of sage, thyme, and oregano. It was in such outwardly perfect circumstances that Julie came to recognize that her marriage was at a crossroads. While she fully respected the path Mark had chosen, which she once described as "a beautiful little practice," it just didn't speak to her as it did to him. So she took her own path and left Mark to his without bitterness.

"If I had to rank the reasons to leave a marriage," Julie told one nosy fan, "I think that's a good one. To pursue a spiritual path is a profound choice to make."

ANYONE WHO HAS as much passion for a spiritual path as Mark has for his yearns to share it with the people he loves. Ironically, the person in Mark's life who was most responsive to his shamanistic evangelism was his father, who listened without uneasiness when Mark talked about it and who asked questions that weren't just polite chitchat.

In 1995 Space called Mark and told him he would like to attend a retreat. A few months later Space dragged Toot, still a good Catholic girl, along to Palm Springs, where Brant hosted a three-day gathering. Mark was busy training for his last Ironman, so he was not present to serve as a bridge to the weirdness, which culminated, as always, in a sweat lodge. Toot refused to enter. Most of those who gave it a whirl staggered out long before it was complete. Space was among the very few who hung tough till the bitter end.

Space was not motivated entirely by an interest in shamanism. There was a second motive, which also induced him to participate in the following year's Ironman—not coincidentally, the first Ironman after Mark's retirement. Space was 65 years old and still afraid of the water when he started preparing for the race. Mark could have coached his dad, but did not, foisting him on Paul Huddle instead. The day before the race, Paul guided Space through a practice loop around the 2.4-mile swim course. The old man was able to complete it just inside the two-hour, twenty-minute time limit. Unfortunately, the next morning brought choppy seas. Space failed to complete the swim before the cutoff time and was humiliatingly dragged from the ocean, vomiting seawater.

That took some courage. Perhaps it was the courage of a repentant father seeking to show his son some kind of acceptance before it was too late.

Mark spends his afternoons working in a home office adorned with colorful Mexican Indian art pieces. Most of his work is triathlon related. While Mark made a clean break from his participation in the sport, he did not cut himself off from triathlon completely. He remains passionate about the swim-bike-run game, and he knows he has much to offer those who continue to practice it. Mark has less interest, however, in entertaining large mobs of athletes as the coach of masters swim classes or running groups, than Dave does. In recent years the sport's competitive ranks have been overrun by training geeks who tend to get on the nerves of old-timers like Mark and Paul Huddle and Scott Molina with their endless talk about power output numbers and body-fat percentages. It is sometimes tempting to shake them by the shoulders and shout, "Wake up! Don't you know you're a human being?"

In 2001 Mark partnered with triathlon coach and professional computer programmer Luis Vargas to create an automated online coaching service. It was the perfect solution. Mark Allen Online provides premium-quality, fully customized training plans based on Mark's "go slow to get faster" philosophy that are delivered online. Each year Mark hosts a celebration in Kona for his customers who, thanks to his coaching, are able to claim coveted Ironman qualifying slots. In 2010 there were more than thirty of them.

Mark also seeks out a select few to help individually. In fact, he has made a cottage industry of counseling elite male triathletes who have come close to winning Ironman several times but who can't quite take the last hard step—in other words, athletes who remind him of himself. Mark believes that the secret to taking that last step is not physical but mental and spiritual, and he believes he holds that secret.

"If you're talking about a top athlete, somebody who's trying to win Ironman, they're already working at 97, 98 percent of their potential," Mark said in a 2010 interview. "But getting that last 2 or 3 percent probably requires them to change the one thing that's most difficult for them to change."

The man who most reminded Mark of himself was Peter Reid. Like Mark, Peter had a difficult relationship with his father and channeled the resulting anger into sport. Peter's father, Ted, scoffed at the idea of his son's becoming a professional triathlete, telling him it wasn't a real career. Peter's racing was about proving him wrong.

Peter's wife, Lori Bowden, also a triathlete, became friendly with Julie Moss during the summer of 1996, when the two women found themselves training in the same group in San Diego. One day Julie invited Lori to dinner. This was before the move north, when Mark and Julie still lived in a gorgeous Spanish Mediterranean house in Cardiff-by-the-Sea, surrounded by bougainvillea, cactus, and willow trees, which was afforded by Mark's success. As symbols of Mark's achievements, the lovely home and grounds intimidated the hell out of Peter as he approached them with Lori, bottle of wine in hand, on the appointed evening.

Conversation around the dining table was dominated by Lori and Julie, both of whom played the talkative yang to the quiet yin of their husbands. Mark, relaxed and comfortable in his early retirement, interjected a remark here and there. Meanwhile Peter, who had met Mark before but never really talked to him, sat frozen in his chair, utterly star-struck, his eyes frequently drifting toward an aboriginal painting titled *Dream Time* that hung on the wall behind Mark. Recognizing a kindred spirit, Mark developed a nascent fondness for the young dreamer that evening.

Peter finished fourth in his first Ironman that October. Two years later, with a little help from Mark, Peter won the race. The next night the new Ironman champion attended a private celebration in Kailua-Kona. He was standing alone in the middle of a room in a kind of daze when suddenly Mark Allen stood before him. Without uttering a word, Mark, who is not a hugger, reached out and embraced Peter. It was not a welcome-to-the-club gesture, motivated by Mark's understanding of what it means to win Ironman. Mark hugged Peter because he knew what it meant for *Peter* to win Ironman.

Prone to depression, Peter went up and down as an athlete and as a human being over the next few years. He lost Ironman in 1999, won again in 2000, then went completely sideways, quitting the race in 2001, almost quitting the sport in 2002, and splitting from Lori. Mark stepped in and became Peter's full-time coach. He taught Peter to approach the sport as a whole person. Mark even convinced Peter to try working with Brant Secunda. While Peter did not talk to any deer, he came away from his first of two visits to Soquel feeling more refreshed and positive than he had in some time.

In 2003 Peter Reid reached the mountaintop one more time. Months later, his dad died. But before he did, Ted sent Peter a letter in which he apologized for his many mistakes as a parent and begged forgiveness. The moment Peter read these words, the fire that had fueled his training and racing was snuffed. It became harder and harder to get out the door and train. He could no longer push himself in races as he once had, and his results told the story. In the spring of 2006 Peter quit the sport cold and disappeared into the northern Canadian wilderness to fly small planes. Since Peter's retirement, only a handful of elite triathletes have so much as nibbled at the spiritual piece of Mark's secret to success.

"Why isn't every triathlete in the world coming to learn from Brant?" Mark asked himself in an interview. "One answer that's come to me is that anything that's going to require people to change is also going to require them to do a certain amount of work. Often that work pushes the sensitive buttons in us that are resistant to change."

In many ways, Dave Scott and Mark Allen could not be more unalike. Their individual secrets to success are very different on most levels. Mark may have summarized those differences best when he said, "At Ironman, to do well takes either supreme confidence or calm. Dave gets there through confidence. I think I've gotten there through calm." But there's one way in which the former star-crossed rivals have become the same. As they grow older, both men have arrived at a place where they feel an increasingly pressing desire to help others achieve great things in the same way that they did. This desire is fueled by both pride and fear—pride in their tremendous accomplishments and in all that went into them, and fear that history will forget these accomplishments and all that went into them. This fear has been justified and exacerbated by a surprising dearth of serious seekers of their wisdom. Each man in his own way suffers a bit of the prophet's loneliness, wondering at times if the convictions he stood for died at his own athletic curtain call. Neither man seems to fully understand that his secret is a secret not for everyone but for very few. This kind of secret fundamentally cannot be shared because it must be inborn, like Dave's, or earned, like Mark's.

ON SEPTEMBER 26, 2010, Mats Allen, then 17 years old, participated in his first triathlon, an Olympic-distance event in Santa Cruz. Mark and Julie then lived two blocks apart and within walking distance of the race site at Santa Cruz Municipal Wharf. They traveled there separately. Signing up for the race had been their son's idea. Throughout Mats's childhood,

Mark had gone out of his way to avoid steering his son toward the sport that had made him famous—that is, to avoid doing what his own father had done to him in medicine. Left to choose his own path, Mats had gotten into water polo. When his team was recruited by the triathlon's organizer to serve as volunteers on race day, Mats thought, *What the heck—why not do the race?* Having never ridden a racing bike before, Mats asked his dad to show him how to clip into and out of the pedals on the eve of the competition. Fortunately, Mark remembered.

A strong swimmer, Mats exited the water near the front end of his starting wave. A frenetically engaged Mark Allen snapped several photos of his son as he emerged through the foam, then raced across the strand to capture images of Mats mounting his bike in transition. Julie hung back, watching the two of them, experiencing one of those moments of dizzying nostalgia that convey the full preciousness of time's losses. She had been present at Mark's first triathlon in 1982. Now here he was, gray-haired, cheering on a first-time triathlete who looked uncannily like his father twenty-two years before.

After completing the race, capturing first place in his age group on the strength of his excellent swim, Mats went home talking about perhaps doing Ironman after he turned 18.

In June 2011 Drew Scott qualified for Ironman. Ryan and Kara Scott have dabbled in triathlon as well. It's possible—not likely but possible—that some combination of these young people will meet one October Saturday on the Queen K Highway and perhaps share a moment of competitive, cooperative suffering that leaves them changed forever.

Another Iron War? Never. History may repeat itself as a new generation takes the reins, but some things happen outside the normal run of history. A few magical moments appear only once in time—and live forever.

We can't all be heroes, because somebody
has to sit on the curb and clap as they go by.
— WILL ROGERS

S even and a half hours after the start of the 2000 Ironman, I left the
makeshift media center that had been set up in a meeting room on
the ground floor of the King Kamehameha Hotel and began walking
toward the Queen Kaahumanu Highway to catch sight of the men's race
leader returning to town. Although I had the required credential, I hadn't
bothered to take a spot on one of the press vehicles that spent the whole
day on the course, choosing instead to hang out in the air-conditioned media center and follow the online coverage provided on ironman.com—the
same online coverage that any schmuck lacking a press pass could watch
anywhere in the world without undergoing the hassle and expense of traveling to the race.

I had ridden on the women's press truck when I'd covered my first
Ironman in 1998 and had learned my lesson. It was the most exhausting
thing I had ever done besides race an Ironman myself. Nine hours of standing and holding on for dear life as we leapfrogged from athlete to athlete
along the highway, shouting my throat sore in the roaring wind, climbing
down from and back onto a flatbed under the hot sun at our many stops,
feverishly scribbling bib numbers and time gaps onto a sweat-sodden notepad, forgetting to eat and to reapply sunscreen. And for what? The total
product of these efforts and privations was a pathetically meager grasp of
what had actually happened in the race.

Watching an Ironman is nothing like watching a football game. The
athletes are obscured and unidentifiable in the swim. On the bike they
quickly spread out so widely that one has to serially ignore most of the rel-
evant players at any given time while paying attention to a single athlete

or small group. The run is like a great card shuffle as bike specialists wilt and superior runners move up. It's impossible to see it all, or even half of it.

So I decided to take a more comfortable approach to my second Ironman reporting experience. But I couldn't resist treating myself to an unmediated view of the climax.

My path from the King Kam to my targeted viewing spot closely traced the first mile-plus of the Ironman bike leg, except that I used the sidewalk on the left side of the road instead of claiming the middle of the outbound lanes on the right side of the roadway as the racers had done in the morning. Starting at the point where Ali'i Drive bends away from Kailua Bay, I walked three-quarters of a mile up Pay-'n'-Save Hill to the Queen K. By the time I topped the hill, my T-shirt was soaked through. It was two forty-five in the afternoon, the air temperature was 90 degrees, and the dew point stood only 10 degrees higher. Although I was less than a month away from running a marathon and in great shape, my heart thumped palpably from the effort of merely walking the hill in such terrific heat and humidity. I couldn't imagine scaling it at a dead run of six and a half minutes per mile after six hours of prior exercise, as the world's best could.

The finish-line area in front of the hotel had been bustling with humanity, but at the intersection of Palani Road and the Queen K, where Mark Allen, running the opposite way, had first looked back after dropping Dave in 1989, there was almost no one—just a traffic cop and a few crowd-averse triathlon fans who, like me, preferred to get a good, long look at the race leader just before he finished rather than fighting for a glimpse of him at the moment he broke the tape. But I continued even farther, walking northward along the Queen K until I reached the high point of Palani Hill—the hill that had decided Iron War. Here, I knew, I would get the most telescopic view of the soon-to-be champion's approach.

As I squinted toward the distant point on the horizon where police lights would herald the coming of the race leader, I suddenly sensed that I was being watched. I looked across the highway, and there stood a woman, looking at me in the tentative way one does when one wishes to be noticed without speaking or seeming weird. I had somehow not observed her as I was walking.

I thought about crossing the road to say hello, but she beat me to it. As she approached I noticed that she was very lean, obviously an athlete, fortyish with ginger-colored hair and freckles.

"How's it going?" she said.

"Good," I said. "Just came out to see the finish."

"Any idea who's leading?"

"Last I heard it was Peter Reid."

We traded information about the race. The woman said she was working as a spotter for NBC. I told her I was reporting for Active.com. Then, belatedly, she reached out a hand.

"Julie Moss," she said.

I blushed crimson. *Why hadn't I recognized her?*

"I can't believe I didn't recognize you!" I blurted after sharing my own name.

"Maybe it's because I'm not on my hands and knees," she joked.

We talked a little longer, and then Julie returned to the far side of the highway. At that moment I saw lights on the horizon. A few minutes passed, and I could distinguish a flatbed press truck followed by a pace car flanked by two police motorcycles. No other entourage. Peter Reid remained hidden behind the press truck until he was almost close enough to touch. He looked terrible. Normally a fluid runner, he now appeared as if running in chains, stiff and tied up. His face was rigid, his eyes locked yearningly on a finish line in his mind. He was clearly exerting as much force of will to keep moving forward as he ever had in his life. Julie called some encouraging words to him, interrupting a near-total silence. Peter took no notice of her. She took no umbrage. As Mark Allen's wife, she knew all about competitive tunnel vision; plus, as a former racer herself, she knew that only two things existed in all the universe for Peter now: unbelievable pain and an unaccountable desire to continue, to finish, to win.

As Peter passed, a lump suddenly lodged in my throat, and my eyes welled. I squelched the ambush of emotion with surprise and wonder.

What the hell just happened?

I reviewed the strange moment in my mind. It wasn't Peter's victory that moved me, I concluded. I'd been rooting for Tim DeBoom, the American hope. It was Peter's lonely display of courage. I knew what he was going through, or the better part of it anyway, and like an old war buddy I felt a sentimental connection to him through a special bond of suffering.

But it was more than that. The feeling was similar to my experience in other moments of transcendent connection, like when I gave my future wife a hug she badly needed or when I listened to one of those sad songs that gets me every time. The particular type of connection I felt to Peter Reid in his isolated agony clearly had a special significance for me. I felt something like it every time I studied a certain photograph, the iconic image of Iron War (shown on the cover), captured by Lois Schwartz at about one minute before three o'clock on the afternoon of October 14, 1989—an image that says it all as words never could. There was a pattern here. Something about the sight and thought of brave men and women grimacing through the voluntary torture of endurance racing squeezed my soul differently than other sources of sentimental feeling. But what was that something, exactly?

Not until a decade later, on my journey to discover the *how* and the *why* of Iron War, did I come to fully understand what that something was. I found the answer in Michael Atkinson's sociological study of triathlon as a pain community that answered a fundamental human need for a certain kind of suffering.

There is no single characteristic that defines human nature or the human condition, but it is tempting to formulate such definitions all the same. Whichever characteristic stands out as the true essence of our condition or nature for any given person depends on his biases. My biases are such that the voluntary suffering of triathlon, borne in pursuit of the triumph of spirit over flesh, seems the most potent metaphor for our nature and condition.

Our earthly lives are doomed. Our lives are, in the long run—the billion-year perspective—utterly meaningless. And in the meantime they are a constant struggle. It takes a lot of courage just to make it from one end to the other. Yet who among us tries merely to make it? Somehow we muster the courage and spirit not only to survive, and bear the suffering required for that, but to create meaning, to pursue greatness, to put on a show, and we willingly bear incalculable additional suffering for the sake of these nonmandatory joys. To paraphrase Dave Scott, something within us just can't resist trying to "see what we can do" with these bodies and minds while we have them, no matter the price.

Human beings are the creatures that try harder and never stop trying. We try when it's hopeless. We try when it doesn't make any sense. And when we succeed in trying harder than we have ever tried before, we try harder still. We are Cinderella, and Rocky, and the Little Engine That Could. We are beautiful in this way. Heartbreakingly beautiful.

I love humanity most when I experience something that makes me feel a sense of solidarity with my human comrades as fellow doomed "triers" (or is it triathletes?). Nothing makes me feel this sense more acutely than watching someone like Peter Reid run through illimitable misery for a reward that is only imagined to matter.

And no experience of this kind affects me more powerfully than Iron War, the race where two men tried as hard as anyone has ever tried for anything.

THERE IS A TENDENCY to treat true stories from the world of sports as vehicles for practical inspiration. Readers and hearers and watchers of true sports stories expect to come away from these tales of others' victories with an impetus toward their own. When I started my journey into Iron War, I harbored a notion that I would find one great lesson at the end of it to distill and pass on. One can, of course, find any number of different lessons and inspirations in the story of the 1989 Ironman, some of them very familiar. The old *never give up* lesson is in fact the chief lesson Mark Allen himself learned from living the story.

"Had I not had those bad experiences," he said in an interview, referring to the six failures that preceded his first triumph in Kona, "and learned those lessons about how to hold it together when it's not going well, I wouldn't have won the other six. That experience of having to drag yourself across the finish line when there's a thousand and one times you want to quit, when you don't feel you can make it, but somehow you do, it gives you a perspective within which to always have a shred of hope that somehow it will turn around for you. And when you have that inside, no matter how bad it looks, there is always a part of you that will continue to give it what you have."

While there are zillions of stories about not quitting, few tellers of such tales ever really explore the source of the will to endure, the substance of trying harder. Most raconteurs of sport just take it as given that any seer or hearer of a story of outrageous persistence can be inspired to try harder, as Julie Moss's stirring crawl in February 1982 inspired Mark Allen to overcome the choker inside him and to do his first Ironman. But, as I learned in my efforts to understand the *why* and *how* of Iron War, modern science has enabled us to put this kind of courage under the microscope as never before, and the results have not been kind to the myth of the communicability of will. Scientists including Samuele Marcora and Stephen McGregor have demonstrated that the bravery of the likes of Dave Scott and Mark Allen is a physical thing subject to physical laws and cannot be freely chosen by just anyone. It is certainly affected by psychological influences, such as poor parenting, but one cannot, in the absence of that kind of influence, simply manufacture the sort of hunger that drives the son of a bad father to practically kill himself to win. And no less important than the life experiences that forge iron will are the biological determinants—such as the freakishly strong anterior cingulate cortex that Dave Scott perhaps inherited from one of his parents, or perhaps not—which are even less accessible to free choice.

So, while the story of Iron War certainly delivers a lesson about the power of persistence, it's not a practical lesson. After all, Julie Moss didn't inspire *everyone* to do what Mark ultimately did, because no one else had what he had inside him. If Dave and Mark inspire others to achieve their own legacy of greatness, more power to them. But what I've taken away from my study of Iron War is a clear appreciation of why I have never achieved and never will achieve acts of greatness like those achieved by Dave and Mark. And no amount of "feeling inspired" by their story can change that for me.

What if *feeling* inspired, versus *being* inspired, is the true value of the greatest race ever run?

Iron War tightens the throat and moistens the eyes and makes one say, "Wow!" Nothing useful in that, but so what? After all, what else is life but a messy unfolding of feelings? And what else do we really seek in life but to feel strongly? Most of life consists of muted background feelings, and necessarily so. It's the occasional bursts of intense sensation that make life seem the miracle that it is. Some of these sensations are bad—but the good ones are impossible without them, so the bad ones have value too.

The powerful feelings that the Iron War legend inspires are a vicarious echo of the feelings Dave Scott and Mark Allen sought in the thing itself. They wanted to feel a greater measure of a special type of suffering than most people ever know, and they wanted to feel the immense satisfaction they would earn in overcoming it—a fulfillment that folks like me can only try to imagine.

One of the first questions Dave Scott was asked after the greatest race ever run was how it felt.

"It was kind of painfully enjoyable," the Man said. "And I'm not sure I want to feel that again."

But he would never regret feeling it once.

NOTES

CHAPTER 1: THE MOMENT

p. 2 in which all are complicit: Dan Empfield, personal telephone interview, November 2010.

p. 2 drink station he's staffing: *ABC Sports* 1989 Ironman television broadcast.

p. 3 radio reports from the field: Mike Plant, personal interview, San Marcos, CA, Nov. 2010.

p. 3 indifferent to his own performance: Paul Huddle, personal telephone interview, September 2010.

p. 3 briefly forgotten: Rich Cruse, e-mail correspondence, May 2010.

p. 3 the greatest race ever run: Bob Babbitt, personal interview, San Diego, CA, 2010.

p. 3 only race that really matters: John Duke, personal telephone interview, December 2010.

p. 3 before the 1987 Ironman: *ABC Sports* 1987 Ironman television broadcast.

p. 4 promptly fulfilled the promise: *ABC Sports* 1983 Ironman television broadcast.

p. 4 living in Davis, California: Babbitt interview.

p. 4 as close as they are now: *Competitor*, cover image by David Epperson, October 1989.

p. 5 now near completing: *ABC Sports* 1989 Ironman television broadcast.

p. 5 a one-time opportunist: Scott Molina, personal telephone interview, July 2010.

p. 6 He meditates: William R. Katovsky, "A Champion Thoroughbred," *Triathlete*, September 1984, pp. 48–55.

p. 6 weaken him as a competitor: *ABC Sports* 1983 Ironman television broadcast.

p. 6 not even good for you: Babbitt interview.

p. 6 seated in adjacent chairs: ibid.

p. 6 weak in any moment: "The Iron War: Mark Allen and Dave Scott," http://www.youtube.com/watch?v=zOVGVMiwPSA.

CHAPTER 2: A DROP TOO MUCH

p. 9 on his three-speed bike: Dave Scott, personal telephone interview, January 2011.

p. 9 five and a half miles away: ibid.

p. 10 fair and square: ibid.

p. 10 into a day, every day: ibid.

p. 10 *Ozzie and Harriet*: Liz Barrett and William R. Katovsky, "It's Lonely at the Top: An Interview with Dave Scott," *Triathlete*, May 1984, pp. 34–43.

p. 10 fierce when necessary: Dave Walker, personal telephone interview, November 2010.

p. 10 results of their sports competitions: Barrett and Katovsky, "It's Lonely at the Top."

p. 10 in the United States: Lew Kidder, personal telephone interview, May 2011.

p. 10 competent yet completely unassuming: Walker interview.

p. 11 of those chores: Dave Scott, 2011 USA Triathlon Hall of Fame induction speech.

p. 11 constituted his exercise: Walker interview.

p. 11 too much perfume: Scott, 2011 USA Triathlon Hall of Fame induction speech.

p. 11 in the lock it was made for: ibid.

p. 11 Patti, Dave, and Jane joined: Dave Scott interview.

p. 11 every lap was competition: Dave Scott, *Dave Scott's Triathlon Training* (New York: Fireside, 1986).

p. 11 give him by example: Endurance Planet, "Hall of Fame Series—Verne Scott—1/14/2009," www.enduranceplanet.com/hall-of-fame-series-verne-scott-1142009.

p. 12 name of Murphy Reinschreiber: Murphy Reinschreiber, personal telephone interview, February 2011.

p. 12 Little League all-star: Bob Babbitt, "Still Lord of the Lava," *Competitor*, October 1991, pp. 18–23.

p. 13 And he didn't: Dave Scott, 2011 USA Triathlon Hall of Fame induction speech.

p. 13 practicing and competing were done: Dave Scott interview.

p. 13 dawn or after dark: Walker interview.

p. 13 the school gymnasium: Dave Scott interview.

p. 13 personality would change: ibid.

p. 13 the freedom to move: ibid.

p. 14 fell apart in his hands: Dave Scott, "The Schedule: One for the Books," *Inside Triathlon*, November 1997, p. 42.

p. 14 stroke is horrendous: Dan Levin, "Gall, Divided into Three Parts," *Sports Illustrated* Ocotober 10, 1983.

p. 14 to be seen shirtless: Bob Babbitt, personal interview, San Diego, CA, 2010.

p. 14 the fear that lives within me: Steve Boga, *Risk! An Exploration into the Lives of Athletes on the Edge* (Berkeley, CA: North Atlantic Books, 1988), p. 44.

p. 14 *crazy*, she thought: Linda Buchanan, personal telephone interview, November 2010.

p. 14 Verne's first choice: ibid.

p. 15 a form of osmosis: Mark Roberts, personal telephone interview, November 2010.

p. 15 wood-paneled weight room: Kirk Hamilton, personal telephone interview, July 2010.

p. 15 backing away: Craig Wilson, personal telephone interview, November 2010.

p. 15 ice cream for dessert: Scott, *Dave Scott's Triathlon Training*.

p. 15 in one sitting: ibid.

p. 16 table for two hours: Roberts interview.

p. 16 his meals and snacks: Scott, *Dave Scott's Triathlon Training*.

p. 16 rice cakes and wheat crackers: Levin, "Gall, Divided into Three Parts."

p. 16 rinsed his cottage cheese: Premiere Speakers Bureau video of Mark Allen corporate speech.

p. 16 bonding with his offspring: Endurance Planet, "Hall of Fame Series—Verne Scott."

p. 16 UC–Santa Barbara: "Swim Coach Raises the Bar for Amateurs," active.com, http://www.active.com/swimming/Articles/Swim_coach_raises_the_bar_for_amateurs.htm.

p. 16 excuses of any kind: Buchanan interview.

p. 17 just to experience Dave: John Reganold, personal interview, July 2010.

p. 17 while others slept: Ken McAlpine, unpublished article written for *Competitor*, 2010.

p. 17 he took it hard: Wilson interview.

p. 18 invited her brother to join her: Endurance Planet, "Hall of Fame Series—Verne Scott."

p. 18 Buck barked: ibid.

p. 18 prize of a frozen turkey: Scott, *Dave Scott's Triathlon Training*.

p. 19 second in his age group: "Waikiki Roughwater Swim, Hawaii," http://waikikiroughwaterswim.com/1978/1978.html.

p. 19 the following January: Dave Scott on Competitor Radio, http://competitorradio.competitor.com/tag/dave-scott.

p. 19 threw it away: ibid.

p. 19 in Los Angeles: Mike Norton, personal telephone interview, July 2010.

p. 20 You could win it: ibid.

p. 20 And it starts now: Endurance Planet, "Hall of Fame Series—Verne Scott."

p. 20 more experienced than he was: Dave Scott on Competitor Radio.

p. 20 In a workout: Reganold interview.

p. 20 dusting everyone: Dave Scott on Competitor Radio.

p. 21 Dave threw a fit: ibid.

p. 21 yelling at her some more: Scott, *Dave Scott's Triathlon Training.*

p. 21 with which he shared it: Dave Scott on Competitor Radio.

p. 21 anyone had done it yet: ibid.

p. 22 across the United States: Dave McGillivray, personal conversation, April 2011.

p. 22 a microphone in his face: McAlpine, unpublished article.

p. 22 with anyone at the end: *ABC Sports* 1980 Ironman television broadcast.

p. 23 women's changing room: McAlpine, unpublished article.

p. 23 within just a year or two: *ABC Sports* 1980 Ironman television broadcast.

p. 23 shoe to the right pedal: Los Angeles Triathlon Club, *A Night with Dave Scott and Mark Allen*, October 5, 2002, videotape courtesy of Bob Babbitt.

p. 23 better pedaling efficiency: Dave Scott on Competitor Radio.

p. 23 blow by him any minute: Los Angeles Triathlon Club, *A Night with Dave Scott and Mark Allen.*

p. 23 carbon-fiber frames: Ironman.com, year-by-year results.

p. 24 the right of way: Dave Scott on Competitor Radio.

p. 24 techniques from movies: ibid.

p. 24 the woman said: *ABC Sports* 1980 Ironman television broadcast.

p. 24 fast-thinking Pat Feeney: Dave Scott on Competitor Radio.

p. 24 relieve himself in some bushes: McAlpine, unpublished article.

p. 25 in Kapiolani Park: Valerie Silk, personal telephone interview, July 2010.

p. 25 just getting started: Scott, *Dave Scott's Triathlon Training;* Dave Scott on Competitor Radio.

p. 25 per one-year plan: Levin, "Gall, Divided into Three Parts."

p. 25 a triathlon in Davis: Endurance Planet, "Hall of Fame Series–Verne Scott."

p. 25 Dave's name and image: Levin, "Gall, Divided into Three Parts."

p. 26 than ultraendurance racing: Endurance Planet, "Hall of Fame Series–Verne Scott."

p. 26 showdown with Mark Allen: *ABC Sports* 1989 Ironman television broadcast.

p. 26 he broke down: Levin, "Gall, Divided into Three Parts."

p. 27 some 3,000 times: Ken McAlpine, "Dave Scott: Man, Myth, or Legend," *Triathlete*, October 1989, pp. 34-38.

p. 27 a moment's hesitation: 26:50: Dave Scott interview.

p. 27 before he got home: Norton interview.

p. 28 give triathlon a try: Herbert Krabel, "Pigg Power: Mike Pigg," http://www.slowtwitch.com/Interview/Pigg_Power_-_Mike_Pigg_353.html.

p. 28 emptied it in minutes: Dave Scott on Competitor Radio.

p. 28 a loaf of bread: ibid.

p. 28 Pigg returned to Davis: Mike Pigg, personal telephone interview, November 2010.

p. 28 pain in his knee while running: Jim Mason, "Ironman Dave Scott Is in Better Shape Than Anybody," *Vegetarian Times*, July 1983, pp. 18-20.

p. 28 turned to apathy: Buchanan interview.

p. 28 gained fifteen pounds: Mason, "Ironman Dave Scott Is in Better Shape Than Anybody."

p. 29 would let go eventually: Buchanan interview.

p. 29 kind, charismatic woman: ibid.

p. 29 I beat Dave Scott: Tim McDonald, "The Other Dave Scott," *Triathlon*, May 1984, pp. 52-53, 92-93.

p. 29 back on track: ibid.

p. 30 Dave was, in fact, single: Anna Scott, personal telephone interview, November 2010.

p. 30 his vulnerable side: ibid.

p. 30 breaking a collarbone: Tracy Dodds, "Dual Exhaustion: Dave and Anna Scott Have Found Success Combining a Personal Life and a Rigorous Training Schedule," *Los Angeles Times*, February 7, 1988.

p. 30 while he rode his bike: Anna Scott interview.

p. 30 other side eventually: ibid.

p. 30 around the bend: Dave Scott interview.

p. 31 making yourself more miserable: Molina interview.

p. 31 laid him low lately: Levin, "Gall: Divided into Three Parts."

p. 31 lonely state to America: Scott Tinley, "The Years with Dave," *Triathlete*, October 1992, pp. 48–52.

p. 31 described him) persisted: Barrett and Katovsky, "It's Lonely at the Top."

p. 32 embarrassments and rumors: Molina interview.

CHAPTER 3: GET A GRIP

p. 33 in Glendale, California: Mark Allen with Bob Babbitt, *Mark Allen's Total Triathlete* (New York: McGraw-Hill, 1988).

p. 33 safely into the world: Ken Allen, personal telephone interview, February 2011.

p. 33 David had Down syndrome: ibid.

p. 33 he has remained ever since: ibid.

p. 34 kept their own counsel: Carole Allen, personal telephone interview, February 2011.

p. 34 moved to the Midwest: Allen with Babbitt, *Mark Allen's Total Triathlete*.

p. 34 in a neighboring apartment: ibid.

p. 34 Space's treatment of him: "The Last Word Unedited: Chris McCormack and Mark Allen, Part Two," Lavamagazine.com, http://lavamagazine.com/features/the-last-word, unedited-chris-mccormack-and-mark-allen,-part-two#axzz1UZVr7uI5.

p. 34 frequent "negative reinforcement": Joel Silverman, "Back to Business," *Inside Triathlon*, July 1995, pp. 19–21.

p. 34 in no uncertain terms: Gary Allen, quoted in ibid.

p. 34 almost a quarter century: Mark Allen, quoted in ibid.

p. 35 That's incredible: Allen with Babbitt, *Mark Allen's Total Triathlete*.

p. 35 two weeks late: ibid.

p. 35 at the University of California-Davis: Ken Allen interview.

p. 35 his inscrutability: Eric Bunje, personal telephone interview, July 2010.

p. 35 Mark Allen shared: ibid.

p. 35 in the entire first grade: Allen with Babbitt, *Mark Allen's Total Triathlete*.

p. 35 residency at Stanford University: Ken Allen interview.

p. 35 took place in Mexico city: "About Mark Allen," InGoofoo, http://www.ingoofoo.com /content/view/46/93.

p. 36 survived the test, but barely: ibid.

p. 36 swim twenty-five yards: Allen with Babbitt, *Mark Allen's Total Triathlete*.

p. 36 *Palo Alto Times*: Mark Allen, Fit Soul, Fit Body presentation, Palo Alto, CA, Nov. 10, 2009.

p. 36 his father became: Allen with Babbitt, *Mark Allen's Total Triathlete*.

p. 36 woman in her mid-20s: Carole Allen interview.

p. 37 lays it on thick, doesn't he: ibid.

p. 37 talk about his swimming: Allen with Babbitt, *Mark Allen's Total Triathlete*.

p. 37 his race was done: Pete Gauvin, "Mind over Suffering—Mark Allen," adventure sportsjournal.com.

p. 37 Mark choked: Mark Allen on Competitor Radio, http://competitorradio.competitor. com/tag/mark-allen.

p. 38 for the first time in his life: Bunje interview.

p. 38 seventy-mile round-trip: ibid.

p. 38 Just do the races: ibid.

p. 38 he faked a stomachache: *Triathlete*, August 1999.

p. 38 a gliding hawk: Bunje interview.

p. 38 lots of questions: ibid.

p. 38 depicted in movies: Mark Allen, "Impacts of Shamanism," Dance of the Deer Foundation, http://blog.danceofthedeer.com/2010/04/impacts-of-shamanism.

p. 38 and other customs: Ken Allen interview.

p. 39 apprenticeship in Mexico: Scott Molina, personal telephone interview, July 2010.

p. 39 chafed against it: Mark Allen, personal conversation, Kona, HI, October 2010.

p. 39 nothing seemed a perfect match: Mark Allen, "Impacts of Shamanism."

p. 39 haze of mellow pleasure: Gary Hardin, personal telephone interview, February 2011.

p. 39 recently learned to surf: John Walters, "Fast Afoot or Fast Asleep?" *Sports Illustrated*, May 31, 1993.

p. 39 riding a unicycle: Gary Hardin, e-mail correspondence.

p. 40 *to offer in this world*: Silverman, "Back to Business." Allen's words: "How many times do I have to win before I feel better?"

p. 40 throughout the summer: Gary Hardin, personal interview.

p. 40 after his first year at UCSD: Allen with Babbitt, *Mark Allen's Total Triathlete*.

p. 40 a few days a week: ibid.

p. 40 get back into the pool: Bill Morgan, personal telephone interview, October 2010.

p. 40 he would fall apart: ibid.

p. 40 what might have been: Ryan Hall, assistant athletic director, sports information director, UC-San Diego Athletics, e-mail correspondence.

p. 41 San Diego lifestyle: Molina interview.

p. 41 being a doctor himself: Allen with Babbitt, *Mark Allen's Total Triathlete*.

p. 41 Not yet: Los Angeles Triathlon Club, *A Night with Dave Scott and Mark Allen*, October 5, 2002, videotape courtesy of Bob Babbitt.

p. 41 he asked himself: Allen with Babbitt, *Mark Allen's Total Triathlete*.

p. 41 his own career in medicine: ibid.

p. 41 from his sire: Los Angeles Triathlon Club, *A Night with Dave Scott and Mark Allen*.

p. 41 Animallen: Julie Moss, personal telephone interview, September 2010.

p. 42 and in the water: Mike Plant, "Mark Allen," *Triathlon*, July 1985, pp. 34-38.

p. 42 challenged him to a race: Morgan interview.

p. 42 thought to before: Moss interview.

p. 42 February 6, 1982: "*Wide World* 'Constant Variety' Milestones and Highlights," http:// espn.go.com/abcsports/wwos/highlights/variety8090.html.

p. 42 apartment in Del Mar: Morgan interview.

p. 42 glimpse or two of Reed: ibid.

p. 42 with a show of grit: *People*, October 11, 1982.

p. 42 eight miles into the marathon: *ABC Sports* February 1982 Ironman television broadcast.

p. 43 turn off the television: Mathias Müller with Timothy Carlson, *17 Hours to Glory: Extraordinary Stories from the Heart of Triathlon* (Boulder, CO: VeloPress, 2010), p. 19.

p. 44 about Julie Moss especially: ibid.

p. 44 the fall and winter months: Brant Secunda and Mark Allen, "Fit Soul—Fit Body: 9 Keys to a Healthier, Happier You," Living Dialogues podcast series, episodes 89 and 90, personallifemedia.com, http://personallifemedia.com/podcasts/212-living-dialogues/episodes/33806-brant-secunda-huichol-shaman-healer-mark. Courtesy of Personal Life Media.

p. 44 do for a living: ibid.

p. 44 Volkswagen Squareback: Morgan interview.

p. 44 inaugural La Jolla Half Marathon: Moss interview.

p. 45 But thanks: ibid. Moss does not recall the exact words of this conversation.

p. 45 Don't tell Reed I said that: ibid.

p. 45 he started with hers: ibid.

p. 45 that Saturday morning: Scott Tinley, *Triathlon: A Personal History* (Boulder, CO: VeloPress, 1998).

p. 46 to execute transitions: Murphy Reinschreiber, personal telephone interview, February 2011.

p. 46 like the one Mark drove: Tinley, *Triathlon*.

p. 46 at the local K-Mart: Mike Plant, "Scott Molina," *Triathlon*, February 1985.

p. 46 none other than Dave Scott: Mike Plant, "13 Minutes down, 13 Miles to Go," *San Diego Running News*, July 1982, pp. 22–23.

p. 47 locating his own Nikes: Reinschreiber interview.

p. 47 he heard footsteps: Mark Allen on Competitor Radio.

p. 47 bib number 6: Tinley, *Triathlon*.

p. 47 to watch out for you: Allen with Babbitt, *Mark Allen's Total Triathlete*.

p. 47 drifted ahead of him: Mark Allen on Competitor Radio.

p. 47 in his first triathlon: Dale Basescu, personal telephone interview, October 2010.

p. 47 play in his head: Los Angeles Triathlon Club, *A Night with Dave Scott and Mark Allen*.

p. 48 the pace another notch: Dale Basescu, personal interview.

p. 48 It rattled him: ibid.

p. 49 greatest triathlete ever," he said: ibid.

p. 49 I know it: ibid.

p. 50 you haven't won anything. Eric Bunje, personal interview.

p. 50 California State Fair Swim Meet: Reinschreiber interview.

p. 50 the grip of death: ibid.

p. 50 outsuffer all comers: ibid.

p. 51 when pedaling hard: Paul Huddle, quoted in Timothy Carlson, "Mark Allen's Dream-Time Transition," *Triathlete*, August 1997, pp. 18–24.

p. 51 at chakra points: Craig Neff, "Triumph of Pigg Power," *Sports Illustrated*, October 5, 1987.

p. 51 when Mark wasn't looking: Kenny Souza, personal telephone interview, October 2010.

p. 51 practiced self-hypnosis: Plant, "Mark Allen."

p. 52 eternity in suspension: Allen with Babbitt, *Mark Allen's Total Triathlete*.

p. 52 left around the house: Souza interview.

p. 52 what you need to do in life: Allen with Babbitt, *Mark Allen's Total Triathlete*.

p. 52 doing what you need to do: David K. Reynolds, "Reality's Reminders," http://constructiveliving.org/works/reminders.html.

p. 52 focus on himself: Allen with Babbitt, *Mark Allen's Total Triathlete*.

p. 52 a few times every week: Souza interview.

p. 52 overtraining fatigue: Molina interview.

p. 53 only a few times a week: Mark Allen, "Working Your Heart," Mark Allen Online, http://www.markallenonline.com/maoArticles.aspx?AID=2.

p. 53 below the prescribed threshold: ibid.

p. 53 at his cleverness: Ray Browning, personal telephone interview, January 2011.

p. 53 dust in his garage: Moss interview.

p. 53 a meditation retreat: William R. Katovsky, "A Champion Thoroughbred," *Triathlete*, September 1984, pp. 48–55.

p. 54 a month of lifeguarding: Allen with Babbitt, *Mark Allen's Total Triathlete*.

p. 54 would recognize him: ibid.

p. 54 slept together in the bedroom: Moss interview.

p. 54 right in front of them: Allen with Babbitt, *Mark Allen's Total Triathlete*.

p. 54 J. David brokerage firm: Donald C. Bauder, *Captain Money and the Golden Girl: The J. David Affair* (San Diego, CA: Harcourt, 1985).

p. 55 the night before the race: Allen with Babbitt, *Mark Allen's Total Triathlete*.

p. 55 *all in front of me*, he thought: Tinley, *Triathlon*.

p. 55 zip codes in America: Bauder, *Captain Money and the Golden Girl*.

p. 55 spare bedrooms, and he did: Scott Molina, e-mail correspondence, January 2011.

p. 55 looking distressed: Allen with Babbitt, *Mark Allen's Total Triathlete*.

p. 56 the scandal broke, at age 25: Tinley, *Triathlon*.

p. 56 the 1984 racing season: Bob Babbitt, "Keith Peters," Competitor Radio, 2009, http://competitorradio.competitor.com/2009/03/298keith-peters.

p. 56 fifty grand a year plus bonuses: Molina interview.

p. 56 to see often at races: Ed Zieralski, "Julie Moss' Agony in Defeat Was Appalling, but Love's Labor Made Her a Star," *People*, October 11, 1982.

p. 56 Go for it: ibid.

p. 56 to stay in his room: Walters, "Fast Afoot or Fast Asleep?"

p. 57 won back his father's support: Plant, "Mark Allen."

CHAPTER 4: PAIN COMMUNITY

p. 59 World Championship is taking place: All information about and quotations from Michael Atkinson come from personal interviews and e-mail correspondence with him.

p. 61 when it's over: Michael Atkinson, "Triathlon, Suffering, and Exciting Significance," *Leisure Studies* 27, 2 (April 2008): 165-180.

p. 62 an otherwise too-easy world: ibid, p. 166.

p. 62 work in different ways: ibid, p. 171.

p. 64 to spend life: ibid, p. 173.

p. 65 Tug's Tavern: Scott Tinley, *Triathlon: A Personal History* (Boulder, CO: VeloPress, 1998).

p. 65 to prevent sunburn: Gaylia Osterlund, "High Above San Diego, Tom Warren Enjoys the Peace and Quiet," Ironman.com, June 4, 2003, http://ironman.com/holdingcell/2003/june-2003/high-above-san-diego-tom-warren-enjoys-the-peace-and-quiet#axzz1U5ZoWcuS.

p. 65 a half mile to shore: Dave Distel, "Ironman Keeps Insanity Firmly in His Grasp," *Los Angeles Times*, October 25, 1991, http://articles.latimes.com/1991-10-25/sports/sp-265_1_tom-warren.

p. 65 the number in his log: Scott Tinley, "Working Stiff Part 2: Working Out and the Empires of Deception," beginnertriathlete.com, January 14, 2011, http://www.beginnertriathlete.com/cms/article-detail.asp?articleid=2169.

p. 66 man-made isthmus: Tinley, *Triathlon*.

p. 66 the first Iron Man: ibid.

p. 67 perimeter of Oahu: Nick Munting, "An Officer and a Gentleman—John Collins," Ironman.com, June 29, 2001, http://ironman.com/holdingcell/2001/june-2001/an-officer-and-a-gentleman-john-collins#axzz1U5ZoWcuS.

p. **67** called Iron Man," he said: ibid.

p. **68** in October 1977: ibid.

p. **68** prize of—nothing: Barry McDermott, "Ironman," *Sports Illustrated*, May 19, 1979, http://sportsillustrated.cnn.com/vault/article/magazine/MAG1094935/index.htm.

p. **69** stumbled upon it: Kara Douglass Thom, *Becoming an Ironman: First Encounters with the Ultimate Endurance Event* (Halcottsville, NY: Breakaway Books, 2002).

p. **69** prove their toughness: McDermott, "Ironman."

p. **69** better that way: ibid.

p. **71** system for Ironman entry: "Ironman Triathlon World Championship," Ironman.com, July 15, 2005, http://ironman.com/mediacenter/history/ironman-triathlon-world-championship#axzz1U5ZoWcuS.

p. **71** tackled alone: Jack H. Wilmore, "Influence of Motivation on Physical Work Capacity and Performance," *Journal of Applied Physiology* 24, 4 (April 1968): 459–463.

p. **72** runner-up $12,000: 1989 Bud Light Ironman official program.

CHAPTER 5: YOU AGAIN

p. **73** Waikiki Roughwater Swim: Dave Scott, *Dave Scott's Triathlon Training* (New York: Fireside, 1986).

p. **73** first year of college: Carole Allen, personal telephone interview, February 2011.

p. **74** objects of Pele's vengeance: Bob Babbitt, *25 Years of the Ironman Triathlon World Championship* (Aachen, Germany: Meyer and Meyer Fachverlag und Buchhandel GmbH, 2003).

p. **74** gifts to Pele: "George Lycurgus," Wikipedia.com, http://en.wikipedia.org/wiki/George_Lycurgus.

p. **74** kick the bucket: Carole Allen interview.

p. **75** jimmy the lock: ibid.

p. **75** put them in storage: ibid.

p. **75** brought in 850: T. J. Murphy, "A Look Back at a Look Back: Ironman's First 10 Years," Ironman.com, January 3, 2003, http://ironman.com/holdingcell/2003/january-2003/a-look-back-at-a-look-back-ironmans-first-10-years#axzz1U5ZoWcuS. Originally published in *Triathlete*, October 1988.

p. **75** greater governmental support: Valerie Silk, personal interview.

p. **75** seven o'clock on race morning: Los Angeles Triathlon Club, *A Night with Dave Scott and Mark Allen*, October 5, 2002, videotape courtesy of Bob Babbitt.

p. **76** and shouted, "Two": ibid.

p. **76** such unexpected success: *ABC Sports* October 1982 Ironman television broadcast.

p. **76** straight to the changing room: Mike Plant, "Long Day's Journey," *Triathlon*, Spring 1983, pp. 24–31, 41, 54, 59.

p. **77** I'm Mark Allen," Mark said: Los Angeles Triathlon Club, *A Night with Dave Scott and Mark Allen*.

p. **77** threat at Ironman: ibid.

p. **77** the annoying gadfly: ibid.

p. **77** one-in-a-million race-ender: Plant, "Long Day's Journey," p. 28.

p. **77** first two-time Ironman champion: Los Angeles Triathlon Club, *A Night with Dave Scott and Mark Allen*.

pp. **77-78** lead on Dave Scott: Mike Plant, "Vive Les Triathletes Américains," *Triathlon*, Winter 1983, pp. 46–51, 73, 75.

p. **78** pleading for him: ibid.

p. 78 on the French Riviera: Mark Allen with Bob Babbitt, *Mark Allen's Total Triathlete* (New York: McGraw-Hill, 1988).

p. 78 salvage the year for myself: Liz Barrett and William R. Katovsky, "It's Lonely at the Top: An Interview with Dave Scott," *Triathlete*, May 1984, p. 38.

p. 78 hot, rank spray: Scott Tinley, *Triathlon: A Personal History* (Boulder, CO: VeloPress, 1998).

p. 79 going to *bury* this guy: *ABC Sports* 1983 Ironman television broadcast.

p. 79 side of the road," he said later: Los Angeles Triathlon Club, *A Night with Dave Scott and Mark Allen*.

p. 79 *Gee, thanks*, Dave thought: ibid.

p. 79 just go away: Timothy Carlson, "How to Win (and Lose) in Kona: Lesson One," Triathlete Europe, March 1, 2011, http://triathlete-europe.competitor.com/2011/03/01/strategy-games-lessons-learned-kona.

p. 79 frustrations in the lava fields: William R. Katovsky, "Hawaii Heat," *Triathlete*, January 1985, pp. 20–43.

p. 80 This was Grip's year: ibid.

p. 80 adoring age-group competitors: Terry Mulgannon, "Ironmania," *Triathlon*, January 1985, pp. 38–50, 64–65.

p. 80 shrinking into himself: ibid.

p. 80 bag of cycling clothes: ibid.

p. 80 ebullience she'd expected: ibid.

p. 80 spectators gathered there: ibid.

p. 81 put on my running shoes: Dave Scott, *Dave Scott's Triathlon Training* (New York: Fireside, 1986).

p. 81 down Ali'i Drive toward town: Brant Secunda and Mark Allen, "Fit Soul–Fit Body: 9 Keys to a Healthier, Happier You," Living Dialogues podcast series, episodes 89 and 90, personallifemedia.com, http://personallifemedia.com/podcasts/212-living-dialogues/episodes/33806-brant-secunda-huichol-shaman-healer-mark. Courtesy of Personal Life Media.

p. 81 out of gas: Los Angeles Triathlon Club, *A Night with Dave Scott and Mark Allen*.

p. 81 off my bike!" he roared: *ABC Sports* 1984 Ironman television broadcast.

p. 82 Mark's advantage: Los Angeles Triathlon Club, *A Night with Dave Scott and Mark Allen*.

p. 82 as he took the lead: Katovsky, "Hawaii Heat."

p. 82 abreast of him: Los Angeles Triathlon Club, *A Night with Dave Scott and Mark Allen*.

p. 82 Mark said at last: ibid.

p. 83 silently into the water: Mulgannon, "Ironmania."

p. 83 asked him later: Mark Allen on Competitor Radio, http://competitorradio.competitor.com/tag/mark-allen.

p. 83 corporate backers: Bob Cooper, "A Dark Future?" *Triathlete*, February 1986, pp. 34–35.

p. 83 married to Anna Pettis: Tom Taylor, "The French Connection," *Triathlete*, January 1986, pp. 36–41.

p. 83 prize purse for the 1986 race: Tinley, *Triathlon*.

p. 83 laugh at the finish line: CJ Olivares Jr., "Encore, Allen," *Triathlete*, January 1987, pp. 32–36.

p. 84 putting out 100 percent: Allen with Babbitt, *Mark Allen's Total Triathlete*.

p. 84 pee from the saddle: Mulgannon, "Ironman X."

p. 84 stopped too: ibid.

p. 85 "Where's Allen?" he barked: ibid.

p. 85 100-degree heat: ibid.

p. 85 feverish with envy: Allen with Babbitt, *Mark Allen's Total Triathlete.*

p. 86 Kellogg said he would: Bob Babbitt, personal interview, San Diego, CA, 2010.

p. 86 won the 1987 race: ibid.

p. 86 in early October: Los Angeles Triathlon Club, *A Night with Dave Scott and Mark Allen.*

p. 86 he said flatly: CJ Olivares Jr., "Toughest Ironman Ever!" *Triathlete*, January 1988, pp. 32–42.

p. 86 *got to get it back*: Allen with Babbitt, *Mark Allen's Total Triathlete.*

p. 87 day before the race: ibid.

p. 87 possibility had ended: Babbitt interview.

p. 87 Or whoever . . . : Mike Plant, "Don't Mess with the Man," *Outside*, February 1988, pp. 38–42.

p. 87 feels that pressure: *ABC Sports* 1987 Ironman television broadcast.

p. 88 before the camera: Allen with Babbitt, *Mark Allen's Total Triathlete.*

p. 88 through his goggles: ibid.

p. 88 Mark chased: Bob Babbitt, "Lord of the Lava," *Competitor*, November 1987, pp. 4–5, 38.

p. 88 wasn't pushing the pace: Allen with Babbitt, *Mark Allen's Total Triathlete.*

p. 88 situation in his gut: ibid.

p. 89 his face, was ready: Olivares, "Toughest Ironman Ever!"

p. 89 soon afterward: Allen with Babbitt, *Mark Allen's Total Triathlete.*

p. 89 turned to water: Olivares, "Toughest Ironman Ever!"

p. 89 lead of five minutes: ibid.

p. 89 victory speech: Los Angeles Triathlon Club, *A Night with Dave Scott and Mark Allen.*

p. 89 tone of a grade school teacher: ibid.

p. 90 the last ten miles: ibid.

p. 90 ever-worsening news: ibid.

p. 90 past heroic wins: ibid.

p. 91 *really good now*: ibid.

p. 91 In fact, he cried: Olivares, "Toughest Ironman Ever!"

p. 91 pissed blood: Allen with Babbitt, *Mark Allen's Total Triathlete.*

p. 91 to stop the bleeding: Charlie Graves, personal telephone interview, October 2010.

p. 91 *missing in my strategy*: Los Angeles Triathlon Club, *A Night with Dave Scott and Mark Allen.*

p. 92 until he fully recovered: "The Last Word Unedited: Chris McCormack and Mark Allen, Part Two," Lavamagazine.com, http://lavamagazine.com/features/the-last-word, -unedited-chris-mccormack-and-mark-allen,-part-two#axzz1UZVr7uI5.

p. 92 did nothing differently: Los Angeles Triathlon Club, *A Night with Dave Scott and Mark Allen.*

p. 92 a knee injury: ibid.

p. 93 a tire puncture: Ken McAlpine, "Dave Scott: Man, Myth, or Legend," *Triathlete*, October 1989, pp. 34–38.

p. 93 he said afterward: Mark Allen on Competitor Radio, http://competitorradio.competitor.com/tag/mark-allen.

p. 93 his undeserved misfortune: Babbitt, *25 Years of the Ironman Triathlon World Championship.*

p. 93 winner, Scott Molina: Richard Graham, "Ironman," *Triathlete*, January 1988, pp. 26–41.

p. 93 ranked eighth: "Triathlete Magazine's 1989 Reader's Poll Results," *Triathlete*, March 1989, p. 11.

p. 93 bet on the right guy: "As the Freewheel Turns," *Triathlete*, May 1989, p. 16.

p. 94 the rest of his days: Mark Allen on Competitor Radio.

p. 94 himself, and his life: ibid.

p. 94 *I'll do it*: ibid.

p. 95 whole different level: T. J. Murphy, "A Space Between Two Thoughts," *Triathlete,* October 1998, pp. 38-43.

p. 95 suburb of Lyttleton: Richard Graham, "Lyttleton: Triathlon's Unlikely Training Center," *Triathlete*, August 1989, pp. 59-60.

p. 95 swimming, riding, and running: ibid.

p. 95 plus a mile: Murphy, "A Space Between Two Thoughts."

p. 95 sunup and sundown: Los Angeles Triathlon Club, *A Night with Dave Scott and Mark Allen.*

p. 95 and back down. Murphy, "A Space Between Two Thoughts."

p. 96 matched that of Ironman: Los Angeles Triathlon Club, *A Night with Dave Scott and Mark Allen.*

p. 96 training on the moon: *ABC Sports* 1983 Ironman television broadcast.

p. 96 level of fitness: Los Angeles Triathlon Club, *A Night with Dave Scott and Mark Allen.*

p. 96 implode in the marathon: ibid.

p. 96 I loved it: ibid.

p. 97 of the day to run: ibid.

p. 97 killing them by exposure: CJ Olivares Jr., "1989 Triathletes of the Year: Mark Allen," *Triathlete*, March 1990, pp. 34-37.

p. 97 by nineteen seconds: CJ Olivares Jr., "Duel in the Sun," *Triathlete*, August 1989, pp. 52-58.

p. 97 And he did: Gary Newkirk, "World Cup Australia," *Triathlete*, August 1989, pp. 38-48.

p. 98 30-kilometer run: ibid.

p. 98 beat him by four: ibid.

p. 99 legitimate athletic endeavor: Ray Browning, personal telephone interview, January 2011.

p. 99 "real" athletes appeared: ibid.

p. 99 engagement to Julie: Newkirk, "World Cup Australia."

p. 100 before my time: Gary Newkirk, "Back to the Future," *Triathlete*, September 1989, pp. 46-53.

p. 100 named Lance Armstrong: McAlpine, "Dave Scott: Man, Myth, or Legend."

p. 100 than his rival: Bob Babbitt, "Face Off in Kona," *Competitor*, October 1989, pp. 8-10, 23.

p. 100 nine weeks before Hawaii: ibid.

p. 100 into a tailspin: Anna Scott, personal telephone interview, November 2010.

p. 100 ran seven and a half: Babbitt, "Face Off in Kona."

p. 101 wanted to save weight: Dave Scott on Competitor Radio, http://competitorradio.competitor.com/tag/dave-scott.

p. 101 the swim in 48:25: "Slowtwitch Forums: Triathlon Forum," http://forum.slowtwitch.com/forum/Slowtwitch_Forums_C1/Triathlon_Forum_F1/Super_Fast_Ironman_times,,,_Canada04_and_sub_8_P193395.

p. 101 he kept stomping: Dave Scott on Competitor Radio.

p. 101 bike course in 4:27:31: "Slowtwitch Forums: Triathlon Forum."

p. 101 total time of 8:01:32: ibid.

p. 101 about this," she said: Babbitt, "Face Off in Kona."

p. 102 out of reach for himself: CJ Olivares Jr., "The Man Is Back," *Triathlete*, October 1989.

p. 102 San Elijo Lagoon: Mark Allen on Competitor Radio.

p. 102 the flight into Kona: ibid.

p. 103 lift her curse: Carole Allen interview.

CHAPTER 6: DIG ME BEACH

p. 105 greatest race ever run: Julie Moss, personal telephone interview, September 2010.

p. 106 known until 1993): "Kona International Airport," Wikipedia, http://en.wikipedia.org/wiki/Keahole_Airport.

p. 106 *could happen here*: Los Angeles Triathlon Club, *A Night with Dave Scott and Mark Allen*, 2002, videotape courtesy of Bob Babbitt.

p. 106 only if you stay with him: Kenny Moore, "Big Splash in Hawaii," *Sports Illustrated*, October 23, 1989.

p. 107 a big mistake: Bob Babbitt, "Face Off in Kona," *Competitor*, October 1989 pp. 8–10, 23.

p. 107 unit for two weeks: Moss interview.

p. 108 and the media: Charlie Graves, personal telephone interview, October 2010.

p. 108 wrenches in the sport: Gary Allen, personal telephone interview, January 2011.

p. 108 the same to Mark's body: Mike Rubano, personal telephone interview, October 2010.

p. 108 known to do in the past: Moss interview.

p. 108 the next day: Dave Scott, personal telephone interview, January 2011.

p. 109 his old college marks: Stephen Walker, "Dave Scott Interview," *Podium Sports Journal*, July 1, 2007, http://www.podiumsportsjournal.com/2007/07/01/dave-scott-interview.

p. 109 headed for town: Anna Scott interview.

p. 109 *could happen here*: ibid.

p. 110 parking lot and stopped: ibid.

p. 110 two and a half stars, officially: "Sea Village Resort," tripadvisor.com, http://www.tripadvisor.com/Hotel_Review-g60872-d273246-Reviews-Sea_Village_Resort-Kailua_Kona_Island_of_Hawaii_Hawaii.html.

p. 110 on that lava beach: Moss interview.

p. 111 Elvis of triathlon: Bob Babbitt, personal conversations, June 2010–May 2011.

p. 111 wanted him close: Anna Scott interview.

p. 111 an adjacent unit: John Reganold, personal interview, July 2010.

p. 111 Monday of race week: CJ Olivares Jr., "The Art of War," *Triathlete*, January 1990, pp. 24–37.

p. 111 workout sequence: Dave Scott interview.

p. 112 over the last four: Walker, "Dave Scott Interview."

p. 112 their eyes dueled: Mark Allen with Bob Babbitt, *Mark Allen's Total Triathlete* (New York: McGraw-Hill, 1988).

p. 112 as this one does: *ABC Sports* 1989 Ironman television broadcast.

p. 112 like to defeat: ibid.

p. 113 swim course backward: Walker, "Dave Scott Interview."

p. 113 Mark Allen's dad: Carole Allen, personal telephone interview, February 2011. Carole Allen does not recall the exact timing of this occurrence.

p. 113 hurry to fix it: Rubano interview.

p. 113 take care of it: George Goldstine, e-mail correspondence, February 2011. Goldstine does not recall the exact timing of this occurrence.

p. 113 having no choice: Rubano interview.

p. 114 equally shocked: ibid. Rubano does not recall the exact timing of this occurrence.

p. 114 cottage cheese, and spices: Dominique Donner, "Training Tips," http://www.ddonner.com/forum.html, accessed August 9, 2011.

p. 114 also high in fat: Scott Molina, personal telephone interview, July 2010.

p. 114 advantage in Hawaii: CJ Olivares, personal telephone interview, October 2010.

p. 115 before and during the race: ibid.

p. 115 soft-walled suitcase: Rubano interview. Rubano does not recall the exact timing of this occurrence.

p. 115 climb inside the bag: Phil Maffetone, personal telephone interview, January 2010.

p. 115 hot dog!" she said: Moss interview.

p. 116 Big Red Wiener: ibid.

p. 116 to win Ironman: Rubano interview.

p. 116 appointment with the chamber: Maffetone interview.

p. 116 Seventy-five minutes: Rubano interview,

p. 116 almost back to normal: Olivares, "The Art of War."

p. 116 along Ali'i Drive: Walker, "Dave Scott Interview."

p. 116 possible for him too: Dave Scott interview.

p. 117 from across the road: Olivares interview. Olivares does not recall the exact timing of this occurrence.

p. 117 ready to *run*: ibid.

p. 117 in the proper direction: Walker, "Dave Scott Interview."

p. 117 cross a room in Kona: Babbitt interview.

p. 117 Kamehameha Hotel: Mark Roberts, personal telephone interview, November 2010.

p. 118 kissing the Wailing Wall: Olivares interview.

p. 118 Tinley between them: Roberts interview.

p. 118 at Mark's table: ibid.

p. 119 remembered as a legend: Tim McDonald, "The Other Dave Scott," *Triathlon*, May 1984, pp. 52–53, 92–93.

p. 119 in different environments: Molina interview.

p. 119 his energy aura: ibid.

p. 119 awkwardness) and brief: Roberts interview.

p. 120 his race packet: ibid.

p. 120 a pint of blood: Graves interview.

p. 120 support on race day: Anna Scott interview.

p. 120 Ryan," Dave said: ibid.

p. 121 back out on the course: ibid.

p. 121 to those details: Los Angeles Triathlon Club, *A Night with Dave Scott and Mark Allen*. Dave Scott does not recall the exact words of this conversation.

p. 122 made a sizzling sound: *Triathlete*, January 1988. This incident actually happened before the 1987 Ironman, but I took the liberty of moving it because Tinley always did something to make people laugh at the pro meeting, and there are no surviving accounts of his antics at the 1989 meeting.

p. 122 important race rules: Gerry Rott, personal telephone interview, January 2010.

p. 122 aid from race watchers: Brian Hughes, personal telephone interview, March 2011.

p. 122 egg on his face: ibid.

p. 122 the Kona Surf Hotel: Rott interview.

p. 123 a.k.a. the Mad Triathlete: John Boyer, personal telephone interview, December 2010. Boyer does not recall the exact timing of this occurrence or the precise wording of the conversation.

p. 123 six-minutes-per-mile pace: Walker, "Dave Scott Interview."

p. 123 the previous day: Moss interview.

p. 124 embody pure peace: Brant Secunda and Mark Allen, "Fit Soul—Fit Body: 9 Keys to a Healthier, Happier You," Living Dialogues podcast series, episodes 89 and 90, personallifemedia.com, http://personallifemedia.com/podcasts/212-living-dialogues/episodes/33806-brant-secunda-huichol-shaman-healer-mark. Courtesy of Personal Life Media.

p. 124 mutual loathing: Reganold interview.

p. 124 certainly possible: ibid.

p. 125 he had been already: Mike Reilly, personal telephone interview, November 2010.

p. 125 of the King Kam: 1989 Bud Light Ironman official program.

p. 125 *before Dave came to town:* Lyrics courtesy of John Boyer.

p. 125 drunk Australian athletes: Boyer interview.

p. 126 1,284 other bikes: Debbie Baker, personal telephone interview, December 2010.

p. 126 he didn't like it: Dan Rock, personal interview, Solana Beach, CA, January 2011.

p. 126 really a Kestrel: ibid.

p. 126 every gear change: Aaron Hersh, commissioned research.

p. 127 to visit a friend: Jim Curl, personal telephone interview, February 2011. Curl does not recall the exact timing of this occurrence.

p. 127 everything in sight: ibid.

p. 127 Kanaloa with Julie: Moss interview.

p. 128 Lagoon at home: Mark Allen on Competitor Radio, http://competitorradio.competitor.com/tag/mark-allen.

p. 128 true destination anyway: ibid.

p. 128 to make offerings: plaque at Kuemanu Heiau, courtesy Department of Parks and Recreation, County of Hawaii.

p. 129 I've been missing: John Brant, "Mark Allen, Astral Jock," *Outside*, March 1991.

p. 129 have to be brave: ibid.

p. 129 Mike said, believing it: Rubano interview.

CHAPTER 7: IRON WILL

p. 131 Frogs of Busto Arsizio: All information about and quotations from Samuele Marcora come from personal telephone interviews and e-mail correspondence with him, June 2010–March 2011.

p. 134 strong, well-trained athletes: S. M. Marcora and W. Staiano, "The Limit to Exercise Tolerance in Humans: Mind over Muscle?" *European Journal of Applied Physiology* 109, 4 (July 2010): 763–770.

p. 135 began to falter: Sharon Robb, "Mike Pigg Wins USTS Championship, Points Title," *South Florida Sun Sentinel*, November 13, 1988, http://articles.sun-sentinel.com/1988-11-13/news/8803060846_1_bike-race-mike-pigg-mark-allen.

p. 135 Yet he did: Gary Newkirk, "Hilton Head: The End of THE Trail," *Triathlete*, February 1989, pp. 30–37, 63.

p. 137 *spit it out:* A. M. Carter, A. E. Jeukendrup, and D. A. Jones, "The Effect of Carbohydrate Mouth Rinse on 1-h Cycle Time Trial Performance," *Medicine and Science in Sports and Exercise* 36 (December 2004): 2107–2111.

p. 139 concentrate for that race: *Triathlete*, May 1984.

p. 139 five-kilometer time trial: M. Amann, L. T. Proctor, J. J. Sebranek, D. F. Pegelow, and J. A. Dempsey, "Opioid-Mediated Muscle Afferents Inhibit Central Motor Drive and

Limit Peripheral Muscle Fatigue Development in Humans," *Journal of Physiology* 587, 1 (January 2009): 271-283.

p. 141 is, in fact, cognitively demanding: S. M. Marcora, W. Staiano, and V. Manning, "Mental Fatigue Impairs Physical Performance in Humans." *Journal of Applied Physiology* 106, 3 (March 2009): 857-864.

p. 142 you as an athlete: Los Angeles Triathlon Club, *A Night with Dave Scott and Mark Allen*, 2002, videotape courtesy of Bob Babbitt.

p. 142 goes on in an Ironman: ibid.

p. 143 work through it: William R. Katovsky, "A Champion Thoroughbred," *Triathlete*, September 1984, pp. 48-55.

p. 143 seems to pay off: Bob Babbitt, "Legend of the Fall," *Competitor*, October 1996, pp. 12-17.

p. 143 his fastest efforts: Kenny Moore, "Big Splash in Hawaii," *Sports Illustrated*, October 23, 1989.

p. 143 as he spoke these words: ibid.

p. 144 and then *explode*: John Brant, "Mark Allen, Astral Jock," *Outside*, March 1991.

p. 144 feeling really strong: Mike Plant, "Mark Allen," *Triathlon*, July 1985, pp. 34-38.

p. 145 circles, waiting, gloating: Mark Allen on Competitor Radio, http://competitorradio. competitor.com/tag/mark-allen.

p. 145 as a young boy: Dave Scott, *Dave Scott's Triathlon Training* (New York: Fireside, 1986).

p. 146 Dave loved it: Dave Scott, 2011 USA Triathlon Hall of Fame induction speech.

p. 146 as everyone else is: Babbitt, "Legend of the Fall."

p. 147 that hurt them: Dr. John Deri, "Fit Soul, Fit Body," Healthy Mind and Body podcast, http://www.blogtalkradio.com/healthy mind-body/2011/05/12/fit-soul-fit-body.

p. 147 temperament and behavior: Suniya S. Luthar, ed., *Resilience and Vulnerability: Adaptation in the Context of Childhood Adversities* (Cambridge: Cambridge University Press, 2005).

p. 148 he won't forget it: Phil Maffetone, personal telephone interview, January 2010.

p. 148 horsepower, escaped: Julie Moss, personal telephone interview, September 2010.

CHAPTER 8: SHOT OUT OF A CANNON

p. 151 the alarm sounds: Dave Scott, personal telephone interview, January 2011.

p. 151 uninterrupted slumber: Anna Scott, personal telephone interview, November 2010.

p. 151 until the race starts: John Reganold, personal interview, July 2010.

p. 152 a third banana: Dave Scott, *Dave Scott's Triathlon Training* (New York: Fireside, 1986).

p. 152 see what he can do: Anna Scott interview.

p. 152 Jane from next door: Reganold interview.

p. 152 Pat says: Reganold interview.

p. 152 stiffness of sleep: Dave Scott interview.

p. 153 tower on Ali'i Drive: Mike Plant, personal interview, San Marcos, CA, November 2010.

p. 153 seven a.m. this morning: *ABC Sports* 1989 Ironman television broadcast.

p. 153 to watch the start: Plant interview.

p. 153 during the night: Scott Molina, personal telephone interview, July 2010.

p. 153 and attacking him: John Brant, "Mark Allen, Astral Jock," *Outside*, March 1991.

p. 153 Scott to catch him: Mark Allen with Bob Babbitt, *Mark Allen's Total Triathlete* (New York: McGraw-Hill, 1988).

p. 154 his stuff together: Julie Moss, personal telephone interview, September 2010.

p. 154 somehow turned itself on: ibid.

p. 154 *worst morning of my life*: ibid.

p. 154 he's weeping: Rob Mackle, personal telephone interview, November 2010.

p. 154 quietly admitted: Mike Rubano, personal telephone interview, October 2010.

p. 154 and Brian Hughes arrive: Charlie Graves, personal telephone interview, October 2010.

p. 155 to catch the start: Rubano interview.

p. 155 slap in the face: Mark Allen on Competitor Radio, http://competitorradio.competitor.com/tag/mark-allen.

p. 155 local dive shop: Plant interview.

p. 156 more up-tempo: *ABC Sports* 1989 Ironman television broadcast.

p. 156 triathlon racing suits: ibid.

p. 156 get ready to go: CJ Olivares Jr., "The Art of War," *Triathlete*, January 1990, pp. 24–37.

p. 156 written on that spot: "Bud Light Ironman Triathlon World Championship XI: Race Results, October 14, 1989," Ironman.com, http://ironman.com/events/ironman/world championship/?show=results#axzz1UeKPUh1o.

p. 156 X of her own: Moss interview.

p. 156 hug and separate: ibid.

p. 157 too many times: ibid.

p. 157 It's working: Mark Allen on Competitor Radio.

p. 157 with black accents: *ABC Sports* 1989 Ironman television broadcast.

p. 157 in their cages: Graves interview.

p. 157 and during the race: Gary Allen, personal telephone interview, January 2011.

p. 157 I have a feeling: Carole Allen, personal telephone interview, February 2011.

p. 158 with her free hand: ibid.

p. 158 a few hours later: ibid.

p. 158 without protest: Dave Scott interview.

p. 158 to dethrone you: Donna de Varona, Facebook correspondence, March 2011.

p. 158 thing he's ever done: *ABC Sports* 1989 Ironman television broadcast.

p. 159 a low chuckle: Reganold interview.

p. 159 in the King Kam: Anna Scott interview.

p. 159 I love you: ibid.

p. 159 into the bay there: Dave Scott interview.

p. 159 out of the gate: Stephen Walker, "Dave Scott Interview," *Podium Sports Journal*, July 1, 2007, http://www.podiumsportsjournal.com/2007/07/01/dave-scott-interview.

p. 159 alone, head down: Mike Reilly, personal telephone interview, November 2010.

p. 160 Thanks: ibid.

p. 160 over the loudspeakers: Plant interview.

p. 161 no countdown: ibid.

p. 161 admonitions over the loudspeakers: ibid.

p. 161 bite someone: *ABC Sports* 1989 Ironman television broadcast.

p. 161 national anthem is sung: Reilly interview.

p. 161 they're on board: Olivares, "The Art of War."

p. 161 from the pier: Chris Hinshaw, personal telephone interview, January 2011.

p. 161 easy to find: Olivares, "The Art of War."

p. 161 going to beat you: Los Angeles Triathlon Club, *A Night with Dave Scott and Mark Allen*, 2002, videotape courtesy of Bob Babbitt.

p. 161: Good luck, Dave: ibid.

p. 161 behind the cannon: Debbie Baker, personal telephone interview, December 2010.

p. 162 be somewhere else: Mike Reilly, e-mail correspondence, November 2010.

p. 162 idly on his lap: Gary Newkirk, personal telephone interview, December 2010.

p. 162 swim over him: Olivares, "The Art of War."

p. 163 off the front: *ABC Sports* 1989 Ironman television broadcast.

p. 163 calling it a day: Scott Tinley, *Triathlon: A Personal History* (Boulder, CO: VeloPress, 1998).

p. 163 very much a race: *ABC Sports* 1989 Ironman television broadcast.

p. 164 *end well for you*: Walker, "Dave Scott Interview."

p. 164 Beast of the East: Ken McAlpine, "The Beast from the East," *Triathlete*, May 1989, pp. 70-73.

p. 164 matter of minutes: Olivares, "The Art of War."

p. 164 swim exit ramp: "Bud Light Ironman Triathlon World Championship XI: Race Results, October 14, 1989."

p. 164 at other vendors: Newkirk interview.

p. 164 beyond the pier: Hinshaw interview.

p. 165 virtually a mirror: Tracy Frankel photograph, "A bird's-eye view of the Ironman's 2.4-mile swim," *Triathlete*, January 1990, p. 26.

p. 165 first Ironman in 1987: "Bud Light Ironman Triathlon World Championship IX: Race Results, October 10, 1987," Ironman.com, http://ironman.com/events/ironman/world championship/?show=results#axzz1UeKPUh1o.

p. 165 that cooperation: Wolfgang Dittrich, personal telephone interview, November 2010.

p. 165 chore of sighting: ibid.

p. 165 each man's head: *ABC Sports* 1989 Ironman television broadcast.

p. 165 even give up: Dittrich interview.

p. 166 reaches the finish line: "Bud Light Ironman Triathlon World Championship XI: Race Results, October 14, 1989."

p. 166 figured it out sooner: Greg Kirkpatrick, "Ironman Canada—1998," ontherunevents .com, http://www.ontherunevents.com/news/0054.sht.

p. 166 in today's race: Patrick Bateman, personal telephone interview, December 2010.

p. 166 a few weeks ago: Hinshaw interview.

p. 166 positions on the bike: "Bud Light Ironman Triathlon World Championship XI: Race Results, October 14, 1989."

p. 166 to touch his rival: *ABC Sports* 1989 Ironman television broadcast.

p. 166 he's still there: Los Angeles Triathlon Club, *A Night with Dave Scott and Mark Allen*.

p. 167 back to shore: Plant interview.

p. 167 behind Dave's group: *ABC Sports* 1989 Ironman television broadcast.

p. 167 anything flamboyant: Bob Babbitt, "IronWar!" *Competitor*, December 1989, pp. 8-10, 33.

p. 168 Sharon Allen, alone: Graves interview.

p. 168 as a single group: Reganold interview.

p. 168 visible at some distance: Scott, *Dave Scott's Triathlon Training*.

p. 168 the final strokes: *ABC Sports* 1989 Ironman television broadcast.

p. 169 like a knapsack: ibid.

p. 169 of a second later: "Bud Light Ironman Triathlon World Championship XI: Race Results, October 14, 1989."

p. 169 spontaneously burst: Gary Allen interview.

p. 169 sense of urgency: ibid.

p. 169 a grizzly bear: *ABC Sports* Ironman television broadcast.

p. 170 vanguard of the group: "Bud Light Ironman Triathlon World Championship XI: Race Results, October 14, 1989."

p. 170 an errant elbow: Mark Roberts, personal telephone interview, November 2010.

p. 170 behind Dave: Gary Allen interview.

CHAPTER 9: BURNING MATCHES

p. 171 the transition area: Dave Scott, e-mail correspondence, July 2011.

p. 171 right behind him: *ABC Sports* 1989 Ironman television broadcast.

p. 171 long metal racks: ibid.

p. 172 ahead of him: ibid.

p. 172 short-course speed: Dave Scott, personal telephone interview, January 2011.

p. 172 ball of the foot: *ABC Sports* 1989 Ironman television broadcast.

p. 173 of the Netherlands: Rob Barel, e-mail correspondence, February 2011.

p. 173 winner Ray Browning: Ray Browning, personal telephone interview, January 2011.

p. 173 stomping on his pedals: Dirk Aschmoneit, personal telephone interview, March 2011.

p. 174 *la folie*, he thinks: Yves Cordier, e-mail correspondence, March 2011.

p. 174 the caboose: Chris Hinshaw, personal telephone interview, January 2011.

p. 174 smelled, from the road: Patrick Bateman, personal telephone interview, January 2010.

p. 175 from his bottle: Mike Pigg, personal telephone interview, November 2010.

p. 175 at Duke University: Scott Molina, personal telephone interview, July 2010.

p. 175 jersey pocket: Dave Scott, *Dave Scott's Triathlon Training* (New York: Fireside, 1986).

p. 175 away from Rob: Wolfgang Dittrich, personal telephone interview, November 2010.

p. 175 his ideal rhythm: ibid.

p. 175 the German drift ahead: Rob Mackle, personal telephone interview, November 2010.

p. 175 down his gullet: Dittrich interview.

p. 175 document his exploits: ibid.

pp. 175–176 other Ironman officials: Mike Reilly, personal telephone interview, November 2010.

p. 176 3:00 at the start: Dave Scott on Competitor Radio, http://competitorradio.competitor.com/tag/dave-scott.

p. 176 antidrafting rules require: 1989 Bud Light Ironman official program.

p. 176 rather not inhale: CJ Olivares Jr., "The Art of War," *Triathlete*, January 1990, pp. 24–37.

p. 176 he is praying: Kenny Moore, "Big Splash in Hawaii," *Sports Illustrated*, October 23, 1989.

p. 177 and Pat Feeney: Anna Scott, personal telephone interview, November 2010.

p. 177 in their Jeep: Charlie Graves, personal telephone interview, October 2010.

p. 177 Waikoloa Beach instead: Brian Hughes, personal telephone interview, March 2011.

p. 177 three-wheel bicycle: *ABC Sports* 1989 Ironman television broadcast.

p. 177 rest of his life: Dick Hoyt, personal telephone interview, January 2011.

p. 177 to deal with it: *ABC Sports* 1989 Ironman television broadcast.

p. 178 disappeared," he said: Hoyt interview.

p. 178 without him, anyway: ibid.

p. 178 from his son's penis: Sam Nall, *It's Only a Mountain: Dick and Rick Hoyt, Men of Iron* (St. Petersburg, FL: Southern Heritage Press, 2002).

p. 179 pull alongside him: Dittrich interview.

p. 179 than to say them: ibid.

p. 179 climb toward Hawi: Cordier e-mail correspondence.

p. 179 not going fast enough: Dan Rock, personal interview, Solana Beach, CA, January 2011.

p. 180 he was doomed: Hinshaw interview.

p. 180 John cheers: John Reganold, personal interview, July 2010.

p. 180 he calls: Dave Scott interview.

p. 181 from the rim: Chris Lieto, *TriCenter*, courtesy competitortv.com.

p. 181 an open window: *ABC Sports* 1989 Ironman television broadcast.

p. 181 We will see: ibid.

p. 182 would be in trouble: Mackle interview.

p. 182 can't see his face: "Iron War Uncut. Dave Scott and Mark Allen," http://www.youtube .com/watch?v=WTeoBJRzUlo.

p. 182 good for business: personal conversations with Hawi proprietors.

p. 183 the portable toilets: *ABC Sports* 1989 Ironman television broadcast.

p. 183 memory of convenience: Dittrich interview.

p. 183 nearly double it: *ABC Sports* 1989 Ironman television broadcast.

p. 183 a fruit smoothie: Mackle interview.

p. 184 bathroom opportunities: Pigg interview.

p. 184 punches the accelerator: Olivares, "The Art of War."

p. 184 on the descent from Hawi: Ken Glah, personal telephone interview, December 2010.

p. 184 margin in check: Olivares, "The Art of War."

p. 185 keep it upright: CJ Olivares, personal telephone interview, October 2010.

p. 185 break her neck: *ABC Sports* 1989 Ironman television broadcast.

p. 185 coming down again: Dave Scott on Competitor Radio.

p. 185 known as the Beast: Harald Johnson, "Beauty and the Beast," *Triathlete*, July 1988, pp. 24-29.

p. 185 front of the train: Pigg interview.

p. 186 they will finish: *ABC Sports* 1989 Ironman television broadcast.

p. 186 gap: "Three minutes!": Dave Scott on Competitor Radio.

p. 187 grade of 7 percent: Mapmyride.com, http://www.mapmyride.com/s/routes/view /bike-ride-map/hawaii/kona/1130454.

p. 187 saddle and launches: Dave Scott interview.

p. 187 and vomits: Olivares, "The Art of War."

p. 187 in his low back: Mackle interview.

p. 187 He does: Dave Scott interview.

p. 188 *Here we go*: Olivares interview.

p. 188 his low back hurts: Babbit, "Kona Countdown: Dave Scott."

p. 188 Mark lowers his head: "Iron War Uncut: Dave Scott and Mark Allen."

p. 188 started to struggle: Dittrich interview.

p. 188 into Wolfgang's face: ibid.

p. 188 intensity just a bit: Dave Scott interview.

p. 188 behind Dave and Mark: Pigg interview.

p. 188 last of the five: Olivares, "The Art of War."

p. 189 everyone goes berserk: Reilly interview.

p. 189 lounge chair: Los Angeles Triathlon Club, *A Night with Dave Scott and Mark Allen*, October 5, 2002, videotape courtesy of Bob Babbitt.

p. 190 into the run: ibid.

p. 190 rest of the way: Dittrich interview.

p. 190 race time: 5:27:17: *ABC Sports* 1989 Ironman television broadcast.

p. 190 stage finish: Mike Plant, personal interview, San Marcos, CA, November 2010.

p. 190 one minute fifty-one seconds later: "Bud Light Ironman Triathlon World Championship XI: Race Results, October 14, 1989," Ironman.com, http://ironman.com/events/ironman/worldchampionship/?show=results#axzz1UeKPUh10.

p. 190 split is 4:37:53: ibid.

p. 190 after Rob: ibid.

p. 190 feel what's coming: Plant interview.

CHAPTER 10: VISION QUEST

p. 191 wear for the run: Mark Allen on Competitor Radio, http://competitorradio.competitor.com/tag/mark-allen.

p. 191 the island day: *ABC Sports* 1989 Ironman television broadcast.

p. 192 only he knows: Mike Plant, *Iron Will: The Triathlete's Ultimate Challenge* (Boulder, CO: VeloPress, 1999).

p. 192 hauling after him: *ABC Sports* 1989 Ironman television broadcast.

p. 192 Ironman bike leg: CJ Olivares Jr., "The Art of War," *Triathlete*, January 1990, pp. 24–37.

p. 192 early run pace: ibid.

p. 193 as the runners pass: John Reganold, personal interview, July 2010.

p. 193 as a spotter: Mike Plant, personal interview, San Marcos, CA, November 2010.

p. 193 and John Martin: Brian Hughes, personal telephone interview, March 2011.

p. 193 and Mike Norton: Reganold interview.

p. 193 first mile: 5:55: Mike Plant, e-mail correspondence, February 2011.

p. 193 hushed by the report: Plant interview.

p. 194 surge to catch Dave: Dave Scott on Competitor Radio, http://competitorradio.competitor.com/tag/dave-scott.

p. 194 decarbonated Coca-Cola: *ABC Sports* 1989 Ironman television broadcast.

p. 194 four and five apiece: ibid.

p. 195 hands on mouths: Reganold interview.

p. 195 lawn chair earlier: Los Angeles Triathlon Club, *A Night with Dave Scott and Mark Allen*, October 5, 2002, videotape courtesy of Bob Babbitt.

p. 195 ten seconds to do: ibid.

p. 196 *take him with me*: "Iron War Uncut: Dave Scott and Mark Allen," http://www.youtube.com/watch?v=WTeoBJRzUlo.

p. 196 stations on Ali'i Drive: ibid.

p. 196 the coming pass: Olivares, "The Art of War."

p. 196 less than four miles: Lars Finanger, "Wolfgang Dittrich—The Rabbit," Slowtwitch.com, October 27, 2008, http://www.slowtwitch.com/Interview/Wolfgang_Dittrich_-_the_rabbit_587.html.

p. 196 Man, oh, man: Mike Plant, personal interview.

p. 196 history in the making: Bob Babbitt, personal interview, San Diego, CA, 2010.

p. 197 into Mark's mind: Olivares, "The Art of War."

p. 197 sole of his shoe: T. J. Murphy, "Shamanism and the Art of Triathlon," *Triathlete*, August 1999.

p. 197 at a parade: Anna Scott, personal telephone interview, November 2010.

p. 197 he jokes: Los Angeles Triathlon Club, *A Night with Dave Scott and Mark Allen*.

p. 198 Paula Newby-Fraser: "Bud Light Ironman Triathlon World Championship XI: Race Results, October 14, 1989," Ironman.com, http://ironman.com/events/ironman/worldchampionship/?show=results#axzz1UeKPUh10.

p. 198 point in the race: Julie Moss, personal telephone interview, September 2010.

p. 198 race for the ages: Mike Reilly, personal telephone interview, November 2010.

p. **198** the final straight: ibid.

p. **198** for third place: Ken Glah, personal telephone interview, December 2010.

p. **198** transition. 58:24: Los Angeles Triathlon Club, *A Night with Dave Scott and Mark Allen*.

p. **199** behind them is running: Lew Kidder, "Bud Light Ironman World Championship," *Triathlon Today*, November 1989.

p. **199** toward the coast: *ABC Sports* 1989 Ironman television broadcast.

p. **199** fail to finish: "Bud Light Ironman Triathlon World Championship XI: Race Results, October 14, 1989," Ironman.com, http://ironman.com/events/ironman/worldchampi onship/?show=results#axzz1UeKPIIh1o.

p. **199** before the race: Sharron Ackles, personal telephone interview, 1999.

p. **200** at this one: Olivares, "The Art of War."

p. **200** at this aid station: Dave Scott on Competitor Radio.

p. **200** increasingly uncomfortable: Brant Secunda and Mark Allen, "Fit Soul–Fit Body: 9 Keys to a Healthier, Happier You," Living Dialogues podcast series, episodes 89 and 90, personallifemedia.com, http://personallifemedia.com/podcasts/212-living-dialogues/episodes/33806-brant-secunda-huichol-shaman-healer-mark. Courtesy of Personal Life Media.

p. **201** feels like a wall: Olivares, "The Art of War."

p. **201** never *win this race*: Mark Allen, personal telephone interview, 2004.

p. **201** two days ago: Los Angeles Triathlon Club, *A Night with Dave Scott and Mark Allen*.

p. **201** his peripheral vision: Murphy, "Shamanism and the Art of Triathlon."

p. **202** *more to life*: Allen interview.

p. **202** into his spirit: Secunda and Allen, "Fit Soul–Fit Body."

p. **202** his station wagon: Mike Adamle, personal telephone interview, December 2010.

p. **202** of the bike leg: John Boyer, personal telephone interview, December 2010.

p. **203** point in the race: Los Angeles Triathlon Club, *A Night with Dave Scott and Mark Allen*.

p. **203** visible to onlookers: Bob Babbitt, personal conversations, June 2010–May 2011.

p. **203** eighteen in 5:40: Plant interview.

p. **203** behind the gladiators: Babbitt conversations.

p. **204** Exceed and Coke: Photo by Gary Newkirk, *Triathlete*, January 1990, pp. 24–25.

p. **204** bib is missing: ibid.

p. **204** can barely watch: Mike Rubano, personal telephone interview, October 2010.

p. **204** memory of the day: Ken Glah, personal telephone interview, December 2010.

p. **204** completed descent: Olivares, "The Art of War."

p. **205** helicopter hanging above: Moss interview.

p. **205** *What will happen*: ibid.

p. **205** *It's too important*: ibid.

p. **206** Hop on: ibid.

p. **206** You can do it: *ABC Sports* 1989 Ironman television broadcast.

p. **206** into his palm: Dave Scott, personal telephone interview, January 2011.

p. **206** behind Grip: Olivares, "The Art of War."

p. **206** zapped his legs: Dave Scott on Competitor Radio.

p. **206** making the catch: Olivares, "The Art of War."

p. **206** Crush him: Mike Norton, personal telephone interview, July 2010.

p. **207** answers in his mind: Dave Scott interview.

p. **207** boarding of the truck: Moss interview.

p. **207** on this hill: Kenny Moore, "Big Splash in Hawaii," *Sports Illustrated*, October 23, 1989.

p. 207 this moment: 7:58:02: Kidder, "Bud Light Ironman World Championship."

p. 207 *Go now!*: Mathias Müller with Timothy Carlson, *17 Hours to Glory: Extraordinary Stories from the Heart of Triathlon* (Boulder, CO: VeloPress, 2010).

p. 207 rival is struggling: *ABC Sports* 1989 Ironman television broadcast.

p. 208 disjointed stilts: ibid.

p. 208 Julie shouts: Moore, "Big Splash in Hawaii."

p. 208 Dave will be on him: ibid.

p. 208 the present hill: Olivares, "The Art of War."

p. 208 top of the hill: John Brant, "Dave Scott, Mere Mortal," *Outside*, October 1992, http://www.outsideonline.com/outdoor-adventure/Dave-Scott--Mere-Mortal.html.

p. 208 along the Queen K: Los Angeles Triathlon Club, *A Night with Dave Scott and Mark Allen*.

p. 208 flies down Pay-'n'-Save Hill: ibid.

p. 208 shouting, "Yes": Moore, "Big Splash in Hawaii."

p. 208 give it to you: Hughes interview.

p. 209 Mark, you won: ibid.

p. 209 for four minutes: Plant interview.

p. 209 whole lot louder: Olivares, "The Art of War."

p. 210 unashamed weeping: *ABC Sports* 1989 Ironman television broadcast.

p. 210 and more personal: Moss interview.

p. 210 champion of Ironman: *ABC Sports* 1989 Ironman television broadcast.

p. 211 of his left hand: ibid.

p. 211 *Not really*: Plant interview.

CHAPTER 11: BREAKING POINT

p. 213 in Angola, Indiana: All information about and quotations from Stephen McGregor come from personal interviews and e-mail correspondence with him.

p. 216 in the AP axis: S. J. McGregor, M. A. Busa, J. A. Yaggie, and E. M. Bollt, "High Resolution MEMS Accelerometers to Estimate VO_2 and Compare Running Mechanics Between Highly Trained Intercollegiate Runners and Untrained Runners," *PLoS One* 4, 10 (October 2009): e7355.

p. 217 robotic, if you will: S. J. McGregor, M. A. Busa, J. Skufca, J. A. Yaggie, and E. M. Bollt, "Control Entropy Identifies Differential Changes in Complexity of Walking and Running Gait Patterns with Increasing Speed in Highly Trained Runners," *Chaos* 19 (June 2009): 026109.

p. 223 of football practice: Curtis Vollmar, personal interview, Ypsilanti, MI, December 2010.

p. 224 top runner on the team: ibid.

p. 224 except to race: ibid.

p. 224 in poor shape: John Goodridge, personal interview, Ypsilanti, MI, December 2010.

p. 224 ran above himself: ibid.

p. 224 can't really race: Vollmar interview.

p. 224 he went all out: ibid.

p. 224 the guys," he suggested: Goodridge interview.

p. 225 other young alumni: Vollmar interview.

p. 225 the same technique: personal observation.

p. 225 VO_2max of 75: ibid.

p. 227 And I beat them: T. J. Murphy, "Listen to What the Man Says," *Triathlete*, April 2000, pp. 52–67.

p. 227 heel wear went away: Dave Scott, personal telephone interview, January 2011.

p. 228 not the whole thing: ibid.

p. 228 early in his career: Mike Plant, "Mark Allen," *Triathlon*, July 1985, pp. 34–38.

p. 228 they ever had: Paul Huddle, personal telephone interview, September 2010.

p. 228 on those subjects: Mark Allen with Bob Babbitt, *Mark Allen's Total Triathlete* (New York: McGraw-Hill, 1988), p. 11.

p. 229 an asset for me: Dave Scott, "Ironman Champion Dave Scott Offers Tri Wisdom," Active.com, www.active.com/triathlon/Articles/Triathlon_Wisdom_From_Ironman_Champion_Dave_Scott.htm, accessed August 9, 2011.

p. 229 most accurate putters: J. Baumeister, K. Reinecke, H. Liesen, and M. Weiss, "Cortical Activity of Skilled Performance in a Complex Sports Related Motor Task," *European Journal of Applied Physiology* 104, 4 (November 2008): 625–631.

p. 229 relaxed and efficient: John Brant, "Mark Allen, Astral Jock," *Outside*, March 1991.

p. 229 And lunch: Dan Levin, "Gall, Divided into Three Parts," *Sports Illustrated*, October 10, 1983.

p. 231 he will later report: Scott interview.

p. 231 I couldn't do it: Mike Reilly, personal telephone interview, November 2010.

CHAPTER 12: THE MAN'S SEARCH FOR MEANING

p. 233 weekend triathlon camp: Dan Rock, personal interview, Solana Beach, CA, January 2011.

p. 234 *I'm losing*: ibid.

p. 234 rest of his life: Jim Curl, personal telephone interview, February 2011

p. 234 fast as you can: Dave Scott, personal telephone interview, January 2011.

p. 235 did not last long: ibid.

p. 235 a fabulous race: ibid.

p. 235 film canister, I think: Anna Scott, personal telephone interview, November 2010.

p. 235 earlier in the race: Dave Scott interview.

p. 236 previous day's insult: Bob Babbitt, personal interview, San Diego, CA, 2010.

p. 236 Next time: Dave Scott interview.

p. 236 Mark won yet again: ibid.

p. 237 Usually nobody had: Ray Browning, personal telephone interview, January 2011.

p. 237 Dave's legendary career: John Brant, "Dave Scott, Mere Mortal," *Outside*, October 1992, http://www.outsideonline.com/outdoor-adventure/Dave-Scott--Mere-Mortal.html.

p. 237 a 15-year-old: ibid.

p. 238 start getting ideas: ibid.

p. 238 consecutive Ironman title: William R. Katovsky, "Gulf Coast Diary," *Inside Triathlon*, July 1994, pp 18–21.

p. 238 not sixth place: Dave Scott interview.

p. 239 in his hamstrings: ibid.

p. 239 continue the race: ibid.

p. 239 He's tarnishing his legacy: Dave Scott interview.

p. 239 than he was then: Linda Buchanan, personal telephone interview, November 2010.

p. 239 at forty miles: *NBC Sports* 1994 Ironman television broadcast.

p. 240 Mark said nothing: Lisa Lax, personal telephone interview, January 2011.

p. 240 The race is here: Greg Welch, personal telephone interview, January 2011.

p. 240 like a life preserver: ibid.

p. 240 regaining the lead: John Smith, e-mail correspondence, January 2011.

p. 241 by thirty-five minutes: William R. Katovsky, "How He Did It," *Triathlete*, February 1995, pp. 31–39.

p. 241 think I was old: Dave Scott interview.

p. 241 breaking a toe: ibid.

p. 241 socially straitjacketed: ibid.

p. 241 he'd sneered: T. J. Murphy, personal interview, San Diego, CA, June 2010.

p. 242 tempted to quit Ironman: Dave Scott interview.

p. 242 ever been in Hawaii: Ironman.com, year-by-year results.

p. 242 so much fun: ibid.

p. 242 pretty darn close: Mike Reilly, personal telephone interview, November 2010.

p. 243 if not *the* best: Dave Scott interview.

p. 243 ahead of their parents: Photograph by Miku, *Triathlete*, January 1997, p. 30.

p. 243 earlier in the season: "Larsen Toys with Triathlon's Long-Course Elite at Half-Vineman," http://www.active.com/triathlon/Articles/Larsen_toys_with_triathlon_s_long-course_elite_at_Half-Vineman.htm.

p. 243 he quit Ironman: Jay Prasuhn, "An All-American Win," *Triathlete*, January 2002, pp. 26-39.

p. 243 publisher Bob Babbitt: Babbitt interview.

p. 243 Dave bellowed: ibid.

p. 243 should be flying: ibid.

p. 244 Ironman course on Oahu: Cindy Luis, "Lourens Wins Ironman Revisited," *Honolulu Star-Bulletin*, August 18, 2003, http://archives.starbulletin.com/2003/08/18/sports/story2.html.

p. 244 to victory: Babbitt interview.

p. 244 took second place: "Results, 2007 Ironman Revisited," Adventurecorps.com, http://www.adventurecorps.com/magnum/2007imr/index.html, accessed August 9, 2011.

p. 244 start line in October: Rob Klingensmith, personal telephone interview, July 2010.

p. 244 Solid: Dave Scott interview.

p. 245 55 to 59 age group: ibid.

p. 245 for an open house: Amy Bounds, "Driver Ticketed in Boulder Ironman Champion Accident," *Boulder Daily Camera*, May 19, 2009, http://www.dailycamera.com/ci_13121459.

p. 245 a bike-blind motorist: Dave Scott interview.

p. 246 found her destination: ibid.

p. 246 broadside, and hard: ibid.

p. 246 he croaked: ibid.

p. 246 Can I call someone: Lars Finanger, personal interview, San Diego, CA, June 2010.

p. 247 lying on the ground: Dave Scott interview.

p. 247 *endorphin lunatic*: ibid.

p. 247 It's gigantic: ibid.

p. 247 divorced five years later: Anna Scott interview.

p. 247 incident to her mother: Murphy interview.

p. 247 swim, bike, or run: ibid.

p. 247 interact with other people: Dave Scott interview.

p. 248 and rightly so: Klingensmith interview.

p. 248 his own bed: Randy Viola, personal telephone interview, July 2010.

p. 248 protect him—from himself: ibid.

p. 248 Dave took it anyway: Klingensmith interview.

p. 248 left in his dust: Dave Scott interview.

p. 249 he deadpanned: Mirinda Carfrae, personal conversation, Chicago, IL, August 2010.

p. 249 little time to train: Dave Scott, personal interview, Boulder, CO, June 2010.

p. 249 *what you can do*: ibid.

p. 249 what her mouth said: personal observation.

p. 249 she had uterine cancer: Dave Scott, 2011 USA Triathlon Hall of Fame induction speech.

p. 250 got to have faith: ibid.

p. 251 this time," he said: personal observation.

p. 251 minutes behind Chrissie: http://www.bamswimteam.org (results no longer available).

p. 251 on the beach: ibid.

p. 251 to start slipping: T. J. Murphy, "Listen to What the Man Says," *Triathlete*, April 2000, pp. 52-67.

p. 251 Dave teased: personal observation.

p. 251 tucked in behind them: ibid.

p. 251 It seemed possible: Dave Scott interview.

p. 252 surged away easily: personal observation.

p. 252 Less than nothing: Dave Scott interview.

p. 252 looking at him: personal observation.

p. 252 refused to stop running: Mike Norton, personal telephone interview, July 2010.

p. 252 Yeah, right: personal observation.

p. 253 He won: ibid.

p. 253 pride in doing that: Dave Scott interview.

p. 253 made it this far: personal observation.

p. 254 out there more: Murphy interview.

p. 254 meet his standards: Bob Babbitt, personal conversations, June 2010-May 2011.

p. 254 out of reach: Dave Scott interview.

p. 254 and every run: Anna Scott interview.

p. 255 high expectations: Dave Scott interview.

p. 255 everything she had to win: ibid.

p. 255 win next time: ibid.

CHAPTER 13: SHAMAN SURFER

p. 257 to win the race: T. J. Murphy, "Shamanism and the Art of Triathlon," *Triathlete*, August 1999, pp. 42-47.

p. 257 nowhere to be found: ibid.

p. 257 permit his attendance: Julie Moss, personal telephone interview, September 2010.

p. 258 about the shaman: CJ Olivares Jr., "1989 Triathletes of the Year: Mark Allen," *Triathlete*, March 1990, pp. 34-37.

p. 258 and Kenny Souza: Kenny Souza, personal telephone interview, October 2010.

p. 258 Pacific Ocean in Mexico: "Earth and Sky," Dance of the Deer Foundation advertisement, *Yoga Journal*, September/October 1989, p. 2.

p. 258 have their hats back: Souza interview.

p. 258 return to sleep: Charlie Graves, personal telephone interview, October 2010.

p. 258 night of his vision: ibid.

p. 258 to Puerto Vallarta: "Mark Allen & Brant Secunda—Fit Soul, Fit Body, Part 3," http://www.youtube.com/watch?v=dJ5Ms7TwPAA&feature=related.

p. 259 the invented Don Juan: Brant Secunda, "Dreamers of the Sun: Huichol Shamanism," Dance of the Deer Foundation, April 25, 2010, http://blog.danceofthedeer.com/2010/04/dreamers-of-the-sun-huichol-shamanism.

p. 260 foolish adventure alone: Fit Soul, Fit Body presentation, Boulder, CO, 2009, video courtesy of Lifestyles of Health and Sustainability.

p. 260 now saving his life: Secunda, "Dreamers of the Sun."

p. 260 left in him: ibid.

p. 260 death in 1990: Chuck Thurman, "The Language of Fire," *Metro Santa Cruz*, May 20–26, 1997, http://www.metroactive.com/papers/cruz/03.20.97/hometown-9712.html.

p. 260 and head scarves: "Earth and Sky."

p. 260 tolerance for suffering: Murphy, "Shamanism and the Art of Triathlon."

p. 261 inner happiness: Mark Allen, "Impacts of Shamanism," Dance of the Deer Foundation, http://blog.danceofthedeer.com/2010/04/impacts-of-shamanism.

p. 261 into the world: ibid.

p. 261 as complete as Brant himself. Moss interview.

p. 262 got used to that: Paul Huddle, personal telephone interview, September 2010; Souza interview.

p. 262 *filled my bucket*: Mark Allen on Competitor Radio.

p. 262 even better in Kona: ibid.

p. 262 position on his bike: Moss interview.

p. 262 his bony frame: Diane Buchta, personal interview, 1998.

p. 262 the Huichol way: Mark Allen on Competitor Radio.

p. 263 broke his collarbone: Joel Silverman, "Back to Business," *Inside Triathlon*, July 1995.

p. 263 conceive a child together: Julie Moss, e-mail correspondence, July 2011.

p. 263 move beyond that: ibid.

p. 263 Space had caused him: ibid.

p. 263 record of 8:09:08: "Countdown to Kona: Con Muchos Bustos," http://triathlon.competitor.com/2009/09/features/countdown-to-kona-con-mucho-bustos-1992_4640

p. 263 for a long time: Moss, e-mail correspondence, July 2011.

p. 264 Free *of* his father: ibid.

p. 264 anything else in life: Richard Graham, "Hawaii," *Inside Triathlon*, December 1993/January 1994, pp. 10–14.

p. 264 thirty-seventh birthday: Mike Rubano, personal telephone interview, October 2010.

p. 264 between Bill and Michael: ibid.

p. 265 television advertisement together: ibid.

p. 265 or sell, or whatever: ibid.

p. 265 from Mark Allen: ibid.

p. 266 and dropped out: Joel Silverman, "Back to Business," *Inside Triathlon*, June 1995.

p. 266 or two, or three: Moss interview.

p. 266 to sustain him: Souza interview.

p. 266 certain kind of cactus: Scott Molina, personal telephone interview, July 2010.

p. 267 *will* talk to you: Souza interview.

p. 267 he would walk away: Mark Allen on Competitor Radio.

p. 267 was this close: Los Angeles Triathlon Club, *A Night with Dave Scott and Mark Allen*, October 5, 2002, videotape courtesy of Bob Babbitt.

p. 267 to dethrone him: ibid.

p. 268 weak field in 8:23 flat: "Allen, Fuhr Win Ironman Japan," *Inside Triathlon*, August 1995, p. 23.

p. 268 who rode 4:21:14: Julian Jenkinson, "Triumph of the Wheel," *Triathlete*, September 1995, pp. 38–42.

p. 268 saw these results: Los Angeles Triathlon Club, *A Night with Dave Scott and Mark Allen*.

p. 268 70 years old: Mark Allen on Competitor Radio.

p. 268 and fasting: "Mark Allen & Brant Secunda—Fit Soul, Fit Body, Part 1," http://www.youtube.com/watch?v=hr2tTSJm_bE.

p. 268 can win Ironman: Souza interview.

p. 269 had already retired: Mark Allen on Competitor Radio.

p. 269 vitality had returned: ibid.

p. 269 since Iron War: Moss interview.

p. 269 in silence, as always: Bob Babbitt, "Keith Peters," Competitor Radio, 2009, http://competitorradio.competitor.com/2009/03/298keith-peters.

p. 269 its girlie splendor: Los Angeles Triathlon Club, A Night with Dave Scott and Mark Allen.

p. 269 mock disappointment: ibid.

p. 269 for 112 miles: ibid.

p. 270 ahead of him: ibid.

p. 270 gusts of 45 mph: Roy Wallack, "The Stalking," Triathlete, December 1995, pp. 18-28, 33-43.

p. 270 by eleven minutes: Bob Babbitt, "Mission Impossible," Competitor, November/December 1995, pp. 16-26.

p. 270 doesn't look so good: Mark Allen on Competitor Radio.

pp. 270-271 on the lava field: plaque at Lekeleke burial ground, courtesy of Keauhou Resort.

p. 271 let alone win: "Mark Allen & Brant Secunda—Fit Soul, Fit Body, Part 8," http://www.youtube.com/watch?v=l4TVIvA8NTM.

p. 271 Quiet your mind: Mark Allen on Competitor Radio.

p. 271 of the race change: ibid.

p. 272 finished off the youngster: NBC Sports 1995 Ironman television broadcast.

p. 272 the medical tent: Wallack, "The Stalking."

p. 272 the next two years: Timothy Carlson, "Mark Allen's Dream-Time Transition," Triathlete, August 1997, pp. 18-24.

p. 272 next day loss still: Mark Allen, personal conversation, Kona, HI, October 2010.

p. 273 except him: Mark Allen with Bob Babbitt, Mark Allen's Total Triathlete (New York: McGraw-Hill, 1988).

p. 273 Sedona, Arizona: Murphy, "Shamanism and the Art of Triathlon."

p. 273 assembled for the event: ibid.

p. 273 broader triathlon community: T. J. Murphy, personal interview, San Diego, CA, June 2010.

p. 273 those deprogrammers: ibid.

p. 274 looked completely sane: ibid.

p. 274 things got weird: ibid.

p. 274 this is happening: ibid.

p. 274 through the high desert: Murphy, "Shamanism and the Art of Triathlon."

p. 274 Mark just smiled: Los Angeles Triathlon Club, A Night with Dave Scott and Mark Allen.

p. 275 fog of heat: Murphy, "Shamanism and the Art of Triathlon," Triathlete, August 1999.

p. 275 earlier in the day: ibid.

p. 275 was now corrected: Murphy interview.

p. 275 connecting with: ibid.

p. 275 in his racing: Murphy, "Shamanism and the Art of Triathlon."

p. 276 stable under pressure: Mark Allen, personal telephone interview, 2004.

p. 276 home with them: Murphy interview.

p. 276 Mona Lisa smile: ibid.

p. 276 riding waves: Moss interview.

p. 276 his existing friendships: Mark Allen on *The Simon Gown Triathlon Show*, LA Talk Radio, December 3, 2009, http://www.latalkradio.com/Players/Simon-120309.shtml.

p. 276 surfing acquaintances: Moss interview.

p. 277 marriage was at a crossroads: ibid.

p. 277 profound choice to make: ibid.

p. 277 attend a retreat: Ken Allen, personal telephone interview, February 2011.

p. 277 refused to enter: Carole Allen, personal telephone interview, February 2011.

p. 277 the bitter end: Ken Allen interview.

p. 277 after Mark's retirement: ibid.

p. 277 vomiting seawater: Dan Rock, personal interview, Solana Beach, CA, January 2011.

p. 278 Indian art pieces: Carlson, "Mark Allen's Dream-Time Transition."

p. 278 a human being: Mark Allen, personal conversation, Kona, HI, October 2010.

p. 278 online coaching service: Luis Vargas, personal telephone interview, March 2011.

p. 278 for them to change: Mark Allen on Competitor Radio.

p. 278 proving him wrong: T. J. Murphy, "Searching for Peter Reid," *Inside Triathlon*, May/June 2009, pp. 16-30.

p. 279 in San Diego: Trilover, "Hungry and in Pursuit . . . Once Again: Interview with Three-Time Ironman World Champion Peter Reid," BeginnerTriathlete.com, http://www.beginnertriathlete.com/cms/article-detail.asp?articleid=362, accessed August 9, 2011.

p. 279 by Mark's success: Carlson, "Mark Allen's Dream-Time Transition."

p. 279 utterly star-struck: Trilover, "Hungry and in Pursuit . . ."

p. 279 the wall behind Mark: Carlson, "Mark Allen's Dream-Time Transition."

p. 279 embraced Peter: Trilover, "Hungry and in Pursuit . . ."

p. 279 in some time: Peter Reid, "Kona #1—Mark, Psycho Kona Camp," http://peterreid.com/journals/journals_2004_01K.htm.

p. 280 told the story: Mathias Müller with Timothy Carlson, *17 Hours to Glory: Extraordinary Stories from the Heart of Triathlon* (Boulder, CO: VeloPress, 2010).

p. 280 fly small planes: Murphy, "Searching for Peter Reid."

p. 280 resistant to change: Mark Allen on *The Simon Gown Triathlon Show*.

p. 280 gotten there through calm: Joel Silverman, "Back to Business," *Inside Triathlon*, July 1995.

p. 280 traveled there separately: Moss interview.

p. 281 eve of the competition: ibid.

p. 281 first triathlon in 1982: ibid.

p. 281 qualified for Ironman: John Meyer, "Drew Scott Wins Boulder Peak Triathlon," *Denver Post*, July 11, 2011, http://www.denverpost.com/running/ci_18452368.

EPILOGUE

p. 287 what you have: T. J. Murphy, "A Space Between Two Thoughts," *Triathlete*, October 1998, pp. 38-43.

p. 288 to feel that again: CJ Olivares Jr., "The Art of War," *Triathlete*, January 1990, pp. 24-37.

FIRST PHOTO SECTION

p. 1: Carol Hogan; **p. 2**: *above*, David Epperson; *below*, Mike Plant; **p. 3**: Diane Johnson; **p. 4**: Mike Plant; **p. 5**: *above*, David Epperson; *below*, Tracy Frankel; **p. 6**: *above*, Tracy Frankel; *below*, Mike Plant; **p. 7**: *above right and below right*, Tracy Frankel; *below left*, Mike Plant; **p. 8**: Mike Plant

SECOND PHOTO SECTION

p. 1: Mike Plant; **p. 2**: Tracy Frankel; **p. 3**: Mike Plant; **p. 4**: *above*, Tracy Frankel; *below*, Mike Plant; **p. 5**: Tracy Frankel; **p. 6**: Tracy Frankel; **p. 7**: Tracy Frankel; **p. 8**: *above*, Mike Plant; *below*, Tracy Frankel

THIRD PHOTO SECTION

p. 1: David Epperson; **p. 2**: Tracy Frankel; **p. 3**: *above left and above right*, Tracy Frankel; *below*, Rich Cruse; **p. 4**: Rich Cruse; **p. 5**: *above left*, Tracy Frankel; *above right*, Rich Cruse; *below*, Timothy Carlson; **p. 6**: *above left and right*, Tracy Frankel; *below*, Rich Cruse; **p. 7**: Timothy Carlson; **p. 8**: Timothy Carlson

IRON WAR COURSE MAP
Ironman® World Championship—October 14, 1989

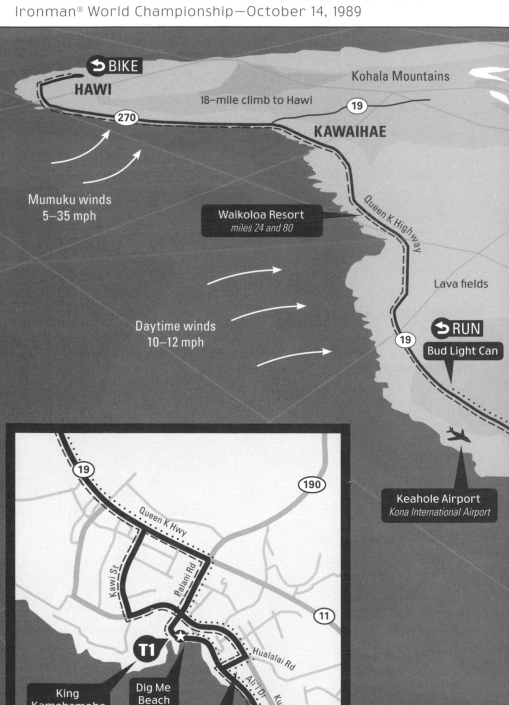

🔄 BIKE

HAWI

Kohala Mountains

18–mile climb to Hawi

270

19

KAWAIHAE

Mumuku winds
5–35 mph

Waikoloa Resort
miles 24 and 80

Queen K Highway

Lava fields

Daytime winds
10–12 mph

🔄 RUN

19

Bud Light Can

Keahole Airport
Kona International Airport

19

190

Queen K Hwy

Kawi St

Palani Rd

11

Hualalai Rd

T1

Ali'i Dr

Kuakini Hwy

King
Kamehameha
Hotel

Dig Me
Beach

Hot
Corner

Mauna Kea
13,796 ft.

Mauna Loa
13,677 ft.

Swim: Counterclockwise, Kailua Pier to Captain Beams party boat and back to the pier.

Bike: Up Palani Road to Queen Kaahumanu Highway, 33 miles through the lava fields to Highway 270, and on up to Hawi (52 miles). Returning the same way until Kawi Street (99 miles) and onto Kuakini Highway. Right onto Hualalai Road, and south on Ali'i Drive. Then 7 miles along the coast to Ehukai Street, and into the Kona Surf Hotel parking lot.

Run: Heading back along the same route to top of Palani Road (8 miles), and then 8 miles on the Queen K to the marathon turnaround. Retracing the route back to Hot Corner, and then right to the homestretch along Ali'i Drive to the finish.

Lava fields

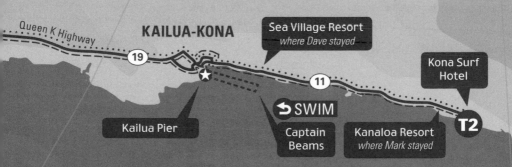

Queen K Highway

KAILUA-KONA

Sea Village Resort
where Dave stayed

Kona Surf Hotel

19

11

↩ SWIM

T2

Kailua Pier

Captain Beams

Kanaloa Resort
where Mark stayed

STATS

140.6 miles—2.4 mile SWIM, 112 mile BIKE, 26.2 mile RUN

Weather		Humidity		Avg. Water Temp.	79°F (26°C)
High	88°F (31°C)	High	85% (evening)	Sunrise	6:15 a.m.
Low	72°F (22°C)	Low	40% (afternoon)	Sunset	5:58 p.m.

The Ironman racecourse has been modified a few times since 1989, but most of it still takes place on the Queen K Highway and Ali'i Drive.

IRON WAR TIMELINE
Ironman® World Championship and Biographical Events

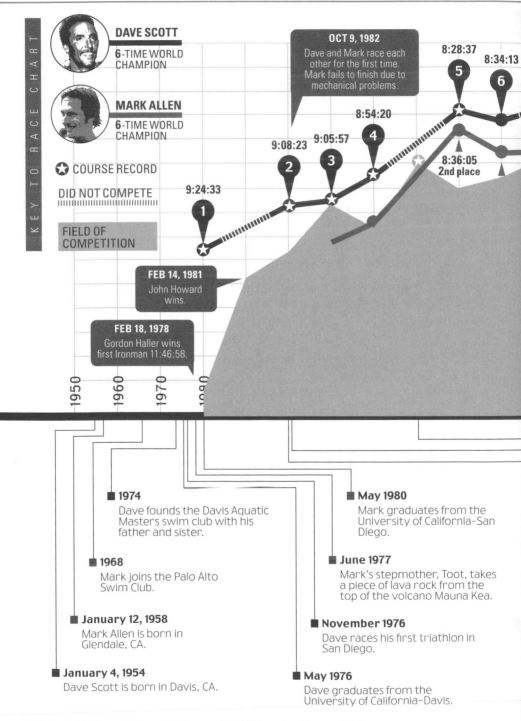

KEY TO RACE CHART

DAVE SCOTT
6-TIME WORLD CHAMPION

MARK ALLEN
6-TIME WORLD CHAMPION

⭐ COURSE RECORD

DID NOT COMPETE

FIELD OF COMPETITION

OCT 9, 1982
Dave and Mark race each other for the first time. Mark fails to finish due to mechanical problems.

8:28:37
5

8:34:13
6

8:54:20
4

9:08:23
2

9:05:57
3

9:24:33
1

8:36:05
2nd place

FEB 14, 1981
John Howard wins.

FEB 18, 1978
Gordon Haller wins first Ironman 11:46:58.

1950 1960 1970 1980

1974
Dave founds the Davis Aquatic Masters swim club with his father and sister.

1968
Mark joins the Palo Alto Swim Club.

January 12, 1958
Mark Allen is born in Glendale, CA.

January 4, 1954
Dave Scott is born in Davis, CA.

May 1980
Mark graduates from the University of California-San Diego.

June 1977
Mark's stepmother, Toot, takes a piece of lava rock from the top of the volcano Mauna Kea.

November 1976
Dave races his first triathlon in San Diego.

May 1976
Dave graduates from the University of California-Davis.

* Note: In 1982 two editions of the Ironman World Championship were held.

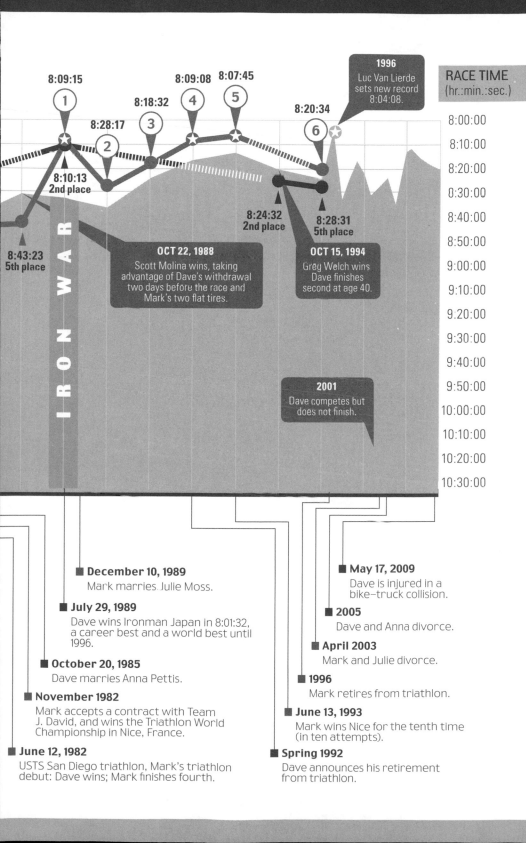

RACE TIME
(hr.:min.:sec.)

8:09:15
(1)

8:28:17
(2)

8:18:32
(3)

8:09:08
(4)

8:07:45
(5)

8:20:34
(6)

1996
Luc Van Lierde
sets new record
8:04:08.

8:00:00
8:10:00
8:20:00
0:30:00
8:40:00
8:50:00
9:00:00
9:10:00
9.20:00
9:30:00
9:40:00
9:50:00
10:00:00
10:10:00
10:20:00
10:30:00

8:10:13
2nd place

8:43:23
5th place

8:24:32
2nd place

8:28:31
5th place

IRON WAR

OCT 22, 1988
Scott Molina wins, taking
advantage of Dave's withdrawal
two days before the race and
Mark's two flat tires.

OCT 15, 1994
Greg Welch wins
Dave finishes
second at age 40.

2001
Dave competes but
does not finish.

■ **December 10, 1989**
Mark marries Julie Moss.

■ **July 29, 1989**
Dave wins Ironman Japan in 8:01:32,
a career best and a world best until
1996.

■ **October 20, 1985**
Dave marries Anna Pettis.

■ **November 1982**
Mark accepts a contract with Team
J. David, and wins the Triathlon World
Championship in Nice, France.

■ **June 12, 1982**
USTS San Diego triathlon, Mark's triathlon
debut: Dave wins; Mark finishes fourth.

■ **May 17, 2009**
Dave is injured in a
bike–truck collision.

■ **2005**
Dave and Anna divorce.

■ **April 2003**
Mark and Julie divorce.

■ **1996**
Mark retires from triathlon.

■ **June 13, 1993**
Mark wins Nice for the tenth time
(in ten attempts).

■ **Spring 1992**
Dave announces his retirement
from triathlon.

ACKNOWLEDGMENTS

THE INSPIRATION TO WRITE THIS BOOK came from my father. Also a writer, Tom Fitzgerald started work in 2002 on an epic fable about Benjamin Franklin. At the outset, he anticipated that it would take him about a year to complete it. One year turned into two, two became three, four, and more, and still he was not satisfied. Tom held the manuscript close to his vest through this long incubation. Finally, after six years, he decided that *Poor Richard's Lament* was ready to be shared with a small number of critical readers, among whom I was lucky to be included.

I expected it to be good. I did not expect to discover that my own father had written one of the best novels I'd ever read (and I read a lot of them). I had known, of course, that he was a capable writer. I'd just had no idea he was capable of such unalloyed brilliance. Nor had he. The book showed me what is possible when a man of mortal gifts makes a total commitment to doing the very best he can. No sooner had I read the last page of *Poor Richard's Lament* than I began to search for my own way of giving 100 percent.

The debt of gratitude that I owe my dad for his contributions to this book begins with the mentoring he offered when I was 9 years old, after I told him I wanted to be a writer too, and does not end with his ardent championing of my most challenging project all the way to the printer more than thirty years later. But I am most grateful to him simply for achieving something great on his own and inspiring me to try to do the same.

The first thing I did after deciding to write this book was to walk fifteen feet from my desk to Bob Babbitt's office at the Competitor Group building in San Diego and ask for his help. Bob had given Iron War its name, after all, and had done more than anyone to build and sustain the legend of the greatest race ever run. He was the unofficial curator of the Iron War Museum, if you will. An eyewitness to the race who was close enough to both of its heroes to have ghostwritten two books for one and served as an agent to the other, Bob knew more about the 1989 Ironman, Dave Scott, and Mark

Allen than anyone, and infinitely more than I did. I would need him on my team to make my telling of the story all it could be.

Bob provided invaluable help in the form of stories and memories; relationships and contacts; and cold, hard documentation of the race, the rivalry, and the lives of the rivals. Beyond that, working with Bob made the project immeasurably more fun and fulfilling for me than it otherwise would have been.

Iron War is unlike anything else I've written. Put another way, I had no idea how to write this kind of book when I started it, and my unpreparedness showed in my early drafts. Every writer needs a good editor, but I needed a *great* editor to avoid disappointing myself, and I was extremely fortunate to have such an editor in Renee Jardine at VeloPress. It would have taken years of fumbling along on my own to get the manuscript to where Renee quickly brought it with her incisive critical readings and spot-on suggestions. What's more, although her name does not appear on the cover, Renee dedicated herself to the book as fully as if it were her own. As a result, it is very much hers too.

Nearly every person whose name is to be found in this volume granted me one or more personal interviews. I am profoundly grateful to all of these men and women for so generously sharing their time and recollections. Scott Molina, Julie Moss, Mike Plant, Anna Scott, and Dave Scott deserve special mention. Others whose names are not seen in these pages made contributions that were no less valuable and are no less appreciated. I am especially thankful to Ted Costantino, Jaime Gamboa, Steve Gintowt, Linda Konner, Connie Oehring, and Dave Trendler for their efforts and support.

ABOUT THE AUTHOR

As a boy in New Hampshire **MATT FITZGERALD** watched ABC's coverage of Ironman every year throughout the 1980s. He was already a competitive runner, having started at age 11 after running the last mile of the 1983 Boston Marathon with his father (who of course had run the whole thing). Partial to underdogs, Matt rooted for Mark Allen.

In 1995, Matt was hired as an editor at Sausalito, California-based *Multisport* magazine by Bill Katovsky, who twelve years earlier had founded *Triathlete* magazine. Bill chose Matt over the only other candidate for the position because Matt knew who Dave Scott was, and the other candidate did not. Several months later Matt met Mark Allen at the Competitor Sports Awards in San Diego, where Mark was named Triathlete of the Year. Matt gushed like a schoolgirl in the presence of his childhood idol.

Matt's first contact with Dave Scott was equally awkward. He was working at *Triathlete* in 1998 when he carelessly described Dave as a "five-time Ironman champion" in an article. Dave later called Matt and gently corrected his error.

In 2003 Matt's first book, a triathlon training guide, was published. Mark Allen contributed the foreword. By then Matt also had a professional relationship with Dave Scott, who was sponsored by a sports nutrition company that Matt served as a consultant. Matt enjoyed the opportunity to ask Dave every question he'd ever dreamed of asking him as the two of them killed time in a few trade-show booths. It was this experience, which left him as great an admirer of the Man as he'd ever been of Grip, that gave Matt the idea to write the story of Dave Scott and Mark Allen's greatest race.

Matt currently lives in San Diego with his wife, Nataki, whom he admires most of all.